Race and Social Difference

Selected Readings

Edited by Paul Baxter and Basil Sansom

Penguin Books

Penguin Books Ltd, Harmondsworth,
Middlesex, England
Penguin Books Inc., 7110 Ambassador Road,
Baltimore, Md 21207, USA
Penguin Books Australia Ltd,
Ringwood, Victoria, Australia

First published 1972
This selection copyright © Paul Baxter and Basil Sansom, 1972
Introduction and notes copyright © Paul Baxter and Basil Sansom, 1972
Copyright acknowledgements for items in this volume will be found
on page 475

Made and printed in Great Britain by
C. Nicholls & Company Ltd
Set in Monotype Times

For Pat and Dianne

Contents

Introduction

Whatever the social scientist writes about race, he may be certain that he will face opponents, most of whom will not be scholars, who contend his view. The arguments about race are popular ones because race is a social issue. The more relevant race relations are in everyday life, the greater the popular interest in the race arguments and the more heated and doctrinaire the discussion. The intensity of opposition to informed discussion is, therefore, greatest in precisely those places where there are race relations for the scientist to study. Where members of different races are accorded differential access to local resources, a theory of race relations that does not accord with local beliefs about race is an attack on the local social order. Evidence which demonstrates the negligible importance of inherited physical differences undermines a structure of belief that provides the rationale for action in day-to-day encounters, and threatens those who are interested in preserving the current state of affairs. In such situations, scientific writings about race which are given any publicity have an immediately disturbing relevance for their readers. They cannot remain merely descriptive statements but become calls to social action.

The readings in this book have been selected in the awareness that there is still an opposition. The first group of readings constitutes a declaration about the general irrelevance of racial differences insofar as the human potential for societal and cultural development is concerned. There is evidence that certain populations have inherited characteristics that, in specific circumstances, can be of advantage for bare human survival: but there are no races of mankind which have been shown to be superior or inferior to any other. The U N E S C O proposals on race, which we reprint, are a series of general statements to which all serious students would subscribe. With that established, the following selections deal with our proper concern which is the sociology of race.

Our central concern is with race as a social fact, rather than with race as a set of biological facts. Race, that is, as it concerns the meanings that men have attached to the physical peculiarities they observe, or believe themselves able to observe, as characteristics of recognizable and distinctive populations. Physical differences between groupings of mankind are thus not considered as important in, or for, themselves, but rather as they provide proud distinctions or stigma that men use as grounds for social discrimination. In the study of society, then, our concern is not with race but with reactions to it.

It follows, therefore, that the sociology of race and race relations begins with a consideration of race in social consciousness, because race becomes a social reality once men define others in its terms. Social consciousness of race is dealt with in the second group of writings from Part Two through to Part Four.

The first readings on the consciousness of race are about social categories. The analysis depends on the proposition that social perceptions of race are categorical. These are put to work as men oppose one racially defined category against another and posit the kind of social relationship that should pertain between the representatives of categories thus set apart by racial division. Stereotypes, to which ready references are made, are constructed to abet those who wish to determine the categorical membership of anyone whose racial identity is in question.

Moving on to race in ideology and literature, we present studies of categorical image-makers at work; the references are mostly to colour, because colour and race are almost synonymous in common thought. The ideologist has patent aims, seeking to win acceptance for his racist definition of the world. In literature, an author's motives are not always evident, and he may unwittingly express and employ the accepted racial definitions of his culture or he may deliberately use his writing as a vehicle for the communication of a racial view of human relationships. Racial definitions in literature work to colour moral images of man and can give to an unfolding plot the significance of a tale of races. Either way, racial thought is communicated to an audience or collectivity of readers while they are being diverted and entertained. At the extreme, ideas of race have come to assume the characteristics of myth, and race becomes what men in society make of it.

Part Five of this reader is headed 'Sex and Colour'. As we all know, marriage and mating (like eating together) are purposive acts of profound personal significance and are highly charged with symbolic content. In the social distance scale constructed by Bogardus, one of the questions used to reckon social distance asks what categories of persons would be acceptable as marriage partners. There are, of course, popular forms of this question. The point is that attitudes towards, and behaviour determining the identity of, sexual and marriage partners are diagnostic of the relationships between social groups, and particularly so when the partners are visibly different in physical type.

Membership of a race is inherited and its physical characteristics are transmitted at the moment of conception. Miscegenation produces social confusion in the local calculus of racial identity. Hence, rules and taboos governing marriage and sexual relations assume signal importance whenever and wherever racial differences have been accorded social significance. A universal in race relations is a concern, sometimes even a popular obsession, with sexual relations across the boundary which demarcates one group from another. The continued 'purity' of a race depends on the regulation of sexual encounters. Hence, in South Africa a whole tribe of 'mixed bloods' have been stigmatized by reference to their collective origin in repeated sets of interracial mating and, in the white man's history books, they are still referred to as the Basters.

In Part Six racial discrimination is considered in relation to dominance and social inequality, where social mobility between racial groups is highly circumscribed or altogether precluded. Discrimination on racial grounds must, by its very nature, be unyielding because the marks of race are indelible and membership of racial groups is ascribed with reference to them. This kind of rigidity cannot exist within the compass of a single society without strong social sanctions to maintain it. Where groups maintain separate racial identities, yet where their members are required to interact with frequency, there is a high probability that any differential allocation of power between the groups will lead to the increasing exploitation of the weaker by the stronger. The greater the number of sectors of social life in which race is used as a criterion for discrimination, the greater the probability that the social system will be one in which one racial group dominates another. Race and social inequality are frequent correlates, and Dr André Béteille found it necessary to devote a section to the topic of Race and Inequality, in his Penguin Reader *Social Inequality*.

A progressive logic has governed the serial order in which we have arranged our selections to the end of Part Six. After Part Six our priorities change as we have selected from the compendious ethnography of race. We have tried to display some of the variety in the patterning of race relations in different localities; the variety of topics which scholars have defined within the field of race relations and the variety of theoretical approaches that have been brought to bear. Race relations are only a special case of group relations in society, and the questions that can be raised are as broad as sociology and social anthropology themselves. Any sociological question that is posed in a local context within which race is a defining element is a question that relates to the conduct of interracial affairs.

In Parts Seven to Ten the selections are arranged on a regional basis. All the contributions deal with localities in which race relations are highly significant and built into the social structure. These societies can themselves be characterized in terms of the way in which racial groups are accommodated within them; and are classifiable under such broad headings as 'segregationist', 'pluralistic' or 'integrationist'. Secondly, as is appropriate, all the authors deal with facts that are generally relevant to social action in a community-wide or societal setting, and have a general relevance for our understanding of the patterns characteristic of particular locales.

In some instances, specialised concepts developed in one locale are applied and elaborated to illuminate by comparison the type of social order which has evolved in another. M. G. Smith discusses Jamaica as a 'plural society' using the concept of 'pluralism' pioneered by Boeke and Furnivall in their studies of Indonesia. Lloyd Warner applies a modified conception of caste, a feature of Hindu societies, in his attempt to typify and analyse the social consequences of segregation in the American South. For the most part, however, authors draw on various aspects of general social theory. Thus, Mitchell's presentation of the racial myths sustained by white Rhodesians derives from an anthropological tradition that goes back to Malinowski's work on the Trobriand Islanders. Gluckman analyses the 'Bonds in the Colour Bar' from the perspective of the theory of conflict. Sprague's account of the contrasting patterns of race relations in the New World is in a tradition that presents contemporary social arrangements as a culmination of rooted historical forces.

The essays in the final part of the book deal with reactions to race in specific places, but they are not so concerned to characterize aspects of the embracing social structure as with the definition of situations and encounters within the larger structure. The sociological consideration of race relations began with the analysis of generalized notions and categories as they are embedded in social consciousness. In situational accounts social typing and categorization are examined as social actors apply general notions to make sense of their individual actions and situations, and race is presented as it operates, as a definitive criterion in interpersonal relations.

One of our difficulties in making this selection was deciding where to draw the boundaries between race and ethnicity and race relations and ethnic relations. We solved this problem arbitrarily by taking race to describe groupings separated by ineluctable physical differences that were emphasized by actors in their social relationships. In contrast, we reserved the label 'ethnicity' for distinctions between groupings made in terms of cultural identity. Two papers, 'Les Races de Kisangani' and 'Anglo-Saxonism and the Irish' straddle this indistinct boundary. Both are concerned with 'racist' definitions of groups whose physical characteristics do not provide unambiguous marks of racial identity. In the two situations described, racial differences can be clearly seen to be fabricated. They strengthen the general point that men talk and act in racist terms even when obvious physical differentiating characteristics are absent.

We have not been able to include a number of papers and extracts which we should have liked but two topical subjects which some readers may have anticipated have been excluded. First, several studies of race relations in Britain are readily available, so their inclusion here seemed unnecessary. Secondly, following Jensen's (1969) article, the hoary topic of the comparative educability of the Negro has had a little fresh life breathed into it. If there were demonstrable differences in intelligence or educability between large populations, then this would be a fact which, like ecological or demographic facts, would be a datum in sociological analysis. But the subject of comparative intelligence itself is not one open to sociological inquiry and is therefore beyond the bounds of this reader; though the revival of interest in the topic is itself one of the curiosities in the sociology of knowledge. Moreover, we have both lived amongst Negro peoples and have been so often abashed by the intellectual abilities of our friends and neighbours that the topic seems not just insulting, but also unreal.

Reference

JENSEN, A. (1969), 'How much can we boost IQ and scholastic achievement?', *Harvard Educ. Rev.*, vol. 39, Winter.

Part One
On Hereditary Human Differences

Tobias provides a succinct and conservative series of
answers to the questions which are constantly raised about the
physical and genetic differences which exist between the
varieties of mankind. He also discusses the relevance
such differences have for mental and cultural achievement.
Peoples as diverse as the Romans and the Fulani have
interpreted the shape of nose they happen to have inherited as
an indicator of their own cultural superiority. Weiner's paper
illustrates the manner in which modern physical anthropologists
approach taxonomic studies. He examines the structure of the
nose in order to examine the purposes it serves in a particular
environment. He also opens up further questions of a cultural
nature. Could those narrow-nosed desert dwellers who wrap
the lower halves of their faces, not only be straining out dust
from the air they breathe, but also be establishing a micro-
climate inside the wrap, in which some of their breath
moisture is re-cycled for re-inspiration? Friedlander
demonstrates how a genetically transmitted immunity to
malaria permitted a transported population to oust
unwittingly a genetically different one; with great demographic,
economic and social consequences.

The UNESCO Proposals summarize the considered findings
of a panel of scholars on the weight which rational men should
give to racial differences.

1 Phillip V. Tobias

The Meaning of Race

P. V. Tobias, *The Meaning of Race*, a lecture delivered to the Union of Jewish Women of Southern Africa, 8 May, 1961, and published by the South African Institute of Race Relations, pp. 5–41.

The definition of race

What is understood scientifically by race? It is a term which is borrowed from biology. We speak of races of dogs or sheep or birds or plants: by that we mean that the species is divided up into a number of populations which are united by heredity. There are no hard and fast boundary-lines between these races of plants or animals; in fact, commonly, one type or race merges into the next through intermediate forms. The 'typical' representatives of the different races are simply those which are most different from the others. But members of one race can and do interbreed with members of another race, producing intermediate forms.

In the same way, we may speak of races of Man. The human species during its evolution has spread over the face of the earth and become divided up into a great number of populations united by heredity. Confronted with an enormous diversity of different-looking people, anatomists and physical anthropologists have classified the varieties into a number of races. As with plants and animals, there are no hard and fast dividing-lines among the various human races: populations occur which are impossible to classify, because they look intermediate between some other two races. Interbreeding can and does occur between the members of one race and those of another and this is one of the ways in which intermediate forms come into being. (Tobias, 1953)

So race is a biological concept which helps us to bring order out of the otherwise meaningless range of human variation. It is a classification of anatomies, used for anatomical purposes. 'Since the ends are anatomical in nature, the methods used are anatomical.' There is no thought of leaping from anatomy to intelligence, language or religion (Washburn, 1945), or level of civilization. Thus, we may accept the definition of race proposed by the distinguished French anthropologist, Henri Vallois: 'A race is a natural group of men displaying a particular set of common hereditary characteristics' (Vallois).

In this sense and strictly in this sense, the ideal of races of man is a valid concept. It is necessary to stress this point, because some scientists have been so alarmed by the rise of political doctrines based upon racial differences and by the enormities and excesses committed in the name of race, that they have gone to the other extreme and claimed that race is a meaningless concept, a myth, a fallacy. It is now generally conceded that the first draft of the famous UNESCO statement on race went too far in this direction (UNESCO, 1952). We need a more balanced view and the present consensus of opinion recognises the existence of races as *valid biological entities*.

Races of mankind

Let me try to give you a bird's eye view of the nearly three thousand million people on earth and the way in which they have been classified for scientific purposes into valid racial categories. Anthropologists are agreed that most of the world's populations can be grouped into three major constellations of races. They are the Negroid, the Caucasoid and the Mongoloid. In addition, two smaller groups are often recognised, the Australoid and the Khoisanoid.

The first major subdivision is the Negroid, the dark-skinned, dark-eyed, strong-jawed, woolly-haired people who make up rather less than two-thirds of the population of Africa. They are to be found, as well, beyond the Indian Ocean in Melanesia and beyond the Atlantic as the American Negroes. Several branches, in Africa, Asia and the Indies, are of diminutive stature: they are the Pygmies, comprising *Negrillos* in Africa and *Negritos* in Asia.

The second racial constellation comprises the Caucasoids, represented mainly by the Europeans. Generally they are light-skinned, straight-faced and have straight, wavy or curly hair. The colour of their eyes and hair varies from very fair to very dark. Even among these Caucasoids there are various types, such as the

Nordic, robust, hairy, tall and fair, long-headed and long-faced; the *Alpine*, squat, medium in stature and dark in hair colour, short-headed and short-faced; the *Mediterranean*, slender, medium in stature, dark in hair-colour and of dusky complexion, long-headed and long-faced. These three – the Nordic, Alpine and Mediterranean – are concentrated in Northern, Central and Southern Europe respectively; the Mediterraneans are found too, on the Southern approaches to the Mediterranean, as far south as Somaliland and as far east as India, where their skin colour is darkest. Other Caucasoid races include the *Armenoid*, the very short-headed, swarthy and big-nosed peoples of South-East Europe; and the *East Baltic*, another short-headed but light-haired people of North-East Europe.

From their population centres in Europe, the Caucasoids have in fairly recent times spread out and colonized almost every part of the globe. The White populations of Southern Africa, Australia and America, are highly-mixed blends of the various Caucasoid races which have populated those parts in historical times.

The third major cluster of races is the *Mongoloid*, yellow- or coppery-skinned, straight-haired and characterized by high cheek-bones, often 'Mongolian eye-folds' and squat faces and heads. They form the great bulk of the Eastern Asian population – the true Mongolian Mongoloids. Some have overflowed into the peninsulas and archipelagos of Southern-Eastern Asia as far as the Phillippines and even across the Behring Straits into the Americas as Eskimos and American Indians.

As I mentioned before, several people do not fit easily into this classification: the Australian aborigines are one example. Some have called them a distinct race – the *Australoids*; other regard them as a blend of various other types. Yet another somewhat anomalous group is the Bushman and Hottentot peoples of Southern Africa: although having some features in common with the Negroid peoples of Africa, it seems rather more likely that they represent the remnants of a distinct race, the *Khoisanoid*, which flourished in Africa before the rise of the Negroes. Today their much-hybridized remnants do not exceed 75,000 in number.

The genetic bases of race

While we have come to recognize the existence of these major constellations of races, it is most important that we define the limitations of the race concept. In his definition, Vallois (1952) stressed that the differences among races are hereditary: that is, the tendencies to show particular racial features are handed on through the spermatozoon and the egg which unite to form a new life. We know today that heredity is based mainly on different kinds of genes, tiny hereditary particles contained within the spermatozoon and the egg. Since the spermatozoon comes from the father and the egg from the mother it follows that a new embryo receives one set of genes from each parent. It thus combines two sets of genes in its make-up. Each gene can exist in two or more forms, thus the genes for hair-colour may be blondness genes, or brunette-forming genes and so on.

By studying genetic features in different populations, we obtain a good idea of how the genic make-up of one population resembles or differs from that of another population. By such studies, it has been found that races generally differ from one another not in possessing different sorts of genes, but in possessing the different forms of each gene in a greater or lesser frequency. For example, we may cite the blood groups, each one of us belongs to a particular blood group and blood-transfusions always have to be preceded by a test of one's blood group. Thus everyone belongs to blood-group A or B or O or AB. That really means, everyone has the genes for Group A or B or O or AB. In this room*, one would expect about four or five people per hundred to possess the gene for Group B. But if I were giving this lecture in India, thirty or forty people per hundred would be found to possess the B gene. In other words, one of the differences between people of India and people of Western Europe is that, although both possess the gene for B, it is much commoner in India. In the same way no matter what genetic feature we chose, we should find races differing in the frequency with which they possess the gene in question. Thus although the genes for black hair among Caucasoids are commonest in Mediterraneans and Alpines, black-haired Nordics are met with and so are blond Mediterraneans, and

* Containing a white audience in South Africa.

even red-haired and blue-eyed Negroids, and blond Australian aborigines. Or, again, the gene for woolly-hair is almost universal among Negroids, but does occur rarely among Caucasoids.

Thus, the modern concept of race is that racial differences are based not on absolute differences, but on different gene-frequencies. And all mankind has far more genes in common than the genes which differentiate the different races. It has been estimated that 90–95 per cent of genes are common to all men: these are the genes which make men men, which give us two legs, an upright stance, a big brain, mobile fingers and a prehensile thumb (Coon, Garn and Birdsell, 1950). Only 5–10 per cent of all our genes are concerned with the little superficial frill of variation which makes for the differences among races.

Perhaps it may surprise you to learn that races differ from one another in such few respects – a mere few thousand genes. But the reason is not far to seek. If we ask, how long have the present races of mankind been in existence we have to admit that, from the fossil remains of man's ancestors, we cannot trace the present-day racial divisions any earlier than about 25,000 years, let us say 50,000 years at the outside. Yet, it is well over a million years since the human line of ancestry separated from the ape line. We are forced to conclude from this that the formation of the present-day races is a comparatively recent phenomenon. It is not so very long since the ancestors of the present races looked very much more alike than do their present racial descendants. In fact, Washburn (1945) has calculated that every living race has had a least 100 times as much of its human ancestry in common with all other races as it has had alone. Small wonder then that living races still share over 90 per cent of their genes in common with one another and that a mere 5–10 per cent of the genes have diversified in the last 2,000 generations to bring about the degree of difference among modern races.

It makes us realise, too, that all of us human beings share far more of our essential humanity in common and differ in far fewer respects than doctrinaire racists would like us to believe!

Are there superior and inferior races?

Behind all racially-discriminating legislation is the assumption, sometimes stated, sometimes tacitly implied, that what is good enough for members of one racial group is too good for members of another. The assumption in a nutshell is that racial differences are degrees of goodness. 'My group is better than your group.' It is a pattern of thinking which one finds wherever a strong group-consciousness is accompanied by a refusal to face reality – that is to check up and see if it really is true what one believes about the members of another group. A drastic demonstration of this failure to test reality in prejudiced people was made by Professor E. L. Hartley: in a study of antagonism to other groups than one's own (out-groups) he included three entirely imaginary groups, which he called *Danireans, Piraneans*, and those hideous monsters the *Wallorians*. A large proportion of those who disliked Negroes and Jews also expressed a dislike of these three non-existent groups and advocated restrictive measures against them (Jahoda, 1960).

Thus, without testing reality, people who discriminate against Africans are liable to say this is because they are inferior, lower class, low in intelligence, they force out the Whites, are lazy, sloppy, dirty, immoral, oversexed, troublesome, childish, they have a bad smell and carry disease.

It is interesting to compare the views of anti-semites: they will admit to disliking Jews because they have all the money, or are always begging, control business, are capitalists but also communists, are clannish, but also intrude on other people's affairs, are smart, intellectuals, think themselves better than others, but also have a dreadful inferiority complex, work too hard but never do manual labour, and are noisy, bad-mannered and emotional (Jahoda, 1960).

The internal contradictions testify that people with such views fail to check their ideas against reality.

Another aspect of the contradictory and unreal thinking of individuals who discriminate against members of other races is that sometimes the selfsame qualities which are deprecated in the out-group are admired in the in-group! Thus, in an American survey, it was asked: did Abraham Lincoln work far into the night? This shows he was industrious, resolute, persevering and eager to realise his capacities to the full. Do the out-group Jews or Japanese keep these same hours? This only bears witness to their sweatshop mentality and their ruthless undercutting of

American standards, their unfair competitive practices (Jahoda, 1960). Such 'double-think' underlies racially discriminating legislation.

It was once very fashionable to avow the physical inferiority of the darker races – and all manner of strange proofs were put forward, such as that the negro has a smaller brain, thicker skull, a less convoluted brain, and so on. Thus, we read

Investigation has proved that the smoothness of the brain and the pigment of the skin go hand in hand. There are exceptions to this rule but they are in the minority. Mental activity has the effect of convoluting the brain and the greatest number of convolutions are found in the brains of individuals of the races with the lightest skins; growing less through the gamut of pigments to the black, at which stage the brain has a smooth surface (The *Star*, 1957).

None of these statements has any basis in fact.

There are those who tried hard to show that some races were nearer the apes: thus the Negro's jutting jaws and long arms must surely show that he is not very far removed from the apes: to which others retorted that, if one judged by hairiness, the Nordic European was far more ape-like than the Negro, while the little hairless Bushman has far shorter arms than the European. All such arguments are unscientific and worthless. If, as I indicated a moment ago, the human line split off from the ape line well over 1,000,000 – and possibly 10,000,000 – years ago, and the modern races of man developed only 25 or 50,000 years ago, it is palpably meaningless to compare living races of man with living apes in order to arrange them in some sort of hierarchical order. Such comparisons are indefensible since the races of man have nearly all their ancestry in common.

We must conclude that there is no scientific basis for arranging the living races of mankind in a series from the more ape-like to the more god-like.

Recently it has become somewhat unfashionable and vulgar to use this sort of argument. In South Africa, a new formula has been found. *Cultural differences* have become the new justification for discriminatory practices. Yet, even now, despite the sophisticated turn in the argument, there is the underlying thought that those cultural differences are unchangeable, are part of a man's nature, his heredity. What has science to say under this head?

Racial differences apply to physical features – what one looks like; one's build, colouring, shape of nose, head, face – all features which are under the control of genes. Mental characteristics are not taken into account in classifying the races. This is because scientists have not yet devised tests for comparing satisfactorily the intelligence, capabilities and other mental attributes of different races. Practically all tests so far devised assess performances which are influenced by the environment in which an individual has grown up and been educated. Such educational and environmental differences among people are not racial differences. As an example of environmental effects: a group of Negro children in rural Tennessee obtained an average Intelligence Quotient (IQ) of 58, whereas Negro children in Los Angeles, California, had an average IQ of 105 (Klineberg, 1951). For the white population as a whole, an IQ of 100 is to be expected; that is the standard with which these results are to be compared. In the inferior environment of rural Tennessee, the Negro score is far below this standard, whereas in the more favourable urban environment of Los Angeles, the Negro score reaches and even exceeds the average 'normal' IQ. If conclusions are drawn about Negroes in general from the Southern experiment, they would be that the Negroes as a race were of inferior intelligence to the Whites; yet conclusions based on the Los Angeles experiment would show exactly the opposite! Considering the two sets of results together, we are bound to conclude that it is the marked environmental difference which accounts for the vastly different performances by the two groups of children of the same racial type.

Race, culture and intelligence

Despite this, there are still some who maintain that race determines all social and mental activities and therefore culture and civilization generally. This view had its origin in the days of slavery, when slave-owners answered those who wished to abolish slavery by suggesting that slaves were ignorant and illiterate because of their race (and not because they were denied schooling facilities!). One remembers the words of John Stuart Mill, who said,

Of all vulgar modes of escaping from the consideration of the effect of the social and moral influences on the human mind, the most vulgar is that of attributing the diversities of conduct and character to inherent natural differences.

It is easy to deny a subservient people the benefits of civilization and then to describe them as uncivilized. The resulting idea of racial superiority and inferiority has been carried to absurd extremes in the present century at the hands of racist-anthropologists and politicians.

Thus, we find Gunther (1927) speaking of the Nordic Man as feeling a strong urge towards truth and justice, prudence, reserve, steadfastness, calm judgment, as though these things were determined by his genes. 'The gift of narrative, with a sense for describing events and landscape and a tendency to roguish humour, is common in the Nordic race. ... Fairness and trustworthiness are peculiar Nordic virtues. ... Passion ... has little meaning for him. In contrast, the Mediterranean man is very strongly swayed by the sexual life, at least he is not as continent as the Nordic ...' Again, Alpines are 'petty criminals, small-time swindlers, sneak-thieves and sexual perverts'; whereas Nordics are 'capable of the nobler crimes'!

This attribution of mental and temperamental traits to members of different racial groups has its parallel in South Africa as well. Who has not heard, as a defence of discriminatory policies, the time-worn question, why has the African not made any great contribution to civilization? The implication of this question is that the African has not got it in him to have made any great contribution. But this indirect imputation of inferiority is no less scientifically unjustified than the more direct slur. It is not difficult to answer this question.

Archaeology and anthropology teach us that civilization has never been the exclusive possession of any one race or people: it has its roots in many ages and many cultures. Western European culture, for example, reached Western Europe late, having come from Asia Minor and Greece. Architectural principles came from Egypt and the fertile crescent; weaving probably from the Nile Valley and silk from China; writing, pottery, the wheel from the Middle East; likewise agriculture and domestication of certain animals. Our list of borrowings and inheritances is a long one yet as Shapiro (1944) has pointed out:

Our debts have not made us humble. We behave as if we had created our civilization singlehanded and had occupied a position of leadership from the beginning of civilization itself. Actually we are not only the inheritors of a varied and complex tradition, but the present protagonists of western civilization are merely the latest of mankind to become civilized . . . All during the prehistoric ages North-Western Europe represented a backwater.

Into these remote regions came the stone age innovations, after they had been invented elsewhere. Similarly the Neolithic techniques and the use of bronze and iron only slowly were diffused to Western Europe centuries after this discovery in Egypt and Mesopotamia. So wild and barbarous were the regions inhabited by the ancient Britons, the Scandinavians and the Germans that the Greeks never knew of their existence. And to the Romans the inhabitants of these far distant corners were uncouth barbarians unfamiliar with the amenities of civilization. In fact, up to the time of the Renaissance the North-Western Europeans could hardly claim parity by any objective standard with a civilization such as the Chinese of the same epoch, or the native civilizations of Mexico or Peru, where substantial achievements in social organization, architecture and art far surpassed contemporary European productions.

But we should be quite wrong to attribute this backwardness of North-Western Europe to racial inferiority: accidents of geography and history are quite sufficient to account for it. Surprising it would indeed have been if the important inventions which started off our civilization had all been discovered at the same time by different peoples. A chance discovery made here does not mean that everyone else who did not happen to chance upon the same discovery at the same moment was congenitally idiotic. So, too, with Africa: after having started everything off initially, after having been the continent where, on available fossil evidence, man first emerged on the face of our planet; where man first started to differentiate himself from the other beasts by his cultural life, through tools of stone and bone; after having given these priceless gifts first to Asia, and then to Europe, it is not to be expected that, with all the physical difficulties of life in Africa, the people of the continent should indefinitely retain a lead over the others. Replete as it is with tropical diseases, malaria, sleeping-sickness, bilharzia, hook-worm and a hundred other scourges, it is not surprising that man survived in Africa at a leisurely tempo. Perhaps we have been too blind and too busy to receive and appreciate Africa's greatest gift to mankind. . . .

There is no justification for invoking any racial inferiority to explain the apparent cultural lag between the people of Africa south of the Sahara and those of the Middle East. The reasons are essentially similar to the reasons why North-Western Europeans lagged behind the Middle East: accidents of time and space. And just as North-Western Europe proved equal to the challenge of the new techniques when finally they reached that area, so have thousands of Africans already proved that their race sets no limits to their educability. Despite hardships of poverty and frustration, those who have risen to the higher levels of education have proved fully equal to the challenge. There is no need to suggest – as was suggested in the Union House of Parliament not so long ago – that the African has to go through the same period of evolution that the White race went through (House of Assembly, 30 April, 1946). This idea that a long, slow apprenticeship to civilization must be served is based on the faultiest of reasoning, as a moment's reflection will show. Europe's civilization evolved comparatively slowly because means of communication were slow; not because the Europeans were racially incapable of absorbing civilization more rapidly. But this is an age of rapid communication, of mass education methods – and what it took Europe centuries to learn from the Mediterranean and the Middle East, Africa will undoubtedly acquire in a decade or two. Such rapidity of change is not without precedent; it happened that way to the backward, ignorant and illiterate peasantry of Russia and Japan. So, too, will it happen in Africa sooner than we might imagine; and in South Africa, where there have been several centuries of contact between Africans and the ways of civilization borne by the White settlers, the civilizing process is going to occur more rapidly than elsewhere in the rest of the continent.

It is impossible to say more at present than that science has not validly demonstrated any inherited mental differences between the races. Our recognition of races remains based upon physical or somatic features. That mental differences may parallel the physical differences is a possibility, but we do not yet possess adequate techniques for distinguishing between those mental characteristics which may be inborn or hereditary or racial, from those which are due to education and the environment generally. Researches on identical twins are helping to elucidate which mental traits are hereditary, but it would be premature to generalize at this stage. Biesheuvel's studies on aptitudes have led him to this interim conclusion:

It may turn out that the intellectual differences between races are a matter of 'bent' towards particular abilities, rather than of general intellectual capacity; there may be a real difference in the mean level that can be achieved; or there may be no difference at all, neither qualitative nor quantitative, given adequate opportunities for development. Only further research can decide between these possibilities (Sonnabend and Sofer, 1948).

It is customary to ascribe personality traits to peoples, especially to national groups (which are by no means co-extensive with racial groups). It is common practice to speak of the 'phlegmatic Englishman', the 'sensuous Frenchman', the 'loquacious Welshman', the 'stolid German'. Such personality traits may indeed characterize many members of the several nations, but we have no evidence that these qualities are inherent in the genetic constitution and do not result from social behaviour patterns. Still less is it possible to demonstrate personality traits extending over whole races (e.g. Caucasoids, Mongoloids), as distinct from national characteristics.

In short, mental characteristics cannot in any way assist the classifying of the races at this stage of our knowledge. Conversely, it is not scientifically sound to base lines of conduct and legislation on the assumption that a particular culture, language or outlook on life is inseparably bound up with particular physical features. This is the fallacy of regarding a civilized African who, despite tremendous difficulties, has succeeded in receiving a decent higher education, as an imitation Englishman. The whole of history and prehistory consists in the adoption by some peoples of the ideas and inventions of other peoples. Formerly this was often the result of conquest, enslavement, concubinage; more recently, it has been conceived by most western men as a duty or mission to pass on the fruits of civilization to those who had not yet come to them by their own resources. It is a change of motivation, but the fundamental process remains the same as it has been for thousands of years. Unfortunately, South African politicians have changed not only the motivation, but even the fundamental process – of passing on the full fruits of our culture to those who do not enjoy it yet, but who are clamouring to be initiated into its ways. The so-called tribal universities are not there to pass on the full fruits of civilization to the African and other non-White groups; they are there rather to pass on just such parts of civilization and modern culture as will not change the African too radically from his African tribal culture. They are truly tribal colleges in more than one sense. The fallacy behind them is the same old one : the idea that race and culture are inextricably linked and we must do nothing to ease them apart.

Science does not provide any basis for this idea; rather it shows exactly the opposite – that race and culture are totally separate concepts, that in time past cultures have diffused from race to race.

Of course, I shall not deny that social and cultural circumstances may influence the biological boundaries of race. For instance, the exchange of genes tends to be greater *within* a race than *among* different races. Man does not need legislation for this to be true; men of one type are simply more likely to marry people of similar type. There will always be some who will wish to marry outside the group, but they are generally a minority. For instance, Sonnabend and Sofer (1948) showed that, in 1946, fewer than 10 per cent of the marriages which could produce Coloured offspring in South Africa were mixed marriages, that is, between Coloureds and others. Over 90 per cent were between Coloured and Coloured. That was the position before there was any Mixed Marriages Act. So we may cite social taboos and also legislation as two social or cultural factors which may limit the amount of gene exchange between groups. Historically, there have been other factors which have *encouraged* the exchange of genes among groups. Thus, warfare and conquest, slavery and concubinage, improved means of transport and migration, have all thrown different races of mankind together in such a way as to promote gene exchange between groups.

In fact, there are those who feel that Man's very culture, which has made his world-wide distribution possible, is changing the direction of his evolution. Whereas, until the last few thousand years, Man's evolution was divergent, tending to produce different races of men, his evolution today has become convergent (de Chardin, 1959); the different races of man are growing together. Racial boundaries are no longer co-extensive with geographical boundaries. Negroes are no longer confined to Negro lands; European Caucasoids are no longer confined to Europe; Mongoloids are no more the people of Mongolia – they cover two-thirds of Asia, much of America and Greenland. Geographical isolation originally made the emergence of the races possible; today that isolation has largely disappeared and men of different races co-exist in most parts of the world. Culturally, this is undoubtedly bringing all men of the world within sight of the same fruits of civilization; the same standards of living and of health and welfare are the goals of almost all men on earth today and they are attainable goals. Racially, in many parts of the world, divergence is giving way to convergence. The mixing of peoples over the face of the globe is no less inevitable than the mixing of cultures. Human racial evolution has turned the corner; in future it will increasingly be convergent. Man differs from all other animals in his dependence on culture. It is this very culture which is enabling him to spread across the globe and makes it inevitable that racial convergence will be an increasing feature in the human populations of tomorrow.

This brings one squarely face to face with two more problems: for the average South African's immediate reaction to what I have just said will be to ask, 'What harm will I suffer if I lose my race purity?' and secondly, 'What are the consequences of race-mixing?' Let us consider each of these soul-searching questions in turn, because on each of them science has something to say.

Purity of race

Many White South Africans believe that they belong to a pure race, this assumption lies behind legislation designed to 'maintain the purity of the race'. What does science have to say on this score? More specifically, are the races I defined above pure, or, if not, can they be traced back to pure races?

The traditional approach of scientists in the past was to relate the living forms of Man to idealized racial types. If a race of ideal types could be found, it would be a pure race. Thus, consciously or unconsciously, anthropologists have envisaged pure races, existing either today or in the past. The quest for pure races has tended to elevate race purity to a sought-after quality. Some anthropologists have, in a measure, been responsible for the over-emphasis on race purity. The extreme example of this tendency is that of the German racist-anthropologists. A few quotations from Gunther (1927), who typifies this class of now completely dis-credited anthropologists, illustrate the lengths to which the ideas of race purity and impurity were carried:

Athens sank in the same measure that the blood of her Nordic upper class ran dry (p. 168).

Where the Nordics, keeping their racial purity, settle over an unbroken area, some kind of popular government must come into being (p. 192).

and, topically and perhaps sternly amusing

For areas with pure race some kind of republican system might well be fitting (p. 192).

Thus, under the Nazi regime, race purity became a fetish; history was re-written to show the alleged part of the Nordic demi-gods in the advance of civilization. It is interesting to recall that these were the last people in Europe to receive the benefits of civilization, just as the Mediterraneans were the first.

But the magic shadow-show of race purity has not been confin-ed to Nazi Germany. South Africans, too, have had this fetish drummed into their heads by the legislators, so that it is possible for a man to write to the *Star* (6th March, 1959): 'The undeniable fact is that the overwhelming majority of people are without foreign admixture', and again, 'To esteem race purity is in itself unobjectionable, and is in conformity with the instinct of self-preservation'; and even to say, 'The evil is not race purity, but in the oppression of one race by another, and in wanton destruction of this purity through miscegenation; for the pure-blooded types of human beings are the most excellent forms of life'.

Let us in South Africa beware lest we become race-purity drunk and go mad in search of the entirely mythical El Dorado of race purity.

For we have no objective scientific evidence that 'pure' races of Man exist anywhere on earth today, nor that a 'pure' race has ever existed. Weiner (1942), surveying the developments in physical anthropology since 1935, concludes:

Prehistoric men (judged from bony remains) were quite as variable as modern populations so that no evidence emerges . . . of the former existence of 'pure' or homogeneous races.

Even the rugged-browed Neanderthal Man, who lived in Europe during the first part of the last (Wurm) glaciation of the Great Ice Age, shows marked variation within his kind. In Southern Africa, we have about a dozen skulls dating from the Middle Stone Age and the intermediate phase which immediately followed it; yet, even at that remote period, more than ten thousand years ago, the earliest human beings of whom we have record in South Africa are not homogeneous, but differ fundamentally among themselves.

To what depths of time must we plumb to find pure races? The ancient *Pithecanthropus* hominids of Java and China and Africa varied among themselves hundreds of thousands of years ago. Of the still earlier South African fossil ape-men, the Australopithecines or Dartians (as Sir Arthur Keith proposed they be called after their first discoverer, Professor Raymond A. Dart), several kinds are known from the caves of the Central and Southern Transvaal, the North-Eastern Cape Province and Tanganyika.

We conclude that, from the dawn of man in the Pliocene-Pleistocene geological epoch, to the present day, there is no trace of a pure human race. Racial purity is a mythical concept, one might almost say a mystical concept. Man himself has created racial categories; he has made a classification of races to try to bring order to his understanding of the variations of man. His racial categories are arbitrary – that is why different workers recognise different numbers of races; although all are striving to reflect the natural relationships of populations of human beings. In such a scheme of categories, purity of race finds no place. Always there are more individuals who do not conform to the so-called ideal type; and by departing from that ideal type, they move nearer to some other ideal type. A shortish, darkish Northern European may thus resemble more a Southern European; a blond, heavily-built Southern European may be quite intermediate between the Mediterranean and Nordic or East Baltic races. Thus, there are no sharp boundaries to any race; there is no rigidly-defined charmed circle within which everyone looks alike. The boundary-lines of race are vague and tail away into the territories of adjacent racial groups. Scientifically, it is impossible therefore to classify each single individual into a particular racial category. Especially is this true where the area of vague and blurred overlap between racial groups has been made so much bigger by the intensity of inter-racial crossing in South African history.

No wonder we were told in 1957 that seven teams had had to be created to classify the races in South Africa – and we have yet to learn that a single physical anthropologist or geneticist was included in these teams. No wonder, too, that it was reported in the *Star* on 13 January, 1958, that the special committee which the Minister of the Interior had appointed four years previously to coordinate the different (and often conflicting) definitions of races in various South African Statutes, had had to report that they found the task impossible. This was a fair report, since they were being asked indeed to attempt the impossible. Unfortunately, the Minister's response was to re-appoint the committee and ask them to have another shot! A year later, the committee was still bogged down on the definition of 'Native' – and had not even started trying to define a 'European' or 'Coloured'.

The great hybrid populations, like the Cape Coloured people, are impossible to classify precisely; some are dark, some light, some Hottentot-looking, some Negroid-looking, some Caucasoid-looking. Our attempt to label every member of our population with a specific racial label is unscientific in the extreme; we are trying to force people who do exist, as real pulsating human beings, into categories of our own creating, which do not exist as clearly-defined entities. All this is being done in the name of a fantasy called racial purity, which science declares has no validity whatsoever.

This brings me to my next theme: racial mixing.

Racial hybridization

At one time or another, every conceivable anatomical disharmony and social evil has been attributed to racial mixing. Recently, we were treated to the spectacle of a White minister of religion expressing himself thus on the Coloured people, an example of a hybrid group:

Here we have a people who came into being through miscegenation with the Whites.[1]
And as a mongrel race, they are, to us, the writing on the wall, a warning against what can happen with intermixture. They are Western in their code of living. They speak our language, sing our songs, live in our country, but they are a people notorious for their moral corruption. Lies are to them second nature. They are absolutely unreliable in any matter, have little ambition and get their greatest pleasure from a bottle of wine and debauchery (The *Star*, 1961).

Unthinkingly, all these features are attributed to the results of mixing of genes; and the good minister is guilty of a threefold inaccuracy – firstly, there is no justification for attributing these characteristics to the Coloured people at large; secondly, he is blaming the genes for features which science has shown are culturally determined, not genetically; and thirdly, he is lightly jumping to the conclusion that these particular effects result from the mixing of genes. No one of these components of this man's thinking could stand up to the cold light of scientific scrutiny and they have a ring about them which is unpleasantly reminiscent of the quotations I gave earlier from one of Germany's leading racist-anthropologists, Gunther.

The views he expressed are all too frequent among South Africans; even, one might be tempted to add, South Africans of different races. Yet, by the same strange process of double-think, to which I earlier referred, we find Professor D. F. du Toit Malherbe in his 'Stamouers van die Afrikanervolk' declaring approvingly, 'Mixed marriages gave our population its unity' – only he meant mixed marriages between White and White!

He found it necessary to add:

Nobody in South Africa need worry about a bit of non-White blood[2] (mostly from Eastern people with a high civilization) which filtered in in the beginning as a result of mixed marriages. It has been diluted by pure blood from Europe with the result that the few families in

1. Notice the peculiar turn of phraseology which makes it look as though the Whites were the innocent and injured party!
2. Note again the confusion of civilization and race!

question today have some of the blondest people among them. The blood composition of the Afrikaner people as a whole is today purer than that of many of Europe's and America's peoples (The *Star*, 1959).

From what I have said earlier, I think it is readily apparent that the writer has been guilty – in this short passage – not only of flying in the face of historical facts, but of perpetrating every single one of the unscientific howlers to which I have already referred.

The tragedy for our young children, the South Africans of tomorrow, is that our school books on History and Race Studies are filled with this sort of thing. Small wonder that young people, nurtured on such pseudo-scientific fallacies, grow up to approve policies based upon these very fallacies.

Nowhere more strikingly demonstrated than in Southern Africa, the principles of racial hybridization have here produced a melange of enormous complexity. Recent studies made from the Department of Anatomy of the University of the Witwatersrand have revealed the variety of racial elements woven into the faces of various South African groups. In 1937, Professor Dart first demonstrated that living Bushmen of the Southern Kalahari included strange foreign facial types, Mediterranean, Armenoid and Mongoloid (Dart, 1937). Similar variability has been found more recently by Eric Williams (1954) and Hertha de Villiers in Kung and Heikum Bushmen, while de Villiers has recognized Mediterranean, Nordic, Armenoid and Bush facial types liberally distributed among the Negro faces of the Ovambo (see Eriksen, 1954). Of course, the possibility cannot be ruled out that some of these features, e.g. the so-called Mongolian eye-fold, may be parallel developments. Nevertheless, in the light of our knowledge of racial movements and contacts in prehistoric Africa over some thousands of years, there is scarcely room for doubt that much of the high incidence of these foreign features reflects ancient hybridization, rather than the recent parallel evolution of features already present in existing racial groups.

This is important because it is by the face that we most commonly judge people. We might look around this room and, our eye lighting on some particular individual, we tend to jump to the conclusion, 'Ha! Obviously an Eskimo!' It is common knowledge that the face betrays a wealth of information about every individual; from it we glean clues, about race, age, sex, family relationships, state of health and even disposition and habits. Raymond Mortimer, in his Essay on Clothes, makes the point neatly: 'If we really had modesty, it is our faces we should conceal. By comparison, our legs are anonymous, our bellies uneventful.'

All this evidence confirms that a search for a 'pure' race in South African would be in vain. Physical anthropologists may still speak of the 'typical Negro' or 'typical Bushman' face; but the studies cited a moment ago reveal that the individual with 'typical' face is exceptional rather than usual. It is most exceptional to find in *one* individual a combination of *all* the features, *each* of which, *on its own*, may occur most frequently in one particular race – features such as the shape of the nose, and protrusion of the jaws, the skin and hair colour, hair form on scalp, face and body, form and colour of the eyes, the architecture of the cheekbones, the forehead and the chin, the body build and stature, and the blood group picture.

As Kroeber has put it (1948), a race is only an average of a large number of individuals.

Where miscegenation has created a large hybrid population, as in the Coloured people of South Africa, a relative stability does tend to emerge; for a new race is being born. Professor J. Keen (1951) has claimed that a relatively stabilized Coloured type may be recognised, at least as regards the skull; but even so, a spectrum of variation exists. Although the Coloured population is emerging as a new race, it intergrades marginally with the intergrading results from the wide range of variation within the Coloured people itself, due to reshuffling and mutation of the genes, and from the small but definite fringe of continued miscegenation between people 'on either side of the line' or who have 'crossed the line'. There are individual Coloured people whom one could not distinguish on their physical appearance from Caucasoid Whites on the one hand and from South African Hottentots and Negroids on the other; while there are individual self-styled Whites and Negroes whom one could not distinguish from Coloureds.

The main difference between the Coloureds and other living peoples, as Sonnabend and Sofer have stressed (1948), is that the particular mixture which produced the Coloured people occurred within historical times and is still fresh in human memory. The earlier miscegenations which have given rise to the other groups in our population are shrouded in the distant past and, indeed, many of them took place before the dawn of recorded history. Furthermore, the Coloured people are still living cheek by jowl with the main racial groups which produced them and, in fact, are still being numerically reinforced from their parent stocks; whereas in the past, hybrid populations have often completely absorbed or supplanted their progenitors.

One of the arguments often advanced against racial crossing is that it is biologically harmful: the particular form of biological harm most commonly stressed is that the hybrids are likely to be sterile. Thus, it has been asserted that in the former Dutch East Indies, Indo-Europeans became sterile in about the third generation. However, it remains a fact that hybrid populations have maintained themselves numerically, whether it be the Pitcairn Islanders, the descendants of Polynesians and English mutineers from the 'Bounty'; or the Cape Coloured folk who today number about one-and-a-half millions; or the Brown people of Jamaica; or the bewildering array of hybrids in Hawaii; or the 28 million Indian-White crosses in South and Central America and Mexico, and the eight million Negro-White hybrids in the New World. In fact, official statistics show that the birth-rate of Coloured people in South Africa is higher than that of any other group in the population, being almost double that of the Whites. So infertility is not a consequence of race-mixture. This is true even between races which may be regarded as opposite extremes. Our recent researches have brought to light fertile crossings between Bushmen and Europeans: in both families the male parent was a Caucasoid of predominantly Nordic physical type. Nordics and Bushmen are physically poles apart, yet crosses between them are completely fertile.

A second form of biological harm which, it has been claimed results from racial hybridization, is physical deterioration. Yet, it has never been adequately demonstrated that hybrids show physical deterioration. In fact, some studies show just the opposite. For example, Eugen Fischer's classical studies of the Reho-both Bastards, a cross between South African Boers and Hottentots, showed that they are a healthy and exceptionally vigorous people. Despite the uninformed claims which frequently feature in the correspondence columns of our daily newspapers, we can only conclude that no reliable documentation exists that race mixture as a biological process is inevitably a deleterious one. It would seem that hybrids are different from others principally because of the way they are regarded and treated by those among whom they live. If there are harmful consequences of race mixture, they are not biological ones but social, and can generally be traced to social factors such as the attitudes between in-group and out-group. The inferiority of the hybrid is in the eye of the observer, especially when the observer happens to belong to one of the parental races and considers himself to be racially pure. As Alexander Pope said, 'To the jaundiced eye, all is yellow.'

Summary and conclusions

Finally, let me recapitulate briefly the main conclusions of this lecture:

1. Race is an idea borrowed from biology. It helps us to classify the endless variety of human beings, in the same way as biologists classify plants or animals.

2. The numerous populations into which mankind may be divided have been classified into major groups or constellations of races, namely the Caucasoid, the Mongoloid, the Negroid, the the Australoid and the Khoisanoid.

3. Races differ not in absolutes, but in the frequency with which different genes occur in different populations.

4. The overwhelming majority of our genes are shared in common by all mankind; a relatively small percentage control those features which differentiate the races from one another.

5. The formation of the modern races of man is a relatively recent process, probably not extending back in time for more than 25 to 50 thousand years. As against this period of recent diversification, at least one hundred times as long a period of its human ancestry has been spent by each race in common with all other races, as it has spent alone.

6. Racially discriminatory practices make certain assumptions about race, sometimes overtly, sometimes tacitly and sometimes

couched under new names, such as cultural differences. These include:

(a) the assumption that races are pure and distinct entities;

(b) the assumption that all members of a race look alike and think and act alike; basic to this one is the idea that how one behaves depends on one's genes;

(c) the assumption that some races are better than others, some indeed falling right outside the magic circle of love and brotherhood, not being worthy of one's finest feelings because they are inferior beings.

7. Science provides no evidence that any single one of the assumptions underlying South Africa's racial legislation is justified.

8. Mental characteristics are not used nor are they useful in the classification of the races; racial classification is based purely on physical (including physiological) features. Science has neither proved nor disproved that races differ genetically in intellect or bent.

9. Science has offered no confirmation that some races are superior to others. Science has failed to confirm that some races are nearer to the apes and others to the angels.

10. Accidents of geography and history are sufficient to account for the different contributions which different populations have made to the sum-total of what we have conceitedly come to call 'western' civilization; conceitedly – for 'western' civilization did not start in the west, but reached the west late from the Middle East! There is no need to blame the tardy, almost reluctant adoption of civilization by North-Western Europeans on racial inferiority; nor is there any need to resort to similar explanations of Africa's late adoption of civilization. Difficulties of terrain, of physical environment and of communication, are sufficient to account for different contributions to the advancement of human culture.

11. It should be recalled that Africa *has* made contributions; it contributed *Man* to the face of our planet and too, it contributed the earliest beginnings of human culture, differentiating the animal Man from the other animals. Perhaps, too, we should

regard its ability to relax as a great contribution which western man has been slow to recognize and slower to emulate.

12. Culture, language and outlook are not inseparably bound up with particular physical racial features. But Man's very culture is today altering the direction of his evolution, as he moves cosmopolitanly throughout the world and cultural and racial divergence gives way over large areas to cultural and racial convergence.

13. The myth of the pure race has been thoroughly disproved. There are no pure human races and, as far as our fossil record goes, there never have been.

14. Racial groups are highly variable entities; intermediates exist between one race and the next; and all races are capable of interbreeding with all others, all that is, that have been tested.

15. Not only is purity of race a non-existent fantasy, but the idea that purity of race is a desirable thing has no evidence to support it.

16. The fallacious beliefs about the alleged evils of race crossing do not bear scientific scrutiny: neither sterility, nor physical deterioration, can be regarded as proved biological consequences of race-mixing. The unfortunate effects, if unfortunate effects there be, are purely social, the results of the way in which others look at and treat the hybrids.

I have tried, all too sketchily, to cover an enormously wide field in the space of one lecture. By way of introduction to the subject, I have tried to show what science thinks about race and, in order to bring these ideas home, I have contrasted with that popular misconceptions about race. You may perhaps wonder: why should I have all this scientific mumbo-jumbo thrust on to me? It is of nobody's concern what I believe about the theory of the expanding universe or the atomic theory. Why therefore should I concern myself with the scientific theory of race? The answer is that these other terms and concepts are emotionally and politically neutral; the term 'race' on the other hand is heavily charged emotionally and politically and full of unsound and even dangerous meanings. It is in the name of race that millions of people have been murdered and millions of others are being held in degradation. That is why you cannot afford to remain ignorant about race.

References

CHARDIN, T. de (1959), *The Phenomenon of Man*, Collins.

COON, C. S., GARN, S. M., and BIRDSELL, J. B. (1950), *Races: a Study of the Problems of Race Formation in Man*, Chas. E. Thomas, Springfield.

DART, R. A. (1937), 'The physical characters of the Auni-Khomani Bushmen', *Bantu Studies*, vol. 11, pp. 175–246.

ERIKSEN, H. (1954), 'Facial features of Kuanyama, Ovambo and Heikum Bushmen', *S. Afr. J. Sci.*, vol. 51, pp. 18–29.

GUNTHER, H. F. K. (1927), *The Racial Elements of European History*, Methuen.

JAHODA, M. (1960), 'X-ray of the racist mind', *UNESCO Courier*, no. 10, Oct., pp. 24–7.

KEEN, J. A. (1951), *Trans. Roy. Soc. S. Afr.*, vol. 33, 29.

KLINEBERG, O. (1951), *Race and Psychology*, UNESCO, Paris, reprinted 1965.

KROEBER, A. L. (1948), *Anthropology*, Harcourt Press.

SHAPIRO, H. L. (1944), 'Anthropology's contribution to interracial understanding', *Science*, vol. 99, pp. 373–6.

SONNABEND, H., and SOFER, C. (1948), *South Africa's Step-Children*, S A Affairs Pamphlet, Johannesburg,

The *Star* (1957), Letter 20 June, Johannesburg.

The *Star* (1959), 24 November, Johannesburg.

The *Star* (1961), 18 January, Johannesburg.

TOBIAS, P. V. (1953), 'The problem of race determination: limiting factors in the identification of the South African races', *J. Forensic Med.*, vol. 1, pp. 113–23.

UNESCO (1952), *The Race Concept: results of an Inquiry: Vaderland* (1961), 18 Maart.

VALLOIS, H. V. (1952), Race Inventory paper for Wenner-Gren Foundation International Symposium on Anthropology, June 9–20, New York.

WASHBURN, S. L. (1945), *Thinking About Race*, Smithsonian Report, pp. 363–78, New York.

WEINER, J. S. (1942), 'Physical anthropology since 1935: a survey of developments', in *A Hundred Years of Anthropology*, Duckworth.

WILLIAMS, E. W, (1954), 'Facial features of some !Kung Bushmen', *S. Afr. J. Sci.*, vol. 51, pp. 11–17.

2 J. S. Weiner

Nose Shape and Climate

J. S. Weiner, 'Nose Shape and Climate', *American Journal of Physical Anthropology*, (N.S.) vol 12, no. 4, 1954, pp. 1–4.

In 1923 Thomson and Buxton demonstrated a close association between the shape of the nose, expressed as the nasal index, and external climatic conditions. They reported, as did Davies (1932) on still larger samples, that the nasal index is more highly correlated with mean annual temperature than with the relative humidity of the air. For 'predicting' the index they recommended the use of both air temperature and relative humidity in the regression formula, since temperature used alone was apt to produce considerable errors. The correlations led them to regard 'temperature as a dominant factor' though 'modified by various degrees of humidity'. Davies also considered that 'temperature exerts a stronger influence than humidity' in view of its higher correlation coefficient.

In their discussion of the functional significance of these relations, Thomson and Buxton made clear that both temperature and humidity were concerned. They suggested that the modifications of nose shape in different climates may reasonably be related to the need for moistening the inspired air; for this reason the humidity of the air is obviously of physiological significance. They indicated also that variation of nose shape might bear some relation to heat loss from the respiratory tract. They argued, for example, that 'in the tropics the loss of lung water from the respiratory tract is undoubtedly of considerable physiological importance. In air containing the highest relative humidity the existence of a free passage of entry is of advantage, in order that sufficient air may be breathed in to absorb water from the respiratory tract.'

That moistening of the air is a prime function of the nasal epithelium appears from the work of Proetz (1941) and Negus

(1949). Negus gives physiological, pathological and clinical reasons for the importance of this moistening on the vitality and activity of the cilia, which are in fact more susceptible to changes in the consistency of the film in which they work (and therefore to drying out) than they are to quite large degrees of heating and cooling. According to Dawes and Prichard (1953), Perwitchscky's findings (1927) also suggest that warming is a less important function than moistening of the inspired air. Dawes and Prichard point out the means by which the inspired air is moistened and cleansed are closely related. In providing moisture additional to that contained in the inspired air so as to bring the moisture content to about 95 per cent relative humidity at body temperature, the mucous membrane of the nose in dry climates may secrete even up to a liter of water per day (Proetz 1941).

It follows from these considerations that if the shape of the nose bears some relation to the moistening of inspired air, the nasal index should be most closely associated with the physical factor primarily concerned in the exchange of water from nasal epithelium to inspired air. This factor is the absolute humidity and can be expressed either as the vapor pressure of the air or in terms of its moisture content (in grains per pound of dry air). The loss of water from the respiratory tract induced by evaporative cooling which according to Thomson and Buxton might also influence the shape of the nose, is likewise governed by the vapor pressure of the inspired air. The amount of heat lost by this evaporative channel especially in hot climates, it may be mentioned, is a relatively small proportion of the total heat loss and the effectiveness of the respiratory tract in desert climates would be reduced by the heat gain from breathing air at temperatures above that of the body. In any case, evaporative heat loss from the respiratory tract and moisture addition to the inspired air would both be functions of the vapor pressure gradient between the external air and the virtually saturated surfaces of the tract. The vapor pressure of the latter may be assumed to remain relatively constant so that nose shape can be directly related to external vapor pressure.

The use of the two separate climatic variates, air temperature and relative humidity, though useful enough for indicating the type of climate associated with variation in nasal index, is thus not entirely adequate to express these postulated functions of water exchange by the nose. To combine them statistically does not furnish the correct physical specification of the outside air.

The data provided by Thomson and Buxton for some one hundred and fifty living population samples have been re-examined in a preliminary way and the indications are that correlations with the external absolute humidity are likely to be as good as, and probably better than, those with air temperature and humidity. It has not yet been possible to assemble the rather formidable amount of meteorological data (and many of these are probably not available) necessary to obtain the true mean absolute humidity for these one hundred and fifty locations, but as an approximation the absolute humidity has been derived from the mean annual temperature and mean annual relative humidity as given in Thomson and Buxton's paper. This approximation involves only a relatively small error for polar regions and is unimportant for hot regions (Sumner and Tunnel, 1949). Table I shows that the original coefficients are appreciably lower than that with the wet bulb temperature or even more so than that with vapor pressure of the air. From the latter the relation between the nasal index and the amount of water to be secreted, say in twenty four hours, to humidify the inspired air could be calculated, if desired.

Table 1 **Nasal Index (146 groups living)**

Correlated with	Coefficient	Standard error
*Dry bulb temp.	0·63	0·050
*Relative humidity	0·42	0·068
*Dry bulb temp. and rel. humidity	0·72	0·040
Wet bulb temp.	0·77	0·034
Vapor pressure of the air	0·82	0·027

* Source: Thomson and Buxton (1923).

It would be worth extending the analysis on these lines to many more groups using more detailed meteorological data. The figures given should be regarded meanwhile as indicative of the functional basis underlying the nasal index-climate relationship, namely, the loss of water to the inspired air.

References

DAVIES, A. (1932), 'A re-survey of the morphology of the nose in relation to climate', *J. Roy. Anthropol. Inst.*, vol. 62, pp. 337–59.

DAWES, J. D. K., and PRICHARD, M. M. L. (1953). 'Studies of vascular arrangements of the nose', *J. Anat.*, vol. 87., pp. 311–22.

NEGUS, V. E. (1949), 'The defence of the air passages with special reference to ciliary action', *Oxford Medical School Gazette*, vol. 4, p. 1952.

PERWITCHSCKY, R. (1927), 'Die Temperatur und Feuchtigkeits-verhältnisse der Atemluft in den Luftwegen', *Arch. Ohr.-Nas.-und Kehlkheilk.*, vol. 117, pp. 1–36.

PROETZ, A. W. (1941), *Essays on Applied Physiology of the Nose*, St Louis, Annals Publishing Co.

SUMNER, E. J., and TUNNEL, G. A. (1949), 'Determination of the true mean vapour pressure of the atmosphere from temperature and hygrometric data', *Meteorological Magazine*, vol. 79, pp. 258–63, 295–301.

THOMSON, A., and BUXTON, D. (1923), Man's nasal index in relation to certain climatic conditions', *J. Roy. Anthropol. Inst.*, vol. 53., pp. 92–122.

3 R. E. G. Armattoe

Lament for the Negro

R. E. G. Armattoe, *Deep Down in the Blackman's Mind*, Arthur H. Stockwell, Ilfracombe, p. 91.

I know naught that's friendly to Negroes
Save earth, sky, storms, rain and mosquitoes.
For the earth is full of their dust,
Which it turns into mud with lust.
And the sky exposes their plight
With its shameless denial of right.
The storms have been full with their sighs,
Despite their attempt at disguise.
And the rains are wet with the tears
They have shed all these many years.
Mosquitoes are brothers by blood
Since they've drink them in such a flood.
There is naught that is friendly to the Negro
Save earth, sky, storms, rain and mosquito.

4 Judith Friedlander

Malaria and Demography in the Lowlands of Mexico: An Ethno-Historical Approach

Judith Friedlander, 'Malaria and demography in the lowlands of Mexico: an ethno-historical approach', in R. F. Spencer (ed.), *Forms of Symbolic Action*, University of Washington Press, 1969, pp. 217–33. (Some maps and tables have been omitted)

The purpose of this paper is to offer an explanation for the presence of a relatively high Negro and surprisingly low indigenous population in the lowlands of Mexico during colonial times. Almost immediately after the Spanish conquest, the Indians thoughout Mexico started to die off in great numbers, causing a severe labor shortage which threatened the Spanish economic system. These deaths were in large part caused by Old World diseases which were introduced by the colonizers and against which the Indians had no resistance. African slaves were therefore imported, proving healthier and more suited to the strenuous work than the Indians.

Even after the arrival of the African slaves, the Indian's mortality rate remained high. In fact they very nearly disappeared entirely in the lowlands and during the early years of colonization the Indians were dying off twice as fast in the lowlands as in the highlands. The black slaves, on the other hand, who came primarily from the tropics of Africa, seemed better adapted to the hot humid lowlands of Mexico than did the original inhabitants. Thus while the Indians were vanishing from everywhere and African slaves were being used throughout Mexico, it was in the lowlands where the Indian's death rate was most dramatic and where the black slaves were in greatest demand. It should be kept in mind that sugar, one of Mexico's most lucrative exports, was grown and processed in the lowlands; therefore as sugar became increasingly important, the plantations and mills required larger and larger labor forces, which, for lack of Indians, depended almost entirely on African slaves.

Such being the case, we are faced with the following two questions:

1. Why should proportionately more indigenous peoples have died in the lowlands than in the highlands?

2. Did the African slaves serve to increase further the mortality of the Indians in the lowlands and if so, why did they not affect the Indians in the highlands as well, for black slaves were numerous there too?

The answers, we suggest, are in part related to the role played by one particular disease, malaria, and the differential immunity to it afforded to the two populations under discussion. Malaria is primarily a lowland disease and its impact was only felt in the lowland areas of Mexico.

We argue that the Indians suffered greater losses in the lowlands than in the highlands because of the deleterious effects of this imported disease, while the Africans thrived, for significant numbers of them had a genetically inherited immunity to malaria. We further postulate that the introduction to Mexico of the malarial parasites coincides with that of the Negro slaves who came from some of the most malaria-ridden regions of Africa. In Mexico, the Anopheles mosquitoes, the necessary vector, fed on the infected blood and thus passed on this disease to the Indian and white peoples who were not immune. As to why the Indians suffered more than the white men will be clarified below.

Unlike many of the other imported diseases that ravaged Mexico after the conquest, malaria does not hit just once, killing large numbers, perhaps, but leaving those who survive immune; rather it attacks the individual repeatedly, wearing down one's general resistance to other diseases as well as causing pregnant women to abort. Malaria, therefore, very easily could have dealt a severe blow to the indigenous population. Once introduced into an area, it could have taken a continuing yearly toll of non-immune Indians, either by being directly responsible for their deaths, by inhibiting normal reproduction, or by making them more susceptible to any disease that might have passed through the region. Epidemics of greater intensity than malaria came and went, leaving many dead, but those who survived were immune; while malaria continued year in and year out, constantly draining the people, never permitting the Indians to recover numerically, even to the meager extent they so succeeded in doing in the highlands. Although the Europeans suffered from malaria also, at least their systems were partially protected against the other diseases which were introduced into the area, for these were primarily of Old World origin. As for the Africans, they suffered neither from the periodic Old World epidemics to any great extent, nor from the omnipresent malaria. Thus the black slave seemed to be the perfect labor substitute for the disease-ridden lowlands of Mexico; however, this solution to the problem was complicated by the fact that with the Negro came malaria, the very disease, we suggest, which caused the further demise of the Indian population.

We may here attempt to support the above argument by bringing together information collected by medical doctors, biological anthropologists, historians and demographers. The problem will be broken down into the following sections:

1. Evidence for the immunization to malaria of significant numbers of Africans.

2. African slaves in Mexico; their origin; their numbers; and where they worked.

3. Evidence that the Indians were dying at a more drastic rate in the lowlands than in the highlands.

4. Evidence that there was malaria in the lowlands during colonial times and that there was a differential immunity to this disease.

5. Evidence of traces of this immunity in modern Negroid populations in the malarial regions of present-day Mexico.

6. Conclusions.

Evidence for the immunization to malaria of significant numbers of Africans.

The Negro's relative immunity to malaria has been the subject of great speculation among both biological anthropologists and medical doctors for years. Recently it has been suggested that there might be a positive correlation between the comparatively high incidence of certain blood deficiencies, most notably sickle-cell anemia and glucose-6-phosphate-dehydrogenase (abbreviated G-6-P-D) deficiency and the fact that the populations in which these are found are living in highly malarial regions. Since the evidence for G-6-P-D deficiency is rather suspect, according to specialists at Billings Hospital at the University of Chicago (Bowman, 1967 and Powell *et al.*, 1966), we will restrict this discussion to sickle-cell anemia alone.

Sickle-cell anemia (Singer, 1962 unless otherwise noted) which is found primarily among Negro or Negro mixed-blood populations, is caused by the presence of an abnormal hemoglobin in the blood of the individual. This is only phenotypically evident when the person is homozygous for this trait, that is, when he inherits a gene for the abnormal hemoglobin from both of his parents. The heterozygote sometimes suffers as well when under great stress. In other words, under most circumstances, it is only the homozygous individual who suffers from this disease. When a person does have sickle-cell anemia, he is not expected to live long enough to have children.

With such an extremely high mortality rate among anemic victims, it would be expected that the incidences of the sickle-cell gene would be selected out of a population. However, this is not the case in malarial regions. It seems that those individuals who are heterozygous for the sickling trait, having inherited the gene from only one of their parents, and who do not usually suffer from the anemia, are favored in such environments. This means that these heterozygous individuals are reproducing at a greater rate than those who do not have this sickling trait at all in areas with malaria; thus the number of sickle-cell anemia cases remains constant, the deaths of the homozygotes being balanced by the higher fertility of the heterozygotes. The explanation for this offered by Neel, Allison and others is that those individuals heterozygous for the sickle-cell trait have a selective advantage over non-sicklers in malarial regions. In simpler terms, heterozygotes do not usually suffer from malaria, a disease which, among other things, is known to cause miscarriages and they are therefore reproducing more rapidly.

In Figures 1 and 2, pp. 61 and 62 it may be seen that the

areas in Africa with the greatest incidence of the sickle-cell trait (designated as HbS in the key), are West Africa, Angola, the Congo and the Sudan. These are also the most intensive malarial zones.

Since findings of paleo-pathologists indicate that malaria is not indigenous to the New World (Dunn, 1965), we suggest that it was transported to Mexico along with the African slaves. It is, however, unlikely that the parasite could have entered Mexico in, let us say, the blood of the 'infected', but 'unaffected' black slaves; for according to one fairly well-accepted hypothesis, individuals with the sickling trait do not suffer from malaria precisely because, for the parasite, this abnormal hemoglobin is an unfavorable medium in which to develop, hence it dies. On the other hand, it does seem reasonable to postulate that malaria could have been contracted by the white slavers who transported the slaves from Africa to Mexico and thus the disease accompanied the slaves to the New World. Another carrier of malaria could have been the large number of Spanish soldiers who served in Italy before coming to the New World, for Italy at that time was seriously plagued by malaria (Sauer, 1966, p. 204).

African slaves in Mexico; their origin; their numbers; and where they worked.

The slaves sent to Mexico came primarily from Cape Verde during the sixteenth century and from Angola in the seventeenth (Aguirre Beltrán, 1946, p. 245). There was also a large number coming from the Sudan as well. As can be observed on the maps, these areas have populations with some of the highest occurrences of the sickle-cell trait today and are highly endemic for malaria. We are assuming that these regions were at least as concentrated during the sixteenth and seventeenth centuries as now.

In Tables 3, 4, and 5, pp. 64 and 66 it may be seen that as early as 1570, there were as many as 20,569 Africans and 2435 Afro-Mestizos in Mexico according to the information quoted by Aguirre Beltrán. By 1742, there were 20,131 Africans and 249,368 Afro-Mestizos, which implies a sizeable population of Negroes and Negro mixed-bloods.

We are left, then, with the problem of establishing that there was a large Negro population in the lowlands areas of Mexico. The bishopric (obispado) of Tlaxcala, which consistently has one of the highest African and African mixed populations in Mexico, is an area which includes the present-day states of Tabasco and Veracruz (Priestly, 1923, p.104), which do have lowland sections. However, the indigenous and European populations are also high in the bishropric. We might assume that the Indians lived in the highlands and the Negroes in the lowlands, but working from these figures alone, that would be mere conjecture. On the other hand, to support such a speculation, Aguirre Beltrán states (1946, p. 192) that by the end of the sixteenth century, the city of Veracruz, for one, had 200 Spaniards, more than 500 Negroes and virtually no Indians, either in the city or in the surrounding lowland region. Furthermore, since the crown as early as 1609 proclaimed that Indian labor could not be employed for certain jobs, such as sugar processing (Harris, 1964, p.15) and sugar was one of the most important exports, as well as the fact that the Indians were dying off at a more drastic rate in the lowlands than in the highlands, it does stand to reason that slaves would be more in demand here than elsewhere and would therefore be found in greater numbers. With no figures to support his statement, Harris maintains just this (1964, p. 17).

Evidence that the Indians were dying at a more drastic rate in the lowlands than in the highlands.

The best information on the population decline in Mexico after the conquest comes from the work of the demographers, Borah and Cook. According to their latest tabulations, the aboriginal population in 1519 was between 20 and 28 million (Borah and Cook, 1963, p. 88). These figures are considered extremely high for the aboriginal population on the eve of the conquest by prehistorians and are questioned on the grounds that prehispanic agricultural techniques could not have supported such a large population (Armillas, 1968). However, everybody agrees that the population loss was catastrophic. Without giving specific numbers, Wolf suggests that six-sevenths of the pre-conquest population of Middle America was wiped out (Wolf, 1959, p. 195). Since in this paper we are not concerned with exact figures, rather with overall patterns, it is enough merely to alert the reader to the fact that the above totals for 1519 are debatable; for there is no question about the fact that the population loss was dramatic. By 1532, the population had dropped to 16,800,000; by 1548, to 6,300,000; by 1580, to 1,900,000; by 1595, to 1,375,000 and by 1605, to 1,075,000. . . . by 1568, only 7·44 per cent of the 1532 population was left in the lowlands and 19·85 per cent in the highlands. African slaves began to be imported in substantial numbers by 1528. After 1580, however, the decline was faster in the highlands than in the lowlands and by 1605, the population was hardly declining at all in the lowlands. At the same time, the rate in the highlands was also abating, but not as quickly. Thus in the earlier years, the rate of population decline in the lowlands was greater than that in the highlands and after 1580, the trend was reversed. When the figures are averaged over the years, however, they suggest that 'the rate of population decline was nearly twice as great in the lowland regions as in the highland ones' (Cook and Borah, 1960, p. 52).

Many factors could account for this sudden leveling off of the mortality rate in the lowlands: the disappearance of epidemic diseases, the improvement of the diet and the migration of highland Indians to the lowlands (Cook and Borah, 1960, p. 56), although the latter was against the law – the New Laws of 1542 (Humboldt, 1811, vol. 2, p. 168). As to why the highland Indians' mortality rate was more constant and hence became greater than the lowlands during the latter fifth of the sixteenth century and into the seventeenth before it too began to level off, is a complex question which we will not attempt to answer fully here. Let us suggest in passing, however, that the highland region had a long history of famines before the Spanish conquest, as is reported in the Nahuatl Codices (Carter, 1931, p. 96) and such food shortages remained a serious problem, for although the Spaniards improved the agricultural techniques, they permitted fewer Indians to attend to farming and irrigation than had formerly been the case because they needed large labor forces to work in the mines. Thus food shortages undoubtedly remained a serious problem, continuing to weaken the Indians even after many of the more dangerous epidemics disappeared. The humid lowland, on the other hand, with its fertile land and sparser population always had abundant food, a situation which lured the Aztecs to conquer the region during pre-hispanic times.

Cook and Borah's statistics for the lowlands are compatible with the argument which is being presented in this paper. As we have stressed earlier, malaria is not necessarily a killer, but causes one to be more susceptible to other diseases by wearing down the individual's general resistance. It follows, therefore, that if the other major epidemics should disappear, malaria would lose some of its force as a lethal catalyst. As Curtin has pointed out, the most numerous immunities to diseases are acquired, not inherited (Curtin, 1968, p. 197). Many diseases, when experienced during childhood are far less likely to be lethal at that time. When the child recovers, he is conferred with a life-long immunity to the disease. 'In general, then, the individual will be safest if he stays in the disease environment of his childhood' (Curtin, 1968, p. 197). Now the Indians' disease environment was radically altered by the Europeans and Africans who were carriers, though often not sufferers of the Old World diseases; hence the fully grown and unimmune Indians fell victim to epidemic after epidemic. During these first sixty years (up to 1580), however, it is perfectly conceivable that a new equilibrium was being defined. In other words by 1580 or so, the majority of the old World diseases had already been introduced and were now a part of the Indians' childhood disease environment and therefore new generations of young Indians were growing up having acquired, during childhood, immunities to these other Old World diseases. Thus, although malaria was still present, for one cannot acquire an immunity to it but must be born with it, this disease no longer posed the same lethal threat that it did before.

By the time the lowland Indian population started to level off, the numbers of indigenous people left was so low and they were so culturally fragmented as a result of the thorough infiltration of the hispanic plantation way of life (Harris, 1964, part 4), that they never regained their cultural identity, even to the meager extent they succeeded in doing so in the highlands where their numbers, in absolute terms, never dropped so low. There are of course exceptions, most notably the Yucatan, which will be discussed later, and a few pockets of Indian communities in other lowland areas. In the Costa Chica area, for one, we will see that these 'Indians' have intermixed with Negroes.

To look at one specific lowland region more closely, we find that the following demographic changes took place between 1519 and 1580 in the environs of the city of Veracruz: at Cempoala, two leagues to the north, there were 20,000 people, by 1580, fewer than thirty houses remained; at Rinconada, five leagues to the west, there were 10,000 Indians, dropping to fewer than fifty houses; other towns left no trace at all aside from their names (letter written by Alonso Hernández Diosado to Viceroy Don Martín, 1580. In Pasquel, 1960, p. 188).

Evidence that there was malaria in the lowlands during colonial times and that there was a differential immunity to this disease

The cause of malaria was not understood during colonial times. However, the disease was recognized and was thought to have been the result of inhaling the putrid air which came from swamps hence its name, 'malaria' – 'mal aria' or 'bad air' in Italian (Prothero, 1965, p. 7). The current Spanish term for the disease is 'el paludismo' coming from the same root as the adjective 'paludoso', *marshy*.

Contemporary accounts of the area describe a malarial environment, which is convincing both in terms of the colonial conception of the disease conditions as well as our own. Diosado pointed out that the region around Veracruz was particularly unhealthy because there were many 'ponds, rivers and marshes and other wet and swampy places from which the aforementioned winds collect the thick and putrid vapors which are blown over the city causing no small inconveniences to those who live there . . .' (Pasquel, 1960, vol. 1, p. 91). A Jesuit priest described the city in similar terms: 'The port of the city is very hot and humid, plagued by mosquitoes to such a degree that hardly any light gets through to the homes and what made (*sic*) this port more uncomfortable was it being infested with diseases . . .' (Aguirre Beltrán, 1946, p. 191).

In sum, it is fairly clear that malaria was a serious problem by at least 1580. That the Negro was able to withstand this disease is supported by statements such as the royal proclamation of 1778 which said: 'In view of the fact that the malaria epidemic has layed up the majority of the Granada Infantry Regiment, give arms to the companies of Negroes and Negro mixed-bloods'

(Aguirre Beltrán, 1946, p. 195), for they alone were healthy enough to perform military duties. Furthermore, as recently as seventy years ago, it was still held that only the Negro was able to withstand tropical diseases, that the Indians and Europeans were not meant to live in such places (Murphy, 1958, p. 183); yet the Indians did live quite comfortably in these lowland regions before the onslaught of Old World diseases, particularly malaria.

Negro slaves were regarded as Herculean in strength; one Negro was thought to be as strong as four Indians (Murphy, 1958, p. 181). Aguirre Beltrán points out that those slaves who arrived in the New World were undoubtedly some of the most physically fit Negroes available, for they had to undergo several screenings before they set foot in the western Hemisphere. Most important, they were chosen in Africa for their superior strength and health (this implies those who were not suffering from malaria).

Evidence of traces of this immunity in modern Negroid populations in the malarial regions of present-day Mexico

Under the direction of Ruben Lisker of the Department of Hematology in the Instituto Nacional de la Nutrición in Mexico, studies have been conducted to determine the prevalence of the sickle-cell trait among the present-day populations of Mexico. His work in the Costa Chica area shows that the population has a significant amount of the sickle-cell trait, directly linked to the Negroes in the area and that furthermore, the trait seems to have been positively selected for in the area which is highly endemic for *vivax* malaria and, to a lesser extent, for *falciparum* malaria (Lisker *et al.*, 1965, pp. 184–5). When we say a 'significant' number of individuals have this trait, we are talking about 10 per cent of the population in the town of Cuajincuilapa, known for having many Negro inhabitants, Negroes having been in this area since the seventeenth century, approximately 4 per cent in Ometepec, 3 per cent in San Pedro Mixtepec and virtually no incidence in Poch-utla. These villages are listed in order of proximity to Cuajin-culapa. Since for Africa, Livingstone considers similar statistics meaningful in determining the genetic resistance of those popula-tions to malaria (Livingstone, 1967), then the figures in the New World are all the more outstanding when we remember that the peoples in the Costa Chica region are the descendants of the miscegenation of three races, two of which (the Indians and the whites) do not have the abnormal hemoglobin S.

Aside from Lisker's work, virtually no studies have been conducted in Mexico which have tested for the sickle-cell trait. Until Lisker or others do more of the kind of work already done in the Costa Chica region, we will not know whether the trait is prevalent throughout the lowlands and whether it might have played a significant role in the demographic changes in the entire coastal region. At this time we can only say the following: the fact that the Negroes coming to Mexico were primarily from malarial parts of Africa whose populations today exhibit a high incidence of the sickle-cell trait and the fact that the historical literature emphasizes the superiority of the Negroes and the Negro mixed-bloods' resistance to malaria which was ravaging the area, both seem to support the hypothesis that the black men's immunity to the disease was genetically based and could very well be linked with the sickle-cell trait. In any case, their general immunity was common enough to merit considerable comment.

There is, of course, the very important qualification to be made, namely that most of the research on the sickle-cell trait has been done in correlation with *falciparum* and not *vivax* malaria. Although both exist in Mexico, Lisker's studies have been conducted in an area more seriously threatened with the latter. It is true that one of the major objectives of his article was to suggest that the sickle-cell trait afforded protection against *vivax* malaria as well, but this is a very recent hypothesis. Therefore, in order to substantiate the role this genetic immunity played in protecting the Negro slave in Mexico, we must determine what form of malaria existed in the area in question and validate the fact that the sickle-cell trait serves as an immunization to it. If we are correct in assuming that malaria accompanied the ostensibly healthy Negro to the New World, i.e. that malaria came from those areas of Africa where the slaves were sold to the white slavers, it then follows that the African slaves were immune to the species imported. For even if the slaves had been captured by black slavers far from the ports where they were ultimately transferred to the white slavers, these slaves could not have remained healthy in the port towns had they not also been immune to the particular species of the area.

Conclusions

The ecological implications for this malaria hypothesis are interesting. It happens that with the advance of agriculture, man has provided the perfect environment for malaria. By cutting down the forests in Africa, the necessary open ground and open stagnant pools were produced, permitting the spread of the Anopheles mosquitoes and hence malaria (Singer, 1962, p. 158). The same situation could have taken place in the lowlands of Mexico as well, for the plantation economy opened up much more land in this area and with the sugar plantation came the Negroes and malaria. Furthermore, it is suggested that certain of the drier parts of the 'tierra caliente' near Veracruz, such as Rinconada, which were opened for agriculture in pre-Columbian times by the introduction of irrigation (Sanders, 1953) would have undoubtedly proved to be an ideal environment for breeding Anopheles mosquitoes in an area which would not ordinarily have suffered from these insects and subsequently from malaria.

In addition, it is interesting to note that the Yucatan lowlands have no malaria (Carter, 1931, p. 115), the reason being that the soil is extremely calcareous and thus very porous, not permitting stagnant water to collect on the surface of the ground. Coincident with this is the fact that unlike the other lowland areas which were ravaged by malaria, the Yucatan was not only free from malaria, but had and has a proportionately higher indigenous population than other lowland regions.

In sum, it has been suggested that as a result of a severe native labor shortage, the Spaniards imported Negro slaves to fill the gap. They were essential in the lowlands to work on the sugar plantations and in the sugar mills. Selected for their superior strength, the healthiest representatives were sent to the Americas; this implies those who were not suffering from malaria at the time they were chosen. Among these slaves, a large number might very likely have had a genetically inherited protection against the disease. Malaria, however, accompanied the Negroes to the New World in the blood of the white slavers and was then spread to the unimmune Indians by the aboriginal Anopheles mosquitoes to the Indians and European colonists. This disease served as an extra catalyst to wear down the already ailing Indians and to help cause the greater indigenous mortality in these regions than in the malaria-free highlands and the Yucatan. As the Indians continued to die out, the Negroes became progressively more in demand and soon, by default, they and the Europeans dominated this area of Mexico numerically. As to whether the sickle-cell trait was diffused among the native and white populations to a

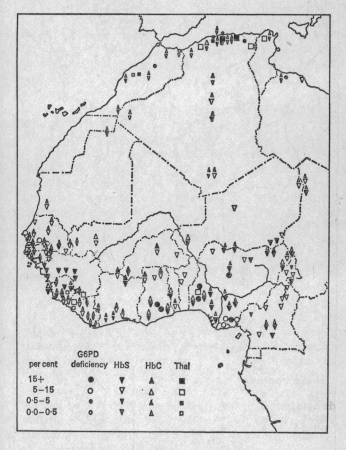

Figure 1 Percentage incidence of the red cell defects in North and West Africa, (Source : Livingstone, 1967)

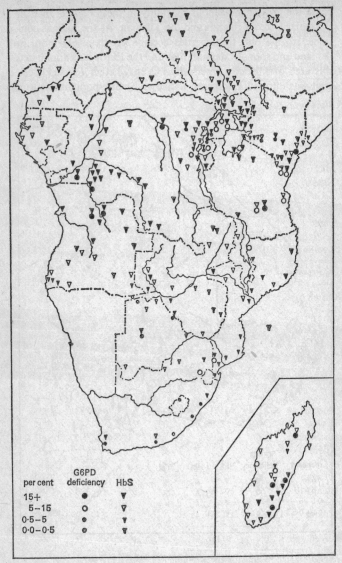

Figure 2 Percentage incidence of the red cell defects in Central and East Africa (Source : Livingstone, 1967)

great enough extent to fortify the progeny of Afro-Indian and Afro-European unions in the area against malaria is still uncertain; however, Lisker's work suggests such a possibility.

Table 1 Population by 'castes' of New Spain in 1570

Bishropric	European	African	Indigenous	Euro-Mestizo	Indo-Mestizo	Afro-Mestizo
Mexico	2794	11,736	1,310,904	8632	1992	2000
Tlaxcala	900	3278	844,828	944	100	100
Oaxaca	420	532	583,600	256	50	50
Michoacan	1000	1955	94,556	247	200	200
Nueva Galicia	1000	2630	108,360	530	75	75
Yucatan	350	293	282,612	156	20	10
Chiapas	180	145	112,000	302		
Totals	6644	20,569	3,336,860	11,067	2437	2435
Percentages	0·2	0·6	98·7	0·3	0·07	0·07

(After Aguirre Beltrán, 1946, p. 213)

Table 2 Population by 'castes' of New Spain in 1646

Bishropric	European	African	Indigenous	Euro-Mestizo	Afro-Mestizo	Indo-Mestizo
Mexico	8000	19,441	600,000	94,544	43,373	43,190
Tlaxcala	2700	5534	250,000	17,404	17,381	16,841
Oaxaca	600	898	150,000	3952	4712	4005
Michoacan	250	3295	35,858	24,396	20,185	21,067
Nueva Galicia	1450	5180	41,378	19,456	13,778	13,854
Yucatan	700	497	150,053	7676	15,770	8603
Chiapas	80	244	42,318	1140	1330	1482
Totals	13,780	35,089	1,269,607	168,568	116,529	109,042
Percentages	0·8	2·0	74·6	9·8	6·8	6·0

(After Aguirre Beltrán, 1946, p. 221)

Table 3 Population by 'castes' of New Spain in 1742

Bishropric	European	African	Indigenous	Euro-Mestizo	Afro-Mestizo	Indo-Mestizo
Mexico	5716	7200	551,488	222,648	100,156	99,756
Tlaxcala	1928	8872	350,604	40,384	39,444	38,228
Oaxaca	416	240	231,892	9220	10,716	9120
Michoacan	171	492	147,808	55,508	45,896	47,884
Nueva Galicia	1028	2913	36,252	44,568	31,256	31,420
Yucatan	498	274	190,032	17,660	35,712	19,588
Chiapas	57	140	32,180	1524	3016	3372
Totals	9814	20,131	1,540,256	391,512	266,196	249,368
Percentages	0·4	0·8	62·2	15·8	10·8	10·0

(After Aguirre Beltrán, 1946, p. 225)

Table 4 Indigenous population by region at certain dates

Region	Year 1532	1560	1580	1595	1608
	Highlands				
1	7,992,307	1,707,758	1,233,032	770,649	
2a	171,984	32,340	21,560	20,200	
4	1,560,931	222,165	150,620	146,740	
8	1,038,668	188,398	161,299	96,913	
9	462,446	80,515	64,618	90,670	
Subtotal	11,226,336	2,231,176	1,631,129	1,125,172	852,224
Region	Lowlands				
2	1,532,860	74,087	42,370	45,690	
3	710,230	37,682	32,207	17,876	
5	681,372	68,076	56,076	37,119	
6	862,687	63,545	43,885	33,729	
7	1,243,163	113,531	64,264	71,158	
10	614,760	61,476	21,336	41,484	
Subtotal	5,645,072	418,397	260,138	247,056	217,011
Total	16,871,408	2,649,573	1,891,267	1,372,228	1,069,255

(After Cook and Borah, 1960, p. 48).

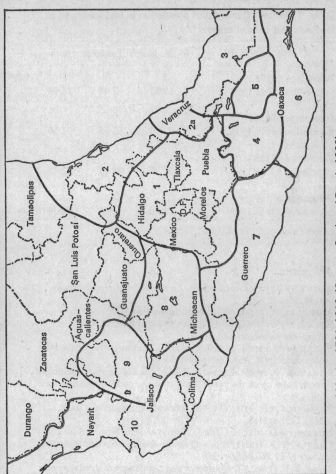

Figure 3 Central Mexico 1581–1610 (Source: Cook and Borah, 1960)

Table 5 Decline of indigenous population in highlands and in lowlands and coastal regions

	Highlands	Lowlands	Both
Percentage of 1532 population left in 1568	19·85	7·44	16·68
Percentage of 1568 population left in 1580	73·10	62·65	71·50
Percentage of 1580 population left in 1595	69·95	94·15	72·45
Percentage of 1595 population left in 1605	75·70	89·90	78·30

(After Cook and Borah, 1960, Table 8)

References

AGUIRRE BELTRÁN, G. (1946), *La población Negra de Mexico*, 1519–1810, Mexico City.

ARMILLAS, P. (1968), personal communication.

BORAH, W. W. (1951), 'New Spain's century of depression', *Ibero-Americana*, no. 35.

BORAH, W. A., and COOK, S. F. (1960), 'The population of central Mexico in 1548', *Ibero-Americana*, no. 43.

BORAH, W. A., and COOK, S. F. (1963), 'The aboriginal population of central Mexico on the eve of the Spanish conquest', *Ibero-Americana*, no. 45.

BOWMAN, J. E. (1967), 'G-6-P-D deficiency and malaria', *Lancet*, May 27; no. 1158.

BUETTNER-JANUSCH, J. (1966), *Origins of Man*, New York.

CARTER, H. R. (1931), *Yellow Fever, an Epidemiology and Historical Study of Its Place of Origin*.

COOK, S. F. (1946), 'The incidence and significance of disease among the Aztecs and related tribes', *Hispanic American Historical Review*, vol. 26, pp. 320–35.

COOK, S. F., and BORAH, W. W. (1960), 'The Indian Population of Central Mexico, 1531–1610', *Ibero-Americana*, no. 44.

CROSBY, A. W. (1967), 'Conquistadory pestilencia: the first New World pandemic and the fall of the Great Indian Empires', *Hispanic American Historical Review*, 47: pp. 321–37.

CURTIN, P. (1968), 'Epidemiology and the slave trade', *Political Science Quarterly*, 73, pp. 190–216.

DUNN, F. L. (1965), 'On the antiquity of malaria in the Western hemisphere', *Hum. Biol.*, vol. 37, pp. 383–93.

HARRIS, M. (1964), *Patterns of Race in the Americas*, New York.

HUMBOLDT, Alexander von (1811), *Political Essay on the Kingdom of New Spain*, vol. 2. Translated from French by John Black. New York.

LISKER, R., *et al.* (1965), 'Studies on several genetic hematological traits of the Mexican population', *Amer. J. Hum. Genet.*, vol. 17, pp. 179–87.

LISKER, R. *et al.* (1966), 'Studies on several genetic hematological traits of Mexicans', *Blood*, vol. 27, pp. 824–30.

LIVINGSTONE, F. (1967), *Abnormal Hemoglobins in Human Populations*, Chicago.

MURPHY, R. C. (1958), 'From Indian to Negro in the Columbian Choco', in E. T. Thompson and E. Hughes (eds.), *Race, Individual and Collective Behaviour*, New York.

PASQUEL, L. (ed.) (1960), *La Ciudad de Veracruz*, (2 vols.), Tucubaya, Mexico.

PI-SUNYER, O. (1957), 'Historical Background to the Negro in Mexico', *J. Negro History,* vol. 42, pp. 237–46.

POWELL, R. D., *et al.* (1968), 'Effects of Glucose-6-Phosphate Dehydrogenase Deficiency upon the host and upon host-drug-malaria parasite interactions', *Military Medicine*, vol. 131, pp. 1039–56.

PRIESTLY, H. I. (1923), *The Mexican Nation, A History*, New York.

PROTHERO, R. M. (1965), *Migrants and Malaria*, London.

SANDERS, W. (1953), 'The Anthropology of Central Veracruz', in I. Bethal and E. D. Hurtedo (eds., *Huastecos, Totonacos y sus Vecinos,* Mexico, pp. 27–79.

SAUER, C. O. (1966), *The Early Spanish Main*, Berkeley and Los Angeles.

SINGER, R. (1962), 'The significance of the sickle-cell in Africa', *The Leach*, 22, pp. 152–61.

WOLF, E. (1959), *Sons of the Shaking Earth*, Chicago.

5 UNESCO

Proposals on the Biological Aspects of Race

This is the full text of proposals agreed at a conference in Moscow in August, 1964. The signatories were brought together by the United Nations Educational Scientific and Cultural Organization.

The undersigned, assembled by UNESCO in order to give their views on the biological aspects of the race question and in particular to formulate the biological part for a statement foreseen for 1966 and intended to bring up to date and to complete the declaration on the nature of race and racial differences signed in 1951, have unanimously agreed on the following:

1. All men living today belong to a single species, *Homo sapiens*, and are derived from a common stock. There are differences of opinion regarding how and when different human groups diverged from this common stock.

2. Biological differences between human beings are due to differences in hereditary constitution and to the influence of the environment on this genetic potential. In most cases, those differences are due to the interaction of these two sets of factors.

3. There is great genetic diversity within all human populations. Pure races – in the sense of genetically homogeneous populations – do not exist in the human species.

4. There are obvious physical differences between populations living in different geographic areas of the world, in their average appearance. Many of these differences have a genetic component. Most often the latter consist in differences in the frequency of the same hereditary characters.

5. Different classifications of mankind into major stocks, and of those into more restricted categories (races, which are groups of populations, or single populations) have been proposed on the basis of hereditary physical traits. Nearly all classifications recognise at least three major stocks.

Since the pattern of geographic variation of the characteristics used in racial classification is a complex one, and since this pattern does not present any major discontinuity, these classifications, whatever they are, cannot claim to classify mankind into clearcut categories; more over, on account of the complexities of human history, it is difficult to determine the place of certain groups within these racial classifications, in particular that of certain intermediate populations.

Many anthropologists, while stressing the importance of human variation, believe that the scientific interest of these classifications is limited, and even that they carry the risk of inviting abusive generalizations.

Differences between individuals within a race or within a population are often greater than the average differences between races or populations.

Some of the variable distinctive traits which are generally chosen as criteria to characterize a race are either independently inherited or show only varying degrees of association between them within each population. Therefore, the combination of these traits in most individuals does not correspond to the typological racial characterization.

6. In man as well as in animals, the genetic composition of each population is subject to the modifying influence of diverse factors: natural selection, tending towards adaptation to the environment, fortuitous mutations which lead to modifications of the molecules of desoxyribonucleic acid which determine heredity, or random modifications in the frequency of qualitative hereditary characters, to an extent dependent on the patterns of mating and the size of populations.

Certain physical characters have a universal biological value for the survival of the human species, irrespective of the environment. The differences on which racial classifications are based do not affect these characters, and therefore, it is not possible from the biological point of view to speak in any way whatsoever of a general inferiority or superiority of this or that race.

7. Human evolution presents attributes of capital importance which are specific to the species.

The human species which is now spread over the whole world,

has a past rich in migrations, in territorial expansions and contractions.

As a consequence, general adaptability to the most diverse environments is in man more pronounced than his adaptations to specific environments.

For long millennia, progress made by man, in any field, seems to have been increasingly, if not exclusively, based on culture and the transmission of cultural achievements and not on the transmission of genetic endowment. This implies a modification in the role of natural selection in man today.

On account of the mobility of human populations and of social factors, mating between members of different human groups which tend to mitigate the differentiations acquired, has played a much more important role in human history than in that of animals. The history of any human population or of any human race, is rich in instances of hybridization and those tend to become more and more numerous.

For man, the obstacles to interbreeding are geographical as well as social and cultural.

8. At all times, the hereditary characteristics of the human populations are in dynamic equilibrium as a result of this interbreeding and of the differentiation mechanisms which were mentioned before. As entities defined by sets of distinctive traits, human races are at any time in a process of emergence and dissolution. Human races in general present a far less clear cut characterization than many animal races and they cannot be compared at all to races of domestic animals, these being the result of heightened selection for special purposes.

9. It has never been proved that interbreeding has biological disadvantages for mankind as a whole.

On the contrary, it contributes to the maintenance of biological ties between human groups and thus to the unity of the species in its diversity.

The biological consequences of a marriage depend only on the individual genetic make-up of the couple and not on their race. Therefore, no biological justification exists for prohibiting intermarriage between persons of different races, or for advising against it on racial grounds.

10. Man since his origin has at his disposal ever more efficient cultural means of nongenetic adaptation.

11. Those cultural factors which break social and geographic barriers, enlarge the size of the breeding populations and so act upon their genetic structure by diminishing the random fluctuations (genetic drift).

12. As a rule, the major stocks extend over vast territories encompassing many diverse populations which differ in language, economy, culture, etc.

There is no national, religious, geographic, linguistic or cultural group which constitutes a race *ipso facto*; the concept of race is purely biological.

However, human beings who speak the same language and share the same culture have a tendency to intermarry, and often there is as a result a certain degree of coincidence between physical traits on the one hand, and linguistic and cultural traits on the other. But there is no known causal nexus between these and therefore it is not justifiable to attribute cultural characteristics to the influence of the genetic inheritance.

13. Most racial classifications of mankind do not include mental traits or attributes as a taxonomic criterion.

Heredity may have an influence in the variability shown by individuals within a given population in their responses to the psychological tests currently applied.

However, no difference has ever been detected convincingly in the hereditary endowments of human groups in regard to what is measured by these tests. On the other hand, ample evidence attests to the influence of physical, cultural and social environment on differences in response to these tests.

The study of this question is hampered by the very great difficulty of determining what part heredity plays in the average differences observed in so-called tests of overall intelligence between populations of different cultures.

The genetic capacity for intellectual development, like certain major anatomical traits peculiar to the species, is one of the biological traits essential for its survival in any natural or social environment.

The peoples of the world today appear to possess equal biological potentialities for attaining any civilizational level. Differences in the achievements of different peoples must be attributed solely to their cultural history.

Certain psychological traits are at times attributed to particular peoples. Whether or not such assertions are valid, we do not find any basis for ascribing such traits to hereditary factors, until proof to the contrary is given.

Neither in the field of hereditary potentialities concerning the overall intelligence and the capacity for cultural development, nor in that of physical traits, is there any justification for the concept of 'inferior' and 'superior' races.

The biological data given above stand in open contradiction to the tenets of racism. Racist theories can in no way pretend to have any scientific foundation and the anthropologists should endeavour to prevent the results of their researches from being used in such a biased way that they would serve non-scientific ends.

Moscow, 18 August 1964.

Editor's note

The UNESCO: *Proposals on the Biological Aspects of Race* reprinted here were not of course the first statements of such sorts made by scholars. The 1951 UNESCO *Statement on the Nature of Race and Race Differences* has been reprinted in: *American Journal of Physical Anthropology*, vol. 10, pp. 363–8; *L' Anthropologie*, vol. 56, pp. 301–304; *Archives Suisses d' Anthropologie Generale*, vol. 17, pp. 81–5; *Qu'est-ce qu'une Race?*, UNESCO, 1952, pp. 83–6; *Le concept de race*, UNESCO, 1953, pp. 11–16; *Man*, vol. 52, article 125, 1952; Juan Comas' *Manual of Physical Anthropology*, Springfield: Charles C. Thomas, pp. 719–23; *Current Anthropology*, vol. 2, no. 4, Oct, 1961, pp. 304–306.

The same issue of *Current Anthropology* (pp. 303–340) contains an excellent article '"Scientific" Racism Again?' by Juan Comas, comments by twenty-one correspondents on his article, a Reply by Comas and a very full Bibliography. The Discussion was continued in vol. 3, nos. 2 and 3 and vol. 5, no. 2.

The *Statements on Race and Race Prejudice, 1950, 1951, 1964 and 1967* are published by UNESCO, Paris.

See also Jean Hiernaux, the introduction to 'The Moscow Expert Meeting', International Social Science Journal, vol. 85, no. 1, 1965, UNESCO, Paris.

Some earlier statements are reprinted as 'Resolutions and Manifestoes of Scientists' in R. Benedict, *Race and Racism*, Routledge & Kegan Paul, 1942, pp. 166–71.

Part Two
Race and Social Consciousness

Our starting point in the analysis of race in society is in the study of social conceptions. Race is a social fact. It is relevant in human relationships only when men conceive of race differences as grounds for discrimination between themselves and others. Kuper discusses how racial categories are integrated into structures of racist thought and action. In his analysis, race consciousness is treated as a phenomenon of the same order as the consciousness of social class. Worsley proposes that the progress of colonization of the Third World by Western powers generated a categorical view of native peoples. Allport defines the nature of stereotypes. The social stereotype, defined in men's minds and used to order their perceptions, is essential if the members of a social group are to maintain a categorical view of themselves in relation to others.

6 Leo Kuper

Race Structure in the Social Consciousness

Excerpt from Leo Kuper, 'Race structure in the social consciousness', *Civilizations*, vol. 20, 1970, pp. 88–103.

Conflict between races in a society finds expression in different conceptions of the racial structure of that society. This applies to formulations of the structure by academicians engaged in purely objective analysis, as well as to the somewhat explicitly ideological declarations of persons caught up in political struggle and committed to specific programs of action.

At the academic level, controversy over the utility and applicability of the concept and theory of the 'plural society' may serve as an example, among social scientists, of divergent conceptions, with different ideological implications. Proponents of the theory emphasize the sharpness of the cleavages between the racial sections and the propensity for violent change, while critics of the theory draw attention to the presence of common institutions and of interracial association, finding in these some indication of a process of, and a potentiality for, evolutionary change.[1] The controversy over the use of the term *caste* to describe white-black relations in the USA (Cox, 1948, pp. 489–538), the acceptance or rejection of the thesis that Negroes in the USA constitute a colonized people in a colonial situation, and the affinity of a theory of polygenesis for social policies of racial differentiation[2] may serve as further examples.

At the political level, the documents presented by Nkundabagenzi (1961), covering political developments in Rwanda during the period 1956–61, disclose the extraordinarily diverse

1. For a general discussion of the controversy, see Smith (1969) and L. Kuper (1969a).
2. Banton (1967, pp. 12–35); Birdsell (1963, pp. 178–85). Theories of monogenesis provide a basis for such concepts as a common humanity and brotherhood of man, but they are also compatible with extreme doctrines of racial separation, as, for example, South African apartheid.

conceptions of the structure of relations between the country's three racial categories,[3] the dominant Tutsi minority, the large and subordinate Hutu majority, and the numerically negligible Twa at the lowest level of subordination. As commonly happens, the third category, in this case the Twa, was often forgotten in the conflict between the other races, resulting in a bi-racial conception.[4] In manifestoes, Hutu leaders proclaimed their conception as one of racial subjection under Tutsi domination (Nkundabagenzi, 1961, pp. 20–32). Some Tutsi leaders expressed the same conception, denying that there was a basis for fraternity between Tutsi and Hutu in a structure of relations which had arisen out of conquest and was always based on bondage (Nkundabagenzi, 1961, pp. 35–6). Other Tutsi conceptions stressed unity though with acknowledgement of differentiation, as in the view that Bahutu, Batutsi, and Batwa were simply nicknames of persons sharing the common family name of Abanyaruanda, or in the slogan, Le Peuple Tripartite (Nkundabagenzi, 1961, pp. 31, 75). Or Tutsi leaders emphasized unity, with rejection of differentiation, based either on perceptions of present reality as in the statement by the King (Mwami Mutara) that he would have no criterion for differentiating the terms Mututsi and Muhutu, or on aspiration for the future, as in the resolution addressed by the National Council for Rwanda to the Belgian government, insisting that the terms Bahutu, Batutsi and Batwa should be

3. Maquet (1961, p. 10) writes that 'a definite physical appearance is considered typical of each group. According to the socially accepted descriptions of the three stereotypes the typical Twa is short, pygmoid rather than pigmy, with a head low in the crown, face and nose flat, cheekbones prominent, forehead bulging, eyes narrow and slightly oblique. Hutu characteristics are woolly hair, flat broad nose, thick lips often everted, and middle stature. Tutsi are very slender and tall. They often have a straight nose and a light brown skin colour. The objective measurements of Professor Jean Hiernaux do not entirely coincide with these stereotypes.'

D'Hertefelt (1964, pp. 219–38) has contributed an interesting analysis of the relationship between myth and ideology in Rwanda.

4. See comments of M. De Schryver, president of a work group appointed by the Belgian government, at a conference in May, 1959. 'Nous avons vu des laïcs en grand nombre et aussi des religieux, des fonctionnaires, des juges des membres du Conseil Supérieur, le Mwami et aussi des Batwa oubliés par les deux autres races Hutu, Tutsi' (Nkundabagenzi, 1961, p. 84).

crossed out in all official documents (Nkundabagenzi, 1961, pp. 1, 37). Or conflict might be acknowledged, but the significance of racial difference for the conflict denied, as in the conception advanced by Tutsi students that the problem was social in itself, but racial in the eyes of the administration and of certain autochthonous elements (Nkundabagenzi, 1961, p. 107).

It is with some aspects of the diverse conceptions of the racial structure in the social consciousness that this paper deals. These conceptions are an integral part of the racial structure of a society. They influence the course of race relations, and they may serve as an index of change, of social forces stimulating sharp conflict and polarization, or contributing to harmonious adjustment and integration. There has been little systematic analysis of conceptions of racial structure, and I therefore start with a preliminary classification before exploring some of the relations among conceptions, and between conceptions and racial structure. The particular themes selected here for comment are first, the description of conceptions in terms of criteria of differentiation, numbers of racial categories identified, and the manner in which they are characterized and structured; second, the interrelations between conceptions, in terms of fluidity, and of transformation from one conception to another; and third, the interaction between different conceptions with reference to their varied structural bases and situational contexts.

The approach derives appreciably from *Class Structure in the Social Consciousness* by Ossowski. His systematic analysis of conceptions of class structures is illuminating for the understanding of conceptions of race structures, in terms both of similarities between the conceptions, and of unique distinctive features. It is for this reason that I develop a comparison between conceptions of class and race structures. I have retained the term 'social consciousness', though it is somewhat archaic, and I follow Ossowski's use of *social consciousness* to refer to concepts, images, beliefs and evaluations that characterize certain milieux, that are more or less common to people of a certain social environment, and that are reinforced in the consciousness of particular individuals by mutual suggestion and by the conviction that they are shared by other people in the same group (1963, p. 6). In the approach to the structure of race relations, I shall use the term to refer to a category that is socially defined, but on the basis of physical criteria (see van den Berghe, 1967, p. 6).

Range of conceptions

Conceptions of the racial structure vary in the numbers of racial categories identified, and I shall distinguish two-category, multi-category and unitary.[5] Conceptions vary also in the criteria by which the categories are defined and described. These criteria may be specifically racial, in the sense of reference to distinguishing physical characteristics (such as black and white); or the racial reference may be indirectly conveyed in geographical terms, such as area of origin (e.g. Africans and Europeans, settler and native, colonist or colonizer and colonized), or by reference to such cultural criteria as level of evolution or civilization, or by group name or ethnic identity (as above, in the case of Hutu, Tutsi and Twa). The criteria may imply continuity (for example, where civilization is the defining characteristic), or discontinuity (as between Negroid and Caucasoid); a related distinction would be that between attributes and variables. Finally, conceptions vary in the manner in which the categories are structured, ranging from conceptions which imply exclusion[6] or a relative absence of linkage, to those which portray the categories as linked, whether harmoniously or antithetically.

Two-category conceptions tend to define the racial categories in terms of attributes, that is to say in terms of qualitatively distinct and discrete characteristics, such as White and Negro, or African and European. If the defining characteristic is a variable, such as civilization, then presumably the tendency would be to treat it as an attribute, distinguishing qualitatively between the categories of civilized and uncivilized, without recognition of

5. 'Two-category' and 'multi-category' are terms used by Banton (1967, p. 287). Alternate usages are dichotomous, trichotomous, multi-divisional (Ossowski, 1963), sociétés bi-communautaires and sociétés pluri-communautaires (Quermonne, 1961, p. 36), or bi-plural and multi-plural. None of these terms is very elegant.

6. Thus, to take an example from caste society, the four *varna* constitute an inclusive system; exclusion is introduced in the conception of pariah castes, and this exclusion becomes more marked in the conception of caste and outcaste.

intervening categories. The criteria are quite varied in their reference and descriptive terminology, including racial, geographical, cultural and ethnic distinctions, as well as animal analogies.

There may be no implication in the two-category conception that the categories are in any way linked. Thus the categories European and African are not related in themselves, and would seem to represent racially exclusive categories, though this is not necessarily so, as in the Pan-Africanist extension of African identity to include all who accept African majority rule and identify with Africans (Kuper, 1965, p. 378). By contrast, the categories of European and non-European link the entire society by a single characteristic, the quality of being (or not being) European. The change from one conception to the other may be an index of basic change within a society, as for example in South Africa, when the law prohibiting 'illicit carnal intercourse' between Europeans and Natives, was changed by the Immorality Amendment Act of 1950 so as to prohibit such intercourse between Europeans and non-Europeans. Thereby a prohibition relating to only two of the categories within the society was extended so as to give effect to a dichotomous conception of the society as a whole, in terms of apartheid legislative planning.

The linking of categories, where this is present, may be conceived as harmonious or antithetical. The conception of White American and American Negro emphasized perhaps exclusion or lack of relationship more than unity, whereas the terms White American and Negro American stress rather the harmonious unity of being American: an analogous case would be the contrast between the terms South African Indian or Indian South African. Antithetical conceptions, such as characterization by opposites (e.g. white-black) are presumably associated with situations of domination and of conflict. The extreme form of antithetical conception would be that defined by Ossowski as the dichotomic conception, namely 'a generalisation for the entire society of a two-term asymmetric relation in which one side is privileged at the expense of the other. In this conception society is divided into two correlative and diametrically opposed classes in such a way that each of these classes is characterized by the relation of its members to the members of the opposed class' (Ossowski, 1963, p. 31). The Marxist conception of the dialectical relationship between bourgeoisie and proletariat is a model of dichotomous conceptions in the class structure, as is Fanon's characterization of the relation between colonizers and colonized in the racial structure (Fanon, 1963, pp. 31–4).

Quite apart from any theoretical or ideological elaboration of a dialectical relationship between the racial categories, the terms by which the categories are identified may become increasingly polarized in a dialectical relationship. Thus South African apartheid legislation, by systematically extending control over race relations in a large number of social situations, under threat of penal sanctions, increasingly weights the racial categories with new social connotations, conceived dialectically. There is an increasing range of social contexts, in which the laws define as legitimate, and presumably desirable, association with members of one's own race, but as criminal, the same acts of association when they are engaged in with members of a different race. This is a similar phenomenon to that mentioned by Ossowski (1963, p. 139) with reference to class, namely that the characterization of class may be more or less rich in content.

Multi-category structures

Where the social structure is conceived in more than two categories, the criteria for identifying the categories are again quite diverse. They may consist of variables, as for example, such shades of color, as *preto, cabra, cabo verde, escuro, mulato escuro, mulato claro, pardo, sarará, moreno, louro, branco da terra* in Vila Recôncavo, Brazil (Banton, 1967, p. 276), or of attributes, such as Africans, Whites, Asiatics and Coloreds in South Africa. They may be discontinuous, or continuous, with the possible implication in the latter case of transformation from one category to another.

As to the structuring of the categories, the conception may be of units largely unrelated. This is part of the *ideological* conception of apartheid, the racial categories being described as having their separate destinies, and a duty to develop along their own lines. Or the categories may be conceived as linked, whether harmoniously or antagonistically. The linking may take the form of a ranked order, in the conception Ossowski describes as gradation, either a simple gradation in which the relations are based on the grading of some objectively measurable character-istic, or a synthetic gradation, where rank is determined by an evaluation resulting from the comparison of incommensurable factors (1963, p. 42). The simple case of gradation would be one, for example, where an intermediate category, arising out of an initial two-category structure, receives recognition, such as a category of Coloreds or Mestizos. Where, as in many colonies, a third category was introduced, Indians under indenture for exam-ple, this category might again occupy a distinctive position in consequence of a synthetic gradation based on such incom-mensurable values as color, culture, national or geographical background and social role. Naturally, simple and synthetic gradations, and conceptions of harmony or antagonism, are likely to vary with the different situation of strata in the social structure.

A unitary conception of the racial structure is only meaningful, in the context of this analysis, in situations, where conceptions of a plural racial structure are prevalent in the society. The unitary conception, corresponding to the conception of the classless society, may consist in the simple denial of racial differentiation, as in the declaration by the Mwami of Rwanda that he would have no criteria for distinguishing Tutsi, Hutu and Twa. Or divi-sion and conflict might be acknowledged, but conceived as based on other than racial division, as for example on social differentia-tion (Nkundabagenzi, 1961, p. 107), or differences in culture or xenophobia, as in many discussions of English attitudes to colored people.[7] Or the exorcism of racial division, and the assertion of the unitary conception, may be expressed in the emphasis on the unifying principle (that all are members of the Abanyaruanda and united in loyalty to the Mwami, or that all are Zanzibari, loyal to the Sultan).

Interrelations between conceptions

The interrelations between these conceptions are quite fluid. I have mentioned the case of a third category arising from the

7. This has always seemed to me, with a different conception of the racial structure of English society, to be a somewhat esoteric rationalization for the rather common phenomenon of racial prejudice and discrimination.

interaction of two categories. These persons of mixed racial ancestry may not be recognized as a category, or they may be recognized under a variety of terms, such as Mestizo, Creole or Colored, or they may be recognized as a category by members of only one racial section (as for example, in the USA where the White withheld status from intermediate strata recognized by the Blacks themselves, such as the light in color). Or the conception of a third category may arise as the result of the introduction of immigrants of different race. Or the recognition of the third category may be a consequence of the intersection of two-category conceptions. Thus, in the French and Portuguese colonial African territories, there was a conception of a two-category structure consisting of French or Portuguese (the colonizers) and the indigenous (colonized) peoples, and a second conception of civilized and uncivilized. From the intersection of these two two-conceptions, arose the legally recognized and privileged category of the 'évolué' in French territories or the 'assimilado' in Portuguese territories. Both the accommodating and revolutionary roles of the members of this category are related to the ambiguity of their position. It would seem that not all the categories arising from the intersection of two conceptions are used. Thus the intersection of Black-White, and African-European, gives rise to Black African, White European, and Black European,[8] but not White African (though perhaps this last category begins to emerge with African political independence and a movement of Whites toward the new centers of power). In the same way, the intersection of Black-White and Christian-Heathen, gives rise to all categories other than White Heathen. From the intersection of White-Negro and Rich-Poor, there arises, in addition to the expected categories of Rich White and Poor Negro, the social problem category of Poor White, conceived as a combination of incompatibles. Rich Negro undergoes a somewhat pompous transmutation to Black Bourgeoisie.

Fluidity is expressed also in changing conceptions resulting from a process of situational selection (Epstein, 1958, p. 235). Thus under apartheid, members of the dominant race define the

8. Jordan Ngubane, an African who settled in a Swazi village, and built himself a latrine, heard himself referred to by Swazi as the Black European. Black Etonian would be a similar conception, but emanating from Whites.

racial categories in some situations as White and Non-White, and in other situations as Afrikaner, English, Bantu, Asiatic, Colored, Malay.[9] In some contexts Africans are conceived as an entity, namely as Bantu, and in other contexts they are fragmented into Zulu, Xhosa, Sotho, Tswana and so on.

There is fluidity also in the reverse process, that is the transformation from multi-category to two-category conceptions. This may result from a process of conceptually obliterating one or more categories, as in the example given above of witnesses before the Belgian work-group in Rwanda forgetting the Twa, or in the conception of the conflict in South Africa as one between African and Afrikaner nationalism, Indians, Coloreds and English-speaking Whites being consigned to distant obscurity or to oblivion. Transformations of this type are no doubt readily effected where there is a dominant cleavage, or where there was an original dichotomy. Again, transformation may arise by a process of situational selection, a range of categories, present for example when the situation is relatively permissive, being reduced to a simple dichotomy in the political sphere, or there may be a coalescence of categories, as in the Pan-Africanist conception of Africans and Non-Africans, the category of Africans, however, including those Non-Africans who identify with Africans.

Unitary conceptions of the racial structure may be quite unstable. There is ambiguity in them – as in the conception of a united people, but divided; or a conception of diversity in unity, or of 'the people tripartite'. The racial divisions may be preserved, but expressed in other terms, thus maintaining the conception of a racially unified society, but the reality of racial differentiation. The conceptions often express the aspiration for unity, in the context of division and conflict, or they constitute a declaration of policy, rather than a belief in unity; and they are highly vulnerable to challenge.

Structural basis and situational context of different conceptions

There would seem to be no specific social *locus* for any of these conceptions. They are carried by the most varied strata in the society. Sections of the *dominant group* in the same society may emphasize different conceptions, dichotomous or unitary.

9. Even the legal definitions of racial entities varied in different situations.

Dominant groups in different societies may have quite different conceptions of racial structures which appear to the outside observer quite similar. Different expectations may be derived by social scientists from the same social context, as for example, a diminution or a heightening of racial consciousness, consequent upon advanced industrialization.

Subordinate categories similarly hold the most varied conceptions. They may seemingly accept conceptions justifying their subordination, and resign themselves to an inferior status in the racial categorization of the society. Or sections may deny the validity of race as a basis for social differentiation, and emphasize other qualities, as did many educated and westernized Africans serving in the role of an auxiliary elite to European colonizers. Or they may proclaim a dichotomous and revolutionary conception of the racial structure, and this whether they are a majority, as in South Africa, or a numerical minority as in the U S A. The controversy between African leaders in South Africa in 1959 over multi-racialism and non-racism, with charges and counter-charges of racism, is a reflection of the somewhat kaleidoscopic conceptions which may arise within a single stratum in an emotionally charged situation (Kuper, 1965, p. 379).

The conceptions held by a *category intermediate* between a dominant racial minority and a subordinate racial majority may perhaps be more predictable, but these also seem to run the gamut of possibilities. Members of an intermediate category may accept the conception held by a dominant stratum, though with revision of their own status within that conception, and they may reproduce the same stereotypes concerning the subordinate majority. Some sections may identify with the dominant groups in politics of accommodation or with the most subordinate categories in a protest or revolutionary struggle of the oppressed races. Others may stress claims to a special significance by virtue of qualities of character or civilization; or they may passionately reject racial conceptions of the structure of the society.

Clearly, there is no simple theory which will explain this great diversity of relationships between the conceptions held by various strata, and the situation of those strata in the structure of the society. This does not mean that we are driven back to the assumption that we are dealing with historically specific relationships.

But it does mean that it is somewhat hazardous to venture general propositions.

There are further difficulties. Not much research has been specifically directed to establishing the conceptions of racial structure held by different sections, and the salience of these conceptions in their social relationships and political movements. Sometimes the evidence may be clear enough, as when a political party repeatedly proclaims a particular conception, and on assuming power, introduces legislative policies in line with that conception. At other times, the evidence as to the social basis and salience of different conceptions is by no means secure.

Moreover, conceptions may have a quite variable relationship to structure in terms of the period to which the conceptions refer. They may express nostalgia for a past golden age, or aspiration for a future Utopia, or manipulative intent, or an image of the present state of the society. There may be no difficulty in discerning the intent and time referent, as in a change of census policy in the recording of data by racial group (see H. Kuper, 1969, pp. 248–9); or there may be a quite ambiguous relationship to present reality. Indeed, the basic distinction between an 'objective' structural reality and a conception of that reality, is in itself troublesome, as discussed below. While all these considerations raise obstacles to generalization, it is nevertheless possible to offer some suggestions.

Dichotomous conception, structure, context

Ossowski relates dichotomic conceptions of class to the objective structure of the society, and to circumstances which foster the image of a dichotomic structure among particular classes (34–5). He comments that revolutionaries tend to view the world in terms of a dichotomy of opposite attributes, while those who defend the existing social order are inclined to present the structure of their own society in terms of a functional scheme or a scheme of non-egalitarian classlessness. But he also shows that the same conception, as far example a dichotomic conception, may be held by representatives of both the privileged and underprivileged class, though serving mutually exclusive purposes (Ossowski, 1963, p. 174).

We may accept in general the proposition that certain characteristics of the 'objective' structure of a society are likely to favor dichotomic conceptions both among the rulers and the ruled. These characteristics would be such as create discontinuity between the racial categories, namely differential incorporation in the polity (as where one category monopolizes the vote and legislative power), cultural diversity raising barriers to ease of association, extensive segregation, inequality in many contexts, and a demographic situation of two racial categories, or a distribution substantially approximating a two-category structure, as for example, a dominant minority, a large subordinate majority of one category and relatively small numbers in other racial categories[10] (Smith, 1969, chaps. 2, 13; Kuper, 1969b, chap. 14). The superimposition of these discontinuities in many varied contexts may be expected to encourage a generalized dichotomic conception in the social consciousness of both rulers and ruled.

There is no necessary implication that this conception would be either revolutionary, or defensive of the status quo. It might simply be embedded in experience, accepted as part of the natural order by the ruling group, and as routine reality by subordinates. In situations of change, where members of different racial categories begin to bridge the discontinuities, or where there is a challenge to the monopoly of privilege, the ruling group, in an aggressive assertion of power, or in defense of that power, may elaborate the ideological potentialities of the dichotomic relationship by such conceptions as the inevitability of conflict, domination and subordination in the contact between races, and the imperative necessity for racial solidarity in the struggle for survival. Conversely, leaders of subordinate groups in situations of change, may elaborate the dichotomic conception in a revolutionary ideology which proclaims the dialectical structure of relationships between the races, and the inescapable necessity for violence to change a system grounded in violence.

10. The presence of these other racial categories does not necessarily exclude dichotomic conceptions by the subordinate racial majority, since the categories may be conveniently eliminated or ignored in political struggle and ideology. A somewhat related phenomenon is the strong attack on White liberals by Black revolutionaries in both South Africa and the U S A. This has the function of eliminating an intermediate category, namely that of Whites who identify in some measure with Blacks. The dichotomy, racial and ideological, is thereby preserved.

The argument as to the influence of discontinuity in structure on dichotomic conceptions of that structure must be somewhat qualified. The 'objective' structure and the conception of the structure cannot be sharply separated. In an important sense, the conception is the structure. Thus structures of racial domination for long periods, supported by sentiments of racial superiority in the ruling group, and by seeming acquiescence in, or resignation before, the assertion of racial superiority and the racial right to rule. But if members of the ruling group or of the subordinate race begin to question these claims, then the structure is thereby immediately modified in some measure.

Now if the challenge of new ideas arises within the society, the stimulus may come from internal changes in social conditions and relationships. There may be increasing pressure on the land, as for example in Rwanda and Kenya; or industrialization and urbanization may provide opportunity for intertribal cooperation in movements of African nationalism against white rule as in South Africa, or a basis for the sharpening of conflict between Black and White by urban guerillas as in the U S A. The structural base, that is to say, remains a condition of primary significance.

But the ideas and support for the ideas, may also come from the outside. A conception of a dichotomic structure, as in a dialectic, or some adaption of a class dialectic to the colonial situation or to a race relations, may be introduced into a society which is by no means dichotomic in structure; and the propagation of the conception and the struggle initiated under its inspiration, may help to create within the society those very conditions of polarization by which it was characterized in the initial conception. Here then it is the dichotomic conception which in some measure creates or increases structural discontinuity in the society. A somewhat mixed case is that in which dichotomic conception and discontinuity in structure develop further and together under the stimulus of some new element, as for example, the introduction of adult franchise in Zanzibar or Guyana, preparatory to independence.

One additional complexity in the projection of dichotomous conceptions from discontinuities in structure, is that the relationship between them may be dialectical. In the same way that a dominant group may react to increasing continuity in the relations between the racial categories by emphasizing rigidity and exclusion, so too, it is precisely under conditions of mobility and increasing continuity that members of the subordinate racial category may mobilize in a revolutionary challenge to the structure of domination, and under a revolutionary ideology proclaiming an unbridgeable racial dichotomy. Sometimes, of course, the mobility and continuity are spurious, being purely token, and this is a condition which may stimulate bitter struggle in a revolution of rising, but frustrated, expectations.

Multi-category conceptions, structure, context

The relationship between 'objective' structure and conception is most complex in the case of multi-category conceptions. These conceptions seem to be favoured by both discontinuity and continuity in structure. Thus the entry of a third category, distinctive in culture, which becomes functionally differentiated, would encourage multicategory conceptions, as for example, in those British colonies where Indians entered under indenture or as immigrants, and became retail traders and artisans. Conversely, where greater racial continuity develops in a two-category structure, so that racial status becomes less of a generalized status, and members of different races begin to hold similar positions in the structure of the society, conditions may favor multi-category conceptions, based on criteria which are not racial in reference or not entirely or exclusively racial, such as culture, class, color or some synthesis of race and other criteria. But these conditions of greater continuity may also stimulate, as we have already suggested, defensive or aggressive dichotomic conceptions among members of the dominant category, or revolutionary dichotomous conceptions among the subordinates. Clearly further conditions need to be specified.

In the interpretation of varied perspectives in class societies, there is often an assumption that upper classes are more conscious of fine class distinctions and that lower classes see the structure as comprising only two classes, those above and those below, ruling class and ruled, or rich and poor. This may be an insight into the social basis of different conceptions in class-structured societies, but it would be misleading if applied to racially structured societies.

A related example of 'multi-tribalism' will serve to illustrate some of the complexity in applying a theory of the greater sensitivity of upper strata to sectional differentiation. Thus in British African colonies, particularly where the policy of indirect rule was applied, the colonial power recognized and utilized 'tribal' diversity in its government and administration. The basic conception of the structure of the society, however, was clearly a conception of two racial categories, rulers and ruled, with sub-divisions within the subordinate racial category. For the subordinate 'tribal' groups, the differences between them remained significant, probably of greater significance than for the ruling race. At the same time, they developed a conception of a two-category racial structure, of rulers and ruled, attaining full expression in the struggles for national liberation, after which the internal 'tribal' differentiation regained significance.

A ruling race may be very conscious of a variety of racial categories, as in the traditional policies of divide and rule, while retaining basically a dichotomic conception of the racial structure. Though the multiracialism is an expression of objective reality, it is related to the exigencies of rule, and does not modify the basic dichotomic conception. Where the ruling race is a numerical minority, its domination may be supported by ideologies which emphasize the unity of the dominant race and the racial or ethnic diversity of the subordinates.[11]

Multi-racialism, instead of being an instrument of domination, may however be a defensive position for a racial group which can no longer maintain its domination. An example of this would be the espousal by white settlers in British African colonies of racial parity in representation, when the introduction of an adult franchise would ensure African majority rule over the European and other minorities.

Members of a subordinate race are likely to be very conscious of the different racial categories in a society, both ruling and other

11. This is substantially the political situation under apartheid in South Africa, though there are many cleavages between the Afrikaans and English-speaking Whites.

categories, and to differentiate between them. A common phenomenon is a specially antagonistic reaction to relatively small stranger or 'pariah' racial categories. They were often introduced in colonial societies, where there was a great gulf in technology and other aspects of culture between the dominant and subordinate race; they remained separated from both the ruling and ruled race by discontinuities in political situation, economic role, religion, family life and so on, and they offered a target for racial tension. Thus, in conflict between the ruling racial minority and the subordinate racial majority, the 'pariah' or stranger racial section readily becomes a scapegoat for both these categories. Even where the subordinate majority develops a revolutionary dichotomic conception of the structure of the society, and ignores or seemingly forgets the stranger group, it is likely, when the revolutionary struggle succeeds, to return to earlier conceptions, and to settle old scores with the 'strangers' in its midst. A subordinate racial category seems unlikely to conceive the racial structure in dichotomic terms, where there is a 'pariah' racial category in the society, or where the third or other category is numerous and a rival for power, as in Guyana. Probably dichotomic conceptions prevail in the consciousness of members of a subordinate racial majority either when other subordinate categories are insignificant in numbers and social functions, or temporarily at the height of revolutionary struggle.

In analysing the conceptions held by third and other racial categories, in situations where there is a dominant minority, and a subordinate majority, a distinction must be drawn between 'stranger' and intermediate racial categories. A 'stranger' category, separated from the rest of the society by discontinuities in structure and culture, and affording a likely target for persecution, can hardly fail to be aware of the multiracial structure of the society. One section may seek to align itself with the dominant race, another with the subordinate majority, and they may attack race as a criterion for social relationships, but they can hardly escape awareness of a separate identity. In an intermediate category, arising out of the intermingling of the dominant racial minority and the subordinate racial majority, and in a situation where there are continuities in structure and culture, some sections may experience a sense of separate racial identity, and perceive the society as multiracial, while other sections identify with either the dominant or subordinate racial categories, and work essentially with a two-category conception. An example of this is given by Zanzibar, where the Shirazi conceived of themselves as Africans who had intermingled with Persians, and where was continuity in structure and culture both between Shirazi and Arabs, and Shirazi and Africans. Okello (1967), the leader of the Zanzibar revolution against the Arabs in 1964, explained his reluctance to recruit Shirazi by reference to his ambivalence in their situation, as follows:

The Shirazis, despite their numerical majority, were always the doubt-ful element in Zanzibar politics. One section identified more with the Arabs, and thus with the Sultan . . . , another section with the non-Shirazi Africans, those of mainland origin, and a third group strove to preserve its specific Shirazi identity. There were no clear reasons why people fell into one or another of these groups (p. 78).

Unitary conception, structure, context

A relatively high degree of racial homogeneity will encourage unitary conceptions of the racial structure, as among Englishmen and Frenchmen for example, even though small racial minorities in their countries are subject to discrimination. These societies are not structured by racial criteria, though this is now changing in England, and racial exclusion was so rationalized as not to disturb the conception that racial differences were of little or no social significance. Where there has been considerable inter-mingling of racial groups, a unitary conception of the racial structure may serve as an ideology of the dominant group, which maintains its racial prerogatives under other rubrics.

A unitary conception, as a defensive measure, may be pro-pagated by small dominant racial minorities, or by sections of these minorities, when there is an effective challenge to their rule, as happened in Zanzibar and Rwanda with the movement toward independence and the introduction of a universal franchise. In these societies, there was a ruler, the Sultan and the Mwami, to serve as a symbol of unity, though identified in both cases with the ruling racial minorities. A unitary conception is not likely to be influential among members of the dominant race, when they constitute a relatively large minority in an industrialized society with marked discontinuities in racial structure, as in South Africa. The reason is that being numerous, members of the dominant group will be distributed at different levels in the economy; the sections at the lowest levels, threatened by competition from members of the subordinate races, provide a social base for extremist racial politics, expressed in dichotomic conceptions.

In the case of subordinate racial categories, continuity in racial structure may be expected to encourage unitary conceptions, under conditions where the continuity has resulted from intermingling and mobility, with consequent ambiguity in racial identification. Conversely, discontinuity in racial structure and racial discrimination are likely to foster dichotomic or exclusive conceptions, but they do not seem to exclude unitary conceptions. These may take the form of a Utopian desire that other criteria of differentiation than those of racial identity should prevail, or the belief that these other criteria are already in some measure operative. An example of this belief was provided during the colonial era by the western-educated among the colonized peoples. It was from this stratum that the colonial rulers recruited an auxiliary elite, and it was in this stratum that there was some acceptance of the belief that cultural differentiation was replacing racial differentiation. It was however also from this stratum that leaders were later recruited in the revolutionary struggle against colonial and racial domination.

Conclusion: class and racial structure

This paper has sketched some conceptions of the racial structure in the consciousness of different strata, distinguishing between two-category, multicategory and unitary conceptions, and analysing the criteria by which categories are differentiated and the principles by which they are structured. The paper commented on the fluidity in these conceptions, and sought to relate them to varied situational and structural contexts.

Ossowski's discussion of the class structure in the social consciousness greatly influenced the approach, and I examined some of his hypotheses and conclusions in the context of the race-structured society. Clearly racial differences are of a more enduring nature than class differences, and there are very extensive social correlates of racial differences in many racially structured societies. In some critical respects relevant to conceptions, class structures and racial structures constitute different systems of stratification, however much they may overlap; and I therefore conclude this paper by offering brief comment on an important distinction between these two systems, as it affects conceptions.

The essence of the distinction is that class structures are intrinsic to interaction in the society, whereas racial structures are in some measure extrinsic, or have a point of reference outside the interaction. Class societies, that is to say, may be viewed as arising directly out of the *interaction of the members* of the society. The concept of class refers to the results of that interaction or describes that interaction from a special perspective at a particular moment in time. Race by contrast, is in some sense *extrinsic to that interaction*. To be sure, the racial structure is also constituted by the interaction, but the *racial differences* which are societally elaborated, *have preceded that interaction*. Race has referents that are independent of the interaction, and it was often associated, as in colonial systems, with previously existing, politically distinct, and culturally differentiated communities. This difference between race and class structure gives race a greater salience and persistence in the conceptions of the social structure held by both dominant and subordinate racial groups, and increases the likelihood of dichotomic and revolutionary perspectives in racially structured societies under conditions of social mobility and increasing social continuity. In the class-structured society, the power, wealth and prestige of the dominant class are constituted by the class structure itself. Upper class position refers mainly to the possession of these prerogatives. Hence, this position may largely be secured without reference to the authority of class. The conception of a classless society or of non-egalitarian classlessness may therefore readily offer an ideological defense for class privilege, which is maintained under the denial of class.

The same position can arise in a race structure where the dominant race is small in numbers, and where its position is entrenched by political and economic power. But race constitutes an independent basis for power, and there is thus a greater likelihood that racial conceptions will be asserted in defense of the status quo. Where the dominant racial minority is relatively large in relation to the resources available, and there is competition for these resources between members of different races, then 'racelessness' can no longer serve as a defensive ideology. On the contrary the defence must remain that of race, and there is an extreme assertion of racism by sections of the dominant race. In the case of the subordinate racial majority, race is an independent basis for exclusion from privilege, and economic and political deprivation flow from that exclusion. Hence the situation encourages perceptions of race as the crucial factor in social discrimination. At the same time, the significance of race is enhanced by the fact that it is the basis for political challenge through the mobilization of the greater numbers of the subordinates.

Increasing progressive continuity in the structure of the society may be expected to encourage fluid and inclusive conceptions of the structure, consonant with evolutionary change. But increasing continuity seems to have different consequences in the two structures. In the class society, the continuity is a product of the interaction. It may give rise to tension, and encourage class conflict, but the tension and conflict are within the class system itself. Continuity in a class-structured society is a transformation of the class system itself. In a racially segmented society, increasing continuity is again a product of interaction, and likely to occasion tension and conflict. But the tension and conflict arise not only in the sectors affected by the mobility, as in the economic or educational sectors; there is tension also between this mobility and the racial identity. This racial identity remains recoverable, and the generalized status of race persists, in appreciable measure, outside the interaction and constitutes an independent point of reference. Under these conditions, and as a result of the tension with the extrinsic status and identity of race, increasing continuity in the 'objective' structure seems more likely to stimulate revolutionary challenge and dichotomic conceptions in racially structured societies, than in class structured societies.

References

BANTON, M. (1967), *Race Relations*, Basic Books.
BIRDSELL, J. B. (1963), 'A review of the origin of races',
  Q. Rev. Biol., vol. 9, 38. (June) pp. 178–85.
COX, O. C. (1948), *Caste, Class and Race*, Doubleday.
EPSTEIN, A. L. (1958), *Politics in an Urban African Community*,
  Manchester University Press.
FANON, F. (1963), *The Wretched of the Earth*, Grove Press.
D'HERTEFELT, M. (1964), 'Mythes et Idéologies dans le Rwanda
  ancien et contemporain', in J. Vansina, R. Mauny and L. V. Thomas
  (eds.). *The Historian in Tropical Africa*, Oxford University Press.
KUPER, H. (1969), 'Strangers in plural societies: Asians in South Africa
  and Uganda', in L. Kuper and M. G. Smith, (eds.), *Pluralism in
  Africa*, University of California Press.
KUPER, L. (1965), *An African Bourgeoisie*, Yale University Press.
KUPER, L. (1969a), 'Plural societies: perspectives and problems',
  in L. Kuper and M. G. Smith, (eds.), *Pluralism in Africa*, University
  of California Press.
KUPER, L. (1969b), 'Ethnic and racial pluralism: some aspects of
  polarization and depluralization', in L. Kuper and M. G. Smith,
  (eds.), *Pluralism in Africa*, University of California Press.
MAQUET, J. J. (1961), *The Premise of Inequality in Rwanda*,
  Oxford University Press.
NKUNDABAGENZI, F. (1961), *Rwanda Politique*, Centre de Recherche
  et d'Information Socio-Politiques, Brussels.
OKELLO, J. (1967), *Revolution in Zanzibar*, East African Publishing
  House, Nairobi.
OSSOWSKI, S. (1963), *Class Structure in the Social Consciousness*,
  translated by Sheila Patterson, Free Press.
QUERMONNE, J. L. (1961), 'Le problème de la cohabitation dans les
  Sociétés Multi-Communautaires', *Revue Française de Science Politique*,
  2 (March) pp. 29–59.
SMITH, M. G. (1969a), 'Some developments in the analytic framework
  of pluralism', in L. Kuper and M. G. Smith (eds.), *Pluralism in Africa*,
  University of California Press.
SMITH, M. G. (1969b), 'Institutional and political conditions of pluralism',
  in L. Kuper and M. G. Smith (eds.), *Pluralism in Africa*, University
  of California Press.
VAN DEN BERGHE, P. L. (1967), *Race and Racism*, Wiley.

7 Peter Worsley

Colonialism and Categories

Excerpt from P. Worsley, *The Third World*, Weidenfeld and Nicolson, 1964, pp. 25–8.

Recent research has emphasized that people tend to see members of other unfamiliar groups in terms of stereotypes precisely because they only 'know' them externally. They do not interact with them as total personalities, and only meet each other in restricted role-capacities. As a result, they do not observe the other's behaviour intimately enough to see the extent of their individuality or the extent to which, in practice, they deviate, being human, from the 'official' norms of their societies. Consequently, the stranger is seen 'in the flat', only as a member of a category; he lacks the idiosyncratic features of an individual human personality. (Hence the common phenomenon of the over-rigid conformity of the recent convert, who knows the official norms, but lacks experience of 'allowable and patterned departures from the norms which the long-established members of the group [...] have acquired... in the course of their socialization' (Merton, 1957, p. 427).)

The social gulf built into the depersonalized official relationship between White ruler and non-White ruled is one which peculiarly facilitates thinking of the Other as insensitive 'submen' by the rulers, and as heartless gods by the ruled. Fanon has remarked that the colon is right in his familiar claim to 'know' the colonized people better than others, precisely because he has created his personality (Fanon, 1961, p. 30).

This misattribution of characteristics to the Other was inevitable in a world where mutual ignorance ran so deep that after centuries of mutual confrontation between the Muslim and Christian worlds, a noted Western student of Islam could write in 1957 that

. . . Muslims do not at all understand the faith of Christians . . . in general, they do not even know that they do not understand (Smith, 1957, p. 108).

Mutual ignorance, however, was not based merely on absence of intimacy. It was grounded in a relationship of power. The domination of Europe over the rest of the world precluded familiarity and fostered hatred as well as illusion.

Political domination made possible not merely the subjection of the non-European, but also a process of reduction and levelling-down. By the late nineteenth century, the rich diversity of cultures and societies in the world outside Europe had been subjected to a process of simplification. The high cultures of the Americas, as we have seen, had long since been wiped out. In India, notably, political domination paved the way for the destruction of the traditional Indian handicrafts industries, particularly textiles, to make way for Lancashire. But the simplification was also a simplification of human categories.

By the late nineteenth century, the 'natural' superiority of Europe was a standard article of faith. The once-respected and diverse cultures of the East had been ground down to common inferiority. The coolie of Canton had his replica on the Hooghly. Today, reading Needham's (1954–62) epoch-making account of Chinese science and civilization, we wonder that the coolie era could have so effectively wiped out the memory of the preceding centuries; that a Macaulay could ever have been so arrogant as to claim that 'a single shelf of a good European library was worth the whole native literature of India and Arabia'.

Yet the great cultures of Japan and China, India and Southern Asia came to be dismissed with contempt – or, at best, as quaint 'orientalism' – by a Europe confident in the ineluctable evolutionary sweep of history towards its summation: 'the steady material and moral improvement of mankind from crude stone implements and sexual promiscuity to the steam engines and monogamous marriage' of the high nineteenth-century Western world (Radcliffe-Brown, 1952, p. 203). The relationship of the rest of the world to Europe had become one of inferiority and backwardness. Even European revolutionaries believed in the coming of socialism in the industrial countries of the West. Non-Europe had been left behind in the evolutionary process, its social institutions and cultural heritages now only so many archaic and bizarre survivals.

The superiority of the West was never seen by the West merely as a matter of technology. It was a total superiority. For Livingstone, Manchester and the Bible went hand-in-hand, not out of rationalizing hypocrisy, nor from any double-dealing crude use of religion as a 'justification' for more sordid material interests, but because each was a part of a cultural whole, ethically superior to what it had displaced.

Technological and military superiority went hand in hand with organizational superiority, increasingly – indeed, often from the beginning – infused with an ethico-religious sense of divinely-ordained inevitability. 'Primitive' now become a label applied indiscriminately to the coloured peoples of the world. Social science grew up reflecting the division of the world: anthropologists largely studied non-Europe, apart from peasant folk-traditions in Europe itself. Though a Tylor might in fact study Mexico, a Bastian Burma, or a Rattray the Ashanti, the tendency was to link the study of these complex cultures with the study of the simple Australian aborigines and the Bushmen of South Africa. Sociologists, on the other hand, studied whites – dockers in the East End, poverty-stricken 'children of the Jago' as primitive in many respects as the nomads at the other end of the earth. The great danger was that the disinherited of Europe might see his image in the dispossessed of Africa or Asia: 'I was in the East End of London yesterday and attended a meeting of the unemployed. I listened to the wild speeches, which were just a cry for "bread", "bread", and on my way home I pondered over the scene and I became more than ever convinced of the importance of imperialism. . . . My cherished idea is a solution for the social problem, i.e. in order to save the 40,000,000 inhabitants of the United Kingdom from a bloody civil war, we colonial statesmen must acquire new lands to settle the surplus population, to provide new markets for the goods produced in the factories and the mines. The Empire, as I have always said, is a bread and butter question. If you want to avoid civil war, you must become imperialists.'

Rhodes's remedy did not necessarily mean shares in superprofits for all, but it certainly meant a greater degree of personal involvement in imperialism for the masses, via emigration, colonial service, or simply through the acceptance of the belief that their interests depended on the maintenance of the Empire . . .

References

FANON, F. (1961), *Les Damnés de la Terre.*
  Translated as *The Wretched of the Earth*, 1965; *L'An V
  de la Revolution Algérienne*, 1962, p. 34.
MERTON, R. K. (1957), *Social Theory and Social Structure*, Free Press.
NEEDHAM, J. (1954–62), *Science and Civilization in China*, vols. 1–4,
  Cambridge University Press.
RADCLIFFE· BROWN, (1952), *Structure and Function in Primitive Society.*
  Cohen and West.
SMITH, W. C. (1957), *Islam in Modern History*, Princeton.

8 Gordon W. Allport

Stereotype Defined

Excerpt from Gordon W. Allport, *The Nature of Prejudice*. Addison Wesley, 1954. Abridged edition, Doubleday, 1958, pp. 187–92.

Whether favorable or unfavorable, a stereotype is an exaggerated belief associated with a category. Its function is to justify (rationalize) our conduct in relation to that category. . . .

At the present time we are ... talking about the ideational content (the image) that is bound in with the category. Thus, category, cognitive organization, linguistic label, and stereotype are all aspects of a complex mental process.

More than a generation ago Walter Lippmann wrote of stereotypes, calling them simply 'pictures in our heads'. To Mr Lippmann goes credit for establishing the conception in modern social psychology. His treatment, however excellent on the descriptive side, was somewhat loose in theory. For one thing he tends to confuse stereotype with category.

A stereotype is not identical with a category; it is rather a fixed idea that accompanies the category. For example, the category 'Negro' can be held in mind simply as a neutral, factual, nonevaluative concept, pertaining merely to a racial stock. Stereotype enters when, and if, the initial category is freighted with 'pictures' and judgements of the Negro as musical, lazy, superstitious, or what not.

A stereotype, then, is not a category, but often exists as a fixed mark upon the category. If I say, 'All lawyers are crooked', I am expressing a stereotyped generalization about a category. The stereotype is not in itself the core of the concept. It operates, however, in such a way as to prevent differentiated thinking about the concept.

The stereotype acts both as a justificatory device for categorical acceptance or rejection of a group, and as a screening or selective device to maintain simplicity in perception and in thinking.

Once again we point to the complicating issue of true group

characteristics. A stereotype need not be altogether false. If we think of the Irish as more prone to alcoholism than, say, Jews, we are making a correct judgment in terms of probability. Yet if we say, 'Jews don't drink', or 'the Irish are whiskey-soaked' we are mainfestly exaggerating the facts, and building up an unjustified stereotype. We can distinguish between a valid generalization and a stereotype only if we have solid data concerning the existence of (the probability of) true group differences.

Stereotypes concerning the Jew

Many studies have been made of the 'pictures' that non-Jews have of Jews. Katz and Braly found in 1932 that college students ascribed the following traits to Jews:

Shrewd
Mercenary
Industrious
Grasping
Intelligent
Ambitious
Sly

With somewhat less agreement, the following traits were also mentioned:

Loyal to family ties
Persistent
Talkative
Aggressive
Very religious

... Interviewing 150 veterans in Chicago, Bettelheim and Janowitz discovered (1950) the following accusations against Jews approximately in this order of frequency:

They are clannish.
Money is their God.
They control everything.

Everybody blames the Jews. They control it all. They are in the right places – in the offices and in politics. They're the ones running things. ... They have power all over the world – in all the industries. They own the radio, banks, movies and stores. Marshall Field and all the big stores are Jewish.

They use underhanded business methods.

They're too tight. If they owe you money, you have to fight to get paid.

They don't do manual work.

They own the factories and get white people to work for them.

Somewhat less frequently mentioned:

The are overbearing.
They are dirty, sloppy, filthy.
They are energetic and smart.
They are loud, noisy, and cause commotions.

A survey conducted by *Fortune Magazine* (1939) asked, 'What do you feel is the reason for hostility toward Jewish people here or abroad?' The leading reasons mentioned were:

They control finances and business.
They are grasping and covetous.
They are too smart or successful.
They are not good mixers.

One notes that in these lists the factor of religion plays little or no part. Originally, of course, this difference (the only J-curve difference characterizing the Jewish group) was all-important. Accusations based on religion, e.g., 'ritual murder,' were formerly more common than now. Today in our secularized society the category of Jew appears to be losing its one real defining attribute. Other attributes have taken its place – attributes that at best rest on slight probability, or are wholly irrelevant and noisy.

The preceding lists of stereotypes seem to be roughly in agreement with one another. That is to say, the same accusations crop up time and again. Technically speaking, there is considerable Jewish 'reliability' (i.e. uniformity) in people's images of what character is like.

But closer analysis reveals a curious situation. Some of the stereotypes are inherently contradictory. Two opposing images are held, and it is unlikely that both could be equally true. We gain considerable light on this matter through the research of Adorno, Frenkel-Brunswik, Levinson, and Sanford (1950). These investigators devised a comprehensive scale to measure attitudes toward Jews, and inserted various propositions that were essentially opposite in type. Thus the subject was asked whether he did or did not agree with each of the following statements:

1. Much resentment against Jews stems from their tending to keep apart and to exclude gentiles from Jewish social life.

2. The Jews should not pry so much into Christian activities and organizations, nor seek so much recognition and prestige from Christians.

An additional pair of statements:

1. Jews tend to remain a foreign element in American society, to preserve their old social standards and to resist the American way of life.

2. Jews go too far in hiding their Jewishness, especially such extremes as changing their names, straightening noses, and imitating Christian manners and customs.

Several items of type (1) comprised a subscale of 'seclusiveness'; several of type (2) a subscale of 'intrusiveness'.

The important finding is that these subscales correlated to the extent of 0.74. That is to say, the *same* people who accused the Jews of being seclusive also tended to accuse them of being intrusive.

It is, of course, conceivable that an individual might in some sense be both seclusive and intrusive (likewise both generous and self-advertising, both miserly and ostentatious, both slovenly and showy, both cowardly and threatening, both ruthless and helpless); but it is unlikely. At least it is unlikely to occur to the extent to which we find these contrary accusations coexisting.

What plainly happens is that people who dislike Jews (for deeper reasons) subscribe to any and all stereotypes that would justify this dislike, whether or not the stereotypes are compatible. Whatever Jews are like, are not like, do, or don't do, the prejudice finds its rationalization in some presumed aspect of 'Jewish essence'.

The fact that prejudiced people so readily subscribe to self-contradictory stereotypes is one proof that genuine group traits are not the point at issue. The point at issue is rather that a dislike requires justification, and that any justification that fits the immediate conversational situation will do.

It will help to understand the mental process involved if we leave the field of prejudice for a moment, and consider the case of everyday proverbs. Compare the following pairs of contradictions:

It is never too late to mend.
No use crying over spilled milk.

Birds of a feather flock together.
Familiarity breeds contempt.

A young monk makes an old devil.
As the twig inclines the tree is bent.

If one state of affairs exists we can call on one proverb to 'explain' it. If the opposite state prevails, we can call on the reverse proverb. And so it is with ethnic stereotypes. If one accusation at a given time seems to explain and justify our dislike, we call upon it; if an opposite accusation at another time seems more appropriate, we invoke it. The need for sequential and uniform logic does not trouble us.

A stereotype is sustained by selective perception and selective forgetting. When a Jew of our acquaintance achieves a goal, we may say quite automatically – 'The Jews are so clever'. If he fails to achieve the goal we say nothing – not thinking to amend our stereotype. In the same way we may overlook nine neat Negro householders, but triumphantly exclaim when we encounter the slovenly tenth, 'they do depreciate property'. Or, take the case of 'Christ killer'. In this cliche we find selective forgetting of many relevant facts; that it was Pilate who permitted the Crucifixion and that the soldiers who executed it were Romans, that the mob was only in part composed of Jews, that Christianity was established and preserved in its precarious early days entirely by men who were ethnically and religiously Jews.

While the scientific problem remains of finding out just what the ethnic and psychological characteristics of a group may be, the fancifulness of many stereotypes is apparent. We therefore conclude that the rationalizing and justifying function of a stereotype exceeds its function as a reflector of group attributes. . . .

References

ADORNO, T. W., *et. al.* (1950), *The Authoritarian Personality,* Harper Row.

BETTLEHEIM, B., and JANOWITZ, M. (1950) *Dynamics of Prejudice; A Psychological and Sociological Study of Veterans,* Harper Row.

FORTUNE MAGAZINE, (1939), vol. 19, p. 104.

KATZ, D., and BRALY, K. W. (1933), 'Racial Stereotypes of one hundred college students', *J. Abnorm. Soc. Psychol.,* vol. 28, pp. 280-90

LIPPMANN W. (1922), *Public Opinion,* Harcourt, Brace & World.

Part Three
Race in Western Thought

Conscious political and social discrimination requires and
generates an ideology to uphold it and race differences can be
used to provide the grounds for ideologies of discrimination. In
this section, Nash provides sets of general propositions which
specify firstly the conditions for the emergence of an ideology of
race and secondly the form that such ideologies take. Nash
derives his argument by using American examples. Curtis and
Curtin deal respectively with British images of Ireland and Africa
in the nineteenth century. Curtin relates the development of an
image of Africa over time to British colonial experience. The
arbitrariness of racial definition is well illustrated by the Irish
situation in which the opposition of 'races' was a matter of Celt
versus Anglo-Saxon.

9 Manning Nash

Race and the Ideology of Race

Reprinted from Manning Nash, 'Race and the ideology of race',
Current Anthropology, vol. 3, no. 3, June 1962, pp. 285–8.

For at least three hundred years, propositions on the inequality of the biological endowments of the varieties of men have been put forth in some 'scientific' guise or other (Cunningham, 1908). The hypotheses come and go, but they tend to cluster in time and to be associated with crises about the relations of different ethnic and/or racial groups. The first bursts of contentions about the natural inferiority of a racially defined population came with the spread of the Europeans into the New World. The discovery of the American Indians, and the domination, exploitation, or extermination of them, precipitated the classic controversy between Las Casas and Sepúlveda at Valladolid in 1550–51 (Hanke, 1959). Other clusters in history turn up at the time of the French Revolution, with Gobineau and the aristocrats decrying the inferiority of the less privileged; the controversy between the abolitionists and the pro-slavery elements in the American South prior to the civil war; the rising howl at the flood tide of Eastern and Southern European immigration to the United States; and now a new burst of literature following the Supreme Court decision to abolish the legal forms of segregation and discrimination.

Is this recurrent construction and reconstruction of hypotheses on the innate, natural inferiority of races of men a response to the fact that 'you can't keep a good hypothesis down'? Or does the activity represent the culmination of social and political forces, rather than the scientific impulse to check out an hypothesis, to fill a gap in the orderly structure of knowledge? The questions are not easily answered. The reply depends upon clearing up some semantic confusion, getting some social and cultural as well as biological and genetic facts straight, and erecting a series of generalizations capable of explaining *both* the differences between human populations *and* the social interpretation of those differences.

In the United States there is currently a growing literature by amateurs and professionals on the problems of race. Comas (1961) wonders if this marks the rise of a new 'scientific' racism. This query raised by an eminent physical anthropologist is the prologue to systematic evaluation of the new assertions on race differences and their meanings. While this is a worthy, even necessary, task for physical anthropologists to undertake, it is the contention of this paper that no amount of sober scientific refutation ever stills the controversy on the meanings of race differences. The interpretation of physical and biological differences between populations is a social phenomenon, and the understanding of how that interpretation is reached and codified is a problem in social and cultural dynamics. In fact, the scientifically responsible student of race is at a distinct disadvantage in trying to confront the propositions on racial inferiority. He is in the unenviable position of trying to defend the null hypothesis, and his adversaries can manufacture plausible arguments much more easily and rapidly than he can refute them. This is not to suggest that refutation is not needed (the toppling of assertions on racial inferiority during the past three hundred years has, in fact, cleared much debris from the storeroom of human knowledge), but that it is now time to wed into one conceptual system the propositions on race and the interpretations of race differences.

An elementary distinction is needed. The study of race is the pursuit of knowledge about a biological phenomenon. Anthropologists and others who are involved in the description and analysis of the population dynamics of groups with differing genetic frequencies and physical features are studying race. They seek to find the scale, origins, causes, distributions, and correlates of the genetic and morphological diversity of the breeding populations called races.

Along with the study of race there may exist the 'ideology of race'. The ideology of race is a system of ideas which interprets and defines the meanings of racial differences, real or imagined, in terms of some system of cultural values. The ideology of race is always normative: it ranks differences as better or worse, superior or inferior, desirable or undesirable, and as modifiable or unmodifiable. Like all ideologies, the ideology of race implies a call to action; it embodies a political and social program; it is a demand that something be done. The ideology of race competes in a political arena, and it is embraced or rejected by a polity, not a scientific community.

The relation of the study of race to the ideology of race is only indirect. The scientific evidence or the 'facts' of race only serve as ammunition in ideological warfare. If one is promoting an ideology, it is better to have most of the facts on your side, but it does not really matter, as long as some of the facts can be absorbed or be made consonant with the ideology. Ideologies are expressions or recipes for the way the world 'ought to be', and the way the world in fact *is*, is tangentially related to the visions and hopes of what it might be made into. On these grounds, that is, the functional consequences of ideologies, no amount of evidence (even were it scientifically impeccable) will destroy an ideology, or even, perhaps, modify it. And so the ideology of race, or 'racism', persistently crops up whenever the political and social circumstances make it functionally pertinent.

The most recent American contribution to the ideology of race is Putnam's book, *Race and Reason* (1961). Lesser contributions come from Garrett (1961) and Shuey (1958). Comas (1961) has treated parts of this effort in terms of the facts of race, and since the ideology of race represents no new research efforts, no new findings on race differences, I let that confrontation stand. *Race and Reason* is a new interpretation of the meaning of race differences in terms of the ideology of the embattled South. Here I want to present a paradigm of the argument of *Race and Reason* and contrast it to the literature that grew up in the pro-slavery controversy prior to the Civil War, also taken from a single book (Jenkins, 1935). This will show the bone structure of racial ideology. Next I will develop the conditions of the emergence of racial ideologies. And finally I shall enumerate the functions of racial ideologies for a social system in which there is marked conflict in the regnant system of values.

The paradigm

Race and reason Pro-slavery literature

1. The attempt to flout natural law by man-made edicts about race relations

To me there is frightening arrogance in this performance. Neither the North, nor the court, has any holy mandate inherent in the trend of the times or the progress of liberalism to reform society in the South. In the matter of schools, rights to equal education are inseparably bound up with rights to freedom of association and in the South at least, may require that both be considered simultaneously.... Moreover, am I not correct in my recollection that it was the social stigma of segregation and its effect upon the Negro's 'mind and heart' to which the court objects as much as to any other, and thus the court in forcing the black man's right to equal education was actually determined to violate the white man's right to freedom of association.

In any case the crux of this issue would seem obvious: social status has to be earned. Or to put it another way, equality of association has to be mutually agreed to and mutually desired. It cannot be achieved by legal fiat. Personally, I feel only affection for the Negro. But there are facts that have to be faced. Any man with two eyes in his head can observe a Negro settlement in the Congo, can study the pure-blooded African in his native habitat as he exists when left on his own resources, can compare this settlement with London or Paris, and can draw his own conclusions regarding levels of character and intelligence which is civilization. Finally he can inquire as to the number of pure-blooded blacks who have made contributions to great literature or engineering or medicine or philosophy or abstract science.... There is no validity to the argument that the Negro 'hasn't been given a chance.' We were all in caves or trees originally. The progress which the pure-blooded black has made when left to himself, with a minimum of white help or hindrance genetically or otherwise, can be measured today in the Congo. (Putnam, 1961, pp. 8–9)

As to the endless declamation about human rights, we have only to say that human rights are not fixed by a fluctuating quantity. Their sum is not the same in any two nations on the globe.... There is a minimum without which a man cannot be responsible; there is a maximum which expresses the highest degree of civilization and of Christian culture. The education of the species consists in its ascent along this line. As you go up, the number of rights increases. but the number of individuals who possess them diminishes. As you come down the line, rights are diminished but the individuals are multiplied. It is just the opposite of the predicamental scale of the logicians; there comprehension increases as you descend and extension decreases. Now when it is said that slavery is inconsistent with human rights, we crave to understand what point in this line the slave is conceived to occupy. There are, no doubt, many rights which belong to other men which are denied him. But is he fit to possess them? Has God qualified him to meet the responsibilities which their possession necessarily implies? His place in the scale is determined by his competency to fulfil his duties. There are other rights which he certainly possesses, without which he could be neither human nor accountable. Before slavery can be charged with doing him an injustice it must be proved that the minimum which fell to his lot, at the bottom of the line, is out of proportion to his capacity and culture. The truth is, the education of the human race for liberty and virtue, is a vast providential scheme, and God assigns to every man . . . the precise place he is to occupy in the great moral school of humanity.' (Address by Dr Thornwell in 1862, quoted in Jenkins, 1935, pp. 230–31)

2. The races differ in their capacities to embrace the complexities of civilization

The essential question in this whole controversy is whether the Negro, given every conceivable help regardless of cost to the whites, is capable of full adaptation to our white civilization within a matter of a few generations, or whether the record indicates such adaptation cannot be expected save in terms of many hundreds, if not thousands, of years, and that complete integration of these races, especially in the heavy black belts of the South, can result only in a parasitic deterioration of white culture, with or without genocide. . . . Yet to my mind it seems obvious that all the facts, and a preponderance of theory, are against Myrdal and his authorities. (Putnam, 1961, pp. 27–8)

If the whole race have but a common original, then common systems may be applied to all; and the greatest license is given to the 'latter day' theorists who would organize the world upon certain uniform bases and fit the same institutions and law to every stage and condition of civilization. If, on the contrary, this assumption be false and groundless, these mad dreamers will at once be refuted, and the world discover that parliament and congress are unsuited to the Hottentot and the African, and the ballot box and trial by jury not altogether the sort of things to flourish in all their vigor among the snows of Russia or the shores of the Bosphorus. Our faith in political theories has never exceeded a mustard seed. (Jenkins, 1935, p. 277)

3. The level of cultural achievement of races indicates their relative innate capacities

To begin with, I know of no period when white men drank blood out of skulls.

Secondly, if one searched through all history for the time when the best pure Negro culture, uninfluenced by white help, was at its peak, and then sought the time when the worst pure white culture, was at its bottom, I suppose one might decide that as a white man, one would have preferred to have lived among the Negroes, although I doubt it. I have not heard of any tribal poetry among Negroes comparable to Beowulf or the Nibelungelied.

Of greater importance, it would be well to examine more closely these so-called 'magnificent Negro civilizations' in Africa. At one time, and a very brief one, there were west Sudan kingdoms with more brilliance than the contemporary one in, say, Scandinavia, but they could not be compared with the contemporary Byzantine Empire or even the troubadour civilization of Provence.

As for the city of Timbuktu, can you mention the Arab-inspired mosque school of that city in the same breath with the University of Paris, also founded in the twelfth century? Which of their medieval professors had the modern influence of St. Thomas Aquinas? Remember also that Timbuktu was ruled by an Arab nobility and a slightly colored Tuareg upper class. Full-blooded Negroes were at the bottom of the social scale. (Putnam, 1961, pp. 42–3)

The social, moral and political as well as the physical history of the Negro race bears strong testimony against them; it furnishes the most undeniable proof of their mental inferiority. In no age or condition has the real Negro shown a capacity to throw off the chains of barbarism and brutality that have long bound down the nations of that race; or to rise above the common cloud of darkness that still broods over them. ... Moreover, when left alone in his native land, he had never of his own initiative advanced from a state of barbarism to develop a civilization of his own. ... The large continent of Africa stood in plain view as an ever present reminder, a rank wilderness, where the various tribes engaged in incessant attempts to subject each other to slavery. ... From the vain search for an indigenous civilization [Cobb drew] the conclusion that the history of the Negro race could not represent a chapter of mere accidents but that it was the fulfilment of manifest destiny. ... The Negro was imitative, but never inventive or suggestive; and by consequence, he could never create a civilization of his own. (Jenkins, 1935, pp. 244–5, 251)

4. Left on their own, inferior races tear down a cultural heritage

What happens to the Negro even after he has had the advantage of long contact with white men and is then thrown on his resources is well illustrated by Liberia.... A glance at Haiti is also instructive. Although bolstered constantly by help from the United States, Haitian civilization is little above that of Africa. Illiteracy and poverty among the masses are almost universal. The remains of the earlier French civilization have fallen into ruin. Except where restored by American business enterprise, the bridges and roads are nearly impassable. The religion is Voodoo. Such is the best example available on earth of what a black civilization, led by mulattoes, can accomplish when left to itself. (Putnam, 1961, p. 89)

[...] The slaveholder pointed out that on every occasion on which the servile race had gained freedom, after once having been held in bondage, it had inevitably within a time lapsed into barbarism. A most vivid illustration of this tendency was found in the history of Santo Domingo and Haiti. The results of emancipation in this island were a powerful object lesson.... An official representative of the United States in Haiti wrote it was a conviction forced upon him by his observation that 'Negroes only cease to be children when they degenerate into savages.' He was convinced that a short residence there would cause 'the most determined philanthropist to entertain serious doubts of the possibility of their ever attaining the full stature of intellectual and civilized manhood' (Jenkins 1935, pp. 245–6).

5. The fight against racial equality is the fight for truth in the interests of all mankind

In a moral sense we are confronted with what might almost be called a trilogy of conspiracy, fraud and intimidation: conspiracy to gain control of important citadels, of learning and news dissemination, fraud in the teaching of false racial doctrines, and intimidation in suppressing those who would preach the truth. To speak of academic freedom in the United States today is to make a mockery of the term. (Putnam, 1961, pp. 49–50)

It is best to be candid on this subject. If they considered the holding of men in slavery as a crime, they would necessarily accuse themselves, a thing which human nature revolts at. I will tell the truth. A large majority of the people in the Southern States do not consider slavery as even an evil. Let the gentleman ... go from neighborhood to neighborhood, and he will find that is a fact. (Jenkins, 1935, p. 56)

6. Those who favor equality are undesirables

Outside the inner Marxist core, there are very few hard-headed realists among the equilitarians. But there are many sentimentalists, and this has led to the perhaps unfairly sarcastic designation 'bleeding heart'. The amateur integrationist has been taught to throw the accusation of emotionalism in the face of his opponents to conceal the fact that it is he, himself, whose case lacks reason. (p. 96)

The Proudhons and Fouriers, French Socialists, Continental Republicans, Northern Abolitionists, who setting out with the perfect equality in every respect of all the nations and families of men, proclaim the doctrines of universal republicanism, universal agrarianisms, and in addition the fullness of liberty and freedom from all restraint, stand ready to fit as in the bed of Procrustes, Hottentot and Bushmen, semi-civilized Negro and Caucasian to institutions of common shape and character. (Jenkins, 1935, p. 277)

These six propositions form the skeleton of any racial ideology, and the same exercise in paradigmatic construction, I suppose, would extend the members to the Nazi ideology, the ideologies of imperial expansion, and other instances. The ideology serves as a basis for a call to action, to do something about the insistence of formerly submerged peoples to get their share of the world's goods, human dignity, sovereignty, and freedom. The calls to action are as varied as the societies from which they issue, but the bone structure of a racial ideology must assent to at least the above six propositions. All of the propositions in a racial ideology are dependent upon the following three logical confusions:

1. The identification of racial differences with cultural and social differences;
2. The assumption that cultural achievement is directly, and chiefly, determined by the racial characteristics of a population;
3. The belief that physical characteristics of a population limit and define the sorts of culture and society they are able to create or participate in.

With these confusions, the empirical findings on racial differences are fed into the ideology where they fit, and ignored where they do not. Building a racial ideology is thus not a function of the state of knowledge about racial differences. It is the response to a situation of social conflict and crisis.

Racial ideologies grow up in situations of conflict, where the participants in the conflict have the hereditary, visible, and physical badges of differences. And even if they do not, symbols, like the yellow stars of Nazi Germany, can be used to mark off a socially visible group with supposed racial characteristics. The conflict is more intense if the parties are not only physically, but culturally different.

The first ideology of race grew up with the expansion of Europe, and it is instructive, for it contains all the necessary ingredients to call forth such systems of ideas. In Africa, Asia, and especially in the New World, men of different appearance and different culture were encountered. The Spaniards, with their legalistic and religious notions, could not slay men, take over an area, and subjugate a people without some sort of rationale or ideology to justify these activities. No group of men is able systematically to subordinate or deprive another group of men without appeal to a body of values which makes the exploitation, the disprivilege, the expropriation, and the degradation of human beings a 'moral' act. In this sense racial ideologies grow up to span a two-sided conflict: the conflict between the privileged, dominant group and the disprivileged, subordinate group; and the conflict within the dominant group itself between the value system and the activities required to keep another group subjugated and deprived. Racial ideologies have the function of defining the subordinate people as 'lesser men', or 'non-men', or 'expendable men'. They thus provide the rationale for the activities or deprivation and heal the breach in the value system.

The conditions for the emergence of the ideology of race in broad terms, then, are (I would hypothesize):

1. A conflict between racial and ethnic groups;

2. The subordination or systematic deprivation of one group;

3. The insistence of the subordinate group on refusing to accept the disprivileges;

4. A system where the division of labor is structured on racial and ethnic lines;

5. The dissent of some of the dominant group to the prevailing facts of disprivilege.

Given the conjunction of these five variables, a racial ideology will emerge, and the intensity of the espousal of the ideology is proportional to the intensity of the social conflict.

The functions of a racial ideology are, of course, related to the factors that gave rise to the ideology, and their specific form depends upon the social system in which the ideology is embedded. In most general terms the racial ideology:

1. Provides a moral rationale for systematic disprivilege;

2. Allows the members of the dominant group to reconcile their values with their activities;

3. Aims to discourage the subordinate group from making claims on the society;

4. Rallies the adherents to political action in a 'just' cause;

5. Defends the existing division of labor as eternal.

In the light of the content, origin, and functions of racial ideologies, it is possible to see that the role of scientific evidence on racial differences is but of marginal importance. Both the attempts to establish and disestablish the 'equalitarian' hypothesis are ideological efforts, for the meaning of racial differences is decided in a political and social context, not in experimental or comparative studies. The paucity of research in the last twenty-five years on racial differences in the anthropological, biological, and psychological sciences is not the result of a conspiracy of silence, but rather of the fact that the question is scientifically uninteresting compared with other questions stemming from theory and real gaps in empirical knowledge.

Furthermore, whatever scientists turned up, one way or the other, would not be a guide to social action. Suppose conclusive evidence were found that a micro-race of inbred Whites had an average variance for twenty points in intelligence below that of a micro-race of inbred Negroes. What then? That depends on your value system and ideology. You might want the whites to try better schools, you might want them to move to urban areas, you might want them to give up exogamy, or you might say, 'So what, plenty of people with that variance function perfectly well in American society. Let them find their places in the social division of labor according to their talents.' You might go on to say all sorts of other things; 'Keep them from mating outside of their group; keep them out of schools where the level is higher; prevent them from entering the labor market on even terms, etc.' But whatever conclusion you drew, it would be based on what your value system told you a twenty-point variance ought to mean. In short, the fact of racial differences (whatever they may mean for performance, and there is no logical or empirical link from the skin surface differences of races to the complex performances of daily life) does not, cannot implicate a social and political program.

Scientists will go on trying to describe and explain differences in all sorts of performances between and among all sorts of categories of persons, but it is not likely that they will ever take the differences they find to be fixed, immutable, or unmanipulable; it is much less likely that they will ever evaluate the meaning of these differences apart from specific environments; and it is impossible that they will recommend courses of social action on the basis of their findings.

It is not the findings of studies of workers in the area of race, but the ideology of race, an ideology which competes with many others in a free and open society, which makes the invidious distinctions and the program recommendations. And of ideologies of race, Reinhold Niebuhr wrote:

[. . .] most rational and social justifications of unequal privilege are clearly after-thoughts. They are created by the disproportion of power which exists in a given social system. The justifications are usually dictated by the men of power to hide the nakedness of their greed, and by the inclination of society itself to veil the brutal facts of human life from itself. (1948, p. 8)

Racial ideologies, like the theory of divine monarchs or the ideology of the transcendant State, will disappear when the social conditions that call them forth no longer obtain. When fuller democracy and equality of opportunity are achieved, racial ideology will move to wherever it is that historical curiosa are stored.

References

COMAS, J. (1961), '"Scientific" racism again?' *Curr. Anthrop.* vol. 2, pp. 203–14.

CUNNINGHAM, D. J. (1908), 'Anthropology in the eighteenth century', *J. Roy. Anthrop. Inst. of Great Britain and Ireland*, vol. 38, pp. 10–35.

GARRETT, H. E. (1961), 'The equalitarian dogma,' *Perspectives in Biology and Medicine*, vol. 4, no. 4, pp. 480–84.

HANKE, L. (1959), *Aristotle and the American Indians*, Chicago.

JENKINS, W. S. (1935), *Pro-Slavery Thought in the Old South*, University of North Carolina.

NIEBUHR, R. (1948), *Moral Man and Immoral Society*, Scribners, New York.

PUTNAM, C. (1961), *Race and Reason, A Yankee View*, Public Affairs Department, Washington, D.C.

SHUEY, A. M. (1958), *The Testing of Negro Intelligence*, Lynchburg, Virginia: J. P. Bell Co.

10 L. P Curtis

Anglo-Saxonism and the Irish

Excerpts from L. P. Curtis, 'The varieties of anti-Irish prejudice' and 'A tale of two races', in *Anglo-Saxons and Celts*, Conference on British Studies, University of Bridgeport, Connecticut, 1968, chapters 2 and 3, pp. 17–48.

In the prolonged debate during the Victorian period about the proper way to deal with the Irish question there were three *leitmotivs* which appeared again and again in varying combinations and proportions in parliament, cabinet councils, newspapers, and on the hustings. These *leitmotivs* represented three kinds of prejudice based on race, class, and religious differences, and together they made up the most active ingredients of Anglo-Saxonism as it affected or impinged upon the Irish Question. These themes may be loosely translated into the negative statement that the real trouble with the Irish was that they were not Anglo-Saxon, upper-class, or Protestant. There are obvious limitations to such a categorization, chief among them being the assumption that any of these types of prejudice can be neatly extricated from the closely woven fabric of Anglo-Saxonism. But it is the constant recurrence of these themes in Victorian society which goes some way to justify an attempt to dissect a corporate prejudice.

To begin with the more modern of these prejudices, the word 'race' always seems to cry out for definition, if only because those who use it so rarely bother to explain their meaning. The word was a far more effective explanation of human affairs when left undefined and unqualified. But one *caveat* is in order. Throughout the nineteenth century Englishmen continued to use the word in a more neutral and traditional sense to designate a particular class or category such as a 'race of kings' or a 'race of yeomen'. This highly ambiguous word must therefore be taken in context, lest the false impression be spread that every Englishman who talked or wrote about 'race' was a racist in the same class as Gobineau, H. S. Chamberlain, or Madison Grant. The word was indeed used in an ever more biological and physiological sense after the 1830s and Anglo-Saxonists usually applied it to any identifiable ethnic unit or group of people possessing a set of apparently unique physical as well as mental characteristics. To most educated Victorians, race, as interpreted in its newer and more scientistic sense, connoted the more or less lasting divisions of mankind into groups of men and women who could claim descent from a common ancestor and who therefore shared the same blood and traits associated with that physiological heritage. After the mid-century, more and more self-styled experts in the science of man saw in race that force or agency which had shaped the destiny of mankind, which accounted for the rise and fall of civilizations, and which dictated almost all forms of change and continuity in human societies. In the 1840s and after, many anthropologists and ethnologists used the word in this sweeping and apocalyptic sense, and educated laymen were not slow to absorb this 'scientific' interpretation and to treat race as the key to understanding not only the past and the present but also the future.[1] [. . .]

When Anglo-Saxonists referred to the Irish race or to Irish Celts, they usually meant by these phrases all Irish-born persons along with their relatives and descendants in other lands who were neither Protestants living in Ulster nor Protestant landlords living in some other province of Ireland. The vast majority of Irishmen were thus considered to be Celtic as well as Catholic, these two categories being taken as almost but not quite interdependent. Those Englishmen who insisted that the Irish belonged to a distinctly different or alien race took it for granted that they possessed a set of permanent traits which marked them off from all the non-Celtic peoples or races of the world. The Irishman, to use an expression that Conor Cruise O'Brien has called the 'pejorative singular', was assumed by Anglo-Saxonists to have a character composed of those traits or attributes which were most deprecated in respectable English society. Like the leopard, the Celt was incapable of changing his spots, save through many

1. P. D. Curtin (1965, p. 28) interprets the word 'race' in this sense – without assigning any date for this usage. For his discussion of earlier race theories in England about the origin of man, and the African in particular, see pp. 28–57, 227–43, 363–87.

generations of intermarriage with some other race. While all Anglo-Saxonists believed that the Catholic Irish were a branch of the extensive Celtic race, and some of them insisted that the Irish were the most 'Celtic' of all the Celts, Unionists were at pains after 1886 to assert that the fact of Irish racial solidarity did not mean that they constituted a nation. Any admission on their part that the boundaries of race and nationhood or nationality coincided would, of course, have gone far to legitimize the Irish nationalist demand for home rule, and that would have been unthinkable for all but a few Anglo-Saxonists. [. . .]

Among the leading apostles of race consciousness in England was Benjamin Disraeli, whose views on race, as expressed in his novels, came close in some respects to those favoured by his Anglo-Saxonist contemporaries. Disraeli espoused the deterministic meaning of race because he wished to establish the fact that the Jews were a supremely gifted people who were head and shoulders above the other races of the world in all important cultural respects. Sidonia, that all-wise and mysterious millionaire who makes such dramatic appearances in *Coningsby* and *Tancred*, personified Disraeli's own fantasies about the genius of the Jewish race. Among Sidonia's many declarations on the importance of race and racial purity, the following passage from *Tancred* must have gratified many an Anglo-Saxonist.

But England flourishes. Is it what you call civilization that makes England flourish? Is it the universal development of the facilities of man that has rendered an island, almost unknown to the ancients, the arbiter of the world? Clearly not. It is her inhabitants that have done this; it is an affair of race. A Saxon race, protected by an insular position, has stamped its diligent and methodic character on the century. And when a superior race, with a superior idea to Work and Order, advances, its state will be progressive, and we shall, perhaps, follow the example of the desolate countries. All is race; there is no other truth.[2]

2. Sidonia went on to explain to his audience of young Englishmen that civilizations declined because the word race was 'worn out'. 'The decay of a race,' he concluded, 'is an inevitable necessity, unless it lives in the deserts and never mixes its blood.' (Disraeli, 1887, pp. 148–50). Chamberlain must have had this passage in mind when he referred to Sidonia's *obiter dicta* on race, (see Chamberlain, 1911). He not only garbled the quotation but assigned it incorrectly to *Coningsby*. This latter work contains some revealing

Half a century later Houston Stewart Chamberlain had occasion to borrow some of the last sentence in order to document his own extravagant theories about racial determinism.

By the 1860s the idea of race as the determinant of both individual and collective behaviour was firmly implanted in the minds of an influential minority of men in the British Isles most of whom read and, in some cases, contributed articles to such periodicals as the *Quarterly Review*, the *Nineteenth Century*, the *Fortnightly Review*, and the various anthropological and ethnological reviews which began publication after the mid-century. The certitude with which many of these men used the concept of race to establish the superiority of the Anglo-Saxon people was matched only by the strength of their conviction that this racial and cultural preeminence was menaced in a number of ways by other races and nations as well as classes. [. . .]

For the Anglo-Saxonists of this period a far more important work than Arnold's essay on national or racial character was Charles Dilke's *Greater Britain*, published in 1868 (See Dilke, 1896). Here the ideal of racial antithesis and conflict loomed large, and there was evidence to spare for the believer in a fundamental struggle between Saxons and Irish Celts. This book was the more remarkable because it had been written by a mere youth, the son of one of the promoters of the Great Exhibition, who had decided to spend the year following his graduation from Cambridge travelling around the world. The young Dilke was fascinated by the extraordinary achievements of the Anglo-Saxon people, and he chose to search for the causes of their success in every important part of that far-flung community which he called 'Greater Britain' or 'Saxondom'. Dilke's mind was saturated with notions about racial distinctions and antipathies. 'Love of race among the English', he wrote, 'rests upon a firmer base than either love of mankind or love of Britain, for it reposes upon a subsoil of things known: the ascertained virtues and powers of the English people (vol. 2, p. 345). Memories of Charles Kingsley's stirring lectures on the exploits of Saxon or English heroes in medieval England still lingered in his mind.

Sidonian aphorisms on the importance of Jewish racial purity. See *Coningsby* (Disraeli, n.d.) pp. 235–6 and 268–9. There is a succinct discussion of Disraeli's views on racial purity in Blake (1966, pp. 202–5).

What inspired Dilke through all his travels was a vision of 'the grandeur of our race' – a race destined to rule and to spread itself over all the earth. Blood was stronger than political ties, national boundaries, or trade agreements. British power and influence did not stop at the edges of the formal empire but spilled over into every region of the world where Anglo-Saxons had settled.

Dilke was a racial imperialist who revered the blood and institutions that bound together Anglo-Saxons throughout the world; the informal empire he recognized was based on blood not trade. His description of America is significant for what it says about the mixture and collision of races there: America was a vast battleground on which the 'dearer' and the 'cheaper' races were waging an all-out war for supremacy. By the 'dearer' races he meant in the first instance the Anglo-Saxons and also the Scandinavian and German peoples. The 'cheaper' races were the Irish and the Chinese – both prolific breeders, hard workers, and inveterate migrants. Dilke even described the Chinese as the Irish of the Orient. What was at stake in this struggle between the principal races of the world was not just the material wealth of America but the survival of Anglo-Saxon civilization. The Irish in America were like the swelling waters of a flood threatening to blot out the Anglo-Saxon landscape. They were gradually taking over New York City and parts of Boston and Philadelphia. In the near future all the great American cities would be Irish while the countryside would remain English (vol. 1, pp. 36–41, 226, 259–60; vol. 2, pp. 346–7). It was the fate of Anglo-Saxons and their culture that troubled him; he could face the prospect of the vanishing tribes of American Indians with equanimity. 'The gradual extinction of the inferior races,' he declared, 'is not only a law of nature, but a blessing to mankind' (vol. 1, p. 109).

Fascinated by the racial antagonism he encountered in America between whites and Negroes in the south, Irish and English in the north and east, and between Chinese and whites in the far west, Dilke wondered at times where this incessant collision would end. He did not lost heart because of his unshakable faith in the superior qualities of the Anglo-Saxon race. Nature, he observed, had intended the English to be a race of officers whose task was 'to direct and guide the cheap labor of the Eastern peoples' (vol. 1, p. 226). There seemed to be no limits to the future of the

Anglo-Saxon race which was marching westward through America and across the Pacific on the way to 'universal rule'. The Anglo-Saxons were, after all, the only extirpating race on earth. They had decimated the Indians of North America, the Maoris of New Zealand, and the aborigines of Australia. If Dilke was not wholly consistent on the subject of racial mixture, if he hedged on the question of miscegenation between conquerors and conquered, he remained convinced that the virile Anglo-Saxons would eventually 'rise triumphant from the doubtful struggle' against the 'cheaper' races.[3] Pride in race and belief in the genius of the English as supreme colonizers and rulers, warriors, and traders animated Dilke's book, and a talent for description of both the people and natural beauty he encountered made it immensely readable. What appealed most to his English readers was his optimism about the ultimate victory of the Anglo-Saxon race over the 'cheaper' races of the world. America, Dilke wrote, offered the English race 'the moral directorship of the globe, by ruling mankind through Saxon institutions and the English tongue. Through America, England is speaking to the world' (p. 268). And through his book Dilke was exhorting the Anglo-Saxon people to be on their guard against the encroachment of 'inferior' or 'cheaper' races like the Irish and to recognize their mission to spread Anglo-Saxon civilization around the world.

The idea of a dichotomy between Celt and Saxon was used by many other Victorians besides Dilke to convey a sense of racial conflict between the two that was never intended by Arnold. In the periodical literature there are many examples of that 'impassable gulf' between these two races. The *Edinburgh Review* (1846) which was generally less susceptible to racial doctrines than most other periodicals, described Ireland and Great Britain as 'among the most dissimilar nations in Europe. They differ in race, in religion, in civilization, and in wealth.' The reviewer of W. S. Trench's book, *Realities of Irish Life* (1868) in the *Quarterly Review* (1869) pointed out that it was foolish for

3. Dilke (1896, pp. 259–60). Like Gobineau, Dilke was not at all consistent about the effects of miscegenation or about the purity of the Irish race in America. He argued that the assimilation of the Irish in America transformed the 'son of Fenian Pat and bright-eyed Biddy' into the 'normal, gaunt American ... whom we have begun to recognize as the latest produce of the Saxon race'. (See also pp. 109, 113, 236, 260–62.)

the political economists to prescribe remedies for the Irish question until the character of the Irish people had completely changed. J. S. Mill's mistake, he maintained, was to treat Irish cottiers as though they were Englishmen. It was time Mill learned that the Irishman was 'not an average human being – an idiomatic and idiosyncratic, not an abstract, man'. Phrases like the 'permanent conditions of human nature' and 'historic anti-pathies of race' occurred frequently in articles on Irish subjects appearing in the *Quarterly*, and most of its reviewers stressed the importance of national or racial character in promoting agitation and disorder in Ireland (see e.g. *Quarterly Review*, 1881).

Such were a few of the theories and beliefs available to those Englishmen who had to pass judgment on Irish questions in the last quarter of the century. There are many other examples of those theories about the antithesis of Saxon and Celt. . . . But what they had in common was the assumption that racial differences and the inequalities stemming from them were facts of life and that the character of a people was more or less bio-logically determined and could not be changed without prolonged crossbreeding or miscegenation. However much disagreement and inconsistency there was among Englishmen about the effects of mixing Celtic and Saxon blood, almost all Anglo-Saxonists agreed that the Irish Celt occupied a rung considerably below themselves on the ladder of human races.

References

BLAKE, R. (1966), *Disraeli*, Eyre & Spottiswood.
CHAMBERLAIN, H. S. (1911), *The Foundation of the Nineteenth Century*, vol. 1, p. 271.
CURTIN, P. D. (1965), *The Image of Africa, British Ideas and Actions, 1700-1850*, University of Wisconsin Press and Macmillan.
DILKE, C. (1896), *Greater Britain; A Record of Travel in English Speaking Countries during 1866 and 1867 (2 vols.)*, Philadelphia.
DISRAELI, B. (1887), *Tancred*, first published 1847, London.
DISRAELI, B. (n.d.), *Coningsby*, Nelson, pp. 235–6.
Edinburgh Review (1846), 84, October, 120, p. 267.
Quarterly Review (1869), 126, January, 251, p. 78.
Quarterly Review (1881), 151, January, 301, pp. 260–61.

11 Philip D. Curtin

British Images of Africans in the Nineteenth Century

Excerpts from Philip D. Curtin, *The Image of Africa: British Ideas and Actions 1780–1850*, The University of Wisconsin Press, 1964, pp. 29–47, 222–57, 337–8, 478–80.

The Africans' 'place in nature'

Even today, when rationalized, 'scientific' racism is no longer tenable, many people of middle age half remember the teachings of their early training and half believe, if only at an emotional level, that physical race is an outward sign of other inborn characteristics. In addition, today as in the eighteenth century, many people are subject to a variety of xenophobic feelings about people who are racially different from themselves. In this same emotional sense, the recognition of racial difference dominated European thought about Africans even before the rise of scientific and pseudo-scientific racism. If 'racism' can be defined as any of the various doctrines holding that human culture and behavior are strongly influenced by physical race, then even this vague xenophobic sentiment is a form of racism. It should, however, be distinguished from the rationalized racial theories attempting to explain the nature of society in racial terms, and even more sharply distinguished from the extreme political creeds which hold that 'racial inferiority' justifies inequality of treatment, enslavement, or genocide for the 'inferior races'. These things may follow from racism, but they are not a necessary part of racist beliefs as such.

Europeans in the later eighteenth century had already had several centuries of contact with Africans, both with the sellers of slaves on the African coasts and with the slaves in the New World. Whatever their views in detail, one assumption was almost universal. They believed that African skin color, hair texture, and facial features were associated in some way with the African way of life (in Africa) and the status of slavery (in the

Americas). Once this association was made, racial views became unconsciously linked with social views, and with the common assessment of African culture. Culture prejudice thus slid off easily toward color prejudice and the two were frequently blended in ways that were imprecise at the time – and even harder to separate after the passage of almost two centuries [. . .]

Even in North America, the confrontation of the English and the Indians was not so much a 'native problem' as a 'frontier problem'. The relatively sparse Indian population was pushed westward, rather than being absorbed into the settlers' society. Before the 1780s, it was only in Ireland that a persistent and troublesome 'native problem' had developed, and here the racial and cultural difference between the metropolis and the empire was much less than that between the overseas world and the West. [. . .]

It was only when imperial control began to tighten in the reign of George III that British imperial theory had to take account of the questions discussed in Spain some two centuries earlier. Especially after 1783, in the shadow of the lost war and in a spirit of general reform, British publicists began to consider the Africans' 'place in nature' and its bearing on imperial policy.

In its early stages, with little background in conscious or rationalized theory, British consideration of African race and African culture was highly dispersed. It was not a central problem discussed as such, but a peripheral question that had to be taken into account by several groups of writers. 'The Negro's place in nature' naturally had a role in whatever reporting came from Africa or the West Indies. It was discussed from another point of view by biologists, who were just then concerned with the problem of explaining human varieties. In quite another context, men of letters used the convention of the 'noble savage' for their own purposes. Finally, the anti-slavery writers of a dominantly Christian and humanitarian turn of mind were forced into a discussion of race by their efforts to reform imperial policy.

Of these four groups, only the travel writers had adequate access to empirical data. Their information therefore, had to serve the others as a store from which they could draw as it suited their needs and interests. Travel reports contained something for everyone, with accounts varying from the most bitter condemnation of Africans and their way of life to an equally broad-minded tolerance. If there was a principal thread running through the whole body of information, it was one of moderate xenophobia. Slave traders, officials, and planters were all men sent out to live in dangerous tropical conditions. They were there to do a job, and one that necessarily brought them into contact with alien peoples whose culture they did not understand. Their resentments were those of foreign visitors in any country. In Africa they often thought they were cheated and they disliked the strangeness of African customs. In America they took the slaves to be obstinate, rebellious, thievish and lazy – which they probably were: these are the expected attributes of slaves in any society.

But for all their xenophobia, the travellers were unusually free of racial antagonism. Most men connected with the slave trade and even the West Indian planters (to say nothing of the enlightened travelers with their ethnographic and humane interests), were less inclined to emphasize racial factors than those who stayed in England. This was especially true of their accounts of day-to-day dealings with the Africans. In 1789, for example, sixteen recent visitors to West Africa reported to a Privy Council Committee on the African trade. While most of them had been concerned in one way or another with the slave trade, none mentioned an assumed African racial inferiority as a bar to future development (Privy Council, 1789). They had little respect for the African way of life, but those who belonged to the Company of Merchants Trading to Africa had in Philip Quaque, their official Chaplain at Cape Coast, an African who was later the most highly paid man on their staff, except the Governor himself.

The travelers often condemned individual Africans as bad men – or all Africans as savage men – but they left the clear impression that Africans *were* men. The African way of doing things might be curious or unpleasant, but individual Africans were shown with abilities, faults, and virtues in much the same proportion as Europeans. Merchants on the African coast (in contrast to planters in the West Indies) dealt with Africans as partners in trade – not, perhaps, equal partners, or the partners an Englishman might choose, but nevertheless men of substance whose views could not safely be ignored.[1] Thus the image of Africans in America was radically different from the stereotype of the servile Africans of the Americas.

Moderate xenophobia, with emphasis on the fact of moderation, was reproduced in the popular attitude toward Africans in England, especially among those in day-to-day contact. Negro servants who came to England from the colonies were popular with their masters and were often valued by the aristocracy in preference to white servants. They were also popular with their European fellow-servants, and with members of the English working class who came to know them. Some racial tension was present, but it came from the normal distrust of strangers, from sexual competition or the belief that Negroes took away employment from Englishmen (Hecht, 1954, pp. 33–6, 45–7). However wrong-headed these attitudes might be, either on the Coast or in England, they arose from the practical concerns of one people dealing with another. As such, they were in touch with social reality. Race as such was a *mark* identifying the group – not a *cause* of the group's other characteristics.

A different kind of attitude emerged when the travelers abstracted from qualities of individuals and began to talk about the group – not individual men but the collective 'Negro'. Reporting of this kind became increasingly common in the 1780s. [. . .]

The tendency to write about the abstract and collective 'Negro' was strongest among biological writers, whose business it was to deal with abstractions of this kind. Where the travelers set out to report what they saw, without the necessity of building their evidence into a system, the eighteenth-century biologists began with a system and used empiricism to make it as accurate as they could. Their principal aim was to examine, classify and arrange the whole order of nature in a rational pattern.

This emphasis on the creation of a large-scale system tended to distract attention from the systematic study of man. The first concern of naturalists like Linnaeus and Banks was the world-

1. The most accessible sample of mid-eighteenth century attitudes is T. Astley (publisher), *A New General Collection of Voyages and Travels*, 4 vols., (London, 1745–7). For representative later works see: Snelgrave (1754); Edwards (1794); Matthews (1788). See also Davidson (1961).

wide collection of specimens to build up a picture of botany and the zoology of the 'lower animals,' which made up the largest part of the whole order of nature. No individual or group of scholars was concerned with anthropology, defined a century later as 'that science which deals with all phenomena exhibited by collective man, and by him alone, which is capable of being reduced to law' (Bendyshe, 1863–4, p. 335). The physical structure of man belonged institutionally to anatomical studies, as a branch of medicine. Data about human culture and society outside of Europe was collected by whatever travelers happened to have the interest to write down what they saw. Analysis of these data was mainly left to a rather vague and still-undifferentiated social science, most often under the rubric of 'moral philosophy'. The scientific study of human varieties therefore fell by default to the biologists, as a kind of appendix to their general systems of nature.

The major eighteenth-century classifications of nature began with Linnaeus' *Systema Naturae*, first published in 1735, and later revised with additions. This work and its successors formed the basic framework of modern biological classification, and they were decidedly set in the eighteenth-century modes of thought. One of the important items of intellectual lumber common to educated men was the ancient belief that God (or Nature, according to taste) had so organized the world that all creation was arranged in a 'Great Chain of Being' – that all living things could be classified and fitted into a hierarchy extending 'from man down to the smallest reptile, whose existence can be discovered only by the microscope'.[2]

Since man had a place as the highest term on the scale, the varieties of mankind had also to be taken into account, and the biologists assumed from the beginning that they too could be arranged in hierarchic order. Linnaeus himself included a racial classification, which changed slightly in different editions of his work. Initially it was a simple system based on skin color, with a white, red, yellow, and black race, each of them placed on one of the four major continents. [. . .]

The attempts to classify and grade human races were damaging enough to the reputation of Africans, but the efforts to explain

2. White (1799) part 1. See also Lovejoy (1936).

the origin of race were more serious still. The traditional and orthodox view was that of Christian revelation: God created man, a single pair, at a finite time in the not-very-distant past. Scientific versions of this belief in a single creation came to be known as 'monogenesis'. If the basic tenets of monogenesis were accepted, all the biologist had to do was explain the origin of later variations among Adam's descendants. [. . .]

The unconscious assumption in all these ideas was that God had created man 'in His image', which was necessarily the image of the biologist. Other varieties must therefore be worse varieties, and thus 'degenerations' from the original stock. Even at its worst, however, the usual monogenetic view allowed all races a place in humanity, and peoples who had 'degenerated' in a few thousand years might well 'improve' again in a relatively short time.

The opposing theory of polygenesis was less favorable. It held that each race was a separate creation, distinct from the children of Adam and permanently so. Although polygenesis was a minority position in eighteenth-century Europe, it has probably been the most common explanation of race throughout human history. Several European suggestions to this effect had appeared from time to time, in spite of the open contradiction of the Bible. One of the most widely read was Isaac Là-Peyrere's *Prae Adamitae*, published in 1655, which held that Adam and Eve had been the last of a series of special creations, and some of the living non-Europeans were descended from the earlier pre-Adamites. Another possibility was that of the anonymous *Co-Adamitae* of 1732, which held that all races were created simultaneously but not endowed with equal ability. The idea was specifically applied to Africans in 1734 by John Atkins, a naval surgeon who had visited the Coast (Bendyshe, 1863–4, pp. 345–9; Count, 1946, p. 158; Atkins, 1734, pp. 23–4).

Polygenesis was especially attractive to the eighteenth century *philosophes* who were concerned to find a plausible and systematic explanation of the world, and not especially concerned either with religious orthodoxy or with the kind of evidence they used. Both Voltaire and Rousseau suggested that Negroes were naturally inferior to Europeans in their mental ability. David Hume argued that,

There never was a civilized nation of any other complexion than white, nor even any individual eminent either in action or speculation. No ingenious manufacturers amongst them, no arts, no sciences ... Such a uniform and constant difference could not happen, in so many countries and ages, if nature had not made an original distinction betwixt these breeds of men.[3]

He thus incorporated the two key assumptions – that white Europeans had a superior culture, and that race and culture were causally connected.

New evidence for polygenesis was brought to light by the publication of Buffon's *Histoire naturelle*, even though Buffon himself was a monogenist. His comparative anatomy showed that there were amazing similarities in physical structure between all animals, and especially between men and certain apes. This information fitted in with the Great Chain of Being and the expected close gradation between species. As early as 1713 naturalists began looking for a 'missing link' between men and apes and speculated on the possibility that Hottentots and orang-outangs might be side by side in the 'scale of life', separated only by the fact that orang-outangs could not speak (Lovejoy, 1936, p. 233; 1904, p. 204). [...]

Another work of 1774 was to be immensely more important in giving a pseudo-scientific base to polygenist theories already in the air. This was the *History of Jamaica* by Edward Long, who, as a resident of the island, was in a position to bring forward 'evidence' about the African slaves. In spite of the title, the book was a multi-volume compendium of history and description, and a guide to future British policy in Jamaica. In a key section, Long tried to assess the place of the Negro in nature, drawing partly on Buffon and partly on the xenophobia natural to his home, where lines of caste and race ran parallel. Africans, in his opinion were 'brutish, ignorant, idle, crafty, treacherous, bloody, thievish, mistrustful, and superstitious people'. Their skins were dark, their features different, and they had 'a covering of wool, like the bestial fleece, instead of hair'. They were inferior in 'faculties of mind', had a 'bestial and fetid smell', and were even parasitized by black lice instead of the lighter-colored lice of the

3. Hume (1898), vol. 3, p. 252. The essay was first published in 1742, but the passage quoted was added as a footnote in the edition of 1753–4. See also Cook (1936).

Europeans. All of this was the common prejudice of the West Indies.

Long's importance in biological thought was not simply his restatement of old prejudice, but the fact that he gave his prejudice the backing of technical biological arguments. He claimed that Europeans and Negroes did not belong to the same species. Since species were generally held to have been created in the beginning by God, while varieties were produced after the creation, it was a distinction of some importance. Species also had a technical meaning that still persists: individuals that can breed together and produce fertile offspring are considered to be of the same species. [. . .]

It is clear that the biologists, as well as the travelers, were influenced by the tendencies of 'diversificationism'. They were actively looking for differences between human races. On one hand, this tended to blind them to similarities. On the other, it made them more willing to accept popular myths. There was, for example, a belief going back to antiquity, that southern people are more lascivious than northerners. It was sometimes re-expressed in racial terms and Negroes were given credit for extraordinary sexual prowess. In the guarded language of a popular pamphlet of 1772: 'The lower class of women in *England*, are remarkably fond of the blacks, for reasons too brutal to mention . .' (Lownes, 1772, p. 49). The biologists were less timid. Both monogenists and polygenists thought the penis of Negro men was larger than that of Europeans, and that Negro women were sexually more desirable for physiological reasons left unexplained (Long, 1774, vol. 2, pp. 383–4; Blumenbach, 1775, p. 249; White, 1799, p. 61). Thus a great deal of the popular xenophobia already prevalent on the fringes of Empire came to be expressed in terms of race difference and endowed with 'scientific' authority.

There were only occasional efforts to redress the balance and recall the unity of mankind. Adam Smith pointed out the relativity of physical beauty: 'What different ideas are formed in different nations concerning the beauty of the human shape and countenance? A fair complexion is a shocking deformity on the coast of Guinea. Thick lips and a flat nose are a beauty' (Smith, 1869, p. 175).

John Hunter held that, 'Travellers have exaggerated the mental varieties far beyond the truth, who have denied good qualities to the inhabitants of other countries, because their mode of life, manners and customs have been excessively different from their own' (Hunter, 1775, p. 392).

But only Blumenbach among the biological writers made a serious effort to correct the dominant tendencies of the science as a whole. [. . .]

In spite of these beginnings of serious scholarly study, the British stereotype of 'the African character' drew far more from the reports of the travelers, than it did from the synthesis of the scholars. But scholars and travelers alike were virtually unanimous about one point – there was such a thing as an 'African character', different in significant ways from the character of man in Europe. There was, of course, disagreement about the exact ingredients of this character, but the range of opinion was somewhat narrower than it had been in the later eighteenth century. There were now more (and more varied) sources of information, and a common image of 'the African' was well publicized. Individual writers could hardly do more than adjust the focus or alter the detail.

It was generally believed that African emotions tended toward extremes: 'The understanding is much less cultivated among the Negroes than among Europeans; but their passions, whether benevolent or malevolent, are proportionately more violent . . . Though addicted to hatred and revenge, they are equally susceptible to love, affection and gratitude' (Leyden, 1799, p. 98).

This belief, with various modifications, was extremely common. It was based more on the general theories of the eighteenth-century environmentalists than on observation. A hot temper and violent passions were the prime characteristics of southerners. The travelers, of course, knew this before they left England, and their reports were influenced accordingly.

Further discussions of the 'African character' tended to list virtues and vices as a kind of balance of good and evil, following a tradition borrowed from moral philosophy. Different lists were surprisingly uniform. The chief African vices were held to be indolence, ferocity, cowardice, and superstition. The virtues were mild manners, a peaceful disposition, politeness, charity, respect for the aged, and sometimes gratitude and nobility of character.[4]

Laziness was the vice most frequently reported, and the emphasis was repeated from several sides. It was believed to be characteristic of Negro slaves in the West Indies. It was reinforced by mistaken observation in West Africa, where the myth of tropical exuberance encouraged the Europeans to think that Africans had no need to work. In addition, agricultural work in West Africa was often seasonal, on account of alternation of dry and wet periods. The usual dry-season under-employment became a wet-season labor shortage. The dry-season pattern might look like simple laziness. Lethargy produced by certain intestinal parasites and other African diseases may also have reinforced the impression.

On the side of virtue, reflections of environmentalism combined with other data drawn from actual observation. A formal politeness is still common in many West African cultures. It must have been all the more striking to travelers who expected to find savages. Respect for the aged is equally characteristic – partly for theological reasons, connected with the veneration of ancestral spirits. The code of African hospitality is often rigorous, and so important to travelers that it could hardly escape notice.

The most significant aspect of the virtue column, however, was the attribution of Christian virtues to the Africans. Faith, hope, and charity had appeared occasionally in the literary image of the noble savage, whether African or not. They appeared again in the Christianized noble African of the anti-slavery writers. The result was not so favorable to Africans as it might appear to be. Europeans always paid lip service to the Sermon on the Mount, but they also admired aggressive self-assertion. The sin of pride was the cardinal sin for theologians, but rarely in the moral attitude of the ordinary person. This moral ambivalence in European thought, however, was not mere hypocrisy. Europeans still retained a genuine respect for child-like simplicity and submissiveness – lost long ago by themselves, according to their own mythology, in the Garden of Eden. [. . .]

4. A convenient summary, based on a wide variety of sources, is found in Abbé Henri Baptiste Grégoire (1810).

Postscript

Perhaps the most striking aspect of the British image of Africa in the early nineteenth century was its variance from the African reality, as we now understand it. There was also a marked lack of the kind of 'progress' one might expect to find in a body of ideas that was constantly enlarged by accretions of new data. This is especially hard to explain, given the fact that nineteenth-century social scientists were trying to be methodical, working to a standard that was conceived as rational investigation.

One source of error has already been suggested: reporters went to Africa knowing the reports of their predecessors and the theoretical conclusions already drawn from them. They were therefore sensitive to data that seemed to confirm their European preconceptions and they were insensitive to contradictory data. Their reports were thus passed through a double set of positive and negative filters, and filtered once more as they were assimilated in Britain. Data that did not fit the existing image were most often simply ignored. As a result, British thought about Africa responded very weakly to new data of any kind.

It responded much more strongly to changes in British thought. The travelers (and, even more, the analysts at home) took the European *weltanschauung* as their point of departure. They did not ask, 'What is Africa like and what manner of men live there?' but, 'How does Africa, and how do the Africans, fit into what we already know about the world?' In this sense, the image of Africa was far more European than African.

In considering the nature of racial differences, for example, the scientists studied African races in order to answer questions posed for them by the existing state of biological theory and knowledge. Some African data were of immense importance, especially the data about differential mortality between blacks and whites on the African coast, but these data were selected because they seemed to answer problems set in their European context. In much the same way, the interdependence of race and culture was assumed because that assumption helped explain something in which the Europeans were very interested – their own leadership in the world of the nineteenth century. It was not built up by careful examination of data from Africa, or any other part of the world overseas.

At a more personal level, many affirmations about Africa were made for political, religious, or personal reasons. Prichard's belief in monogenesis came, first of all, from his desire to prove that science was congruent with Scripture. Nott and Gliddon's polygenesis came from their desire to prove that Negro slavery was licit. It is hard to avoid the conclusion that some of the wilder ravings of Knox's 'transcendental anatomy' came from a blighted career, not merely from the currents of evolutionary thought.

In this way, the British image of Africa was intimately related to other strands of Western thought and life, and all the particular facets of that image were more closely related to one another than can be briefly stated. All these bodies of thought – about medicine, race, history, or political and economic development – were equally integrated with the world of events, both as cause and effect. They helped to form the plans for Sierra Leone or the Niger Expedition. They responded, in turn, to the lessons of experience, though these lessons were filtered in the same manner as other data.

The image of Africa, in short, was largely created in Europe to suit European needs – sometimes material needs, more often intellectual needs. When these needs allowed, it might touch on reality; as it did in the empirical victory of tropical medicine. Otherwise the European *Afrikaanschauung* was part of a European *weltanschauung*, and it was warped as necessary to make it fit into the larger whole. To say this, however, implies neither a moral nor an intellectual judgment of the nineteenth-century Europeans. They sought knowledge for their guidance, and the very magnitude of the effort remains as a kind of monument. Their errors, nevertheless, did as much to mold the course of history as their discoveries.

References

ATKINS, J. (1734), *Navy Surgeon*, London.

BENDYSHE, T. (1863–4), *The History of Anthropology*: Memoirs read before the Anthropological Society of London, vol. 1.

BLUMENBACH, J. F. (1775), *De generis humaine varietate nativa*, Göttingen, trans. T. Bendyshe for the Anthropological Society of London, 1865, pp. 209–13.

COOK, M. (1936), 'Jean Jacques Rousseau and the Negro', *J. Negro History*, vol. 21 (July), pp. 294–303.

COUNT, E. W. (1946), 'The Evolution of the Race Idea in Modern Western Culture During the Period of the Pre-Darwinian Nineteenth Century', *Transactions of the New York Academy of Sciences*, vol. 8, 2nd series.

DAVIDSON, B. (1961), *Black Mother*, London, pp. 101–2.

EDWARDS, B. (1794), *The History, Civil and Commercial, of the British Colonies in the West Indies*, second edition, 2 vols, London.

GREGOIRE, ABBÉ HENRI BAPTISTE (1808), *De La Literature des Nègres, ou Recherches sur leur Facultés Intellectuelles, leur Qualités Morales, et leur Literature*, Paris. Translated by D. B. Warden as *An Inquiry Concerning the Intellectual and Moral Faculties, and Literature of the Negroes*, Brooklyn, N.Y., 1810, pp. 89–106.

GREGOIRE, H. B. (1810), *An Inquiry Concerning the Intellectual and Moral Faculties, and Literature of the Negroes*, Brooklyn, N.Y. Translated by D. B. Warden from the original published in Paris as *De le Literature des Nègres ou recherches sur leur facultés*, les Qualites Morales et leur literature, (1808).

HECHT, J. J. (1954), *Continental and Colonial Servants in Eighteenth Century England*, Northampton, Massachusetts.

HUME, D. (1898), 'Of national character', in *The Philosophical Works of David Hume*, 4 vols, London.

HUNTER, J. (1775), *An Inaugural Dissertation on the Varieties of Man*, London, pp. 366–7, trans. by T. Bendyshein, *Anthropological Writings of Johan Friedrich Blumenbach*, London, 1865.

LEYDEN, (1799), *Historical and Philosophical Sketch of the Discovery and Settlement of Europeans in Northern and Western Africa at the Close of the Eighteenth Century*, London.

LONG, E. (1774), *A History of Jamaica*, 2 vols.

LOWNES, T. (1772), *Candid Reflections upon the Judgement Lately Awarded by the Court of King's Bench in Westminster Hall on What is Commonly called the Negro Cause*, by a Planter.

LOVEJOY, A. C. (1904), 'Some eighteenth century evolutionists', *Popular Science Monthly* vol. 65, pp. 238–51; 323–40.

LOVEJOY, A. C. (1936), *The Great Chain of Being*, Cambridge, Mass.

MATTHEWS, J. (1788), *Voyage to the River Sierra Leone*, London, pp. 91–4.

PRIVY COUNCIL, (1789), *Report of the Lords of the Committee of Council for … Trade and Foreign Plantations … concerning the present state of Trade to Africa, and particularly The Trade in Slaves*, Part 1.

SNELGRAVE, W. (1754), *A New Account of Guinea and the Slave Trade*, London.

SMITH, A. (1869), *The Theory of Moral Sentiments*, essays first published 1757.

WHITE, C. (1799), *An Account of the Regular Gradations in Man*, London.

Part Four
Literary and Folk Images

Insofar as imaginative writers represent the most conscious point of the thought and feeling of their time, they can serve us as guides to the cultural responses, both the explicit and implicit, made by less fluent people in different places and at different times. Isaacs lays bare a continuing set of assumptions about colour which run through a great deal of English literature, even innocent children's stories. Boskin traces the history of Sambo, the comical nigger, until the time he was finally driven from the popular stage when the social position of the Black Americans became more secure. Irele discusses the themes of alienation, revolt and rediscovery as they declare themselves in the work of the group of black Francophone intellectuals who participated in the *négritude* movement.

12 Harold R. Isaacs

Blackness and Whiteness

Excerpt from Harold R. Isaacs, 'Blackness and Whiteness',
Encounter, August 1963, pp. 12–15.

In wanting to become like those who have dominated, despised, and rejected them, Negroes have been behaving like members of many other dominated, despised and rejected groups. All our various cultures and subcultures are filled with examples. It became part of the common experience of certain sections of the colonized peoples during the Western imperial epoch; it was even shared for quite a while by certain kinds of Chinese. In the American culture, it has been plainly visible in the experience of successive immigrant groups as they went about relating themselves to the dominant group in the society. Jews, who have been despised and rejected for a longer time than anybody, have a number of chapters of this kind in their long history. Bruno Bettelheim's interpretation of what happened to some Jews in the Nazi extermination camps suggests a recent and extreme example. More familiar and more common has been the behaviour attached to the idea of 'assimilation', the effort to shed all vestiges of the Jewish identity by disappearing entirely into the dominant group. The equivalent among Negroes is, of course, 'passing' into the white population. But to 'pass' is possible only for relatively few. More generally people have to find other ways of assimilating the majority view of themselves and of expressing the self-rejection and self-hatred that follows from this. Among Negroes the forms and modes of this process are endlessly varied. One of the most pervasive of these has been the institution of colour caste which raised 'whiteness' to the highest value in all aspects of life. This meant everything pertaining to civilization, culture, religion, and human worth. It became among Negroes an intricate system of social, group and personal relationships based directly on degrees of relative darkness and other degrees of physical Negro-ness, the shape and kinds of features, hair, lips, and nose which were 'good' if they resembled the white's, 'bad' if they did not. This was carried to the point of using artificial means – hair straighteners and skin whiteners – in the effort to close the gap between the two.

In coming to terms with himself, every Negro individual has had in one way or another to cope with the infinity of ways in which 'white' is elevated above 'black' in our culture. The association of white and black with light and dark and the translation of these quantities of light into polarities of 'good' and 'evil' and 'beauty' and 'ugliness' has taken place in the conventions and languages of many cultures, but in few has this conversion of physical facts into religious and aesthetic values been worked harder than in our own.

These concepts and usages of black evil and white goodness, of beautiful fairness and ugly blackness, are deeply imbedded in the Bible, are folded into the language of Milton and Shakespeare, indeed are laced into almost every entwining strand of the art and literature in which our history is clothed. They can be traced down the columns of any dictionary from white hope to whitewash, from the black arts to the Black Mass, from black-browed and blackhearted to blacklist and blackmail. 'I am black *but* comely', sang the Shulamite maiden to the daughters of Jerusalem and on that *but* hangs a whole great skein of our culture.

The Bible's central theme of good and evil is constantly represented by the symbolism of 'black' and 'white' and 'dark' and 'light'. In the Scriptures the use of 'black' as a negative word is consistent throughout, standing for sin, ignorance, wickedness and evil. 'My skin is black', cries Job in his great self-arraignment, using this figure to show how heavy was his burden of sin. Again in *Job*: 'Let darkness and the shadow of death stain it; let a cloud dwell upon it; let the blackness of the day terrify it.' Or in *Jeremiah*: 'For this shall the earth mourn and the heavens above be black.' And in the *Epistle of Jude* the famous phrase about 'the wandering stars to whom is reserved the blackness of darkness forever'.

The word 'white' is apparently used a good deal less in the Bible, and less consistently. Thus 'the great white throne' of God in *Revelations*, the 'white raiments' of the elders in *Judges*. But 'white', though most often signifying beauty, purity and elegance, is also more rarely used – as a literally descriptive word – in connection with leprosy, and has been associated in the language with pestilence and death. More consistent is the juxtaposition of 'light' and 'dark', the dark being always bad and light always good, from the original creation of light to divide it from the primeval dark and to show the way for men to see truth and good works and glory and the light of God himself: 'In *Thy* light', sang the Psalmist, 'shall we see light.' There can be no question that when the Lord looked upon his work and found it good, it was the light that pleased him, not the dark. Where the references occur in the Bible to a literal blackness of skin, the association seems to retain its negative cast. 'Look not upon me', adds the Shulamite maiden in the *Song of Songs*, 'because I am black'. A second such allusion is rather more equivocal. This is the reference in *Numbers* to the Lord's anger at Aaron and Miriam after they had spoken against Moses for marrying 'an Ethiopian woman', the term 'Ethiopian' signifying a person of black skin. The text suggests that the Lord was angry primarily because the offenders were jealous of Moses' special role as the Lord's man. If the issue here *was* colour, then his anger was ironically vented: his punishing finger touched Miriam and she became '*leprous, white as snow*'. I suspect, however, that Aaron was objecting to the Ethiopian woman not because she was black – the Israelites who came out of Egypt could hardly have been a lily-white race – but because she was gentile. In this case God either knew more about Moses' origins than Aaron did or was simply being less orthodox than his high priest, a not unfamiliar state of affairs.

The carry-over of the Bible's imagery into the common usage, visible in Chaucer and Milton, is richly illustrated in Shakespeare, whose own impact on the English language has hardly been less great than that of the Bible itself.

Black is the badge of hell,
The hue of the dungeons and the suit of night.

says the King in *Love's Labour's Lost*, in a passage of raillery in which the beauty of Rosaline (French and therefore presumably brunette) is called 'black as ebony' and her admirer Biron chided for loving 'an Ethiope'. In quite another tone, in *Macbeth*, we come on: 'The devil damn thee black—', again the symbolic joining of sin, the devil and the blackness of skin which runs continuously from Job and the prophets through centuries of our literature. (Thus Fitzgerald in *Omar Khayyam*: 'For all the sin wherewith the face of man is blackened . . .'). In Shakespeare's first tragedy, *Titus Andronicus*, the villain is a black man. In *Othello* Shakespeare treats the theme with far greater subtlety. No doubt is left that Brabantio's rage is due in part to the thought that his daughter would run 'to the sooty bosom of such a thing as thou', but the direct allusions to Othello's colour are few. Perhaps the most ironic are those Shakespeare puts in the mouth of Othello himself, as where in the rage of his rising jealousy he says:

Her name, that was as fresh
As Dian's visage is now begrimed and black
As mine own face.

and where he cries out: 'Arise, black vengeance!' He looks upon the sleeping Desdemona not wanting to shed her blood,

Nor scar that whiter skin of hers than snow
And smooth as monumental alabaster.

When he has done the deed, the servant Emilia shrieks at him: 'You the blacker devil!'

One might travel many paths into some of the mysteries of this little-studied matter, whether in other cultures, including the African, or in our own. These could run, in the latter case, from tracing the notions and characteristics attached to blondness or brunette-ness (over the whole course of the Anglo-Saxon romantic tradition on down to the Hollywood illustrations, from Mary Pickford – contradicted, to be sure, by Garbo and Dietrich – and Theda Bara, and the convention requiring cowboy heroes always to wear a white hat and ride a white horse and cowboy villains always a black hat and a black horse). One might pursue these themes into some of their deeper and more enigmatic courses, as Professor Harry Levin did in *The Power of Blackness*, in which he examines the imagery of black and blackness in Hawthorne, Poe and Melville. But to lead us back to the aspects of the matter that touch us here most directly let me only follow an allusion from his pages to William Blake's poem, *The Little Black Boy* – part of a collection published in 1789 – in which the outlook imposed by the white society on the black child is quite neatly capsuled:

My mother bore me in the southern wild,
And I am black, but O! my soul is white;
White as an angel is the English child,
But I am black, as if bereav'd of light.
My mother . . . began to say:
. . . And we are put on earth a little space
That we may learn to bear the beams of love;
And these black bodies and this sunburnt face
Is but a cloud, and like a shady grove.
For when our souls have learn'd the heat to bear,
The cloud will vanish; we shall hear His voice,
Saying: 'Come out from the grove, My love and care,
And round my golden tent like lambs rejoice.'
Thus did my mother say, and kissed me;
And thus I say to little English boy.
When I from black and he from white cloud free,
And round the tent of God like lambs we joy,
I'll shade him from the heat, till he can bear
To lean in joy upon our Father's knee;
And then I'll stand and stroke his silver hair,
And be like him, and he will then love me.

This raising of 'white' and debasement of 'black' has been marked deep on the minds of all through time and every 'white' person has more or less unconsciously imbibed it as a nourishment for his self-esteem. Like the English child in Blake's poem, he was already the colour of the angels, while the black man could only yearn after whiteness, whether of character, soul, or of skin, and hope that by becoming 'like' the white man – whether on earth or in heaven – he would come at last to be loved. This arrangement of things was communicated to all in our culture by all its modes and means, passed by osmosis through all the membranes of class, caste and colour of relationships, caressingly and painlessly injected into our children by their school texts and, even more, their storybooks.

Consider only one contemporary example, out of the Dr Dolittle stories, written by an Englishman, which have delighted

European and American children since 1920. Dr Dolittle, an animal doctor who travels with an entourage of a dog, a duck, a pig, an owl, a monkey and a parrot, goes to Africa to cure monkeys of a plague. Dolittle and his animal helpers become the prisoners of a black king. In the king's garden the parrot and the monkey meet the king's son, Prince Bumpo, who is pictured as an ugly-gnome-like black man with a huge nose that covers most of his face. They hear him yearn aloud: 'If only I were a *white* prince!' The parrot promises that Dr Dolittle will change his colour if he helps them escape. To Dr Dolittle, the unhappy prince tells his story:

Years ago I went in search of The Sleeping Beauty, whom I had read of in a book. And having travelled through the world many days, I at last found her and kissed the lady very gently to wake her – as the book said I should. 'Tis true indeed that she woke. But when she saw my face she cried out, 'Oh, he's black!' And she ran away and wouldn't marry me – but went to sleep again somewhere else. So I came back, full of sadness, to my father's kingdom. Now I hear that you are a wonderful magician and have many powerful potions. So I come to you for help. If you will turn me white, so that I may go back to The Sleeping Beauty, I will give you half of my kingdom and anything besides you ask.

Bumpo refuses to settle just for blond hair and says: 'I would like my eyes blue, too, but I suppose that would be very hard to do.' The doctor concocts a paste which whitens Bumpo's face and keeps it that way long enough for him and his friends to escape, having first refused to give Bumpo a mirror because he knew that the medicine would wear off and that Bumpo would be 'as black as ever in the morning'. As they escape, the doctor says, 'Poor Bumpo'. The parrot says: 'Oh, of course he would know we were just joking with him.' The duck says: 'Serve him right if he does turn black again. I hope it is a dark black.' Dr Dolittle decides that instead of apologizing he will send Bumpo some candy when he gets back home.

I do not know if Negro children have been readers of Hugh Lofting's Dolittle stories, but vast numbers of white children apparently have – it came up in the first place when a discussion of these matters in a seminar stirred the recollection of a graduate student of thirty, and an indirect question brought immediate recall of the story to my own daughter, then sixteen. It is not hard to imagine the effect on white children who, as they chortle over the good doctor's adventures with the animals, also take in this vignette of the ugly black prince who wanted to be white in order to be loved. It takes no great art either to imagine how this tale might stab a black child or help give him all unknowingly the same love for whiteness that it nourishes in the white child.

The imprint on Negroes of this whole system of ordering 'black' and 'white' has been seen and experienced by many but studied by very few. Every 'black' person obviously has been called upon to reject or somehow deflect from himself the associations of evil and inferiority so powerfully attached to blackness. He has been called upon to do this, moreover, under conditions in which his ego was kept under constant assault from all the conditions of his life. That so many Negroes in every successive generation found the ego strength to meet and resist these identifications is in itself no small miracle. That a greater number accepted the white man's images as the truth about themselves is no wonder at all.

13 Joseph Boskin

Sambo: The National Jester in the Popular Culture

Excerpts from Joseph Boskin, 'Sambo' in G. B. Nash and R. Weiss, (eds.) *The Great Fear: Race in the Mind of America*, Holt, Rinehart and Winston, 1970, pp. 165–85.

'The subtlest and most pervasive of all influences,' wrote Walter Lippmann (1922, pp. 89–90) 'are those which create and maintain the repertory of stereotypes. We are told about the world before we see it. We imagine most things before we experience them.' Once implanted in popular lore, a stereotype attached to a group, an issue, or an event pervades our senses and affects our behavior. A standardized mental picture representing an over-simplified opinion or an uncritical judgment, a stereotype is tenacious in its hold over rational thinking. Its power is gained by repetitive play, so that the image it projects becomes firmly imbedded in reactive levels of thought and action.

Although images can serve a positive function, many are deleterious in their effect. As an integral part of the pattern of culture, a stereotype, by its very nature, will operate within and at most levels of society. It will affect the thoughts and actions of those who aware of its existence; more importantly, it influences those who are not. Indeed, stereotypes are often so powerful that they can be dislodged only after a series of assaults on them.

In the history of race relations in the United States, stereotypes have been particularly pernicious. Of the various images assigned to darker-skinned persons by whites, two were developed and flourished almost simultaneously for more than three centuries: Sambo and the Brute. Their functional presence and constant refurbishment in the face of vast social and economic changes attests not only to their tenacity but to the deeply rooted prejudices of those who had developed them in the first instance. Both images were originated by white Americans and were utilized as a means of maintaining their superior position in society.

To a considerable extent, the concepts of Sambo and the Brute complemented each other. Both derived from the view of other racial groups as inferior – either for religious, biological, anthropological, or historical reasons. With respect to the Brute, it was contended that the black man was a primitive creature given to fits of violence and powerful sexual impulses. It was argued, often with quasi-scholarly data, that such dark-skinned peoples as the Africans were stunted in their intellectual capacities because of physical limitations or their slow ascent up the evolutionary ladder. This argument gave rise to myths about the characteristics of black men. Most whites spoke and wrote of the Negro's 'natural rhythm', his sexual prowess, 'flashy' dress habits, and proneness to rioting and fighting.

The Negro as a Brute, albeit an integral part of the fiction of whites, was not always explicit in the popular culture. Movies such as D. W. Griffith's early classic, *Birth of a Nation*, portrayed Negroes as ignorant legislators and sexual violators, but the image of the black as a violent man was usually implicit. This was partly due to the fear of whites that constantly to portray the Negro as the Brute was to affect a possibility of its realization. Not wishing to encourage black violence and retaliation, white society generally stressed the other side of the stereotype. By emphasizing the Sambo image, white America hoped to minimize black hostility and develop a character amenable to the institution of slavery and, after emancipation, to second-class citizenship.

Although the name of Sambo predominated in the mass culture, other folk expressions were used over the centuries. At various times, the Negro was referred to as 'Tambo', 'Rastus', 'Sam', 'Pompey', 'Mammy' and 'Boy'. In popular songs, he was called 'Old Black Joe' and 'Uncle Ned'. He could be found in advertising in the form of 'Uncle Ben's Rice', 'Aunt Jemima's Pancakes', 'Ben the Pullman Porter', and the 'Gold Dust Twins'. In literature, the most famous expression of the character was developed by Joel Chandler Harris in 'Uncle Remus' and his stories. In the development of the mass media in the twentieth century he became 'Stepin Fetchit', 'Amos 'n Andy', 'Rochester' and a host of other characters.

What were the essential features of the Sambo stereotype which became so deeply imbedded in the popular culture? A southern novelist and poet, Robert Penn Warren, summed up the various aspects of the personality type:

He was the supine, grateful, humble, irresponsible, unmanly, banjo-picking, servile, grinning, slack-jawed, docile, dependent, slow-witted, humorous, child-loving, childlike, watermelon-stealing, spiritual-singing, blamelessly fornicating, happy-go-lucky, hedonistic, faithful black servitor who sometimes might step out of character long enough to utter folk wisdom or bury the family silver to save it from the Yankees (1965, p. 52).

The Sambo figure had two principal parts. In the beginning he was childish and comical. Given to outlandish gestures and physical gyrations, he was the buffoon par excellence. Later, he was depicted as the 'natural' servant and slave, nonviolent and humble. There were variations on the theme of Sambo but in the main he emerged as the national jester.

The origins of the Sambo type are uncertain. Several significant characteristics, however, are related to the Negro's position of servitude. The status of the slave evoked strong expressions of disdain and intolerance. The psychology of the situation worked automatically against the servile man. As long as he remained at the lowest level of society, he could barely hope to improve his status; and unable to improve his status, he was powerless to change the white image of him as less than human. Thus the traits ascribed to Sambo are found in other cultures where slavery existed. 'The white slaves of antiquity and the Middle Ages', states Davis (1966), 'were often described in terms that fit the later stereotype of the Negro. Throughout history it has been said that slaves, though occasionally as loyal and faithful as good dogs, were for the most part lazy, irresponsible, cunning, rebellious, untrustworthy, and sexually promiscuous.' There existed, then, an historical precedent for anticipating the character of the black slave in America.

The debut of Sambo

The child-Sambo apparently made his debut into the popular culture in the dramatic theater in the latter half of the eighteenth century. English plays often featured a white actor who wore blackface and who performed the role of a Negro. For example, in *The Padlock*, a play by Isaac Bickerstaff performed in 1769, the character of Mungo, a Negro servant, suffered the insults of his master. In the English plays by George Colman, *Inkle and Yarico* (1791) and *The Africans; or, War, Love and Duty* (1808), comic black figures spoke in dialect and sang nonsensical choruses.

The American contribution to the blackface tradition appeared immediately following the termination of hostilities with England in 1815. The Negro song and singer, as illustrated by a burnt-cork sailor who sang 'The Siege of Plattsburg' or 'Back Side Albany', was apparently the first staged Sambo type. The songs were written by Micab Hawkins, an American composer. Blackfaced performers also were seen in circuses where they sang and danced before delighted audiences.

By the 1820s, the characteristics of the Sambo form were clearly delineated in act and song. In 1822, a broadside 'Sold by the Flying Booksellers' was circulating in Boston on the same day that the Negro population was parading through the city to celebrate the anniversary of the abolition of the slave trade. The statement was a parody of the event and was a ludicrous imitation of the black's dialect. The sheet contained instructions detailing the toasts to be made at a banquet, with the added ridicule: 'Forty cheer – four grin all round de mout', 'three guess – five sober look', 'two wink – seven sly look', and so forth. An example of the political barbs foreshadowed the type of statement which would be found in the minstrel act:

De day is one of dose great nashumnal hepox which will call fort de sensumbility and de herhaw of good feelum of ebery son and daughter of Africa in dis world, and good many udder place beside, which you no find tell of in de jography, cause I spose Massa Morse what make um, dont know wedder deir any such place or not. De committee of derangement hab gib me full power to make de debiltry marshal mind what I say – else dey stand chance to get shin kick cause he no take de hint and act just like raw soger, who know nothing bout milintary dissumpleen (Nathan, 1962, p. 49).

At the close of the decade, two songs heralded the development of a new American comic form. In 'Coal Black Rose' and 'My Long-Tail Blue', performed by comedian George Washington Dixon, two types of black men were impersonated. The two figures –

the plantation hand and the city dandy – would become an integral part of the minstrel theater. [. . .]

It was with the advent of Thomas D. Rice's 'Jim Crow' that minstrelsy was initiated into the theater. Every study of the minstrel show acknowledges the importance of the song and dance of 'Jim Crow' – a name which would become synonymous with segregation in later years – as one of the most important contributors to the tradition. Rice was a well-known performer acting with a theatrical company which was booked at the Columbia Street Theater in New York in 1828–9 when he observed the antics of Jim, a stable hand who worked in a livery stable owned by a man named Crow. The slave, lame and aging, entertained himself by dancing a funny little jig to an original tune which he sang,

Wheel about, turn about,
  Do jis so,
An' ebery time I wheel about
  I jump Jim Crow.

Verse was added to verse, the ending always the same. Rice one day conceived the idea of using the old slave's jig and song for an act of his own. He appeared wearing an outlandish costume which was wrinkled, ill-fitting, and 'bumish'. Singing new verses to new tunes, Rice basked in instantaneous success. From the moment of the first audience response, Rice became one of the foremost exponents of the minstrel character. [. . .]

The heyday of the minstrel lasted for more than fifty years, from the 1830s to the 1880s. It was one of the most popular forms of theater, reaching into all sections and into the most remote corners of America. By the early twentieth century, almost every community boasted of a minstrel group. Books, pamphlets, and scores provided minstrel compendiums from which schools, civic groups, church organizations, and others could chose materials to produce a show. *The Newsboys and Bootblacks Minstrel Show Book*, published in 1919, contained a complete show for 'unchanging voices for boys and girls of the upper grammar grades and junior high schools'. Among the various characters in the show were Rastus, Rufus, and Mose. Typical of the hundreds of published shows was 'The Masonic Lodge'. The picture on the front cover depicts a young Negro woman wearing a funny cap, flanked by cabins with a watermelon patch on the left side and cotton bales and a steamboat on the other side. The words of the characters, Obediah, Spoffit, and Jabez Fishpole, are grossly exaggerated as illustrated by 'cum erlong', 'inishiated', 'arribe' and 'serlissister'. Common folk expressions were transposed into dialect as in 'Punctiosity c'n be tief o' time.'

The minstrel as a neighborhood production continued to the 1940s and reached millions of persons who rarely had first-hand knowledge of the black man. Indeed almost the only contact the immigrant groups who settled in the northern urban areas and midwestern towns had with the Negro was that acquired through the mass media. The minstrel show, in emphasizing the peculiarities of Negro dialect and in creating the vehicle for foolishness, buffoonery, and dance, transformed regional differences of language into signs of racial inferiority. As sociologist Arnold Rose stated regarding the speech pattern of the black man:

To the Northern white man, although seldom to the Southern white man, the speech of the Negro seems unusual. In fact the 'Negro dialect' is an important cause of the Northern white's unconscious assumption that Negroes are of a different biological type from them (1944, pp. 300–301). [. . .]

Twentieth-century Sambo

The electronics industry in the twentieth century made heavy use of stereotypes developed in the previous century. Animated cartoons, stereoscopic slides, moving pictures, photographic stills, radio, and television are, by their very nature, intended to synthesize thoughts and attitudes into a visual pattern. Without doubt, the visual and oral media have been able to create a collective consciousness regarding people, ideas and events. They have demonstrated their power to create, perpetuate or destroy stereotypes and thus to influence reality.

For the Negro, the medium has been the message which, until the 1950s, reproduced and reinforced the illusion of Sambo. From their earliest development in the first half of the nineteenth century, visual devices employed images of Sambo as an aspect of their entertainment. Before the innovation of the moving picture, receptive audiences peered into gadgets which contained scenes of churches, exotic peoples, historic buildings, geographic wonders and humorous events. The stereoscope, a device which permitted the viewer to look at two drawings simultaneously by moving the holder back and forth along a stationary wooden track, was a popular device used to convey visual images. Among its educational and entertainment subjects was the comic black man. In the stereographics, blacks were shown working in the fields, harvesting cotton, and cavorting in pranks. The photographs used were both of black and white actors in blackface with wide eyes and prominent lips, which were consistent with the popular view. One scene staged by blackfaced actors involved a man and a woman in an overturning boat. The man is half way in the water; the woman is trying to prevent his complete immersion. 'Golly', she exclaims, 'I jest can't hole dat nigger.' Other scenes involve subjects such as thievery, a comical wedding ceremony and horseplay between 'darkies'.

Sambo moved from the stereoscope to the silent movie. From its earliest years, the film industry made movies in which the black man's fondness for watermelon, chicken, dice, razors, and funny antics seemed to define his nature. In the 1890s, Thomas Edison's company used Negroes in several of its early films, particularly in the *Black Maria* series and in comic shorts. The titles of the movies provide insight into their plots: *Negro Lovers*, *Chicken Thieves*, and *Colored Boy Eating Watermelons*.

Several years later, Edwin S. Porter, who had completed the classic film *The Great Train Robbery* in 1903, made a short film based on Harriet Beecher Stowe's novel *Uncle Tom's Cabin*. The movie was a series of short vignettes followed by a cakewalk scene. As in the minstrel theater, the characters were mainly white actors performing in blackface. Regardless of the script, the Afro-American in the silent film era was depicted in a manner virtually identical with his counterpart in the printed media. A series of short slapstick films, highly popular prior to World War One were the *Rastus* shorts. In *Rastus in Zululand* and *How Rastus Got His Turkey*, the main character was a buffoon of low intelligence. A black clown named 'Sambo' represented the same caricature in a number of similar shorts. *Sambo* was also the title of a series of all-Negro comedies produced in Philadelphia which included *Coon Town Suffragettes*, a movie which burlesqued the organizing antics of a group of southern 'Mammys' bent on keeping their irresponsible husbands out of saloons.

In the 'silents and sounds' of the 1920s and 1930s, the minstrel tradition was continued by such performers as Al Jolson and Eddie Cantor. Chorus lines and singing groups in the extravaganza movies of the 1930s also wore blackface. When Negroes were hired for parts, they were usually seen singing spirituals and dancing happily in movies whose plots centred on the Old South. They bubbled with gaiety in kitchens while serving food in dining cars, smiled broadly as they red-capped bags at railroad stations, and tap-danced snappily in a variety of scenes.

Several dimensions of the stereotype were particularly mimed in the movies. The superstitious black, whose fear related to the concept of the black man as a child, received featured billing in detective stories such as the Charlie Chan film series. Fear of natural and supernatural phenomena such as earthquakes and ghosts were accentuated and carried to comical heights by such actors as Mantan Moreland and Willie Best. Moreland, who played Charlie Chan's chauffeur, was adroit in the role. Upon encountering a ghost, his eyes bulged, his body swayed, his feet began to move quickly, and off he went exclaiming: 'Tain't no disgrace to run when you git skeered.' Hollywood displayed its ingenuity in inventing techniques to highlight the Negro's alleged fear of ghosts; hair stood on end, speech became incoherent, the face turned white and then black again. In one movie, a frightened black man outran people and animals, shouting to them as he passed, 'Git out de way an' let a man run whut can *run*.'

The epitomization of the stereotype in the movies was achieved by Lincoln Monroe Perry whose stage name, Stepin Fetchit, became synonymous with Sambo. Perry performed in more than a dozen films as a stammering, foot-shuffling, lackadaisical, slack-jawed comic. His motto, according to a Fox studio release, was 'take your time – time ain't gonna take you'.

Not all movies, however, pictured the Negro in Sambo form. There were exceptions to the traditional role. A few films treated the servant with dignity and approached the problem of race seriously. In an occasional movie the Negro appeared as a middle-class professional. During World War Two, the film industry departed from convention by making nearly a dozen important movies in which Negroes were more realistically portrayed. Nonetheless, these films were the exceptions. The more sympathetic portrayal of the black was far outweighed by the popularity of the Sambo stereotype. [. . .]

Such was the grip of Sambo that the inner voices of the black communities rarely were heard. For the most part, the Negro, as Ralph Ellison has powerfully written, was 'invisible'. With the exception of the beat of the jazz groups and dixieland bands, the sorrows of the blues singers and the steps of the dancers, the everyday activities of the black man and woman were virtually unknown. Caucasian conceptions and sensitivities were well protected. Indeed, such was the irony of the separation of the races that while the white man was laughing at his Sambo, the black man was often laughing at his detractor. Within the concentric circles of humor, which overlapped infrequently, the tragedy of race relations in the country could be seen. Caucasian deafness was an integral part of the denial of the Negro as an equal.

The demise of Sambo

The life of Sambo was dependent upon the willingness of the black man to contain his anger and his own laughter from the white and upon the ability of the white to disavow the dual feelings of the oppressed blacks. While blackfaced comedians were strutting in front of the stage lights and across the film, and white actors were mispronouncing so-called Negroid words, blacks were organizing for the end of such demeaning activities. Opposition to the Sambo figure had always existed; its strident voice was heard far back into the eighteenth and nineteenth centuries. Conditions conducive to the elimination of Sambo, however, became considerably more favorable during and after World War Two. The stark contrast between the combatants, a fascist nation which derived much of its sense of being from racist ideas and a democracy whose sense of identity derived from egalitarian ideas, proved to be a catalyst for many black individuals and organizations. The Supreme Court decision in *Brown* v. *the Board of Education of Topeka*, nine years after the conclusion of the war, threw the national spotlight on the practice of segregation.

In 1955, the curtain rose on the act which would bury the stereotype. In that year, Mrs Rosa Parks, a weary seamstress in Montgomery, Alabama, refused to relinquish her seat to a white man in a crowded bus. The driver ordered Mrs Parks to move to the back of the vehicle. When she refused, the driver called a policeman who arrested her. The following day, after a night of meetings, the black community of Montgomery decided to boycott the buses until the restrictive regulation was removed. Led by Dr Martin Luther King, Jr, the action was one of the first successful *communal* acts on the part of the black. It contributed significantly to the revolt of the late 1950s and 1960s.

The activities of black Americans during the civil rights and black power movements – the thousands of meetings, sit-ins, motel-ins, wade-ins, jailings, and beatings – profoundly altered the Negro's conception of himself. A powerful sense of group identity arose, pride in accomplishments grew, and a communal direction only rarely achieved in the past appeared. The new sense of self- and group-identity created an aggressiveness and a determination to bring about social change. In innumerable ways, blacks protested the white's conception of the past. Students at Hyde Park High School in Chicago in 1964 protested the use of the traditional triumphal march from 'Aida' at graduation exercises because the central figure of the opera was a Negro slave. When the white principal of the school gave the students a choice of 'Aida' or nothing, they chose to march in silence.

Similar episodes were repeated many times in the 1960s. More than a hundred Negro high-school students in Bridgeport, Connecticut, turned in their social studies textbooks to protest the books' treatment of the Negro in American history. The young blacks in the 1960s manifested their fierce pride in race in the wearing of natural hairdos, the cult of 'soul', the African dress, the slogan 'black is beautiful' and the clasp of 'brothers'' handshake.

The mass actions of the period created an ethos in which Sambo was attacked and subsequently demolished. There is little doubt that the cry of black power meant the termination of Sambo. The Shriners' traditional blackface Mummers Parade held annually on 1 January was challenged for its perpetuation of

Sambo. After considerable protest from the National Association for the Advancement of Colored People and other local groups in Philadelphia, the Mummers replaced black with gold in 1965. A more amusing episode occurred in Rocky Mountain, North Carolina, in 1966 when Negro employees of a laundry firm refused to clean Ku Klux Klan robes. So adamant were the workers that the owner was forced to subcontract the dirty laundry.

Civil rights workers, black power ideologists, community leaders, comedians, performers of various types, and many others made ringing denunciations of the Sambo tradition. Comedian Godfrey Cambridge, twitted the stereotype in his act. Rushing onstage, Cambridge would pantingly tell his audience: 'I hope you noticed how I rushed up here. No more shuffle after the revolution. We gotta be agile.'

The efforts of blacks, coupled with the changing climate of opinion in the late 1950s and early 1960s, effected changes in the mass media as well. The use of the stereotype in the radio, movies, television and short subjects was gradually phased out. Bowing to pressure from the NAACP, and other civil rights groups, stereotypic symbols of Uncle Rastus were eliminated. In 1963, MGM announced that the 'Tom and Jerry' cartoons would no longer feature the Negro maid. With some exceptions, Africans depicted as cannibals disappeared from animated and other forms of short subjects. The 'Stepin Fetchits' as a movie type were not reintroduced after the war.

Mounting pressure from blacks also forced the mass media to modify or eliminate specific programs, the most prominent being the 'Amos 'n Andy' television show. Though audience interest had waned considerably, *Ebony* magazine clearly signaled the demise of both the radio and television programs in an article in 1961. 'Perhaps the progress of the American Negro in the last ten years,' wrote Edward T. Clayton,

can be measured in the disapproval and final demise of the radio show of A & A. For it is certain that in this age of youthful protestation, of sit-ins and freedom rides, Negro America is no longer amused by the buffoonery of the Mystic Knights of the Sea or the bungling machinations of such as the Kingfish (1961, p. 73).

Consequently, the trappings of the minstrel, such as the use of the blackface and dialect, as well as the minstrel show itself, became a relic of past attitudes.

By the mid-1960s, attractive and light-skinned Afro-Americans were slowly beginning to make their way into various levels of the mass media. The first major use of blacks on a television network commercial occurred in 1963 on Art Linkletter's 'House Party' show. On this inauspicious occasion, three Negroes were planted in the audience and one of them was drawn into the commercial for an instant. Billboards and magazines began to feature blacks in large ads; television news shows hired blacks as sports announcers and later as interviewers; black models made their appearance in all the media and in model shows. Importantly, major television shows utilized blacks in leading roles, the first being comedian Bill Cosby, who co-starred in the 'I Spy' series. Interview and talk shows, such as the popular 'Tonight' program, were hosted by well-known black entertainers and more blacks became members of panel shows. Black specials were produced by singer-actor Harry Belafonte which dealt with Harlem in the 1920s and black humor. By the end of the decade, more black actors were included in the network series shows.

The increasing emphasis on documentary coverage of black-white problems, which introduced the white audience to the highly articulate black leaders, made the Sambo image an irreconcilable contradiction. Similarly, films portrayed the blacks in a more realistic manner. More importantly, however, many black actors and writers such as Ossie Davis, author of the satirical play, *Purlie Victorious* began to produce their own films in a move to interpret their own past and present. Sensitive whites joined them in the reinterpretation of American attitudes and behavior as well. The increasing use of darker-skinned performers indicated a greater willingness among white Americans to deal with their own attitudes toward color.

The rise to national prominence of black comedians and humorists in the late 1950s and 1960s further reflected the changing concept and image of the Negro on the part of both blacks and whites. Before the 1960s, few whites had heard of talented black comics such as 'Moms' Mabley, Redd Foxx, Dusty Fletcher, and Pigmeat Markham, who had been limited to all-black audiences, having been denied access to the popular stage.

Within a few years, however, white Americans became aware of the bitterness and sweetness of Negro humor as it related both to themselves and to the black community. Beginning with Dick Gregory, who, like many Negro comics, began his career in a small night club but quickly gained fame on television, a series of talented men – Bill Cosby, Godfrey Cambridge, Nipsey Russell, Bill Pryor, Stu Gillam, and others – were piquing and regaling national audiences. Their materials were far removed from blackface or Sambo gyrations.

Thus the black revolt of the post-World War Two period and the pressure of the drive toward egalitarianism brought an end to the Sambo image in popular culture. His demise was mourned only by those who had become enmeshed in its psychological labyrinths and who had utilized it as an instrument of racial denigration. A surge of events made the Sambo stereotype a ludicrous caricature of its own creators; only in the smallest way did it correspond with the reality of black life in America. Whatever the outcome of the conflict between blacks and whites in the twentieth century, it was thus no longer possible for the Sambo image to obfuscate the more complex social, economic, and racial problems.

References

CLAYTON, E. T. (1961), 'The tragedy of Amos 'n Andy', *Ebony*, no. 16, 21st October.

DAVIS, D. B. (1966), *The Problem of Slavery in Western Culture*, Ithaca, New York.

LIPPMANN, W. (1922), *Public Opinion*, New York.

NATHAN, H. (1962), *Dan Emmett and the Rise of Early Negro Minstrels*, Norman, Oklahoma.

ROSE, A. (1944), *The Negro in America*, New York.

WARREN, R. P. (1965), *Who Speaks for the Negro?*, New York.

14 Abiola Irele

Négritude – Literature and Ideology

Reprinted from A. Irele, 'Négritude – literature and ideology', *Journal of Modern African Studies*, vol. 3, no. 4, 1965, pp. 499–526.

Pan-Africanism has been described as 'essentially a movement of emotions and ideas' (Legum, 1962, p. 14), and this description is equally applicable to *négritude*, which is its cultural parallel. Indeed, no better phrase could be found to sum up its double nature, first as a psychological response to the social and cultural conditions of the 'colonial situation',[1] and secondly as a fervent quest for a new and original orientation.

In the former respect, the imaginative writings of the French-speaking Negro intellectuals offer a precious testimony to the human problems and inner conflicts of the colonial situation; in the latter respect, their propaganda writing and other activities represent an effort to transcend the immediate conditions of this situation by a process of reflection. *Négritude* is thus at the same time a literary and an ideological movement.

The literature

The literature of *négritude* is dominated by the collective consciousness of the black writer as member of a minority group which is subordinated to another and more powerful group within the total political and social order. The literary preoccupations of the movement revolve around this central problem, the Negro predicament of having been forced by historical circumstances into a state of dependence upon the west, considered the master society and the dominating culture. The

---

1. The term 'colonial situation' will be used here to denote the global situation of black people as it affected the writings of French-speaking Negro intellectuals. The first part of this study (Irele, 1964) has already spelt out how the Negro in the United States was readily assimilated to the domination of other Negro peoples by the west.

literary themes of *négritude* can be seen as a counter-movement away from this state: they constitute a symbolic progresions from subordination to independence, from alienation, through revolt, to self-affirmation.

Alienation

The theme of exile is the point of departure of the whole literary expression of *négritude*, and in it is involved the most pathetic aspect of the French-speaking Negro intellectuals' specific situation, which derives from the political and cultural uprooting of black people in general by colonial conquest. The over-whelming sentiment that dominates in this connection is the black man's sense of separation from his own world and of being thrown into a social system with whose cultural values he can strike no personal relation. The black man recognizes himself as belonging to an 'out-group', an alien in relation to the west, which controls the total universe in which he moves. For the French-speaking Negro writer, this situation is signified by his physical exile in Europe.

Bless you, Mother,
I hear your voice when I am given up to the
    insidious silence of this European night
Prisoner under the white cold sheets tightly drawn,
prisoner of all the inextricable anxieties that
    encumber me.[2]

This sentiment of belonging no longer to oneself but to another goes together with an awareness of inferiority, which becomes translated in social terms into a caste and class consciousness. The association between race and servitude is a constant theme in Negro literature, and occupies a prominent place in *négritude*:

I am a docker in Brooklyn
Bunker-hand on all the oceans
Labourer in Cuba,
Soldier in Algeria. (Camille, 1956, p. 53).

The economic exploitation of the race which defines it as a community and give its members a group consciousness is a consequence of its original humiliation by conquest and slavery.

2. Senghor, 'On the Appeal from the Race of Sheba', (1964, p. 29).

The memory of slavery thus has a particular significance for Negro writers, especially for those of the Caribbean.

And they sold us like beasts and counted our teeth . . . and they examined our genitals, felt the gloss and the roughness of our skin, pawed us, weighed us, and put around our neck like tamed animals the strap of servitude and of nickname (Césaire, 1956, p. 93).

The black man's principal role in western history, has thus been as an economic tool (cf. Williams, 1964). This is what Césaire, echoing Marx, has called 'the reduction of the Negro into an object' (*la chosification du nègre*) (Césaire, 1955, p. 22). But although the Negro experience forms, in this light, part of the general Marxist conception of the 'class struggle', the prevailing preoccupation of these writers was with the black people as a race, and not as a class.[3] They were concerned with the collective image of the black man in the west and with his human status in the world.

The colonial system was based on a social division determined by 'the colour line',[4] and it was maintained by a racial ideology which defined the black man as inferior. The social relationship between colonizer and colonized was thus converted, as far as the black man was concerned, into an opposition between *white* and *black*, which acquired the moral values summarized by the South African, Bloke Modisane, in these words:

White is right, and to be black is to be despised, dehumanized . . . classed among the beasts, hounded and persecuted, discriminated against, segregated and oppressed by government and by man's greed. *White is the positive standard, black the negative* (1960, p. 26).

[Italics mine].

The cultural and political ascendancy of the white man over the black man, combined with the active denigration of the black man, has thus had the effect of vitiating the latter's self-esteem,

3. Gunnar Myrdal (1944, p. 667) has observed that racial solidarity is more marked among US Negroes than class consciousness. He speaks therefore of a 'caste struggle', thus making the economic status of the American Negro secondary to the ethnic classification, in his analysis of the Negroes' place in US society.

4. cf. Raymond Kennedy (1945, p. 308) 'The colour line, indeed, is the foundation of the entire colonial system, for on it is built the whole social, economic, and political structure'.

with profound psychological consequences, which involve shame and self-hatred.[5] The demoralizing effect of the caste system on the black man has been expressed by Léon Damas:

My todays have each one for my yesterdays
Wide eyes that roll with rancour and with shame. (Damas, 1963, p.45).

The black man in the world suffered his negation as a human being. This was the external reality with which the literature of *négritude* was concerned. But there is a more personal and intimate side to this theme of alienation, which has to do with the cultural situation of the assimilated Negro intellectual.

The colonial enterprise was presented as a 'civilizing mission', aimed at transforming the black man by his progressive approximation to the ideals of western civilization through education. This implied in most cases his dissociation from the basic personality pattern imprinted in him by his original culture. Western education was thus an instrument of imposed acculturation, aimed at replacing the black man's original modes of thought and feeling, which were attuned to his native norms, by another personality structure corresponding to western norms.[6] The French policy of *assimilation* probably went furthest in this cultural policy, which was to some extent common to all the colonizing powers, of attempting to fashion the black man – or at least a black elite – in a foreign image.

This problem is at the heart of the cultural and spiritual dilemma of the French-speaking Negro intellectual. For in order to be acceptable socially in the western world, it was necessary for him to deny a part of himself. Conformity to white ideals was only possible at the cost of a repression of his original self (cf. Mannoni, 1950, pp. 10–30).

5. The psychological implications of racial discrimination for the black man in white society have produced numerous studies. This question seems to have been best summarised by John Dollard (1949, p. 184) 'The upshot of the matter seems to be that recognizing one's own Negro traits is bound to be a process wounding to the basic sense of integrity of the individual who comes into life with no such negative views of his own characteristics.' The genesis of Negro 'self-hatred' is discussed at length by Bastide (1950, p. 235) in his chapter on 'Le heurt des races, des civilisations et la psychanalyse'.

6. For the theoretical basis of these remarks, see Kardiner (1946), and Dufrenne (1953).

I must hide in the depths of my veins
The Ancestor storm-dark skinned, shot with
   lightning and thunder
And my guardian animal, I must hide him
Lest I smash through the boom of scandal.
He is my faithful blood and demands fidelity
Protecting my naked pride against
Myself and all the insolence of lucky races.[7]

The result was a division in his personality. The Haitian poet
Léon Laleau has expressed this sentiment of the divided self in
remarkable poetic terms:

This beleaguered heart
Alien to my language and dress
On which I bite like a brace
The borrowed sentiments and customs of Europe.
Mine is the agony
The unutterable despair
In breaking with the cold words of France
The pulsing heart of Senegal.
(Laleau, 1963, p. 195).

We touch here upon what Roger Bastide has called the
'pathology of the uprooted man' (1963, vol. 2, p. 319), and which
Park has observed in the 'cultural hybrid' (1950, p. 356) as
part of the psychological results of culture contact and the accul-
turative process: 'spiritual instability, intensified self consciousness, restlessness and malaise'. Damas has put this sentiment of
malaise into verse:

I feel ridiculous
in their shoes
in their evening suits,
in their starched shirts,
in their hard collars
in their monocles
in their bowler hats.
(1963, p. 39)

This is a problem that was even more accentuated in the case
of the Caribbean writers, whose non-western cultural background
was marginal, and whose racial stock, because of the total orien-

7. Senghor, 'Totem' (1964, p. 10).

tation of their society towards western values, symbolized by whiteness, was more a source of shame and frustration than for the Africans. The pressure upon them to deny their racial connections and to identify with Europe was even greater, though they were subject to the same discrimination as the Africans (cf. Henriques, 1951; Mittelholzer, 1950, and Lamming, 1955, offer sensitive inside views of this Caribbean problem). The West Indians' sentiment of exile is thus intensified by a feeling of rootlessness, which Césaire expresses with the symbol of the island itself.

Island of the blood of Sargossoes
island, nibbled remains of remora,
island, backfiring laughter of whales,
island, specious word of mounted proclamations,
island, large heart spread out

island ill-jointed, island disjointed,
all islands beckon
all islands are widows.
(Césaire, 1961, p. 90)

The black man, and especially the intellectual, found himself a man no longer in his own right, but with reference to another, thus estranged from himself; in exile, not only in a political and social sense, but also spiritually. The whole colonial existence appears as one long paling of the black self, an 'Ambiguous Adventure' as Kane has put it. A man divided between two worlds, his overriding aspiration thus became, in the words of Kane's tragic hero, Diallobé, 'nothing but harmony'.[8]

Revolt

A situation of oppression offers to the victim a range of reactions limited by two opposite poles – total submission, or total refusal – but the exact nature and degree of this reaction will depend upon the experience and the disposition of the individual. The colonial situation as a whole was a collective political and cultural oppression of black people yet it cannot be said that it was felt uniformly as such. The black intellectuals were in fact privileged in comparison with the masses, as far as the more external

8. Kane (1961, p. 88). cf. Reed 'Between two worlds', (1963) for an analysis of the theme of cultural conflict in the African novel.

conditions of life were concerned, and it is quite conceivable that their consciousness of the fundamental injustice of the system in which they lived was limited, if it existed at all.

But the mental conflict into which the French-speaking Negro intellectuals were plunged as individuals probably made them aware that their dilemma was inherent in the whole colonial situation. Thus they were forced, despite assimilation, into an identification with the colonized rather than with the colonizer:

But if I must choose at the hour of testing,
I have chosen the verses of streams and of forests,
The assonance of plains and rivers, chosen the
    rhythm of blood in my naked body,
Chosen the trembling of balafongs, the harmony
    of strings and brass that seem to clash,
    chosen the
Swing swing yes chosen the swing

I have chosen my toiling black people, my
    peasant people, the peasant race through
    all the world.
'And thy brothers are wroth against thee, they,
    have set thee to till the earth.'
To be your trumpet![9]

The literature of *négritude* became, as a result, a testimony to the injustices of colonial rule and an expression of the black man's resentment:

An immense fire which my continuous suffering
and your sneers
and your inhumanity,
and your scorn
and your disdain
have lighted in the depths of my heart
will swallow you all.
(Bernard, 1962, p. 81)

The tone changes often from this kind of menace to one of accusation. The poetry of David Diop illustrates best this indictment of colonial rule:

In those days
When civilisation kicked us in the face

9. Senghor, 'For Koras and Balafongs', (1964, pp. 13–14).

When holy water slapped our tamed foreheads,
The vultures built in the shadow of their talons
The blood-stained monument of tutelage
In those days
There was painful laughter on the
    metallic hell of the roads
And the monotonous rhythm of the
    pater noster
Drowned the howling on the plantations.[10]

Accusation in turn becomes a criticism of western society as a whole, and in this respect the contradiction of 'war and civilization' became a powerful weapon. Senghor's *Hosties Noires*, for example, are a collection of war poems in the tradition of Wilfrid Owen, but he reveals a particular view of European war when he speaks with sarcasm of having been 'delivered up to the savagery of civilized men' (Senghor, 1948, p. 115).

The shortcomings of western society, both within and without, furnished that element of disenchantment which made it possible for *négritude* to develop an attitude of refusal towards the colonial system:

I shout no
no to class
no to the taint of soot
no to the humid floor
no to the glass furnace
no to damped lights
no to love paid for in bank notes.
(Depestre, 1963, p. 191)

Protest, accusation, and refusal lead inevitably to a call to arms:

But when, O my people,
winters in flames dispersing a host
of birds and ash,
shall I see the revolt of your hands?[11]

Protest and threats of revolt are in themselves an indirect form

10. Diop, 'Les Vautours', (1960, p. 8).
11. Roumain, 'Prelude' to *Bois d'ébène* (1945). The titles of the collections of poems by French Negro writers speak manifestly of this mood: *Les Armes miraculeuses* (Césaire), *Coups de pilon* (Diop), *Feu de brousse* (Tchikaya U. Tam'si), *Balles noires* (Guy Tirolien), and so on.

of defence, a verbal means of projecting violent reaction which cannot be realized physically. Although the militancy of *négritude* was an explicit response to a real situation (and the agitated character of a good deal of this writing indicates that the situation was often felt as real personal experience), it has no more than a symbolic value. Its real significance, however, lies elsewhere, for it does reveal in fact the hidden mechanism of response to oppression. The resentment of the black man against domination tends towards retaliation and, as Fanon has shown, his consciousness as a colonized man is suffused with violence.[12] In the work of Césaire, this element is translated in poetic terms into an apocalyptic vision:

And the sea lice-ridden with islands
breaking under rose fingers
flame shafts and my body
thrown up whole from the thunderbolt.
(Césaire, 1946b, p. 25)

The surrealist technique is here employed in a manner appropriate to the alienated condition of the black man. It offers the black poet a means of projecting his dream of violence, and becomes in fact a symbolism of aggression. A corresponding side to this aggressiveness is the way in which the black poet responds by wilfully identifying himself with western symbols of evil:

I seek the thousand folds of the oceans
witnesses of savageness
and rivers where beasts go to drink
to make for myself a face
that would scatter vultures.
(Bélance, 1963, p. 178)

Négritude here borders on nihilism. Yet nihilism is not characteristic of the movement as a whole; more often than not, it represents a defiant truculence, as in this passage where Damas operates a literary reversal of situations in a way reminiscent of Nietzsche:

12. Fanon (1961, ch. 1). Georges Balandier and Roger Bastide have both drawn attention to this phenomenon, highlighted by the influence of the Apocalypse on 'messianic' movements. See Balandier (1963), and Bastide (1950, p. 262).

The White will never be negro
for beauty is negro
and negro is wisdom
for endurance is negro
and negro is courage
for patience is negro
and negro is irony
for charm is negro
and negro is magic

for joy is negro
for peace is negro
for life is negro.[13]

In this respect, one of the most striking technical innovations of *négritude* has to do with the reversal of colour associations in the western language which was the only tongue accessible to most of them, namely French, as in this example from Césaire's *Cahier*:

a solitary man imprisoned in white
a solitary man who defies the white cries of
   white death
TOUSSAINT TOUSSAINT LOUVERTURE
He is a man who bewitches the white hawk of
   white death
He is a man alone in the sterile sea of white sand.[14]

A reversal of western symbols implies as well a reversal of the concepts associated with them. The revolt of *négritude* appears also as a refusal of western values, regarded as oppressive constraints. The Christian religion in particular comes in for continual attack, and this theme has had an original and refreshing treatment, though mainly in strident notes, in the comic novels

13. Damas (1962, p. 52). The same reversal of situations occurs in Laye (1959), where Clarence the white man goes through a succession of adventures in supplication of the attention of a black king.

14. Césaire (1958, p. 46). Sartre observed, in connection with the problem posed to the black poet by his use of a European language: 'Let him open his mouth and he condemns himself, except in so far as he sets himself to destroy the hierarchy' (that is, of the 'coupled terms black-white'). *Black Orpheus*, p. 27.

of Mongo Beti, in particular *Le Pauvre Christ de Bomba*.[15] Western morality is also set in contrast to the African's unbridled sensuality.[16]

It can be remarked that, in general, the theme of revolt in the literature of *négritude* represents a reinforcement of the antagonism created by the colonial situation, between the white master and the black subordinate. It is a way of underlining an opposition that was implicit in the colonial human context. It is not, however, an end in itself, as Sartre has observed, but rather part of a movement towards a more constructive vision.[17]

Rediscovery

The refusal of western political and cultural domination in the literature of *négritude* represents also a severing of the bonds that tie the black man to western civilization. The corollary to this claim for freedom from the west is a search for new values. Revolt becomes not only a self-affirmation but also an instrument of self-differentiation:

For myself I have nothing to fear I am before
Adam I belong neither to the same lion
nor to the same tree I am of another
    warmth and of another cold.
(Césaire, 1946, p. 32).

The quest for new values thus leads the black writer to self-definition in terms that are non-western, and the association

15. This theme is also a favourite one with English-speaking African writers. Okigbo (1962, p. 35) calls the Angelus 'the bells of exile'. Clark (1962, p. 46) writes in 'Ivbie', almost a poem of *négritude*:
Is it ruse or truce
That peace which passeth all understanding?

16. cf. Soyinka (1963) for a parallel treatment of this theme by an African writing in English.

17. Sartre (1963, p. 60) speaks of *négritude* as 'the weak stage of a dialectical progression: the theoretical and practical affirmation of white supremacy is the thesis; the position of *négritude* as antithetical value is the moment of Negativity. But this negative moment is not sufficient in itself and the blacks who use it well know this; they know that it serves to prepare the way for the synthesis or the realization of the human society without racism'. *Black Orpheus* (Paris, 1963), p. 60.

between the black race and Africa acquires a new meaning: instead of being a source of shame, it becomes a source of pride. This is the ultimate end of *négritude*, and much of the literature is dedicated to a rehabilitation of Africa, a way of refurbishing the image of the black man. The psychological function of this, as well as being a counter to the Negro's inferiority complex, is to permit an open and unashamed identification with the continent, a poetic sublimation of those associations in the Negro's mind which constitute for him a source of mental conflict in his relationship with western culture: a process of self-avowal and self-recognition. This view of the movement is best justified by the writings of the West Indians, whose collective repression of Africa, as has been pointed out, has been the more painful:

Africa, I have preserved your memory, Africa
you are in me
like the splinter in a wound
like a totem in the heart of a village.
(Roumain, 1945, p.5)

A myth of Africa developed in consequence out of the literature of *négritude*, which involved a glorification of the African past and a nostalgia for the imaginary beauty and harmony of traditional African society, as in Camara Laye's evocation of his African childhood (1954).

This strain in *négritude* is probably charged with the greatest emotional force. Senghor for instance infuses into his well-known love poem, *Black Woman*, a feeling that is more filial than erotic, due to his identification of the continent with the idea of woman, in a way that lends to the image of Africa the force of a mother figure:

Naked woman, black woman,
Clothed with the colour which is life, with
    your form which is beauty,
In your shadow I have grown up; the gentleness of
    your hands was laid over my eyes
And now, high up on the sun-baked pass, at the heart
of summer, at the heart of noon, I come upon you,
    my Promised Land,
And your beauty strikes me to the heart like the
    flash of an eagle.

Naked woman, black woman,
I sing your beauty that passes, the form that I
  fix in the Eternal,
Before jealous Fate turns you to ashes to feed the
  roots of life.
(Senghor, 1964, p. 6).

In a poem by another writer, Bernard Dadié, despite the use of conventional western imagery, Africa is celebrated in cosmic terms:

I shall weave you a crown
  of the softest gleam
bright as the Venus of the Tropics
And in the feverish scintilation
  of the milky sphere
  I shall write
  in letters of fire
  your name
  O, Africa.
(Dadié, 1956)

The romanticism of the African theme in *négritude* illustrates certain of the functions and characteristics of 'nativistic movements' as analyzed by Linton (1943, 1940, ch. 10), but in literary rather than ritualistic form, that is, at a sophisticated level. Yet a purely sociological and 'realistic' view would miss the profound significance of this aspect of *négritude*. In any case, realism is a purely relative term applied to literature, and has little relevance to poetry,[18] but apart from this, the African theme went far beyond a purely compensatory mechanism in that it was also a genuine rediscovery of Africa, a rebirth of the African idea of the black self. This opening up of the African mind to certain dimensions of its own world which western influence had obscured appears to be in fact the most essential and the most significant element in the literature of *négritude* as *the principal channel of the African Renaissance*. For the way in which the best of these poets

18. It is not suggested by these remarks that the romanticism of *négritude* was without its abuses. But this is a question for literary criticism, which must content itself with judging the aesthetic value of the finished product rather than legislating for the writer about his raw material. Besides, *négritude*, like any other literary school, has produced its uninspired writers, and like any other movement its lunatic fringe.

came to root their vision in African modes of thought has given a new meaning to the traditional African world-view (cf. Jahn, 1961, chs. 5 and 7; Taylor, 1963 for an extensive discussion of this question).

Césaire's poetic formulation of *négritude* is in fact taken from a Bambara symbol of man in a telluric union with the universe:

My *négritude* is not a stone, its deafness hurled
   against the clamour of the day,
my *négritude* is not a speck of dead water on the
   dead eye of the earth,
my *négritude* is neither a tower nor a cathedral
   it thrusts into the red flesh of the earth
   it thrusts into the livid flesh of the sky.
(Césaire, 1958, p. 71)

The West Indian is of course at one remove from the living centre of traditional African humanism, which is essential to the poetry of the African writers of *négritude*, as in Senghor's works;[19] and it has perhaps been expressed in its purest and most authentic form by Birago Diop in his famous poem, *Souffles*:

Listen more often
To things than to beings;
The fire's voice is heard,
Hear the voice of water.
Hear in the wind.
The bush sob
It is the ancestor's breath.

Those who died have never left,
They are in the woman's breast,
They are in the wailing child
And in the kindling firebrand
The dead are not under earth.

They are in the forest, they are in the home
The dead are not dead.
(Drachler, 1963, p. 95)

The literature of *négritude* tends towards a point where it can

19. cf. Beier (1959). Beier concludes his study with the following observation: 'Senghor is not merely a Frenchified African who tries to give exotic interest to his French poems; he is an African who uses the French language to express his African soul.'

coincide with the traditional mythical system of thought in Africa. This does not imply that the coincidence is perfect nor that it is always genuine; what is significant about it is the 'backward movement' towards an end from which western culture had originally pulled the African. *Négritude*, as literature, retraces a collective drama as well as a spiritual adventure, involving a quest for the self, with the conquest of a lost identity as the prize.

From a social angle, its importance is mainly symbolic and functional. In the historical context in which it developed, the black writer incarnating his despised and oppressed race is the mediator of a new self-awareness. The racial exaltation of the movement is mainly a defence (cf. Memmi, 1957, p. 174); the use of an African myth represents black ethnocentrism, an attempt to recreate an emotional as well as an original bond beneath the contingencies of a particularly difficult historical experience.

The alliance of the imaginative and the political in *négritude* relates the movement to African nationalism. Nationalism hardly ever corresponds to an objective reality; but is, none the less, a powerful emotional attitude, and literature has always been an outstanding vehicle for dominated people to give voice to their group feelings.[20] But imaginative writing, even with an explicit political content, implies a group mind rather than group action; it is essentially inactive. At the literary level, *négritude* remains largely subjective, and it was the ideology that attempted to establish objective standards of thought and action for the black man in general, and for the African in particular.

20. cf. Kohn (1946). The analogy between *négritude* and other nationalist literatures has been drawn, principally by two writers: Fonlon (1961) who compares *négritude* to similar movements in Irish nationalism and Melone, (1962), in which *négritude* is compared to the literature of the German revival in the eighteenth and nineteenth centuries.

References

BALANDIER, G. (1963, 2nd edn.), *Sociologie Actuelle de l'Afrique Noire*, Paris.
BASTIDE, R. (1950), 'Le heurt des races, des civilizations et la psychanalyse', in *Sociologie et Psychanalyse*, Paris.
BASTIDE, R. (1963), 'Problèmes de l'entrecroisement des civilizations et de leur oeuvres', in G. Gurvitch (ed.), *Traité de Sociologie*, Paris.

BEIR, U. (1959), 'The theme of the ancestors in Senghor's poetry', in
Black Orpheus, 5 May, Ibadan.
BÉLANCE, R. (1963), 'Moi Nègre', in Survivances, quoted in N. Garret
(ed.), The Renaissance of Haitian Poetry, Présence Africaine.
BERNARD, R. C. (1962), 'Nègre', in G. R. Courthauld, Race and Colour,
in Caribbean Literature, London.
CAMILLE, R. (1956), Assaut à la Nuit, Paris.
CÉSAIRE, A. (1946a), Les Armes Miraculeuses, Gallimard, Paris.
CÉSAIRE, A. (1946b), 'Soleil Serpent', in Les Armes Miraculeuses.
Gallimard, Paris.
CÉSAIRE, A. (1955), Discours sur le Colonialisme, Présence Africaine, Paris.
CÉSAIRE, A. (1956), Et les Chiens se Taisaient, Présence Africaine, Paris.
CÉSAIRE, A. (1958), Cahier d'un Retour au Pays Natal', Paris.
CÉSAIRE, A. (1961), 'Dit d'errance, in Cadastre, Paris.
CLARK, J. P. (1962), Poems, Ibadan.
DADIÉ, B. (1956), 'Couronne à l'Afrique', in La Ronde des Jours, Paris.
DAMAS, L. (1962), Black Label, Introduction page 20, translated by
G. Moore in Seven African Winters. Originally published in 1956, Paris.
DAMAS, L. (1963), 'La complainte du Nègre', in Pigments, Paris.
DEPESTRE, R. (1963), 'Quand je crie non', in Gerbes de Sang, quoted
in N. Garret (ed.), The Renaissance of Haitian Poetry, Paris.
DIOP, B. (1963), 'Souffles', in J. Drachler (ed.), African Heritage,
translated by A. Atik.
DIOP, D. (1963), Coups de Pilon, Paris. Reprinted in
translation by Ulli Beier in J. L. Hughes (ed.), Poems from Black
Africa, 1963, p. 145, Indiana University Press.
DOLLARD, J. (1949), Caste and Class in a Southern Town, 2nd edn,
New York.
DUFRENNE, M. (1953), La personalité de base, Paris.
DRACHLER, J. (1963), African Heritage, New York.
FANON, F. (1961), Les Damnés de la Terre, Paris.
FONLON, B. (1961), La Poésie et le Reveil de l'Homme Noire,
unpublished Ph.D dissertation National University of Ireland, Cork.
HENRIQUES, F. (1951), 'Colour values in Jamaica', Brit. J. Sociol.,
vol. 2, no. 2, Reprinted in C. Wagley and M. Harris, Minorities in the
New World, 1958,
IRELE, A. (1964), 'Négritude or Black Cultural Nationalism',
J. Modern African Studies, vol. 3, no. 3.
JAHN, J. (1961), Muntu, Faber.
KANE, C. H. (1961), L'Aventure Ambigue, Paris.
KARDINER, A. (1946), The Psychological Frontiers of Society, 2nd edn,
New York.
KENNEDY, R. (1945), 'The colonial crisis and the future', in R. Linton
(ed.), The Science of Man in the World Crisis, New York.
KOHN, H. (1946), The Idea of Nationalism, New York.
LALEAU, L. (1963), 'Trahison', in J. Drachler (ed.), African Heritage,
translated by S. Allen. Originally published in French in L. Senghor
(ed.), (1948) Anthologie de la Nouvelle Poésie Nègre et Malagache, Paris.

LAMMING, G. (1955), *The Emigrants*, London.
LAYE, C. (1954), *The African Child*, Collins.
LAYE, C. (1959), *The Radiance of the King*, Collins.
LEGUM, C. (1962), *Pan-Africanism*, Pall Mall Press.
LINTON, R. (1943), 'Nativistic movements', *Amer. Anthropologist*,
    vol. 45, pp. 230-40.
LINTON, R. (1940), 'The Distinctive Aspects of Acculturation', in
    Acculturation in Seven American Indian Tribes, New York.
MANNONI, O. (1950), *Psychologie de la Colonization*, Paris.
MELONE, T. (1962), *De la Négritude dans la Litterature Negro-Africaine*,
    Paris.
MEMMI, A. (1957), *Portrait du Colonisé*, Paris.
MITTELHOLZER, E. (1950), *A Morning at the Office*, London.
MODISANE, B. (1960), 'Why I ran away', in J. L. Hughes (ed.), *An
    African Treasury*, New York.
MOORE, G. (1962), *Seven African Writers*, Oxford University Press.
MYRDAL, G. (1944), *An American Dilemma*, 9th edn. New York.
OKIGBO, P. (1962), *Heavensgate*, Ibadan.
PARK, R. E. (1950), *Race and Culture*, Chicago University Press.
REED, J. (1963), 'Between two worlds', *Makerere Journal*, no. 7.
ROUMAIN, J. (1945), *Bois d'Ebène*, Port au Prince.
SARTRE, J. P. (1963), *Black Orpheus*, Paris.
SENGHOR, L. S. (1948), *Hosties Noires*, in *Anthologie de la nouvelle poésie
    nègre at malagache*, Presses Universitaires de France.
SENGHOR, L. S. (1964), *Selected Poems*, translated by
    J. Reed and C. Wake, Oxford University Press.
SOYINKA, W. (1963), *The Lion and the Jewel*, Ibadan.
TAYLOR, J. V. (1963), *The Primal Vision*, London.
WILLIAMS, E. (1964), *Capitalism and Slavery*, University of
    North Carolina Press.

15 Wole Soyinka

Telephone Conversation

W. Soyinka, 'Telephone conversation', in G. Moore and U. Beier,
Modern Poetry from Africa, Penguin (1963), p. 144–5.

The price seemed reasonable, location
Indifferent. The landlady swore she lived
Off premises. Nothing remained
But self-confession. 'Madam', I warned,
'I hate a wasted journey – I am African.'
Silence. Silenced transmission of
Pressurized good-breeding. Voice, when it came,
Lipstick-coated, long gold-rolled
Cigarette-holder pipped. Caught I was, foully.

'HOW DARK?'... I had not misheard...'ARE YOU
  LIGHT
'OR VERY DARK?' Button B. Button A. Stench
Of rancid breath of public hide-and-speak.
Red booth. Red pillar-box. Red double-tiered
Omnibus squelching tar. It *was* real! Shamed
By ill-mannered silence, surrender
Pushed dumbfoundment to beg simplification.
Considerate she was, varying the emphasis –

'ARE YOU DARK? OR VERY LIGHT?'
  Revelation came.
'You mean – like plain or milk chocolate?'
Her assent was clinical, crushing in its light
Impersonality. Rapidly, wavelength adjusted,
I chose, 'West African sepia' – and as an afterthought,
'Down in my passport'. Silence for spectroscopic
Flight of fancy, till truthfulness clanged her accent
Hard on the mouthpiece 'WHAT'S THAT?', conceding,
'DON'T KNOW WHAT THAT IS.' 'Like brunette.'

'THAT'S DARK, ISN'T IT?' 'Not altogether.
'Facially, I am brunette, but madam, you should see
'The rest of me. Palm of my hand, soles of my feet
'Are a peroxide blonde. Friction, caused –
'Foolishly, madam – by sitting down, has turned
'My bottom raven black – One moment madam!'
– sensing
Her receiver rearing on the thunder clap
About my ears – 'Madam', I pleaded, 'wouldn't
you rather
'See for yourself?'

Part Five
Sex and Colour

Members of the same 'race' produce children in their own
racial image while cross-breeding is the consequence of
interracial mating. Cross-breeding must lead to ambiguity in any
social calculus of race. Races are defined by sets of physical
characteristics attributed to their members and interracial
mating brings the very bodies that carry the substance of
difference into the intimacy of physical contact. Hence, racial
boundaries cannot be maintained without taboos that govern
sexual and marital relations. Bastide discusses the meaning of
interracial mating in Paris and São Paulo while Mason indicates
the various ways in which social practices that relate sex to race
may be combined in local social structures.

16 Roger Bastide

Dusky Venus, Black Apollo

Reprinted from Roger Bastide, 'Dusky Venus, Black Apollo', in *Race*, vol 3., 1961, pp. 10–18, translated by Michael Wood.

Racial conflict is one of those total social phenomena defined by Mauss, where economic, structural, religious and sexual aspects are inextricably linked. In this article however we shall consider only the sexual aspect of the conflict. Not that this has been entirely neglected. Quite the reverse, in fact, for psychoanalysis has given rise to a whole series of investigations into the sexual roots of racialism – which may have been controversial in their findings but which have nevertheless made valid contributions towards a deeper understanding of the prejudices and facts of discrimination.[1] We should note however that these sexual roots, at least in the field of relations between black and white, have been observed for the most part in countries where the colour bar is at its strictest, like the Southern States of North America, or South Africa. But there are other countries like those of Latin America where miscegenation is the rule, and this mingling of races has in fact been held up as proof of a 'racial democracy' which distinguishes the Latin countries from the fiercely endogamous Anglo-Saxons. But is this really so? A striking feature of our two enquiries made at the request of Unesco, one in São Paolo, Brazil, into racial relations between black and white, the other in Paris, into the growth of an African elite in French universities, was that in the course of a great number of interviews the question 'race' always provoked the answer 'sex'. This hiatus between question and answer reveals the problem, the confusion between racial and sexual competition in countries where prejudices are not institutionalized. The vindication of the

1. We considered the contribution of psychoanalysis to the problem of racial relations between black and white (Bastide, 1950, pp. 235–47). May we then leave this question for the present?

Dusky Venus in the states of Latin America, and the inverse phenomenon found in Europe, the vindication of the Black Apollo, bringing the sexes together across the barriers of colour, are not, as is often suggested,[2] a proof that prejudice does not exist, but another manifestation of such prejudice, sometimes masked, but sometimes revealed in a harsher light.

For in the lovemaking of partners of different colour, in the courting which went before, in those privileged instants which seem to destroy race and rediscover the unity of the human species, we find this paradox: the insinuation of racialism in its most savage, most withering forms. In these bodies finding each other, fusing, there are two races at each other's throats. But in order to understand this strange phenomenon which produces the maximum prejudice where all prejudice seems to be abolished, we must, of course, since we have defined racial conflict as a 'total phenomenon', replace sexuality in its total social context – and by total social context we mean not only the present situation but also all the heritage of the past, of that more or less distant past which has sketched the pattern for the present, for human beings joined in the sexual act are not only bodies, but persons in a society, social beings, and endowed each of them with what Halbwachs called a 'collective memory'.

Miscegenation in America arose within the framework of slavery, and remains profoundly marked by it. Broadly speaking, the black woman was the property of her white master, who might use her freely to satisfy his desire, and leave her when he had had enough – and on the other hand the black woman realized that her sexual attraction was a weapon to help her rise in a society based on force: to improve her condition as a slave, moving from work in the fields to domestic service, and to improve the lot of her children, who would be free, educated, by the white father, and who, being lighter-skinned than she, would the more easily be admitted into the white man's world. Sexual relationships in multiracial societies today are still conditioned by these former characteristics.

2. For example by Gilberto Freyre, in his two classic works, *Casa Grande e Senzata* (translated into English as *Masters and Slaves*) and *Sobrados e Mucambos*.

Now if miscegenation were to take place in the form of marriage, and thus in mutual respect and equality between the sexes, it would indeed show an absence of racial prejudice. But as it is practised it effectively reduces a whole race to the level of prostitutes. For just as the middle classes of Europe created prostitution in order to shield their daughters from the lubricity of the male, so the whites spare their own women by channelling their desire towards the condemned race. So that behind miscegenation is exactly what was behind the institution of prostitution in the West: the defence of one group considered as superior, and therefore untouchable, to the detriment of another racial or social group.

The coloured woman is considered not as a woman but simply as an object of pleasure, an easy prey for the white male. A whole series of preconceived ideas are in play here. First of all the idea of the more unbridled sexuality of the black woman, in comparison with the white: the black woman will make love at any time, and with anyone. Secondly, the idea that making love to a coloured woman does not mean anything, will have no consequences, for 'the blacks don't marry, they just pair off' (*O preto nao se casa, junto-se*), as a Brazilian proverb has it. So that underlying sexual relationships between different colours is this most terrifying of prejudices, which sentences a whole race to immorality in order to preserve the virginity of the women of the other race. But there are still other forms of prejudice at work, even within the operation of sexual selection. In the choice of a partner, the mulatto is preferred to the really dark-skinned woman. This means that in making love to a black woman, the desire was not for a Negress but simply for a woman as an object of pleasure, since the woman most desired will be the one who most resembles the white woman. Broadly then, as in the time of slavery, the really black woman is seen as ordained for the sexual initiation of adolescents, still shy and needing the easy conquest; the mulatto is seen as the companion of adult frolics, or those of husbands anxious to escape the constraints of the marital bed. There is the story of the family who took on a little black housemaid as a very young girl, so as to be able to watch over her puberty and be certain of her health, thinking to offer her to their son, who would thus learn the practice of sex without any risk of venereal diseases, and, since she was only a servant, without any risk of a possible mesalliance.

The black woman accepts all this and we find here the second characteristic of slavery which has persisted into modern society. For in a society controlled and directed by whites, it is obvious that the people who will rise most easily in the social scale will be those who come closest to being white – or are most closely connected with the white man's society. We may consider two aspects of this phenomenon. There is first the idea of the progressive 'whitening' of the blacks by the mingling of blood. This is accepted by the black mother wishing her children to have a better life than herself – she calls it 'purifying her blood' (*limpar o sangue*). 'Look at my children,' a coloured woman said to me. 'They're white already. What's the use of fighting, forming leagues for the defence of the Negro and all that?' She had grasped that the best means of getting on in society lay not in political and racial resistance, which will only put the white man's back up, but in producing a line of little mulattos. The counterpart of what this mother says is in the words of a mulatto refusing his consent to the marriage of his children with people darker-skinned than themselves: 'Aren't you ashamed to think of marrying Negroes?' The other aspects of the phenomenon is its 'appropriation' not so much by the black man as by the white, who defines miscegenation not as 'love knoweth no race, it bloweth where it listeth', but as a policy, the conscious and deliberate policy of progressively eliminating the black race by dissolving its African blood in the mass of the population. There is a name for this policy: it has been called the 'progressive aryanization of Brazil'. Now in these two aspects, prejudice is very clearly to be seen. The term 'aryanization' is itself explicit enough: the dark taint is shameful, it must be erased; or even if it is not shameful, the black is certainly inferior to the white. But what is even more serious is that the coloured woman, as a mother wanting a better lot for her children, is forced to accept this ideology, and is thus made to lose her pride in her colour, her sense of the dignity of her race, is brought to treachery, to denial.

If miscegenation is practised chiefly within concubinage, this does not mean that marriage between different colours does not exist. But such marriages are not between opposite colours, but between neighbouring shades. We shall return to this shortly.

Our intention was first to show that the cult of the Dusky Venus does not mean an absence of prejudice. Now we must show that it is because the prejudice of white superiority is here seen in its most clear-cut form that this cult must inflame rather than temper the racial struggle, translating it into terms of the bitterest sexual competition.

This can be observed at all levels of society – even among prostitutes. A survey conducted in the Negro dance-halls, called '*gafieiras*', clearly showed this element of combat. The black males questioned were certain of their superiority over the white: 'The white man has a quick orgasm. The black woman prefers to go to bed with a black man. If she takes a white, it is out of pride or for money, she prefers the Negro in bed.' The replies of the black women did not contradict those of the males but underlined another point of view: 'If I sleep with a Negro, he gives me no peace all night and in the morning he wants his coffee and roll and butter, and on top of that, I have to give him some money for his bus. Look, black women choose Negroes to dance with, but afterwards they always go to bed with a white.' The battle of the sexes here assumes its most vulgar form. The black refuses to pay for his companion for a night, the white is the one who has to pay.

Let us now in contrast move to the highest level, that of the mixed marriages mentioned a moment ago. These take the form of hyper- (or hypo-) gamy (a similar phenomenon is seen in the US, cf. Warner, Junker and Adams, 1941), where the husband, darker-skinned, offers a superior position (money, social standing, etc.) and the wife a lighter colour of skin, which will lead to the whitening of the children. 'The black man, in his eagerness to marry a white woman, will take anyone he can find.' He has no choice, the only women he can find to marry him are gold-diggers, white prostitutes, housemaids, or little mulatto working-girls longing to escape from poverty-stricken lives.

In multiracial societies then, the choice of a partner, whether for marriage or for a night of pleasure, is a form of racial combat. 'The black male doesn't appreciate Negresses,' a coloured woman once complained to me. 'He's always chasing white women.' And in fact the black man's ideology is the reverse of that of the white, is a vindication of the 'White Venus'. But in this vindication the dominating factor is less an attraction than a sense of revenge for slavery, the will to possess, to *have*, the white woman who was 'taboo', 'forbidden', to steal her from the white man – and on the other hand, since the white man chases black women, to avenge their honour in bringing about the 'fall' of the white woman in her turn. This idea of revenge is clearly seen in the history of inter-racial relations. In the 'Balaio' War, which was a revolt of black groups armed by a political party ousted from power, the black leader, on taking a town, slept with all the most handsome girls, and forced the Catholic priests to marry the rest to his soldiers (Correa, n.d.). The Governor of São Paolo, in 1809, noted in his annual report that freed slaves were assaulting white women, and slaves violating their own mistresses (Nardy, 1940). The black folklore of 'Father John' is full of white girls giving secret rendezvous to young slaves, or of white women slipping into the hammocks of their Negroes while their husbands are away.[3] And this folklore is by no means dead; it appears today in various forms. We found one story both in Brazil and in the French West Indies, but not told as a story; each time it was offered as an account of fact. It tells of a white woman climbing a ladder, ostensibly to hang some curtains at her window, and asking her black chauffeur to hold the ladder for her; the chauffeur is at a loss, caught between the temptation of those white legs brushing deliberately against him, those secret parts half-glimpsed, offered even, and the respect he owes his mistress. All the Negroes we questioned affirmed without exception their superior masculinity, claiming that white women preferred them to whites. 'But they don't give in to us because of the pressure of society, the collective control which stops them.'

Which means that in the end the Negro has to make do with the coloured woman. But there he has to face the often successful competition of the white. As we said, the black woman prefers the white man, she sees herself as escaping in this way from the

3. Gomes (n.d.). For examples, cf. this Negro song collected by Teixeira (1941):
The white women all go crazy
Whenever I come near.

atmosphere of her racial milieu, from encystment in her colour, she lives in a kind of dream for a moment, she is courted, flattered, by a white man who, by definition, is 'distinguished' (*branco fino, branco distinto*), she has broken the barrier. But in the end she will be abandoned, perhaps left pregnant, and, in spite of laws offering theoretical protection to the woman, she will be able to do nothing. Her mother will get no satisfaction from the police, who will always say: 'What do you think we can do? Can we force her lover to marry her? She should have been more careful.' So that this black woman, no longer a virgin, even if she has had no children from her relations with the white man, will find herself rejected by the black males, who in their struggle against the white man have erected a 'virginity taboo' for their future wives: 'We're not in the old days now, when the Master used to deflower his slaves and then pass them on to his Negroes as their lawful wives. The Negro today has his honour as a man.' He will no longer accept girls of his race who before marriage have passed through the hands of a white man.

Conflict between the colours in Brazil then appears more strongly in sexual than in professional competition. A taste for the Dusky Venus on the part of the white has its counterpart in the pursuit of the white woman by the black man – so that each race surrounds its women with a maximum of interdictions, checks, defensive bulwarks: 'No white woman, not even a prostitute, will dance with these scruffy Negroes'; *a fortiori*, then, no 'decent' white woman either. And the black for his part will refuse to marry a Negress who has been with white men; the Negress must remain a virgin to her wedding day.

In France the phenomenon which strikes observers is the reverse of the one found in Brazil and, since in the former slave countries we speak of the Dusky Venus, we may perhaps call the inverse phenomenon that of the Black Apollo.

This phenomenon has as yet been little studied from the sociological standpoint. Fanon has something on the question, but he adopts the psychopathological standpoint: desire on the part of the Negro to whiten himself, desire for rape on the part of the white woman, the orgasm springing much more from the idea of a black man's embrace than from the actual physical contact

(Fanon, 1952). We have no wish to question Fanon's affirmations; but we would like to make certain reservations. First, Fanon is a West Indian, not an African. This desire that he writes of to whiten oneself is no doubt valid for West Indians, since it is a result of slavery, which forms in the Negro the ideal of the white man; but it is not valid for Africans. As for the desire for rape, it is probably found more often among intellectuals than in the lower classes of society (where hypergamy offers a more convincing explanation) and we should compare it with, for example, its male counterpart in Baudelaire's erotic images for his Dusky Venus: our civilization has associated the colour black with the devil, so that we may find in the arms of a partner of this colour a subtle refinement of the sense of sin. But this refinement can exist only for persons of a certain cultural level. Fanon's psychopathological explanation, if it is accurate, confines us to certain social groups, to the West Indian group on the one hand, to intellectuals on the other. Sex can be properly understood only in its social context. We shall therefore restrict ourselves to the analysis of this social context.

What are the motives most often suggested to explain the attraction of the Black Apollo for the white woman? The people interviewed all agreed on this point. The Frenchmen pointed out that since the white woman is taboo in Africa she becomes an object of desire for the Africans. Then the Africans said: 'When we got here the first thing we wanted, partly out of curiosity, partly out of a desire for vengeance, was to go with white women. Sometimes we were disgusted with ourselves, but we carried on, saying that this was a way of avenging our African sisters.' And certainly the curiosity is there; the discovery of French 'femininity' (a term borrowed from black students) played an important part; so many young Africans told me that African women 'behave like men', and that they were very susceptible to 'charm', to 'coquetterie', and all the other novelties of sex which they found with Frenchwomen.[4] But for our purpose let us retain only the second argument. It is the undisguised admission that closer relationships between the colours (relationships in any case

4. This feeling, as against the feeling of vengeance, has given rise to mixed marriages. It is well expressed in Zankou-Lango's interview (1954–5), which provoked such violent argument.

described as 'disgusting') are only another form of racial struggle, and not elimination of racialism. Another fact confirms the virulence of this. The basic reason for any miscegenation is the lack of balance between the sexes in the various racial groups in a country. The African arriving in France could have only white women, and very occasionally a black girl. At first he went with the black girls, had children by them, and never thought of marriage. Although such a situation was no catastrophe, since Africans love children more than anything in the world, and the parents soon forgave their daughters, the black students themselves, as they gradually assimilated the puritan values of the Europeans, began to feel remorse. This remorse they themselves have significantly characterized as a 'feeling of incest', which they say is the feeling of those who have had pre-nuptial relations with African girls who are being educated and will tomorrow constitute the female elite of their countries. Hence the redirection of their desire exclusively towards white women.

The ideal that they seek is a double one. Aesthetically, she will be the Nordic type with blonde hair and blue eyes – which means that German or Scandinavian girls will do as well as, or better than, Frenchwomen;[5] and socially, she must be a girl from a good family. Here the expression of revenge will be more clearly defined. But the French girl is not an easy conquest, the Africans say; they complain of her prejudices, her repugnance, the demands she makes. And in fact, dances become a kind of battlefield where the girls are divided into two groups – those who will dance only with whites, and the others, called 'Negro-chasers' by jealous white males. Healthy relationships between the sexes and the colours are thus very difficult to establish. It is understandable in these conditions that white students react violently

5. It is clear that, in spite of appearances, there can be no confusion between cases which at first sight seem identical: those where the black male pursues the white woman, something common to both Americas and to Europe. The American Negro, who in the South is refused even by white prostitutes, because their market-price would be lowered (Dollard, 1937), will on his arrival in the North look for a 'white chick' as a symbol of his liberation, (McKay, 1922). The Brazilian Negro is looking for a symbol of his rise in the social scale, his victory over the regime of slavery. The African in Europe, out of duty rather than love, is inflicting a humiliation on the woman.

to this sexual competition; and they do this in two ways: (i) by attributing ulterior motives either to the Africans or to the French girls: the black student who is not on a grant is after his pocket-money, or free digs if he lives with his girl, and the French girl is after a rich student who will shower her with presents. 'The Frenchman is mean, but an African who feels flattered to be seen out with a beautiful blonde girl is especially kind and considerate to her'; and (ii) by using scurrilous epithets to 'devalue' girls who go out with black students – and this 'devaluation' has certainly had its effect, creating as it has in certain girls, as we found in the course of our survey, a sense of guilt which expresses itself as an aggressive superiority complex. These girls are full of praise for the African's virility, combined with his gentleness in sexual play, but this is more than anything praise of these qualities *against the whites*, at least against certain categories of whites who have not, they say, the carefree, simple nature, the generosity of the African. Then, moving to the attack, they profess their desire to revolt against the conformity of European society, to rise above 'stupid prejudice'. The psychoanalyst would not be slow to see behind this rather peevish anti-racialism a revolt against the family and the discipline of childhood.

We have already said that miscegenation would show an absence of racial prejudice only if it took place legally in marriage. And even then the marriage would have to be between partners of equal standing. Now mixed marriages exist in France too. A few years ago they were quite widespread; they are becoming rarer today. And when they occur, they are for the most part made necessary by the arrival of a child. They do not express the general wish of the African, which is: 'I don't want to marry a white woman; but if I were to have a child by one, I would claim my rights as a father, and I would even make the thing legal to ensure control over the child; on no account would I give up the child.' 'Making the thing legal', then is a last resort. Sexual relationships are accepted only as between lover and mistress, or in brief affairs; they aggravate the prejudice rather than diminish it. As for the mixed marriages, the number of which is becoming steadily smaller, they are, as in Latin America, again a kind of hypergamy. Since members of 'castes' in Africa (smiths, *griots*, or their descendants) can marry only within their own group, they see in a mixed marriage a chance to break the closed circle which fettered their free choice, and consequently a form of hypergamy. The white girl mostly marries above the class of her own family: a nurse of peasant stock, or a factory worker, will marry a medical student, a doctor-to-be; a post-office clerk will marry an African student who in his holidays works at the Post Office (sorting letters) to earn some money, but who will return to his studies in law, in the arts, or in engineering. Our survey did not cover the question of mixed couples. But – at least in some cases that we could find out about – it seems that the African, who knows very well that his wife will never get used to his African family, and that in any case she would be looked down on by the white 'colony', finds himself forced to remain in France. And the sense of piercing regret at having left Africa can poison marital relations, even where there is sincere love on both sides. An African student who had beaten his wife felt that he had added to his stature by this gesture, of which he proudly told his black friends. But how can the wife, accustomed to the 'gentleness' of her lover, understand the drama that lies behind this change in his behaviour? We know of one such wife who found suicide the only solution.

It seems then, in conclusion, that contrary to a widely-held opinion, closer relationships between the colours, whether in marriage or in simple sexual pleasure, are not a sign of absence of prejudice: the Dusky Venus hides the debasement of the black woman as a prostitute; and the Black Apollo is seeking revenge on the white man. It is not so much that love breaks down barriers and unites human beings as that racial ideologies extend their conflicts even into love's embraces.

References

BASTIDE, R. (1950), *Sociologie et Psychanalyse*, Presses Universitaires de France.
CORREA, V. (n.d.), *A Balaiada*, São Paulo.
DOLLARD, J. (1937), *Caste and Class in a Southern Town*, Yale University Press.
FANON, F. (1952), *Peau Noire – Masques Blanc*, Editions du Seuil, Translated as *Black Skin – White Masks*, McGibbon & Kee, 1968.
GOMES, L. (n.d.) *Contos Populares*, São Paulo
MCKAY, C. (1922), *Harlem Shadows*, Harcourt, Brace & World.

NARDY, F. Jr (1940), 'Receio infundado', *Estado de são Paulo*, 15 September.

TEIXEIRA, J. A. (1941), *Folclore Goiano*, São Paolo.

WARNER, W. L., JUNKER, B. H. and ADAMS, W. A., (1941), *Color and Human Nature*, Washington.

ZANKOUS-LANGO (1954–5), *Afrique Nouvelle*, no. 380, 7 November and no. 382, 12 January.

17 Philip Mason

Sexual Attitudes

Excerpt from Philip Mason, *Race Relations*, Oxford University Press, 1970, pp. 154–8.

Sexual Attitudes ... are doubly important in race relations, as a distinguishing mark of the kind of relationship that exists, and also as a cause of racial feeling. Where the men of a superior group make free with the women of a socially lower group but jealously guard their own, resentment will obviously be acute among men of the lower group. But the initial shock may be deadened by long and brutal custom. In the Caribbean and the Deep South a stage of degradation was sometimes reached when men regarded the prostitution of their women as a matter for congratulation, this being the way to social progress. Of all the legacies of slaving, this has been psychologically the most far reaching; for the Negro male, it has meant a second-rate status in the family as well as in society; it lies at the heart of hopelessness in the lower class Negro and of bitterness in the Negro intellectual. [...]

The mere fact of sexual contact does not imply any warmth of feeling; indeed, it may convey a deep contempt for the woman thus used, and may confirm the male of the upper group in the arrogant conviction that he really is, by nature, the superior of the man whose woman he takes. We have also noticed that paternity is acknowledged in some societies but that in others the stain of the mother's status is passed on to the child. These points suggest that we have two different sets of attitudes in a counterpoint; one concerns equality and social stratification, the other concerns attitudes to sex, feelings of guilt, shame or prudery on the one hand, of pride in sexual potency on the other. Among the upper-middle classes of Victorian England, feelings about sex which we may inadequately describe as prudery were strong; on the other hand, the society was stratified and the 'premise of inequality' was nervously guarded. The one set of values forbade incontinence outside marriage, the other marriage with anyone but an equal. A hundred years earlier, attitudes in respect both of sex and inequality had been different; both had been taken for granted more readily and in general there had been much less anxiety about sexual contacts outside marriage. The Portuguese showed little anxiety about sex outside marriage, which they did not regard as implying equality; they were firmly hierarchical and therefore confident that free Negroes would stay at the bottom of the social ladder and could thus be freed without danger. But marriage with Negroes, which would imply a formal equality, was practically unknown in colonial times.

To illustrate the counterplay of the two sets of attitudes, it is worth considering four relationships, marriage, concubinage, exploitation and acknowledgement of paternity. Clearly only marriage recognizes full equality, but there is a world of difference between the kind of friendly long-standing concubinage which has been described in Burma and the brutal exploitation of a Negro woman in the Deep South by a white policeman, whose interest is momentary and purely sexual. And there is clearly a division between societies in which the children belong to the same group as the father and those in which they are relegated to the lowest social group.

The chart which follows, like all such attempts, necessarily simplifies relationships which are much subtler than it can show. Indeed, one of its chief interests is the difficulties of classification which it presents; another is the change which takes place in time.

The classification, I must again emphasize, is necessarily crude. The word 'condoned' means that there is some degree of disapproval but that the practice is widespread and not seriously condemned. The Brahman prohibition was social and religious, not legal, but extremely strong and offspring could not be acknowledged. I find it extremely difficult to include Brazil or Jamaica because there are so many nuances of meaning in the words used. Various studies of Brazil report university students – who are expected to be less conventional than most of the population – expressing themselves overwhelmingly against marriage with a *preto* – a black – but how exactly would they define him? The word really has come to mean 'belonging to the lower classes and looking as though of slave origin'. The table adds force to the distinction between 'dominant' and 'paternal' societies, but shows variations within both. It is notable that, in recent years, South Africa is more rigid than the Deep South, though this was not always so. The difference must be due mainly to the insecurity of the Afrikaners, a minority in their own country, threatened by a whole black continent, with no powerful ally that does not express disapproval of their racial policies.

In the paternal type of society there is much less rigidity and great variations in attitude to sexual contact between races. In British society there was obviously a great change in both moral and aesthetic tone between the periods of Tom Jones and Tristram Shandy and the writings of Jane Austen and Thackeray. Sex had become something that could not be mentioned in polite literature or a lady's drawing-room; it had gone underground. At the same time, since the French Revolution, there was a nervousness about equality. Marriage with someone of a markedly lower social status was disgraceful – particularly of a lady with a man of lower status – but the aristocracy still retained some memories of the feudal past and a lady's maid might find a way to a competence and an establishment of her own by the same path that brought freedom to a slave woman in the Caribbean. A lord might keep a chorus girl but such behaviour would be shocking to the middle classes. All this was reflected in attitudes abroad and accounts for the change in British behaviour in India.

Burma and West Africa, in contrast with India, indicate that a permissive attitude to sex on the side of the subordinate group make a difference to the relationship. There are parallels to this in the Pacific. Apart from this, the chart speaks for itself. It serves as a summary and a guide to the multiplicity of situations and relationships.

Table 1. Social attitudes to sex and race: various societies classified in respect of four relationships

Society	Marriage	Concubinage	Exploitation in casual encounter	Classification of children
South Africa, 1968	Forbidden by law	Forbidden by law	Forbidden by law	Lower group
Deep South, 1960	Forbidden by law	Disgrace	Condoned	Lower group
Brahman village, 1910	Forbidden	Forbidden	Forbidden	Lower group
Tutsi, 1960	Disapproved	Accepted	Accepted	Father's group, if married
British India, 1780	Accepted but rare	Accepted but rare	Accepted	Intermediate
British India, (Officers, 1880)	Very rare; disgrace	Very rare; kept secret	Rare; secret	Intermediate
British India (Non-commissioned, 1880)	Rare; condoned	Rare; condoned	Accepted	Intermediate
British India, 1947	Accepted	Condemned	Condemned	Follows one parent or other
British Burma, 1880–1940	Accepted	Accepted	Condoned	Intermediate but, if wealthy, follows father
British West Africa, 1955	Accepted (doubtfully)	Condoned	Condemned	Intermediate but, if wealthy, follows father
Mexico (time of Cortes)	Accepted	Accepted	Accepted	Father's group, if known
Mexico (Spanish-Indian), seventeenth century	Condoned if heiress wealthy	Accepted	Accepted	Intermediate
Mexico, 1950	Accepted	Accepted	Accepted	Upper group
New Zealand	Unwillingly accepted	Disapproved	Disapproved	Follows one parent
Victorian class system	Disgrace	Disapproved (except for aristocrats)	Disapproved	Follows father if acknowledged
Britain, 1968	Disapproved by relatives	Disapproved	Disapproved	Not yet known

Part Six
Power and Domination

Cox says most of the things that need to be said about race and dominance when the dominant group is capitalistic, western and white. Maquet discusses an indigenous system of dominance in Ruanda where the ruling Tutsi distinguished themselves from subordinate Hutu and Twa by referring to physical stereotypes. Maquet concludes his study of Ruanda by propounding a set of theorems about the premise of inequality. These theorems have more than local applicability. In Maquet's words, the theorems are general propositions that are not self-evident. They stimulate thought about racial dominance wherever it occurs.

18. Oliver Cromwell Cox

Race and Exploitation: A Marxist View

Excerpt from Oliver Cromwell Cox, *Caste, Class and Race: A Study in Social Dynamics*, Doubleday, New York, 1948, pp. 319–22, 332–5, 345–51, 353–4, 380–82, 425–6. (Some footnotes have been omitted).

The concept–race relations

It is evident that the term 'race relations' may include all situations of contact between peoples of different races, and for all time. One objection to the use of this term is that there is no universally accepted definition of race. The biologist and the physical anthropologist may indeed have considerable difficulty with this, but for the sociologist a race may be thought of as simply any group of people that is generally believed to be, and generally accepted as, a race in any given area of ethnic competition. Here is detail enough, since the sociologist is interested in social interaction. Thus, if a man looks white, although, say in America, he is everywhere called a Negro, he is, then, a Negro American. If, on the other hand, a man of identical physical appearance is recognized everywhere in Cuba as a white man, then he is a white Cuban. The sociologist is interested in what meanings and definitions a society gives to certain social phenomena and situations. It would probably be as revealing of interracial attitudes to deliberate upon the variations in the skeletal remains of some people as it would be to question an on-going society's definition of a race because, anthropometrically speaking, the assumed race is not a real race. What we are interested in is the social definition of the term 'race'. To call that which a group has been pleased to designate a race by some other name does not affect the nature of the social problem to be investigated.[1]

1. cf. Brown (1930). It should be made patently clear that the laboratory classification of races, which began among anthropologists about a hundred years ago, has no necessary relationship with the problem of race relations as sociological phenomena. Race relations developed independently of anthropological tests and measurements.

We may think of race relations, therefore, as that behavior which develops among peoples who are aware of each other's actual or imputed physical differences. Moreover, by race relations we do not mean all social contacts between persons of different 'races', but only those contacts the social characteristics of which are determined by a consciousness of 'racial' difference. If, for example, two persons of different racial strains were to meet and deal with each other on their own devices – that is to say, without preoccupation with a social definition of each other's race – then it might be said that race here is of no sociological significance. But if their behavior tended to be fashioned by ethnic attitudes toward each other's actual or purported physical differences, then the situation may be called a social contact between ethnics, and it may be also referred to as race relations. However, these ethnic attitudes are based upon other and more fundamental social phenomena.

Race relations: a definition

In a discussion of 'the origin' of race relations it should be well to determine at the outset exactly what we are looking for. We shall proceed, therefore, by first eliminating certain concepts that are commonly confused with that of race relations. These are: *ethnocentrism, intolerance*, and '*racism*'.

Ethnocentrism, as the sociologists conceive of it, is a social attitude which expresses a community of feeling in any group – the 'we' feeling as over against the 'others'. This attitude seems to be a function of group solidarity, which is not necessarily a racial phenomenon. Neither is social intolerance racial antagonism, for social intolerance is social displeasure or resentment against that group which refuses to conform to the established practices and beliefs of the society. Finally, the term 'racism' as it has been recently employed in the literature seems to refer to a philosophy of racial antipathy. Studies on the origin of racism involve the study of the development of an ideology, an approach which usually results in the substitution of the history of a system of rationalization for that of a material social fact (see Arendt, 1944, pp. 36–73; Detweiler, 1932, pp. 738–47). Indeed, it is likely to be an accumulation of an erratic pattern of verbalizations cut free from any on-going social system.

What then is the phenomenon, the beginnings of which we seek to determine? It is the phenomenon of the capitalist exploitation of peoples and its complementary social attitude. Again, one should miss the point entirely if one were to think of racial antagonism as having its genesis in some 'social instinct' of antipathy between peoples. Such an approach ordinarily leads to no end of confusion. [. . .]

Slavery

Sometimes, probably because of its very obviousness, it is not realized that the slave trade was simply a way of recruiting labor for the purpose of exploiting the great natural resources of America.[2] This trade did not develop because Indians and Negroes were red and black, or because their cranial capacity averaged a certain number of cubic centimeters; but simply because they were the best workers to be found for the heavy labor in the mines and plantations across the Atlantic.[3] If white workers were available in sufficient numbers they would have been substituted. As a matter of fact, part of the early demand for labor in the West Indies and on the mainland was filled by white servants, who were sometimes defined in exactly the same terms as those used to characterize the Africans. Although the recruitment of involuntary labor finally settled down to the African coasts, the earlier kidnappers did a brisk business in some of the most enlightened European cities. Moreover, in the process of exploiting the natural resources of the West Indies, the Spanish conquistadors literally consumed the native Indian population.

This, then, is the beginning of modern race relations. It was

2. In a discussion of the arguments over slavery during the Constitutional Convention, Charles A. Beard (1943) observes: 'South Carolina was particularly determined, and gave northern representatives to understand that if they wished to secure their commercial privileges, they must make concessions to the slave trade. And they were met half way. Ellsworth said: "As slaves multiply so fast in Virginia and Maryland that it is cheaper to raise than import them, whilst in the sickly rice swamps foreign supplies are necessary, if we go no farther than is urged, we shall be unjust towards South Carolina and Georgia. Let us not intermeddle. As population increases, poor laborers will be so plenty as to render slaves useless."'

3. In a discussion of the labor situation among the early Spanish colonists in America, Diffie observes: 'One Negro was reckoned as worth two, four, or even more Indians at work production', (1945, p. 206).

not an abstract, natural, immemorial feeling of mutual antipathy between groups, but rather a practical exploitative relationship with its socio-attitudinal facilitation – at that time only nascent race prejudice. Although this peculiar kind of exploitation was then in its incipiency, it had already achieved its significant characteristics.[4] As it developed and took definite capitalistic form, we could follow the white man around the world and see him repeat the process among practically every people of color. Earl Grey was directly in point when he described, in 1880, the motives and purpose of the British in one racial situation:

Throughout this part of the British Dominions the colored people are generally looked upon by the whites as an inferior race, whose interest ought to be systematically disregarded when they come into competition with their own, and who ought to be governed mainly with a view of the advantage of the superior race. And for this advantage two things are considered to be especially necessary: first, that facilities should be afforded to the white colonists for obtaining possession of land heretofore occupied by the native tribes; and secondly, that the Kaffir population should be made to furnish as large and as cheap a supply of labour as possible (quoted by Morel, 1920, p. 30).

But the fact of crucial significance is that racial exploitation is merely one aspect of the problem of the proletarianization of labor, regardless of the color of the laborer. Hence racial antagonism is essentially political-class conflict. The capitalist exploiter, being opportunistic and practical, will utilize any convenience to keep his labor and other resources freely exploitable. He will devise and employ race prejudice when that becomes convenient.[5]

4. Francis Augustus McNutt describes the relationship in Hispaniola: 'Columbus laid tribute upon the entire population of the island which required that each Indian above fourteen years of age who lived in the mining provinces was to pay a little bell filled with gold every three months; the natives of all other provinces were to pay one *arroba* of cotton. These amounts were so excessive that in 1496 it was found necessary to change the nature of the payments, and instead of the gold and cotton required from the villages, labor was substituted, the Indians being required to lay out and work the plantations of the colonists in their vicinity." Bartholomew De Las Casas (1909).

5. In our description of the uses of race prejudice in this essay we are likely to give the impression that race prejudice was always 'manufactured' in full awareness by individuals or groups of enterpreneurs. This, however, is not quite the case. Race prejudice, from its inception, became part of the

As a matter of fact, the white proletariat of early capitalism had to endure burdens of exploitation quite similar to those which many colored peoples must bear today.

However, the capitalist spirit, the profit-making motive, among the sixteenth-century Spaniards and Portuguese, was constantly inhibited by the philosophy and purpose of the Roman Catholic Church. A social theory supporting the capitalist drive for the impersonal exploitation of the workers never completely emerged. Conversion to Christianity and slavery among the Indians stood at cross-purposes; therefore, the vital problem presented to the exploiters of labor was that of circumventing the assimilative effects of conversion to Christianity. In the West Indies the celebrated priest, Las Casas, was touched by the destructive consequences of the ruthless enslavement of the Indians, and he opposed it on religious grounds. But work had to be done, and if not voluntarily, then some ideology had to be found to justify involuntary servitude.

The Indians were represented as lazy, filthy pagans, of bestial morals, no better than dogs, and fit only for slavery, in which state alone there might be some hope of instructing and converting them to Christianity.[6]

The capitalist exploitation of the colored workers, it should be observed, consigns them to employments and treatment that is humanly degrading. In order to justify this treatment the exploiters must argue that the workers are innately degraded and degenerate, consequently they naturally merit their condition. It may be mentioned incidentally that the ruling-class conception of degradation will tend to be that of all persons in the society, even that of the exploited person himself; and the work done by

---

social heritage, and as such both exploiters and exploited for the most part are born heirs to it. It is possible that most of those who propagate and defend race prejudice are not conscious of its fundamental motivation. To paraphrase Adam Smith: They who teach and finance race prejudice are by no means such fools as the majority of those who believe and practice it.

6. (McNutt, 1909, p. 83). It should be kept clearly in view that this colonial movement was not a transference of the feudal manorial economy to America. It was the beginning of an entirely different economic enterprise – the dawn of colonial capitalism, the moving out of 'white' capital into the lands of colored peoples who had to be exploited unsentimentally and with any degree of ruthlessness in the interest of profits.

degraded persons will tend to degrade superior persons who attempt to do it.

In 1550, finally, the great capitalist interests produced a champion, Gaines de Sepulveda, brilliant theologian and debater, to confront Las Casas in open debate at Valladolid on the right of Spaniards to wage wars of conquest against the Indians. Sepulveda held that it was lawful to make war against (enslave) the Indians:

1. Because of the gravity of their sins. . . .

2. Because of the rudeness of their heathen and barbarous natures, which oblige them to serve those of more elevated natures, such as the Spaniards possess.

3. For the spread of the faith; for their subjection renders its preaching easier and more persuasive [and so on].
(McNutt, 1909, p. 288)

It is not surprising that Sepulveda won the debate. His approach was consistent with the exploitative rationalizations of the time. He contrived a reasonably logical justification for the irrepressibly exploitative situation. This clearly was in answer to an urgent necessity for such an authoritative explanation; the whole world, so to speak, was calling for it. As a characteristic, it should be observed that no explanation at all need have been made to the exploited people themselves. The group sentiment and feeling of the exploited peoples were disregarded entirely.

Sepulveda, then, may be thought of as among the first great racists;[7] his argument was, in effect, that the Indians were inferior to the Spaniards, therefore they should be exploited. Yet the powerful religious interest among the Spaniards limited the establishment of a clear philosophy of racial exploitation. Some years earlier an attempt was made to show 'that the Indians were incapable of conversion', but this was finally squelched by a

7. Among the Spanish writers of the time (about 1535 onward) who were in rather complete accord with the drastic methods of human exploitation in the New World was Gonzalo Fernández de Oviedo, whose prolific works have been collected in the commentary, *Historia General y Natural de las Indias*, 4 vols. It was Oviedo's opinion, even after visiting America on a royal commission, that the Indians were not far removed from the state of wild animals, and that coercive measures were necessary if they were to be Christianized and taught the uses of systematic labor.

threat to bring the advocate before the tribunal of the Inquisition (McNutt, 1909, pp. 94-5). It remained for later thinkers, mainly from northern European countries, to produce the evidence that 'native peoples' have an inferior, animal-like capacity for culture.

In the years to follow there will be unnumbered sermons preached and 'scientific' books written to prove the incapacity for cultural conversion of exploitable peoples, and always with the implied or expressed presumption that this incapacity should stand as a bar to movements for the cultural assimilation of such peoples. (The ultimate purpose of all theories of white superiority is not a demonstration that whites are in fact superior to all other human beings but rather to insist that whites must be supreme.) [...]

The progress of racial antagonism

This, then, is the nature of racial antagonism; developing in Europe, it has been carried to all parts of the world. In almost fateful terms Kipling's celebrated poem written in 1899 describes a desperate conflict, 'the white man's burden', a like obligation, incidentally, never assumed by any other race in all the history of the world:

Take up the White Man's burden –
  Send forth the best ye breed –
Go bind your sons to exile
  To serve your captives' need;
To wait in heavy harness,
  On fluttered folk and wild –
Your new-caught, sullen peoples,
  Half-devil and half-child.

The Europeans have overthrown more or less completely the social system among every colored people with whom they have come into contact. The dynamism and efficiency of capitalistic culture concluded this. The stability of color and inertness of culture, together with effective control over firearms, subsequently made it possible for whites to achieve a more or less separate and dominant position even in the homeland of colored peoples. 'The white man's conception of himself as the aristocrat of the earth came gradually through the discovery, as surprising to himself as to anyone else, that he had weapons and organization which made opposition to his ambition futile.'[8]

It should be made clear that we do not mean to say that the white race is the only one capable of race prejudice. It is probable that without capitalism, a cultural chance occurrence among whites, the world might never have experienced race prejudice. Indeed, we should expect that under another form of economic organization, say socialism, the relationship between whites and peoples of color would be significantly modified.

The depreciation of the white man's color as a social gift goes hand in hand with the westernization of the conquered peoples of color. The Hindus, for example, are the same color today as they were in 1750, but now the white man no longer appears to them to be the cultural magician of other days. His secret of domination has been exposed, and the Hindus are now able to distinguish between his white skin and that secret. Therefore, he is now left with only his nationalism and superior might, for should he pull a cultural rabbit out of his hat, some Hindu would promptly pull another, which might even overmatch the first. Krishnalal Shridharani puts it thus: '[The Saxon] has been accustomed to regarding himself as a supreme being for centuries. Now he faces a world which refuses to recognize him as such. With all his civilized values, he will have to go on the role of military tyrant' (1942, p. 274). There is no assumption, then, that race prejudice is a biological heritage of the white race.

But we should not lose sight of the fact that whites have preempted this attitude.[9] Since the belief in white superiority – that is to say, white nationalism – began to move over the world, no people of color has been able to develop race prejudice independent of whites. It may be, however, that the Japanese have now

8. Hall (Upton Close), (1927) p. 4. In this early period there was a more or less conscious development of the exploitative system. In later years however, the infants that were born into the developed society had, of course, to take it as they found it. The social system determined their behavior naturally; that is to say, the racial exploitation and racial antagonisms seemed natural and the conscious element frequently did not exist. In other words, the racial fate of the individual was determined before he was born.

9. Buck (1942, p. 540) likes to repeat the fact that 'we differ in one important regard from the peoples of Asia. Race has never been a cause for any division among those people. But race prejudice divides us deeply.'

reached that stage of industrial development, nationalistic ambition, and military power sufficient to question their assignment to inferior racial rank; no other colored race has ever dared to do this. Indeed, since 1905 the Japanese have known how it felt to overcome the white man and make him like it. [. . .]

Of course one should not mistake reactionary racial attitudes for prime movers. One has only to imagine a situation developing in Asia in which whites come to recognize themselves as inferior to, say, Japanese – in which whites come to look upon Japanese as a master race in the same sense in which Europeans have been looked upon – to realize what a tremendous revolution in nationalistic feeling and power relationships must transpire. It would involve an exchange in the exploitative position of the races, which could not be fully established until the yellow and brown people actually subdued the Europeans in their homes and there, in Europe, directed the economy in the interest of great capitalists living in the East. Hall (Upton Close) (1944, pp. 109–10) states graphically the nature of white superiority in the East:

The white man walked as a god, above the law . . . secure in exploitation. In his 'sacred cities' there were parks, into which no native was allowed to come. His clubs excluded the native, however high-born or well educated. His person was sacrosanct. . . . He could pass through contending armies – carrying any information he might wish. He could shelter any native political criminal and assist in any plot and remain inviolate. He could exert himself at will to tear down native custom, religion and industry and still be protected according to treaty stipulations.

Then, too, it is even more difficult to conceive of a race becoming superior in the East without being so also in the West.

Still another primary consideration serves to indicate the insuperable difficulties in the way of any other race aspiring either to duplicate the racial record of Europeans or to dominate them. Today communication is so far advanced that no people of color, however ingenious, could hope to put a cultural distance between them and whites comparable to that which the Europeans of the commercial and industrial revolution attained in practical isolation over the colored peoples of the world. And such a relationship is crucial for the development of that complex belief in biological superiority and consequent color prejudice which Europeans have been able to attain. Therefore, we must conclude that race prejudice[10] is not only a cultural trait developed among Europeans, but also that no other race could reasonably hope to duplicate the phenomenon. Like the discovery of the world, it seems evident that this racial achievement could occur only once.

The color prejudice of whites has other potentialities; it functions as a regulator of minor racial prejudices. Whenever there are two or more races in the same racial situation with whites, the whites will implicitly or explicitly influence the relationship between these subordinate races. In other words, the whole racial atmosphere tends to be determined by the superior race. This is a consideration of highest significance in understanding race relations. In the more or less tacit admission of white superiority and in competition among subordinate races for white favor, the situation is set for channelization.

The race against whom the whites are least prejudiced tends to become second in rank, while the race that they despise most will ordinarily be at the bottom. Thus more or less directly the superior race controls the pattern of all dependent race prejudices. However, the whites are not entirely free in the exercise of their prejudice. The actual cultural advancement or national power of the subordinate races may not be without some reciprocal effect in the final adjustment of the races. Referring to the South African situation, Joshi declares:

The whites estimate all non-whites as inferior to themselves. The natives are the 'untouchables' of their country. The Asiatics rank lower than whites, and claim to be higher than the colored or natives. This caste-phobia is a derivation of the color bar.
(Joshi, 1942, p. 28).

Europeans have mixed their blood with that of practically every colored people in the world. In no situation, however, where whites have interbred with colored races have they

10. It should be borne in mind that race prejudice is not simply dislike for the physical appearance or the attitudes of one person by another; it rests basically upon a calculated and concerted determination of a white ruling class to keep some people or peoples of color and their resources exploitable. If we think of race prejudice as merely an expression of dislike by whites for some people of color, our conception of the attitude will be voided of its substance.

accepted the mixed-bloods without discrimination. The tendency has been to accept the mixed-bloods according to their lightness of color, and this notwithstanding interracial laws socially proscribing all persons of colored blood. The anti-color codes merely limit acceptability.

Caste prejudice is an aspect of culture prejudice; while race prejudice – as distinguished from culture prejudice – is color-and-physique prejudice. The latter is prejudice marked by visibility, physical distinguishability; it is not, however, caused by physical differences. We may repeat that precise anthropometrical definitions of race are not of crucial significance. Racial attitudes are based upon simple obvious criteria, and the findings of anthropometry, whether genuine or spurious, may simply provide a basis for their rationalization. Color prejudice, as a psychological phenomenon, is a complex emotion manifested by a positive attitude of distance and a reaction; specifically it is an insistent attitude of white superiority and dominance and an accommodating reaction of persons of color. It is a cultural trait of Western society which took form during the era of explorations. [. . .]

Situations of race relations

Let us now examine some modern situations of free relationship between whites and persons of color; situations, to repeat, in which the aggressive whites have sought most conveniently and efficiently to exploit the human and natural resources of the colored peoples.

1. Situations in which the colored person is a stranger in a white society, such as a Hindu in the United States or a Negro in many parts of Canada and in Argentina – we shall call this the 'stranger' situation.

2. Situations of original white contact where the culture of the colored group is very simple, such as the conquistadors and Indians in the West Indies, and the Dutch and Hottentots in South Africa – the 'original-contact' situation.

3. Situations of colored enslavement in which a small aristocracy of whites exploits large quantities of natural resources, mainly agricultural, with forced colored labor, raised or purchased like

capital in a slave market, such as that in the pre-Civil War South and in Jamaica before 1834 – the slavery situation.

4. Situations in which a small minority of whites in a colored society is bent upon maintaining a ruling-class status, such as the British in the West Indies or the Dutch in the East Indies – the ruling-class situation.

5. Situations in which there are large proportions of both colored and white persons seeking to live in the same area, with whites insisting that the society is a 'white man's country', as in the United States and South Africa – the bipartite situation.

6. Situations in which colored-and-white amalgamation is far advanced and in which a white ruling class is not established, as in Brazil – the amalgamative situation.

7. Situations in which a minority of whites has been subdued by a dominantly colored population, as that which occurred in Haiti during the turn of the eighteenth century, or the expulsion of whites from Japan in 1638 – the nationalistic situation. [. . .]

Personality factors

Two recognizable attitudes of superiority seem to develop in the ruling-class and bipartite situations. In the ruling-class situation colored people are not hopelessly depressed; for them the ceiling of opportunity is high, but attainable. Although the color ranks are practically checkmated by color cliques, color is never explicitly accepted by the group as a whole as a consideration limiting success. There are ordinarily sufficient instances of brilliant victories over color barriers to warrant sanguine illusions that they do not exist. Exemplifying cases of colored persons holding positions of enviable dignity are always available. As a consequence, colored people assume the bearing of freemen; indeed, not infrequently, success is accompanied by a show of exaggerated importance. The successful are impatient with the 'degenerate masses', and they tend to remain aloof from any idea which seeks to identify them with the problems of colored people as a whole. The Negro leader, Marcus Garvey, on returning to Jamaica from the United States, realized the latter fact more vividly than he had expected.

Not so, however, in the bipartite situation. Here people of

color tend to be humbled, not only by the engrossing importance of their color but also by the fact that the color interest is inevitably common to them all. Here the colored person of lowest class has an intuitive way of quickly establishing rapport with the most advanced colored gentleman, for the basis of their sympathy is elemental. It tends to keep the social-class hierarchy among them quite obtuse.

It is interesting to observe the pattern of behavior which develops when colored persons from these two cultures meet on common ground. In the United States, West Indian Negroes are likely to be first admired by American Negroes for their intractability to color restrictions and for their relative absence of a sense of inferiority in the dealings with white people as such. Later, however, the West Indian who has been accustomed to picking his friends and who puts emphasis upon family status is likely to arouse resentment among Americans. The West Indian frequently finds the American wanting in dignity and class refinement; Americans, on the other hand, are likely to find him conceited and boring. The pattern of relationship is by no means thus limited, but we shall not dilate upon it.

In the case of whites, attitudes of superiority are more likely to arise in the bipartite situation. Here white gentlemen and aristocrats, who despise all forms of menial work, are developed. The upper classes assume a condescending, paternal attitude to all lower-class persons, and their sense of power tends to be fully supported by the obsequiousness of the colored masses. In the ruling-class situation, on the other hand, the white man is generally compromising. He is living in a colored man's country and his attitude toward white people 'from home' tends to be apologetic. The latter usually have great prestige among them, and the need for explaining their position usually puts whites in such a situation on the defensive. Usually they are working toward the end that they shall be able to merit retirement and a comfortable life 'back home'.

Probably the most significant difference between the ruling-class and the bipartite situations is to be found in their segregation practices. In the ruling-class situation there is ostensibly no segregation; in the bipartite situation, however, the races are segregated both in custom and in written law. There is what might be called white exclusiveness in the ruling-class situation; that is to say, the whites segregate themselves in residential areas and in their social activities. Overtly the practice is made to rest on the presumption that every man has a right to choose his own associates and to live exclusively if he so desires. Yet the occasional acquisition of residential property by a colored family in a white community never results in a public disturbance; it never results even in a public discussion. Such notices as 'For Whites Only' or 'Colored and White' do not appear in this situation, while both colored people and whites ordinarily attend schools and churches without overt segregation.

In the bipartite situation, on the other hand, explicit segregation is at the foundation of all the racial discrimination and exploitative practices of the whites. In fact, segregation is here absolutely necessary to maintain white ruling-class dominance. The colored zones, belts, and camps are fundamental restrictions upon the colored people. They restrict the latter's freedom of physical movement, the *sine qua non* of a normal life under capitalism.

It would be an egregious error to think of imposed racial segregation as a mutually desirable spatial limitation between the races. What segregation really amounts to is a sort of perennial imprisonment of the colored people by the whites. Moreover, this imprisonment provides the proper milieu for the planned cultural retardation of the colored people. Here they may mill and fester in social degeneracy with relatively minimal opportunity for even the most ambitious of them to extricate themselves.

In this situation, also, the concrete evidence of what is known as white racial superiority is at hand. Gobinesque contrasts between whites and colored people can now be easily supported by even mensurative data. In the ruling-class situation there is the stark fact that the lighter the color of the individual the greater, other things being equal, his economic and cultural advantage. Ordinarily the colored people take this fatalistically; that is to say, they attribute it implicitly to some inherent misfortune of being born colored. But they will not understand an ideology built about the assumption of mental inferiority of colored people as a whole, for the evidence developed in this situation is ordinarily opposed to it.

In the bipartite situation, on the other hand, the cultural

limitations achieved by segregation are so pervasive that color inferiority could be pointed out on almost any count. The ocular proof of this inferiority, of course, serves to justify the continued exploitation and discrimination of the colored people; it never serves to support a conclusion that, the greater the social handicap of a people, the greater the need for social assistance. [. . .]

Race and caste

Race problems, then, are social problems which have reference to groups physically identifiable. Therefore, we should expect two races in contact and having some basic racial antagonism to develop different problems for persons with different degrees of admixture. And such is, in fact, the case. For instance, in the United States a white person with very little Negro blood is confronted with different problems from those which either the pure white or black person must meet. Ordinarily the disinterested public treats this white Negro like a white man and insists that he behave like one. Thus he may be forcibly prevented from sitting among Negroes in public conveyances, while a dark-complexioned Negro may be assaulted on the highway because his Negro wife looks white.

These are but crude indices of the mental conflicts of these people. And so, too, for the various grades of physical distinguishability, the racial problems tend to vary. In the caste system we should not expect to find any such group of marginal persons because the criteria of belonging are not physical marks. A man either belongs to a caste or he does not. There are no half-caste persons in the sense that there are half-race men. The problem which a caste has of knowing its members is of the same order as that of a family's knowing its constituents.

A caste, should it desire to affiliate outsiders, must admit them as new members. On the other hand, if a person has the physical marks of another race, he may without any formality whatever assume that race. A white Negro, for example, may decide to 'pass', and he will if his appearance does not betray him. But a person may not 'pass' into a caste; he can get into it only by formal admission.[11]

11. We should mention that reference is here made to the primary endogamous circle and not to the wider class group, such as Brahmans, Chamars, and so on.

After a certain pattern of race relations has been developed official or even scientific classification of the races has little, if any, effect upon their social relationship. In the caste system, however, an official scale of caste precedence is of considerable importance to the castes concerned. Whether we call all Hindus Caucasians or not, for instance, a light- and a black-complexioned Hindu in the United States must not expect to receive similar social treatment. But in the caste system it is of tremendous difference whether the census labels a caste clean or unclean Sudra. A man in the caste system is known for what he is; in a race system he is known primarily by how he looks.

When a Hindu girl marries into a higher caste her success is not reckoned in terms of physical criteria, for, according to Western ideas of race superiority, her caste may be physically superior. She marries, so to speak, into a higher culture; into a caste, say, of merchants, priests or landowners. Inter-racial marriage, however, always involves problems of amalgamation; and the more pronounced the physical distinction, the more insistent the problems. Race prejudice rests upon physical identifiability; caste prejudice is preoccupied with cultural distinction. [. . .]

References

ARENDT, H. (1944), 'Race-thinking before racism', *The Review of Politics*, vol. 6, pp. 36-73.

BEARD, C. A. (1943), 'An economic interpretation of the constitution of the United States', in M. Farnand, *Records*, vol. 2, p. 371, New York.

BROWN, W. O. (1930), 'Race prejudice', Ph.D. thesis, University of Chicago.

BUCK, P. S. (1942), 'The spirit behind the weapon', *Survey Graphic*, vol. 31, no. 2, November.

DETWEILER, F. G. (1932), 'The rise of modern antagonism', *Amer. J. Sociol.*, vol. 37, pp. 738-47.

DIFFIE, B. W. (1945), *Latin American Civilization*, Harrisburg.

HALL, J. W. (1927), (Upton Close) *The Revolt of Asia*, New York and London.

HALL, J. W. (1944), (Upton Close) 'Life looks at China', *Life*, May, pp. 109-10.

JOSHI, P. S. (1942), *The Tyranny of Colour*, Durban.

McNUTT, F. A. (1909), *Bartholomew Las Casas*, New York.

MOREL, E. D. (1920), *The Black Man's Burden*, New York.

SHRIDHARANI, K. (1942), *Warning to the West*, New York.

19 Jacques Maquet

Inborn Differences and the Premise of Inequality.

Excerpts from Jacques Maquet (a) 'The Kingdom of Ruanda': in
*African Worlds: Studies in the Cosmological Ideas and Social Values
of African Peoples*, Oxford University Press, 1954, pp. 165–87.
(b) *The Premise of Inequality in Ruanda: A Study of Political Relations
in a Central African Kingdom*, Oxford University Press, 1961,
pp. 129–31, 135–8, 143–7, 165–72.

Ruanda is a highland country in East Africa lying in the region
delimited by lakes Kivu, Victoria, and Tanganyika. Its area is 24,500
square kilometres; its population amounts to almost 2 million inhabitants, the highest density in Africa south of the Sahara. Three
socio-'racial' castes are to be distinguished among its peoples: pasto-
ralist Batutsi (about 10 per cent of the population), agriculturalist
Bahutu (about 85 per cent), and Batwa, hunters and potters (about
5 per cent) . . .

Human relations

Two principles dominate the field of human relations in Ruanda:
inequality of men and indefinite reciprocity.

For the Banyarwanda all men have indeed a common nature;
they are ultimately the descendants of the same ancestor. But
this notion does not seem to be very significant, for Banyarwanda
are much more impressed by the differences displayed by the
various castes. The characteristics of these castes are stereotyped
and repeated in many folk-tales. Batutsi are intelligent (in the
sense of astute in political intrigues), apt to command, refined,
courageous, and cruel. Bahutu are hard-working, not very
clever, extrovert, irascible, unmannerly, obedient, physically
strong. Batwa are gluttonous, loyal to their Batutsi masters, lazy,
courageous when hunting, lacking in restraint. These characteristics, with differences in stress and shading, are generally
recognized by all Banyarwanda. As they reflect the Mututsi
point of view, it appears that the superior caste has been able
to make other people see themselves in important respects as
Batutsi see them. Moreover, those qualities are considered to be

innate, not acquired. A Mututsi is born clever and a Muhutu impulsive. Some tales, more widely known than those concerning the creation of man, relate how the first Batutsi came to Ruanda from the heavenly world. According to some versions of this tale, they came with their servant, Mutwa, who mated with a forest ape. From that union all Batwa are descended. Such tales clearly reveal the fundamental differences which the Banyarwanda see among their castes.

When such a picture of 'natural' differences, so significant from the point of view of power, is accepted, the inevitable consequence is that some men are born chiefs and others labourers. Inferiority and superiority are due not to personal qualities but to membership of certain groups. By belonging to different castes, people have fundamentally unequal rights. If an ordinary Mututsi kills a Muhutu, one kinsman of the murderer could eventually be killed in retaliation if the king authorized it. If the murderer was a Muhutu and the victim a Mututsi, two lives were taken.

The principle of the fundamental inequality between social groups thus established in Ruanda has spread from the original inter-caste relations to intra-caste situations. A man superior to another member of his class because of his functions or his wealth, or even his ability, tends to assume towards his inferior an attitude similar to that of a Mututsi *vis-à-vis* a Muhutu. Of course the conception of inequality between superiors and inferiors of the same class is not so rigid as that between the castes, but it permeates all hierarchical situations in Ruanda.

The theme of inequality was embodied in the indigenous political organization, so that political relations clearly express the attitudes socially expected from superiors and inferiors. They are quite understandable if one bears in mind that they originate from an intercaste situation. Authority as such is all-embracing. [...] there is almost no sphere of life in which an inferior is free from the interference of his superior. Because Batutsi are considered fundamentally superior to the Bahutu, there is no field in which they can feel equal. This attitude has been transferred to any hierarchical situation. The complementary attitude of dependence is, of course, expected from the inferior. Inferiority is the relative situation of a person who has to submit to another in a clearly defined field; dependence is inferiority in the totality of life. The dependent person has to submit to his master in any question. There is no domain where he is free even to express a contrary opinion. As the dependent has always to acquiesce even when orders are quite impracticable, he has to conceal his opinions and find excuses for not doing what has been ordered. Double-dealing, politeness, or a utilitarian conception of language are the only defences of the dependent. [. . .]

Any superior is a protector and his protection is of the same character as his authority: all-embracing and limited only by his own convenience. In any difficulty, the inferior may ask the help of his master, and, if help is refused, it will not be on the grounds that the superior is not concerned with that aspect of the life of the subordinate. On the other hand, the superior himself will be the only judge of the limits of his intervention, for the dependent has no right to require anything from his superior.

Everywhere men in authority enjoy advantages denied to those whom they command, but it is often felt that justification is needed for these privileges. In Ruanda such rationalizations do not seem to be required. It is taken for granted by everybody, the subjects included, that superiors as such should derive profits from their position. The very high standard of living of Europeans is accepted without any criticism by 'traditional' Banyarwanda not yet imbued with egalitarian principles.

The conception of authority as all-embracing, unlimited, protective, profitable, and of inferiority as dependent, devoid of rights, fundamentally weak and generally exploited, is exactly suited to a structure of castes composed of human beings who are thought to be fundamentally different and unequal. On these inter-caste relations all hierarchical relations have been modelled. This means that the conceptions and attitudes which have just been sketched pervade most human relations in Ruanda. Indeed, very many human interactions involve persons who, in Ruanda, are placed on a hierarchical scale: man and woman, husband and wife, mother and child, father and son, old and young, craftsman and apprentice, etc., and when there is also a superiority–inferiority situation, even though confined to one aspect of the relation, the whole of that relation is impregnated with inequality. [. . .]

A description of the 'buhake' system

The *buhake* is an institution to which anthropologists who have studied Ruanda social structure have devoted a great part of their attention, if not the greatest. The name is not easily translated. *Buhaka* comes from *guhakwa*, a verb meaning 'to pay one's respects to a superior in his court' (Sandrart, 1930, p. 151). It has been called cattle-lease (*bail à cheptel*) (Vanhove, 1941, p. 18; Bourgeois, 1958), recommendation (in the sense of the mediaeval latin *recommendatio* (De Lacger, vol. 1, 1939, p. 45), and contract of pastoral servitude (Kagame, 1952, p. 18).

The *buhake* denoted the relation which existed between a person called *garagu* and another called *shebuja*. That relationship was created when an individual, Hutu or Tutsi, who had an inferior social prestige and who was less well provided with cattle, offered his services to and asked protection from a person whose status was higher and whose wealth was greater. The following sentences were usually, but not ritually said by the man offering his services, after he had given a jug of beer or hydromel to the other: *urampe amata* (I ask you milk), *urankize* (make me rich), *uramenye* (always think of me), *urambere umubyeyi* (be my father), *n'ange nzakubera umwana* (I shall be your child).

If the offer was accepted, the man in the superior position bestowed on the other one or several cows. From that time on, they were in the institutionalized relation of *shebuja* (which I translate 'lord' or 'patron') and *garagu* ('client'). [...]

Caste structure

As our descriptions and analysis of Ruanda proceed, it becomes more and more certain that there was there a caste structure or something very similar to it. Sociologists usually define a caste society as one composed of several graded groups, each of which is endogamous and practising an hereditary occupation, membership of which can be obtained only by birth (Lowie, 1948, pp. 10, 273).

Birth was, indeed, the usual way in which one became a Tutsi, a Hutu or a Twa. This does not mean that the three strata were 'racial' units, but that an individual was a Tutsi, a Hutu or a

Twa when his father was a Tutsi, a Hutu or a Twa. In the same way was his father a Tutsi, a Hutu or a Twa. But in order to avoid such expressions, which could go on *ad infinitum*, a definition other than an hereditary one should be found. But it does not seem that there is any other than that a Tutsi, a Hutu or a Twa is a person who regarded himself, and was regarded by all those who knew him, as a Tutsi, a Hutu or a Twa, the usual way for a person to fulfil this social definition being to realize the hereditary one. In some cases, however, it was possible to be socially recognized as a Tutsi without having been begotten by a Tutsi father. For instance, a Twa who had been ennobled or the son of a rich Hutu cattle owner and of a Tutsi woman, was sometimes regarded as a Tutsi. But these were exceptional cases and we may say that the caste criterion of membership by birth held in general for all the three Ruanda groups.

The same may be said of the criterion of endogamy ... marriages between Hutu and Tutsi were not banned but ... they were neither favoured nor frequent. Marriages between Twa and the two other groups were prohibited.

Since cattle rearing, agriculture, and hunting, with pot making, were the main activities characteristic of our three strata, the criterion of hereditary occupation was certainly realized in Ruanda.

The fourth criterion, the hierarchy of the groups within the society, was certainly to be seen in Ruanda. [. . .]

The three Ruanda castes were in a hierarchic order, then, from the standpoint of social power, both collective and individual. The Tutsi caste could as a group inflict severe deprivations on the Hutu or Twa castes, and any individual Tutsi could exert strong pressure on any Hutu or Twa irrespective of their personal qualities and possessions.

Let us now turn to the function of the feudal system in Ruanda.

Protection by identification

To live in a society where several castes very unequal in their social power coexist, frequently puts the individuals of the weaker groups in a very difficult position. Indeed, anybody may be at any time confronted with an exacting demand made on him by somebody possessing higher social power. To be protected against such a demand, it is indispensable for the person submitted to it to increase his own social power. It is impossible to do this directly as he cannot, except very rarely, enter into the upper caste, but he may obtain it indirectly by succeeding in identifying himself with a person endowed with great social power. Feudality is an institutionalization of that identification of an individual socially weak, with another, socially powerful, who secures for the former the necessary protection against other socially powerful individuals.

Is it not possible, in a caste society, to protect the persons enjoying little social power by other means than a clientage system?

The political power of the superior group could be limited by preventing that group from using the pressure of legitimate physical force. For instance, it could be made illegal for a person of the upper group to force somebody to work for him under the threat of having him imprisoned or beaten if he refused. This solution was aimed at in the nineteenth-century Western liberal state. There the groups were not castes but classes, defined both by amount of wealth and the type of its usage (capital investment versus consumer goods buying). The difference between classes and castes is irrelevant at this stage of our argument. According to its Marxist critics, that solution has not succeeded in preventing the domination of the economically weak group by the economically powerful one. If, they said, a rich man is not allowed to force another one to work for him under the threat of police, he may force him as effectively by the threat of taking his livelihood from him. Consequently, the Marxists proposed another solution to make the economic power of all individuals equal.

It is clear that both solutions attempt to solve the problem of the protection of socially weak individuals by changing the hierarchic structure of the society. In the liberal solution the dominant group is stripped of its political privileges, which makes it weaker as a superior group; in the Marxist solution, it is deprived of its preponderant social power, and completely disappears. It seems that a clientage institution is the only means permitting the protection of socially weak individuals without destroying the unequal participation of the groups in social power. In that system the groups continue to be endowed with an unequal collective social power, whereas the range of variability in individual social power is made narrower in order to give everybody the opportunity of obtaining sufficient personal security. [. . .]

The problem of the Tutsi domination

This system of the social domination of a caste and of the political domination of a group within that caste seemed to be successful and stable at the beginning of the twentieth century. How did the Tutsi achieve the difficult task of keeping such a large caste kingdom a working concern? Before considering the social structural factors which were operative one must take into account the frame in which and the background against which the problem of domination had to be solved. By frame and background, is understood here the totality of circumstances which appeared to the Tutsi, and were for them, unalterable. Tutsi had to adapt their pattern of domination to these circumstances as they were in any event beyond their control. These circumstances were very numerous, pertaining to physical environment (ecological), to human biology, and even to the culture of the group. What these very various elements had in common was that, at the time referred to in this study, they set limits to the action and ways of life of the group. Some of these limits were not immutable in themselves but they were so none the less for the Tutsi at the beginning of the twentieth century.

From this vast congeries of natural, biological, and cultural factors, I shall review only a few which appear most significant from the present point of view: that of the conditions of domination.

Frame and background of the domination system

A first relevant background fact was that, apart from the ultimate control of a most valuable resource, namely, cattle, the difference between the equipment of Tutsi and Hutu was not very considerable. [. . .]

Except for cattle, Tutsi material equipment did not allow them to impress on Hutu minds, to a comparable extent, the idea of their superiority. Certainly they had more spacious compounds, they were better dressed than the Hutu, they drank better beer, and when travelling, instead of walking, they were frequently carried on a litter by Hutu or Twa servants. All these differences, important as they were, were only, however, differences of quantity and degree, characterizing two strata which had not the same access to the good things of life, rather than essential differences. By 'essential' is meant here that the Tutsi equipment did not include elements such as steam-machines, electricity or gunpower, which, when possessed exclusively by a group, are sufficient to secure an easy domination. Tutsi power did not rest on a superiority in material culture.

Another relevant background factor was the ratio between Tutsi and Hutu. As was previously stated, it is not possible to know that ratio very accurately. It is very likely, however, that it was never greater than ten or fifteen per cent. This fact was extremely important, because an economic exploitation of land tillers for the benefit of cattle-raisers would have been impossible if the Tutsi had numbered much more than this percentage of the total population. If, for instance, the Tutsi had constituted fifty per cent of the population, the Hutu would not have been able to provide them with the foodstuffs and labour necessary to comfortable subsistence. Oberg makes similar comments on the ratio between pastoralists and agriculturalists in Ankole (Oberg, 1940, p. 126). [. . .]

A third factor which made the second so crucial was the type of economy of the country. Because of the relatively poor soil, the irregularity of the rains, and the methods of cultivation, there was not a very considerable surplus. Having to subsist on a very limited national income, the rulers had to cope with an economic problem in the fundamental meaning of the term – that is, they had to organize a way of life with means insufficient to meet needs. This emphasized the capital importance of compulsory labour and tributes, of regular and efficient collection, and of an apportionment of levies which did not let any prospective tax-payer escape. [. . .]

A biological element also has been significant in the establishment and maintenance of Tutsi power in Ruanda. This was the difference in physical appearance between Tutsi and Hutu. Whatever may be the objectivity of physical caste characteristics, it is certain that there were (and still are) Tutsi and Hutu physical stereotypes socially recognized. Such characteristics regarded as significant were, for the Tutsi, to be slender, tall and light skinned; for the Hutu, to be short and stout with coarse features. To conform to one of these types was not sufficient to make of a man a Tutsi or a Hutu. Indeed there were some Tutsi and Hutu who did not possess the physical characteristics of their caste.

Sociological and psychological studies devoted to racial problems, and particularly to anti-semitism, have stressed the importance of the physical stereotypes of groups. It is immaterial whether the stereotypes are verified in the majority of cases, or only quite rarely. What is important is that they provide a basis on which many moral, psychological, and occupational characteristics are crystallized and form a simple picture. This picture, haunting the imagination of those it is supposed to represent as well as of the others, makes everyone extremely conscious of his group participation and of the differences that separate his group from the others.

The fact that a group is characterized by a physical type differentiating it from the others is a factor which may act both ways from the standpoint of social and political power. A minority endowed with a stereotyped physical appearance will have a very great social visibility. If that minority is at the bottom of the hierarchy, its members are constantly despised, and develop attitudes characteristic of those who are looked down on by those with whom they have to live. Consequently, they are hopelessly confined to their group and enjoy almost no opportunity to increase their power. This was the case of the Twa. Their physical stereotype stressed all the features which could be interpreted as ape-like.

If, on the contrary, that physically stereotyped minority is at the top of the power structure, it avails itself of its appearance, regarded as 'beautiful', to support its claims to an innate superiority. Consequently, it is an asset to its power.

Tutsi have been able to use the three different stereotypes of the physical characteristics of the Ruanda castes as a confirmation of their superiority: they have convinced all Ruanda that to be slender and light skinned is much better than to be stout and dark (this was even aesthetically translated in the patterns used in the ornamentations of baskets: they manifested a preference for elongated slim forms). They used the stereotypes also as a proof of their different nature which entitled them to rule and as a guarantee against social mobility: because a Hutu was usually not endowed with the Tutsi physical characteristics he could not easily pass the line.

Two other important elements related to the political power system of Ruanda were its extent and its orographic configuration. [. . .]

The small extent of Ruanda was indeed an asset from this point of view but this was largely neutralized by the relief which made communications extremely difficult. Notwithstanding these unfavourable physical factors, the *mwami* [king] had been able to establish and maintain his political network connecting all the subordinate authorities of Ruanda to himself.

These five elements are among those which more significantly affected the domination system of the Tutsi. They are the only ones. Three of them refer to the social power of the Tutsi caste (type of material culture, Tutsi-Hutu ratio, physical appearance), while two others (economy with a small surplus, area, and relief) were operative rather in the sphere of political power. Only two of these background facts (demographic ratio and physical type) were favourable to the domination pattern whereas one (absence of a different material equipment apart from cattle) was neutral and two (lack of a great surplus, geographic configuration) were obstacles. [. . .]

The Ruanda principle of inequality could be expressed in the following terms: people born in different castes are unequal in inborn endowment, physical as well as psychological and have consequently fundamentally different rights.

That premise, closely connected with the caste structure, is suggested by the analysis of the political and feudal structures. Indeed, when a principle of inequality exists in a society with respect to a certain type of relations, it does not fail to spread to other relations more or less similar. In Ruanda, the inegalitarian premise of inter-caste relations has permeated the intricate relations which could be regarded as analogous in certain respects. A Tutsi who was lord over another Tutsi was thought to be superior over his client in a way comparable to the manner in which he was superior over his Hutu clients. Of course, significant differences remained between inter- and intra-caste relationships of superiority, but the latter tended to be patterned on the former ones.

The extension to intricate relations of the premise of inter-caste inequality made it a principle of integration with a very wide bearing as it could, and did, in fact, pervade all the human relations in which a superiority of one actor over the other was implied. It could be the relation between a mother and her young child, a father and his son, a man and his wife, an old man and a youngster, a craftsman and an apprentice, etc. These relations constituting the texture of social life, the impact on collective living of the premise of fundamental inequality, cannot be over-estimated.

The theorems

In order to understand better how the inequality premise influenced the whole of Ruanda social life, the different aspects of that influence must be made explicit. They will be expressed as a set of theorems, by which is meant general propositions or statements which are not self-evident.

Theorem 1

When two persons are involved in any kind of social relation, it is their mutual hierarchical situation which is regarded as the most relevant element of the relation.

Superiority and inferiority were *foci* of the Ruanda social structure to such an extent that as soon as they entered as a component in the content of a social intercourse, other components were regarded as less important and were coloured by the hierarchical situation of the two actors. [. . .]

This first theorem is a consequence of inequality conceived as essential. When two persons are considered unequal by nature, the superiority of one over the other cannot be limited to a certain sphere. Obedience in everything must be required: there is no field in which a father could be wrong and his son right.

Theorem 2

As in almost any human relation there is some superiority of one actor over the other, as that aspect is always stressed and as inferiority relations are patterned on inter-caste relations, paternalistic, and dependent attitudes were to be found in almost every human relation in Ruanda. [. . .]

Theorem 3

There is no private sector in the life of the inferior *vis-à-vis* his superior. The superior has the right to control the whole of his subordinate's activities. This is not resented by the inferior as unbearable meddling. On the contrary, it is expected by the inferior who feels that such interference is a proof of the interest his superior extends to him. [. . .]

Theorem 4

Strictly contractual relations are not possible. To enter into a contract implies that the intended parties are previously independent of one another. If one is submitted to the other for the whole of his life, how could he freely commit himself to give the other certain services? And how could the other promise to secure his inferior a counterpart that the latter can legally claim? When entering into contractual relations, it is necessary that each prospective partner should be a person independent of and equal to the other in that context. [. . .]

Theorem 5

With such socially accepted conceptions about inequality, those who occupy the superior positions in most of the social relations in which they are involved, tend to develop a permanent authoritarian behaviour. This is characterized by a propensity to command, to be self-assertive, arrogant, protective and compassionate.

Chiefs, rulers, and other superiors try to extend not only the size or range of their power (the number of people controlled) but its density (the degree of control of the subordinates) (Russell, 1938, p. 165). Any independence manifested by the inferior will be resented as rebellious.

This leads to intolerance. The superior's opinions should never be opposed by the inferior who is always and everywhere expected to manifest his dependence by attitudes of compliance. [. . .]

Theorem 6

Even if the caste system and political and feudal institutions have succeeded to a large extent in moulding personalities in such a way as to make inferiors self-effacing, submissive, compliant and dependent, the conditioning has not been perfect. Often the inferior wants to disagree with his superior's opinions, to avoid executing an order or obeying his commands. A straight refusal being regarded as insulting, disrespect or revolt, the only way out for the inferior is to appear to behave always as expected: to fall in with any desire of his superior while concealing his own opinion, never to say no to any order but to find clever excuses for not doing it. Consequently dissimulation is very highly thought of and a skill necessary to master for someone wanting to live more or less securely under such a political regime. [. . .]

Theorem 7

[. . .] In a society in which human relations are imbued with some cultural premises as the one being considered in this chapter, 'truth' cannot be recognized as a dominant value. Indeed, one is supposed to use language not to say what is thought to conform to reality but what is thought to conform to the ruler's opinion. Nobody, the ruler included, entertains many illusions on the sincerity of what is said, but submission has been expressed at the right time and this is felt to be most important.

This theorem could be formulated in this way: the verbal behaviour towards a superior must express dependence rather than 'truth'.

Theorem 8

Once it is taken for granted that in hierarchical relations, behaviour must conform to the superior's expectations even to the point of agreeing with all his opinions, a similar attitude tends to spread to other fields. Each time there is a conflict between what is useful to the speaker or expected from him and what he thinks, he is apt to say rather what is useful or expected.

Thus, a dependent attitude in hierarchical relationships favours the extension to all social relations of a utilitarian usage of language. [. . .]

The origin of the inequality premise

[...] A conquest evolving into a caste structure is sufficient to account for an inegalitarian premise. Even if prior to the conquest each of the two groups concerned has an egalitarian ideology, the establishment of hereditary groups, whereby the status of vanquishers and vanquished is perpetuated, suffices to give birth to a theory of inequality.

I am of the opinion that such a theory is a necessary 'super-structure' (in the Marxist sense) of a caste system. Undoubtedly, a body of inheritance laws, opportunities for a certain kind of education restricted to the wealthiest, a difference in languages, etc., may maintain for some time a high social power in the hands of the conquerors' descendents, even if the cultural ideology is that all men are born equal. But such a lack of internal coherence ('all men are born equal' versus 'political and economic power is restricted to those who are descendants of the conquerors') is very likely to result rapidly in an evolution from a caste system to a class society. A 'racial' theory seems the only ideology perfectly consistent with a caste structure. [...]

It should be understood that when we speak of 'the adoption of an ideology by the conquerors', it is not meant that one day the conquerors made a conscious choice among various possible ideologies. Rather, once a caste system operates, the patterns of political domination and of economic exploitation require people to behave as if the upper caste members were by nature different from that of the lower caste members. When the 'idea behind' these behaviours is made more or less explicit, as in tales and proverbs, it is rationalized in terms of fundamental and inborn inequality.

If there is such a necessary link between caste systems and the premise of inequality, then to know whether the conqueror's ideology, prior to the conquest, was egalitarian or not is only an historical question; when the vanquisher settles and establishes a caste system, the inegalitarian ideology is produced, as its corollary.

References

BOURGEOIS, R. (1958), *Banyarwanda et Burundi: L'Evolution du contrat de Bail à cheptel*, Bruxelles.

KAGAME, A. (1952), *Le Code des Institutions Politiques du Ruanda Précolonial*, Bruxelles.

LACGER, L. de (1939), *Ruanda: Le Ruanda Ancien, le Ruanda Moderne*, two vols, Namur.

LOWIE, R. (1948), *Social Organization*, New York.

OBERG, K. (1940), 'The Kingdom of Ankole in Uganda', in M. Fortes and E. E. Evans-Pritchard (eds.), *African Political Systems*, pp. 121-62, London.

RUSSELL, B. (1938), *Power*, London.

SANDRART, G. (1930), *Cours du Droit Coutumier*, Astrida, mimeograph.

VANHOVE, J. (1941), *Essai de Droit Coutoumier du Ruanda*, Bruxelles.

Part Seven
Race in the Caribbean and South America

Colonial conquest imposes a social structure which regulates
relationships between the colonizers and the indigenous
population. Both contributions in this section deal with the setting
up and management of such relationships in the New World.
Sprague's analysis represents an academic tradition in which the
social heritage of New World countries is typified as either
Iberian or Anglo-Saxon. Distinctive trends in race relations
are developed in terms of the transplanted culture of the colonising
group. In contrast, Smith presents Jamaica as a plural society.
Pluralism is a currently influential concept, originally developed
by Boeke (1953) and Furnivall (1948) in their respective works
on economic and social relationships in Indonesia. The
difference in the two types of analysis is absolute. The Anglo-
Saxon versus Iberian thesis gives analytical priority to culture;
the thesis of pluralism gives priority to the economic relationships
of the market place.

References
BOEKE, J. H. (1953), *Economics and Economic Policy of Dual Societies*,
    Institute of Pacific Relations.
FURNIVALL, V. S. (1948), *Colonial Policies and Practice*, Cambridge
    University Press.

20 Theodore W. Sprague

Anglo-Saxons and Iberians

Reprinted from T. W. Sprague, 'The rivalry of intolerances in race
relations',* *Social Forces*, vol. 28, 1949, pp. 68–76.

In a recent small but very stimulating volume comprising a comparative study of the status of Negroes in the Western Hemisphere, Frank Tannenbaum (1947) seeks to account for the
following facts: In the United States the Negro's present position
is that of a lower caste, which was preceded by a system of slavery
that was finally abolished only through violence and which was
characterized by considerable harshness of treatment, a minimum
of restrictions upon the rights of the slave owner over his property,
and a tendency to discourage manumission, following which,
when it did occur, there was accorded to the ex-slave a minimum
of rights; while in radical contrast to this was the situation in the
areas colonized by Iberian peoples, most notably Brazil, in that at
present there is a virtual absence of caste, with a general expectation and desire for eventual racial amalgamation, preceded
likewise by a system of slavery (but here peacefully abolished),
with, however, in some respects less harshness, regulations
restricting the breaking up of families and limiting other rights
of the owner, and the widely prevalent practice of manumission,
after which the status of the ex-slave was nearly that of any other
free citizen. By way of interpretation he offers the suggestion
that

. . . if one thing stands out clearly from the study of slavery, it is that
the definition of man as a moral being proved the most important
influence both in the treatment of the slave and in the final abolition of
slavery. Once it was believed that all men are free by nature and equal
in the sight of God, once the doctrine of the spiritual identity of all
men, slave or free, came to rule men's minds and condition their

* For criticism and suggestions in the preparation of this article, I am
greatly indebted among others, to my colleague Professor Louis Schneider.

legal systems, then the very nature of slavery came to reflect the accepted doctrine.
(Tannenbaum, 1947, pp. vii, viii).

On the view here expressed I think we should expect to find the type of ideal described turning out to be a notably more important force 'conditioning legal systems' and 'ruling men's minds' in the Iberian countries than has been the case in the United States. But Tannenbaum's description of the ideal he has in mind – with such phrases as 'all men are free by nature and equal in the sight of God' – will surely remind one of ideals, couched in similar verbal formulae, which have been conspicuous elements in the traditions of the United States and which Myrdal (1944) calls 'the American Creed'. [See Reading 26 - Eds.]. While as, stemming from the Enlightenment and thus not unrelated to important currents in the Western European tradition, it is hardly unique to the Anglo-Saxon-American scene, nevertheless this ideal is, according to Myrdal, preeminently associated with the tradition of these countries. He presents it as having been in constant conflict with the values of the American caste system, continually exerting pressure to undermine it and to mitigate its severities. That it has been insufficient to destroy the system is testimony less to its weakness – certainly not to its non-existence or unreality at other than an ideological level – than to the strength of the opposing forces which have been involved in a constant and sharp conflict of values, not only as one or another of the latter is espoused by rival factions, but also within individual personalities.

The seeming divergence of viewpoint which we have here appears less marked when we consider some of Tannenbaum's other statements. For example:

Wherever the law accepted the doctrine of the moral personality of the *slave* and made possible the gradual achievement of freedom implicit in such a doctrine, the slave system was abolished peacefully. Where the *slave* was denied recognition as a moral person and was therefore considered incapable of freedom, the abolition of slavery was accomplished by force – that is, by revolution (Tannenbaum, 1947, p. viii).

The implication here seems clearly to be that the relevant peculiarity of the Iberian tradition, rather than an *overall* ideal of the equality of *all* men, is the application of such an ideal specifically to *slaves*. There is nothing especially incompatible between such a view of the situation and that of Myrdal; but it raises the further question as to why, given that there is no greater or even a weaker, *overall* strength of the equality ideal in the Iberian than in the Anglo-American tradition, it should be that one particular group, the slaves, should nevertheless have benefited more by the application of this ideal to them in the one area than in the other. The present article largely concerns an attempt to answer this question.

It is in this connection that Tannenbaum offers the very interesting and suggestive thesis that among Northern Europeans slavery had been virtually extinct for a number of centuries prior to the commencement of the period of European colonization in the Western Hemisphere, so that the institution among them was a thing newly developed in their relations with Negroes; while slavery in the Iberian colonies represented the transfer to the New World of pre-colonial patterns. Whether because the institution had never completely died out, implying a direct historical continuity, or because Catholicism was able to function to perpetuate the memory and hence to effect the reimplementation of earlier patterns, features of the ancient, classical institution of slavery were retained as elements in that of the Iberians, most notably legal and moral restrictions on the rights of owners over their slaves, restrictions which had been developed and codified centuries earlier.

Furthermore, both the ancient institution and the immediately pre-colonial one had developed, according to Tannenbaum, as a pattern governing relations among peoples who were not sharply distinguished from each other racially, slaves like their masters often being 'white'. Thus we find Spaniards enslaving Moors, and *vice versa*, while both enslaved Jews. Hence eligibility for enslavement tended to be determined, not by 'race', but by religious or other cultural differences, or by conquest, a fact which opened the door to traditions of manumission following conversion or the obliteration with the passage of time of other cultural differences. In the Iberian colonies, then, the Negro was fitted into a pattern of slavery which had already crystallized and which had developed under circumstances such that 'race' was not an essential element in it; whereas in the Anglo-Saxon colonies slavery developed anew and specifically in relation to the Negro, in consequence of which it was easy for the slave status to become identified, not merely with religious and other cultural differences, but also with differences in 'race'.

Since the point will be basic to the subsequent argument, I must here pause to give a rough clarification of the assumptions which I shall make concerning *status*. With no necessary implication of rank or invidious comparison, I shall use this term, following Linton (1936, ch 8), in reference to a position in a social system or structure. I shall further assume that two principal ways in which institutional elements operate in relation to status may be analytically distinguished, in that these function to determine: (a) the criteria of status – the particular characteristics of a person which are recognized by the members of a given society as defining him as indeed an occupant of a particular status; and (b) the particular rights and duties recognized by the society as devolving upon the occupant of the status – and hence the expectations as to the role to be played by him.

In terms of this scheme, then, we may now lay it down that even Tannenbaum's own discussion implies that one main contrast between the Iberian and the Anglo-Saxon traditions lies in the kind and degree of emphasis placed upon 'race' as a criterion of status. Not only is this suggested by the history of slavery in the two areas, but recent studies (for example, cf. Pierson, 1942), especially of Brazil, have shown that in sharp contrast to the racial caste system of the United States, we find in Latin America rather a system of class stratification, in which undoubtedly there is a disproportionately large number of whites at the top and of Negroes at the bottom of the ladder, but in which there is not a rigid segregation into categories of the population according to 'race' and in which white color, while not lacking in value as a prestige symbol, is merely one among many such symbols which give its possessor something of a social advantage.

In the Anglo-Saxon countries, in short, 'race' is like a badge which has absolutely decisive meaning, while in the Iberian tradition it is at the most merely one among other symbols. There seems to have been a lack of any special 'impulse' to treat it as highly meaningful; and certainly the evidence does not suggest the presence of strong forces in conflict with such an impulse and preventing its expression. But precisely this, as Myrdal shows, is exactly the situation in the United States. To recognize this, at any rate at the level of verbal behavior, it should suffice to recollect the constant iteration by politicians and writers of slogans appertaining to the 'American Creed'. All this verbalization would be meaningless if it in no way corresponded to actively functioning currents of sentiment. For a matter of centuries the inferior status of the Negro in the United States has never been simply 'accepted', but has always been viewed by sizeable sections of both the white and Negro population as a 'problem', showing that values have always been active in terms of which the situation has been defined as 'bad', 'unjust', and demanding of action by way of 'remedy'.

On the other hand, evidence seems to be lacking of the existence of such a value conflict in the Iberian tradition. Thus the peaceful character of the evolution away from slavery implies an absence of sharp conflict at any rate between rival factions espousing different values. The very men who were slave owners, it appears voluntarily rather than only under compulsion, were often active in the manumission of their slaves. That slavery in Brazil survived its abolition in the United States by over twenty years, and allegedly (Harris, 1913) persisted in the Portuguese African colonies well into the twentieth century, suggests that there may have been more, rather than less, toleration for the institution in these very areas where the institution was also in general milder.

But, above all, if we compare the Anglo-Saxon and the Iberian traditions with respect to features other than the status of the Negro *qua* Negro, we shall not find evidence that the latter are simply 'more democratic', not that they comprise stronger or more radical ideals of the 'spiritual equality of all men' – they will in fact appear, if anything, to be less 'democratic'. Thus, the cruelties of the Court of the Inquisition, for which the Iberians are famed, suggests the radical importance they attached – not indeed to racial – but to religious distinctions. Again, until long after its abandonment by most other Europeans they retained virtually a fuedal type of class stratification[1]. Students of modern

1. Freyre (1946), repeatedly uses the term 'feudalism' in speaking of Brazil.

Brazil (see Freyre, 1946 and Pierson, 1942) have forcibly emphasized the enormity of the gulf separating the very rich from the very poor and the sharpness of the class lines drawn between the corresponding strata. The Iberians, in short, are at least as inclined as Anglo-Saxons, probably more so, to draw radical status distinctions and to accord the occupants of these statuses a radically unequal distribution of rights and duties; but they do this on the basis of different criteria and in somewhat different ways.

But, beyond this, the central thesis of this article is to the effect that it is in part precisely because of – not in spite of – the fact that the Iberians make other status distinctions that they are less interested than Anglo-Saxons in doing so on the basis of 'race'. What evidence is there for this hypothesis?

One of the principal functions of a status system is as a main determinant of social distances, for the roles institutionally prescribed for the occupants of many statuses carry the expectation of relationships of mutual identification between persons of the same status; they will constitute members of a *group*, persons of other statuses being the objects of 'out-group' attitudes. Thus the status system is a factor in answering a question that always arises for any individual in any society – the question as to 'who are my kinds of persons, belong to my crowd?' and the like. These matters will be variously determined, the questions variously answered, according to the status criteria emphasized in the culture, the possession in common of various criteria establishing a bond of identification – whether of the same degree of wealth, the same language, religion, or other behavioral characteristic, the same ancestry, the same 'race', or whatever. Furthermore, the groups or categories thus segregated on the basis of such criteria will often be ranged in a stratified order implying differential rank, according as possession of the criteria is evaluated in terms of a recognized scale of stratification,[2] thus conferring prestige.

Now, both segregation and rank appear to be correlative notions, implying contrast with opposite states. In order that 'out-group' attitudes may develop, there must be implied as present other

2. This is the normative pattern, an integrated set of standards, on the basis of which persons are ranked in terms of moral evaluation. (cf. Parsons, 1940, p. 844).

persons toward whom 'in-group' attitudes are entertained. To the very extent that I have a vivid sense of certain persons as being 'not my kind', or a 'fundamentally different sort of person', I must by the same token have a sense of certain *others* as being 'of the same kind as I am'. If I feel that there is a 'barrier' separating me from persons of other kinship groups, social classes, 'races', or religions, to the same extent I shall feel a bond between myself and persons of my own kinship group, class, 'race', or religion. In short, *'intolerance' for certain persons tends to imply 'tolerance' for certain others* – or *'segregation from' implies 'segregation with'*. And a similar line of reasoning may be applied to rank: To the extent that I feel superior to certain persons, to that extent I shall treat as my peers (except where my status is one of which I am the sole occupant) those persons who resemble me with respect to the relevant criteria. In short, superiority or inferiority to certain persons tends to imply equality to certain others.

From these principles there follows the further corollary: Segregation or ranking on the basis of one criterion will tend to inhibit the attaching of a similar significance to another criterion the incidence of which does not happen to coincide with that of the first one. For under such circumstances some persons would resemble each other in their common possession of one criterion while differing from each other with respect to the other, leading to the paradox of their being segregated both from and with the same persons at the same time, or at the same time ranked above, below, or on a par with the same individuals. Group lines would cut across each other, confusions as to the appropriate behavior in social relations would arise (should the rule based on which of the criteria be allowed to prevail?), divided loyalties, as also vacillation as to who it is who should be treated as 'friend' and who as 'stranger', as to whose interests (e.g. those of one's class or of one's 'race') are the same as one's own, and the like. To take an extreme example, imagine what the situation would be if American whites, within whose families red-headedness tends to crop up at any time, were to treat this feature as criterion of a 'pariah' status. The conflicts which such a rule would entail with traditionally-prescribed kinship loyalties and with the traditional imputation of equality to members of a family are obvious.

On these general analytical grounds, then, wherever there are recognized two or more non-coinciding status criteria, we may expect to find signs of conflict and mal-integration in the normative patterns governing segregation and stratification, and hence of structural instability and strain. Thus, in the United States we find chronic conflict between two systems of stratification – caste and class; while in the Iberian countries, as I shall try to show, alternative criteria of status have so far inhibited the development of emphasis on 'race' – exemplifying what Smullyan has called the tendency toward 'status equilibrium' (Benoit-Smullyan, 1944, pp. 151–61) – that conflict and strain have been at a minimum. But before returning to an examination of the situation in these two areas, let us briefly and in a tentative way consider, as so many ideal types, some of the possible reactions to these strains and some of the mechanisms which function to minimize them and maintain a semblance of status equilibrium:

1. The roles associated with two statuses, even though their criteria are non-coinciding, may be so defined and limited that conflict will not occur. Indeed, everyone occupies innumerable statuses and plays many non-conflicting roles. In the majority of instances this becomes possible because the statuses do not function to segregate the occupants of the same status into any *actively functioning* social group properly so-called, but merely to determine relationships with the individual occupants of other, correlative statuses. Thus, the roles of husband, uncle, or even that of 'woman',[3] most of the time do not primarily involve one in playing a part as a member of a *group* of persons occupying the same status. Or a genuine group may be defined, but with loyalties to each limited to non-conflicting spheres, social contacts being 'partial' or 'segmentalized'. It is in this way that the potential conflict between loyalty to an international religious organization and the duties of national citizenship are minimized – though at times, as especially with the more 'radical' sects, the compromise is not easily achieved.[4] Again, modern Western society is

3. For a literary picture of what can happen when sex is taken to define two genuinely functional groups, cf. Aristophanes' *Lysistrata*.

4. For a discussion of such a case, involving a sharp conflict between the demands of faith and those of family, political, and other 'wordly' ties, cf. Sprague, (1946, pp. 109–140).

characterized by a host of special-purpose associations with much overlap in membership both with each other and with groups of other types.

But efficient as this type of mechanism can be in restricting conflict, it can show instability, for partial identifications based on the common possession of a criterion have some tendency to 'spread over' into a more complete identification and hence to motivate behavior contrary to a prescribed limitation, as where on the basis of a similarity in rank and situation a bond of identification, leading to fraternization, develops between the personnel of opposing military forces[5] – a situation, significantly enough in the present connection, giving rise to conflict, as is attested by the attempts of commanders to prevent its occurrence. Even the American class-caste conflict is somewhat attenuated by limitations on caste and class roles according to which there is some discrimination of situations in which class is to take precedence over caste, and *vice versa*, class being more dominant than in other contexts in purely commercial dealings, while caste tends to become the more dominant in proportion as a relationship assumes a Gemeinschaft-like character.[6]

2. The very common reaction to conflict – that of denying or ignoring it – finds exemplification here, where it takes the form of denying or ignoring the fact that the criteria differ in incidence. This, of course, in no way removes the conflict. Thus, in the face of the American class-caste conflict, a familiar white stereotype imputes lower-class attributes to *all* Negroes – while, significantly, in Brazil we find the reverse: the imputation of 'whiteness' to upper-class persons wherever in any way plausible (cf. Pierson, 1942, p. 127).

3. Apparently somehow in reaction to the conflict, obstacles to the further development of divergences in the incidence of the criteria may develop, whose effect is thus to prevent, minimize, or

5. cf. Waller (1944, p. 46). Waller even suggests that at times soldiers feel a stronger bond of identification with their opposite numbers on the enemy side than with civilians of their own nation.

6. Hughes (1945, pp. 353–9) has discussed status 'dilemmas' as they arise especially in connection with occupational in relation to racial and sexual status. He distinguishes a number of typical 'solutions' most of which imply limitations on roles, and hence would belong under the present heading.

delay the occurrence of social changes entailing an accentuation of the conflict. This has been a conspicuous phenomenon in the Anglo-Saxon countries in sharp contrast to the Iberian, in that during the colonial period in the former there was definite hostility to attempts to effect the conversion of Negroes to Christianity, while at present they are under great handicaps in their attempts to secure higher education, desirable employment, superior housing, and other symbols of a relatively high class status. It is as if society 'defends' the pre-eminence of those criteria most emphasized by it through resistances to developments whereby other criteria might disturb the equilibrium.

4. Let A and B respectively represent the high prestige values of two status criteria – e.g. 'aristocratic birth' and the possession of a relatively high degree of wealth, and let a and b represent contrasting values of the corresponding criteria – e.g. 'low birth' and poverty. Let us first assume that the two criteria coincide in their incidence – i.e. that all A's are B's and *vice versa*, and all a's are b's and *vice versa*, yielding two groups, AB and ab. Under these circumstances, there will be no conflict of the type we are investigating. Now assume that all the a's come into the possession of wealth, so that our two groups become AB and aB. Now we will have a conflict. One possible mechanism of resolution of it is the re-definition of the 'meaning' of a – e.g. an ancestry formerly regarded as 'bad' comes to be regarded as 'good'. This appears to be what not infrequently happens in India (e.g. Hutton, 1946; Mukerjee, 1937, pp. 377–90), when the greater proportion of the members of a caste or sub-caste gain possession of wealth or other prestige-bearing symbols, the whole group in consequence moving up in rank relative to other castes; while the group will still claim its distinctive ancestry, thus showing a has not lost all status-defining significance, this ancestry, perhaps through the 'discovery' of hitherto unrecognized mythical ancestors, will be re-defined, status equilibrium being thus restored. But notice that under such circumstances, while it is not lost, the force of the A v. a contrast is somewhat weakened; whereas it formerly segregated from each other two groups differing widely in rank, it now merely segregates, in so far as equal rank has been assumed by the two groups.

5. Similar is the more complex situation where only a part of the

a's have come into the possession of B – yielding three groups, AB, aB, and ab. Under these circumstances, a frequently in India becomes re-defined so as to effect the formation of a new sub-caste of aB's segregated from the ab's, which may even attain amalgamation with another initially higher sub-caste of AB's. There has been at times a perceptible tendency in the United States towards the consolidation of sub-castes of well-to-do mulattoes within the Negro caste,[7] but it has never gone very far, doubtless partly because the notion that there are or can be more than two castes has never become a part of the tradition of the dominant white caste, which has persistently maintained the myth of two radically discrete 'races'.

6. A theoretically conceivable occurrence is that all possible combinations of criteria be allowed to define distinct statuses – yielding, for example, AB's, Ab's, aB's, ab's. Probably the nearest realization of this situation that could be found involves a hierarchical arrangement of groups and sub-groups – say, two main groups of A's and a's, each divided into comparable sub-groups of B's and b's. This is the situation we find in the division of two armies each into comparable sub-units and ranks. But such situations involve a very special sort of definition of roles and limitations on loyalties, and thus really a special case of the type considered above under section 1. It might be suggested that we find another example in the division of the Negro caste in the United States into classes – a thesis which, if validated, would effectively refute the entire argument of the present discussion. Up to a point it must be admitted that this is the case, for upper-class Negroes do largely function as leaders or spokesmen for the whole Negro group. But class also functions – not merely, as with units within an army, to demarcate functions and articulate social relations *within* a caste – but to articulate individuals in relation to the whole of society. Since both class and caste function in this way, at some crucial points they amount to 'alternative ways of doing the same thing'. Furthermore, conflict is accentuated by the fact that virtually identical normative patterns are involved in the class stratification of each caste; where, as occurs with some

7. cf. e.g. Davis, Gardner, and Gardner (1941, p. 245), for a discussion of a so-called 'blue-vein' group of light mulattos holding itself more or less aloof from even upper-class Negroes.

American ethnic groups, high prestige is accorded to prominent racketeers (Whyte, 1943) on the basis of norms not recognized by the larger society, the claims of these individuals to special recognition can be ignored by outsiders to the group with no sense of conflict. The distinctions remain purely internal to the ethnic community and are accorded by outsiders a minimum of recognition and even less of respect. But Americans have been conditioned to accord respect on the basis of certain class symbols *whoever* possesses them – hence the conflict.

As perhaps we find exemplified in the recognition of a variety of 'races' on the basis of characteristic combinations of traits, and in the treating of each as defining a social group, all combinations of criteria might be reacted to and perceived as so many unanalysed and characteristic *Gestalten*. But in so far, in contrast to this, as I, being an *A B*, were to treat *B*, for example, as a separate symbol and hence were to have a vivid sense of the social meaning of the *B v. b* contrast, it would be difficult for me to develop strong and stable ties of loyalty to the *Ab*'s, or to refrain from doing so in the case of the *aB*'s; and in so far as I were to do either or both of these things, the implication would be that actually to that extent my sense of the force of the *B v. b* contrast would have become attenuated.

7. Finally, this conflict may be minimized for me in that I may react to the symbols, as a sort of 'compromise', by making a kind of implied 'summation' of their values, treating a person as near or far from me socially, according as his several ratings taken as a whole seemed to approximate mine, allowing an 'inadequacy' in one symbol to be compensated for by a pre-eminence in another. For example, it appears that there is a tendency for skin-color to function more or less in this way within the American Negro caste, as one among other symbols carrying prestige and class-status value. In fact, class position generally may be thought of as a sort of 'resultant' of a number of criteria. But notice that here again this 'solution' implies the very great attenuation of the sense of the force of the several symbols – in particular, to the point where each taken singly has lost its *decisiveness* as a status criterion.

Now it is a central thesis of the present discussion that it is precisely of this last mechanism that we find a further exemplification in the Iberian countries. Here we have seen there is a highly-developed system of class stratification, based, as inevitably with this system of ranking, upon the combined force of a number of criteria, no one of which is absolutely crucial. So important are these latter felt to be as determinants both of rank and of social distance that 'race' never developed into more than just one along with other criteria, to be 'averaged in' along with them. Negroes, so long as they 'behave like savages', tended to be 'treated like savages'. But, as we have seen is attested by Latin customs of manumission and otherwise, when a Negro ceased to 'behave like a Negro', he tended to be treated as a European, allowed and expected to play virtually a European's role. Similarly, the attaching of enormous importance to religion as a segregator implies that community of religion really 'counted for something' in the establishment of a bond even in the face of racial differences. So clearly preeminent, indeed, has been the emphasis upon criteria other than race that from the start conflict has been kept at a relative minimum.

But in the United States and other Anglo-Saxon countries the situation has been more or less the opposite. The bond arising from common class, religion, and the like has been insufficiently strong to override the force of 'racial' segregation. Conflict for long was minimized by the fact that differences in the incidence of the criteria were at first relatively slight (cf. above under section 3). But as gradually the Negroes were converted to Christianity and as increasing numbers of them came into the possession of attributes traditionally recognized as criteria of higher class status, potentialities for conflict became manifest. And conflict there has been; for, although less strongly developed than in the Iberian countries, class stratification and segregation along religious lines is far from lacking in the United States. While these alternative bases of segregation have been insufficiently strong to prevent the development of caste, as I submit they have in the Iberian countries, they have nevertheless been sufficiently so to have given rise to constant, chronic conflict – a conflict which has only been partially resolved by one or another of the several 'mechanisms' discussed above. Especially Warner and his collaborators have shown the great extent to which class and caste are in conflict, a situation which comes out most clearly in the cases of upper-class

Negroes and lower-class whites, with each of which prestige ranks different in class from what it is in caste. But there is not a lack of signs of at least an incipient tendency for racial segregation to yield, at certain points anyway (cf. above under 1), to other criteria, class taking precedence in these contexts, yielding something more akin to a classical 'Marxian class struggle' situation, as in the formation of mixed Negro-white trade unions, with employers, Negro and white, aligning themselves *vis-à-vis* workingmen, Negro or white. These effects have been especially clearly evidenced in the class-induced weakening of ethnic segregation.[8]

It is relevant in the present connection to note that there is at least one area of interracial contact in which Anglo-Saxon colonists failed to develop a racial caste system – viz., Hawaii. But in this case it was not the Europeans but the 'natives' which supplied a highly developed, alternative system of stratification along class lines, a system characteristic generally of Polynesian culture. Early white settlement of the islands took place under circumstances which did not involve the immediate disruption of the structure of native society; the evidence seems to indicate that the whites were, one might say, 'fitted into' this structure, attaining status in this system by marrying women of chiefly rank, thus achieving what amounted to this rank themselves and acting as advisers in the service of the native rules. Thus, in so far as these whites enjoyed high rank, it was not so much in virtue of their 'race' as such as in virtue of their position in terms of the native, non-racial system of stratification. In treating Hawaiians of chiefly rank more or less as 'equals' to themselves they were thus not 'putting themselves on a level with *all* natives', but only with those of high rank (cf. Adams, 1937, chs. 5, 6, 9). It is further relevant that at present Hawaii has a more highly developed class system than has the United States as a whole.

Let us now attempt to see how the sentiments and values of the 'American creed' type have tended to function in the United

8. 'Paradoxically, the force of American equalitarianism, which attempts to make all men American and alike, and the force of our class order, which creates differences among ethnic peoples, have combined to dissolve our ethnic groups,' while 'until now these same forces have not been successful in solving the problem of race'. Warner and Srole (1945, p, 295 et seq). My thesis is that the second of the forces mentioned has been relatively 'successful' in countries like Brazil.

States in relation to caste. The tendency is to assume that, since caste is 'undemocratic' while the creed is 'democratic', obviously the creed must function merely to weaken caste. But it may not be that this argument rests largely, in Paretian terminology, on a mere 'accord of sentiments'?[9]

As applied *directly* to the inferior status of the Negro – in so far as it functions to define caste as 'bad', as constituting a 'problem' demanding remedial action, as a factor in motivating Negroes to refrain from meekly accepting their status and whites to feel guilt in relation to it and to recognize its 'injustice' – the creed has probably been subversive of caste. But it must be remembered that the creed also operates counter to class, religious, and other kinds of segregation, whence it should follow from what I have indicated in this discussion that *to the extent that the creed has operated in this way it has*, paradoxically, *tended to support caste rather than the reverse*; for since, as I have tried to show, rival non-coinciding bases for segregation tend to inhibit each other, any force which tends to undermine one basis will to that extent tend to support those incompatible with it.

The American creed has probably operated at least as strongly to weaken class as it has caste. Furthermore, its effects have probably been most strongly felt through a certain *obscuring* of class. American class seems to differ from class as found elsewhere less in the actual presence of class distinctions or of wide gulfs separating the several strata, than in the extent of class *consciousness*.[10] It is a thing about which, in consequence of the values of the creed, guilt is felt, in relation to which there is a sort of 'conspiracy of silence' and in regard to which there is consequently a relative lack of deliberate self-consciousness. Americans typically

9. Hughes (1945), mentions the 'temptation' which the Negro professional man, like the marginal man generally, is under to foster 'the idea that he is unlike others of his race', implying a 'heavy moral burden'. However, the present discussion offers a measure of comfort to consciences uneasy on this score, since caste would tend in the long run to be weakened by anything – however seemingly 'undemocratic' or disloyal – tending to promote 'exceptions' to its rule and alternative criteria of segregation and stratification.

10. 'In contrast to the situation in Middletown recorded by the Lynds, and by Warner in Yankee City, every individual who grows up in Sucre admits his recognition that his society is stratified'. Hawthorn and Hawthorn, (1948, p. 24).

show a certain reluctance *frankly* to take a stand on the basis of class interest – to do so would make a man a 'snob'. The traditionally 'open' character of the American class system, with the conviction that everyone has a *right* to rise in it if he can, may be expected to breed in Americans a status anxiety in the face of pressure from mobile persons in lower positions. Hence in part the tendency of many whites to feel that, if accorded more political rights, Negroes would 'take over the country'; the possibility that as in Brazil, the bulk of Negroes would 'join forces' with lower class whites while those of higher class status would make common cause with white elites does not seem even to occur to most white Americans.

Furthermore, the American creed has operated with especially thoroughgoing effect in relation to religious 'toleration'. Especially among Protestants, this has been the case to the extent that distinctions of denomination have become unimportant as segregators, with a consequent lack of strong feelings of group solidarity among co-religionists. The result is that community of religion of a white and Negro is practically without force[11] in relation to the strength of segregation based on 'race'.[12]

11. Except – very significantly – for some of the more radical sects.

12. Two possible objections to the formulations I have given may be briefly considered:

(a) It may be objected that class is more highly developed, and especially a thing about which there is more self-consciousness, among American Southern whites than among Northern whites, although caste is more highly developed in the South. But other factors are operative here. Most important, probably, is the far greater numbers of Negroes in the South. But also – and this is in line with the present discussion – the presence in the North of ethnic minorities, segregated mainly on the basis of linguistic, religious, and other cultural features, has perhaps tended to foster a tradition of segregation on the basis of certain criteria in addition to both 'race' and class. Incidentally, as certain ethnics rise in the class system, we can see ethnic segregation tending to become weakened, as would be expected in the light of the present paper; cf footnote 8.

(b) It may be objected that class and class consciousness are highly developed in Great Britain; yet Englishmen, when they come into contact with appreciable numbers of 'native races', tend to become highly 'race conscious'. In this connection I would suggest the following: The English are a highly cohesive people with a strong sense of national unity. However, the common features on which this sense is based are very obscure. Largely under the influence of traditions of tolerance for differing opinions, it certainly is not based upon a self-conscious adherence to any *highly specific*

In summary, I have tried to show that a highly developed system of class stratification, or a segregation of groups of any kind on the basis of religious, ethnic, or other cultural differences, tends to inhibit the according of great importance to 'racial' features as a criterion of status; and that consequently in this country we have the paradox that the ideals of the 'American creed', to the extent that they have tended to weaken the development of class stratification and ethnic and religious segregation, have actually functioned to perpetuate and intensify, rather than the reverse, the caste disabilities of the American Negro.[13]

views. Foreign visitors to the House of Commons have often been struck at the manner in which members will attack each other in ways that would imply in other cultures that they were mortal enemies. In spite of radical differences in views and apparent aims, a vague but very important spirit of unity, of whose exact basis the participants are completely ignorant, has always been present as an important factor in the 'smooth' functioning of the British Parliamentary system. By these same lights, adherence to certain *specific* and even characteristicly British views will be insufficient to guarantee that a 'native' will be treated as an Englishman. Since no one knows exactly what an Englishman is, yet an Englishman is felt to be something very real, it becomes easy to deny status as an Englishman to a person who doesn't look like one.

13. Some of the problems raised here in the context of more inclusive social systems it would be worthwhile to investigate also in microcosm. Ready opportunity to do this should be available in work-groups in industry where such various and not always coinciding status criteria as formal rank and title (in turn determined by various criteria), seniority, sex, 'race', type of work (clerical or bench), education, efficiency, etc., all receive varying degrees of emphasis. The tendency of workers, according as their individual interests happen to lie, to emphasize different criteria is discussed by Roethlisberger and Dickson, (1939, Chapter 16).

References

ADAMS, R. (1937), *Interracial Marriage in Hawaii*, Macmillan.
BENOIT-SMULLYAN, E. (1944), 'Status, status-types and status-interrelations', *Amer. Soc. Rev.*, vol. 9, pp. 151–61
DAVIS, A., GARDNER, B. B., and GARDNER, M. R. (1941), *Deep South*, University of Chicago Press.
FREYRE, G. (1946), *The Masters and the Slaves*, Knopf.
HARRIS, J. H. (1913), *Portuguese Slavery: Britain's Dilemma*.
HAWTHORN, H. B., and HAWTHORN, A. E. (1948), 'Stratification in a Latin American city', *Social Forces*, vol. 27, p. 24.
HUGHES, E. C. (1945), 'Dilemmas and contradictions of status', *Amer. J. Sociol.*, vol. 50. pp. 353–9.

HUTTON, J. H. (1946), *Caste in India: Its Nature, Functions and Origins*, Cambridge University Press.

LINTON, R. (1936), *The Study of Man*, Appleton-Century.

MUKERJEE, R. (1937), 'Caste and social change in India', *Amer. J. Sociol.* vol. 43. pp. 377–90.

MYRDAL, G. (1944), *An American Dilemma*, McGraw Hill.

PARSONS, T. (1940), 'An analytical approach to the theory of social stratification', *Am. J. Sociol.*, vol. 45.

PIERSON, D. (1942), *Negroes in Brazil*, University of Chicago Press.

ROETHLISBERGER, F. J., and DICKSON, W. J. (1939), *Management and the Worker*, Harvard University Press.

SPRAGUE, T. W. (1946), 'The "World" concept among Jehovah's Witnesses', *Harvard Theological Review*, vol. 39.

TANNENBAUM, F. (1947), *Slave and Citizen; The Negro in the Americas*, Knopf.

WALLER, W. (1944), *The Veteran Comes Back*, The Dryden Press.

WARNER, L. W., and SROLE, L. (1945), *The Social Systems of American Ethnic Groups*, Yale University Press.

WHYTE, W. F. (1943), *Street Corner Society*, University of Chicago Press.

21 M. G. Smith

The Plural Framework of Jamaican Society

Reprinted from M. G. Smith 'The plural framework of Jamaican society', *The British Journal of Sociology*, vol. 13, no. 3, 1961, pp. 249–62.

Contemporary Jamaica is relatively complex and internally diverse. Although four-fifths of its population are black, and nine-tenths of the remainder are colored persons of mixed ancestry, there are structurally significant groups of Chinese, Syrian, Jewish, Portuguese, and British descent, and in several instances these ethnic groups are also differentiated by special statuses, organizations and occupational interests.

Apart from this racial complexity, Jamaica includes a number of significantly different ecological areas: the expanding urban area around Kingston; the sugar belts with their large plantations and landless labor force; the rural highlands settled by small-holders; and the tourist coast along the north shore. Community types and organization in each ecological area tend to be somewhat distinct. So do community interests, which now compete for influence on the island government. Of the 1.6 million persons who live in Jamaica, perhaps one-quarter are to be found in Kingston and the other main towns, and nearly one-half live in the hilly interior. The plainsfolk dependent on sugar probably exceed 400,000. Rural-urban differences are important already and will tend to become more so. The rate of population growth is very high.

Jamaica's racial diversity strikes the visitor immediately, but local 'nationalism' has developed a convenient mythology of 'progress' according to which race differences are held to be irrelevant in personal relations. Although it is difficult to state the precise significance of racial difference in a few words, it can be said categorically that race and its symbol, color, do play a very important part in structuring relations between individuals within Jamaica, and the study of this aspect of local life can throw a great deal of light on the island-society (Henriques, 1953). Nonetheless, race concepts are cultural facts and their significance varies with social conditions (Smith, 1955). To understand the local attitude to race, we must therefore begin with the society and its culture. Accordingly, in the following summary of Jamaican social structure, I shall avoid direct reference to ecological or racial differences as far as possible, while presenting a general account which incorporates this racial complexity fully within the frame of social and cultural difference. This procedure permits a shorter description than is otherwise possible and reveals the basis of Jamaican thinking about race.

The most appropriate approach to the description of Jamaican society is that of institutional analysis. An institution is a form or system of activities characteristic of a given population. Institutional activities involve groups and these groups generally have clearly defined forms of relations among their members. Moreover, institutional activities and forms of grouping are also sanctioned by normative beliefs and ideas, and social values are expressed in institutional rules. The basic institutions of a given population are the core of the people's culture; and since society consists of a system of institutionalized relations, a people's institutions form the matrix of their social structure. Thus the description of social structure consists in the analysis of the institutional system of the population under study.

In the following account of Jamaican social structure, I shall therefore describe the institutions of local society and their variety of alternative forms, as systematically and briefly as I can. In Jamaica, each institutional subsystem such as the family or religion is represented by a number of diverse alternatives. Moreover, each group of institutional alternatives characterizes a different segment of the local society. Although usually described as a social class, the population which practices a distinctive set of institutions is best described as a cultural or social section. The three distinctive institutional systems characteristic of contemporary Jamaica therefore define a society divided into three social sections. For initial reference, we may think of these sections as the white, the brown and the black, this being the order of their current and historical dominance, and the exact reverse of their relative numerical strength. Although these color coefficients are primarily heuristic, they indicate the racial majority and cultural ancestry of each section accurately. The white section which ranks highest locally represents the culture of mid-twentieth century West European society. It is the dominant section, but also the smallest, and consists principally of persons reared abroad from early childhood. The black or lowest section may include four-fifths of the population, and practices a folk culture containing numerous elements reminiscent of African societies and Caribbean slavery. The brown intermediate section is culturally and biologically the most variable, and practices a general mixture of patterns from the higher and lower groups. This mixture seems to involve a combination of institutional forms as often as institutional syncretism. Thus the culture of the middle section includes coexistent institutional alternatives drawn from either of the two remaining traditions, as well as those forms which are peculiar to itself.

Kinship institutions differentiate the three sections clearly. The general pattern of kinship throughout this society is bilateral, but its operative range increases as we move from the first section to the second, and its matrilateral range and emphasis are predominant among the lowest group (Clarke, 1957). Differences in family types correspond with these differences in the kinship systems of the social sections; and these differences of family organization are both formal and functional. In the small dominant section, families have a bilateral authority structure and are small, tightly knit groups with important functions of status placement and training. In the intermediate section, families have a patriarchal authority structure, the division of labor between husband and wife is quite distinctive, and the composition and range of the family are more various. In the lowest-ranking section, family authority and responsibility is modally matriarchal, and the composition of domestic units reflects the primacy of uterine kinship and descent.

These sectional differences of family organization are linked with other differences of mating pattern. The small dominant section observes contemporary West European norms of marriage. It includes more divorcées than bastards. The intermediate section practices a creolized version of Victorian marriage, and distinguishes men's legal and illegitimate issue most sharply. The third section typically mates outside the context of marriage, which is usually postponed among them until middle age, very often after the birth of grandchildren. In the top section, mating, marriage and cohabitation imply one another; and family and household normally coincide. At the opposite social extreme, coresidence is certainly not a necessary condition of mating, marriage even less so; and there is no equation between family, household, and mating relation even as a social ideal. In the intermediate section, the mating and family forms characteristic of the other two sections are often found together, men living with their wives and lawful issue respectably, apart from their current or former mistresses and illegitimate children. These three differing forms of domestic organization, mating, family, and kinship are integrated as separate institutional systems which differentiate the three social sections. None fully understands or approves the kinship institutions of the others.

In their magico-religious systems, the three social sections are similarly differentiated. At one extreme, we find the agnostic attitudes characteristic of contemporary British society, and this religious agnosticism is coupled with operational faith and skill in modern science and administration, the dominant values of this world-view being those of materialism. At the other extreme, African-type ritual forms, such as spirit-possession, sacrifice, obeah or magic, are common, together with a liberal variety of beliefs in sorcery, witchcraft, divination, spirits and their manipulation, and several substitutes for *rites de passage*. Among the intermediate section, the typical religious form is denominational Christianity; and the church creed, ritual, theology, organization, and modes of recruiting members differ remarkably from the corresponding revivalist forms which are current among the lowest section (Simpson, 1956). The fundamentalist world-view of this intermediate section contrasts sharply with the moral and cosmological systems of the other two. Basically, these three types of magico-religious system are organized about competing principles of action and explanation. Agnosticism abides by materialist notions of causality and is normally coupled with faith in science. Fundamentalist Christianity believes in an omnipotent Christian God, whose actions are morally perfect and who can be appealed to but not manipulated. Revivalism and other Afro-

Christian cults are based on a belief in good and bad spirits which can affect the living directly, and which may be manipulated for personal evil or good. In the agnostic view there is no room for revelation, but scientific method guides us to valid conclusions. In the fundamentalist view the decisive revelations occurred long ago in Palestine, especially during the life of Christ. In Revivalism and other folk cults, revelation occurs presently through dreams, divination, omens, and especially through spirit possession with its prophecy 'in tongues'. Agnosticism is an outlook which has no institutional organization or membership. Denominational Christianity normally recruits members by infant baptism. Revivalism and other Afro-Christian cults do so by adult conversion and baptism. The priesthood and organization of Christian denominations differ in like measure from that of the revivalist groups.

Education also differentiates the three sections sharply; and there is a positive correlation between the differing sectional experiences of education on the one hand, and their differing magico-religious or kinship practices on the other. The small dominant section consists mainly of professionals with university training, of entrepreneurs, and of landed proprietors, who could easily take such training if they wished, or finance it for their dependents independently. Members of the intermediate section normally undergo instruction in local secondary schools; while members of the third or lowest section have so far had little chance of formal education beyond the level of the elementary school. However, education and schooling are not coterminous, and among all sections the informal component in education varies inversely in its significance with the amount of schooling received. Thus the peasant's lore of herbal medicines, proverbs, folk stories, and the like, his skill in certain manual operations, and his knowledge of cultivation techniques have no parallel among the secondary school or college graduates. Thus the content as well as the form of these sectional educational experiences is quite dissimilar.

In adult life these differences find expression in differing occupational and employment patterns. The entrepreneur exercises managerial functions in personal or corporate organizations. The professional typically finds remunerative long-term appointment in some large corporation, such as government, or else conducts his own practice alone or in partnership. The secondary-school graduate whose education proceeds no further, typically finds clerical employment in business or government.

The great majority of Jamaica's school-leavers come from the elementary or primary schools, where tuition is provided free by government, and where efforts at ensuring attendance sometimes involve compulsion. Most of these elementary-school children later find manual employment on the farms in the rural areas or in menial capacities in the towns. Recent surveys by the Jamaica Social Welfare Commission indicate that a high proportion of those persons who have only had elementary school education are unable to read or write. Another recent survey by Moser (1957) points out that less than one-quarter of the children attending elementary schools do so for the full eight years of the course. A fair proportion of rural and urban children simply do not attend school at all. Certain militant cult-groups such as the Ras Tafarites (Simpson, 1955, pp. 133–49) condemn these elementary schools as agencies of sectional propaganda, in much the same terms as Kerr (1952), who found that they produced disorganized personalities.

In effect, the technology which adults manipulate varies with their early educational experience. In Jamaica, these sectional differences of occupation are in part effects of the differing content and significance of informal education in childhood, in part they are due to the historical inequalities of formal education. The longer a child stays in school receiving formal education, and the greater the stress on his proficiency therein, the shorter and less significant his informal training. The professional is normally just as ignorant of the peasant's knowledge and skills, as is the latter of the former's speciality.

The economic system places special emphasis on the techniques and knowledge transmitted by formal education, and the resulting occupational groups enjoy differing rewards of income and status. Proprietors and professionals who receive the largest incomes also enjoy higher status than other occupational groups; unskilled or semiskilled workers who receive very low incomes rank at the bottom of the occupational scales. These local scales of income and prestige are correlated with employment patterns; and, at least in recruitment, employment is closely related to the system of differential education. Thus the inequality of educational opportunities in Jamaica is an important condition of social and economic differentiation. The local system of differential education governs the distribution of those skills and aptitudes which are conditions of recruitment to occupations of different types. In this way the Jamaican educational system bolsters the social structure, and distinguishes three social sections.

The relation between the systems of occupational differentiation and education tends to be self-perpetuating, since the less-well-paid manual occupations do not allow parents to pay for their children's education at secondary schools. Moreover, children at elementary schools have not had adequate educational facilities or sufficient scholarship opportunities of free secondary education; these conditions have produced sufficient frustration to discourage many parents from sending their children to school regularly. Historically, the propertied sections of the Jamaican population have monopolized the local franchise on the basis of their educational and property qualifications. They have used their political influence to secure high government grants per pupil at the secondary schools while keeping expenditure on elementary education very low. Thus the differential allocation of political rights which was based on educational and economic differences was used by its beneficiaries to maximize the sectional differences in education which underlay these economic and political inequalities. Thus the educational system and the sectional order were integrated, and the one tended to perpetuate the other. Moreover, within Jamaica, the division of labor directly reflects these differences in the educational careers of the population, and serves to maintain them.

The three cultural sections already defined differ also in their economic institutions. Banking, currency, insurance, export-import commerce, and such large-scale agricultural undertakings as sugar or banana estates are controlled by that section which represents contemporary Western culture locally. Overseas marketing is controlled by overseas agencies, normally those of the metropolitan power. The forms of government finance and their development follow current metropolitan forms and changes. To a considerable degree, local branches of foreign economic organizations are managed by expatriates, or by persons of recent expatriate origin. Jews, Syrians, and Chinese are Jamaica's most important entrepreneurial groups; but the values which these groups attach to the maintenance of ethnic identity and cohesion only emphasize the extent to which economic control in Jamaica is separated from the 'native' population, or Creoles as they are called (Rottenberg, n.d).

If we consider employment, saving, property, or marketing, the differing institutional forms and roles of the three Jamaican sections are equally clear. The top-ranking section consists of a hard core of employers and own-account professionals, together with superior civil servants, whose employment conditions are such that dismissal or demotion are virtually inconceivable. Most members of the intermediate section are themselves either employees of 'middle-income' status, or small proprietors, businessmen, farmers, contractors or such lesser professionals as teachers. The majority of this group are also themselves employers, hiring domestic labor and other types of service attendants by unwritten contracts and directing them in a personal fashion which involves heavy reliance on prompt dismissal and casual recruitment, but does not lend itself easily to trade-union action. In the lowest section, the typical employment status is a combination of wage and own-account work, and underemployment or unemployment is widespread. Such institutions as partnership, lend-day, and morning sport, which serve to redistribute labor on a cooperative reciprocal basis, are as distinctive and typical of the lower section as are the systems of regular or casual recruitment for task, job or daywork used by the first and second sections respectively (Smith, 1956).

Saving and credit forms differ likewise. In urban areas, the lowest section saves either by means of African-type credit-thrift associations, such as 'partner' or *susu* (Bascom, 1952, pp. 63–9); or individually by loans to market vendors and others who 'keep' the money placed in their care while turning it over in trade; or cash is hoarded or put in government post-office banks. For members of the lowest section credit facilities are usually available only from those shops and persons with whom they have regular business dealings. In the intermediate section, credit is obtained through solicitors against security in property or insurance, or by hire-purchase and other accounts with various firms. Among the dominant section, credit is sought overseas or through local branches of banks established overseas, and it is advanced by them typically on mortgage, in the form of trading materials and stock, or against produce designed for sale on the world market. Savings among the top section are mainly invested in stocks, business, or land; at the intermediate level the main forms of investment are in houses purchased for rent; among the third section, animals or small holdings predominate.

The three sections differentiated by these economic characteristics are also distinguished by the forms and roles of their economic associations. The dominant section is typically organized in employer associations, chambers of commerce, certain farmers' societies, and the like. Some of these associations have long histories. The lowest section is now organized in trade unions and friendly societies, the former being of recent growth. The intermediate section has hitherto avoided explicit economic organizations of its own, and has also avoided direct participation in the conflict between labor and capital. Its membership in these unions and associations is accordingly marginal, and in this respect its organization reflects its intermediate economic position. However, this intermediate section does control a number of important occupational societies, such as those for teachers, small farmers, or civil servants, which represent its major economic interest-groups.

Property concepts and distribution also differentiate these three sections. Among the economically dominant section, property takes the typical form of productive enterprise, such as commercial businesses, firms, factories, estates, or the like. Typically also these enterprises are limited liability companies, joint-stock or partnership organizations being in the majority, and in them the personalities of shareholders are sharply distinguished from their interests in the enterprise. Thus, for the dominant section, property principally connotes some interest or share in an enterprise, with corresponding rights to a fixed portion of the profits of its operation. Among the intermediate section, property is mainly held on an individual or family basis, by freehold or under mortgage; and it typically consists in land, homes and own-account enterprises, whether small businesses or professional practices.

Among the lowest section, the dominant property form is 'family land', that is, land held without proper legal title, and without precise personal distribution of rights, by the members of a family and their dependants (Clarke, 1953, pp. 85–119). At this level also, personalty consists mainly of small stock, tools, clothes and the like, while the homes which their owners regard as realty have the legal status of 'chattels', being often movable structures, or otherwise of temporary character. The property concepts of each section are thus quite distinctive, those of the dominant section being defined mainly by company, contract, and commercial law; while those of the intermediate section are governed by the law of real property and debt; and the property concepts of the lowest section require such novel enactments as the 1955 Facilities for Titles Law to be accommodated to the prevailing legal code.

Similar differences characterize the sections in regard to marketing. Jamaican markets fall into three types:

1. The local shop or market, at which consumer meets vendor and in which 'the Chinaman' or the 'higgler' (market woman) are the specialist traders (Mintz, 1955, pp. 95–103).

2. Intra-island produce marketing which is oriented to the collection of produce for shipment abroad, and wholesale shopkeeping which distributes imports.

3. Overseas import-export dealings which are controlled by large merchant houses that handle a variety of commodities traveling in either direction and typically operate a monopolistic system of commission agencies.

There are also a number of recently developed crop associations, each exporting a particular commodity. The organization and processes of this large-scale overseas traffic are institutionally as different from those of the intra-island produce trade in their details of insurance, brokerage, shipping, customs, credit and commission agency, and in their relation to the world market, as is the local produce trade from the higgler-dominated trade in community markets. The specialist personnel who dominate each of these three different marketing systems are also drawn from distinct social sections.

The legal positions of the different sections are also different. Jamaican legal forms are typically imitations of the law of the metropolitan power. These imitations have been locally administered by British personnel. In their content and application Jamaican laws have hitherto reflected the interests of the dominant section in controlling the subordinate ones: and even today, when the political bases of this historical order have been partly removed, local laws relating to obeah, bastardy, praedial larceny, ganja (marijuana), and the like are sectional in their orientation, content, and administration. The participation of the intermediate section in law-making and administration is relatively recent, and their typical role is still that of jurors or lawyers. Participation of the lowest section in legal administration has been limited to subordinate police capacities, while the local police and law courts have historically been administered by members of the dominant minority.

Both during and since slavery, the members of the lowest section of Jamaican society have tried to settle their community disputes by informal arbitration or adjudication, in order to prevent such issues from going to court. Obeah, family land, the village lawyer, the peacemaker, or the revivalist priesthood are among the institutions which serve these ends. During slavery, informal courts were held by the slaves under their headmen (Carmichael, 1833); after slavery, missionaries and other prominent persons acted as arbitrators in community disputes (Curtin, 1955, pp. 32–3, 114–16, 163, 169). Even today court cases involving members of the lowest section only are mainly criminal in character, and usually include some verbal or physical violence. Cases brought by members of the intermediate section against their social inferiors are mainly for misdemeanor or for recovery of debts. The judicial maladministration of intersectional issues was especially important in producing the Jamaica 'Rebellion' of 1865 (Smith, 1954, pp. 239–90). Even today the high cost of legal advice and procedure effectively deprives the lowest section of justice in civil issues against their superiors. Illiteracy and wide spread unfamiliarity with the details of the law are equally disadvantageous to them. The dominant section always employs legal aid in its litigation; the lower section can only do so rarely; the middle section may do so half the time (Evans, 1956, p. 12). Like almshouses and approved schools, prisons are primarily populated by the lowest section and are administered by members of the intermediate section under the supervision of the metropolitan power and its nationals.

Government is the institutional subsystem that expresses the conditions of social stability and change in Jamaica most directly. Historically, all important governmental institutions – law, the judiciary and magistracy, the militia and army, the administration and the legislature, were monopolized by the dominant section at the parochial and island levels, and these rulers were assisted in subordinate executive roles by members of the intermediate section. The lowest section remained outside the pale of political life until 1944. Until then they were denied the chance to develop their own political institutions or to imitate any other models. After Emancipation, restrictive property franchises maintained the disenfranchisement of the ex-slave section; and with this was associated control of administration and law by the other two sections. Under this system the dominant section directed policy, and the intermediate section executed it, while control of the lowest section was both the object and condition of many policy decisions.

In the historical development of Jamaican society the majority of its members have had no active role or status formally assigned to them in any phase of its political or legal systems. Under and since slavery, this massive subordinate section has only been able to express itself politically by riots, rebellions, and the like. The 'disturbances' of 1937–38 which produced Bustamante's charismatic leadership and hothouse unionism were the inevitable result of this political order and sociocultural pluralism. These social eruptions led to the introduction of adult suffrage, and this has since been followed by the establishment of the ministerial form of responsible government in the colony. However, the revocation of the British Guianese constitution in 1953 repeats the pattern of constitutional abrogation so familiar in Caribbean history, and shows that the formal transfer of power is hedged about by reservations and can be reversed by force if necessary.

One most interesting reservation held that economic independence is a prerequisite for political autonomy, and it is argued that since only a Federation of the British Caribbean colonies may develop this economic self-sufficiency, this is a *sine qua non* of Caribbean self-government. Within Jamaica, sectional sentiment has contributed greatly to acceptance of the federal idea, notwithstanding its contradiction of nationalism and certain other obvious disadvantages. From the popular point of view, perhaps the most far-reaching disadvantage is that the federal association will reduce the political power of the lowest section within Jamaica. This follows because the island government will now operate under surveillance of the federal legislature and administration, within limits set by federal policy, and under a federal constitution which places conservative political forces and values in a stronger position than they have recently occupied in Jamaica.

The question has been asked how the colonial elite can still maintain control of policy and their dominant status in the face of strong desires for rapid change among the newly enfranchised section. The answers to this question are many and various; they may do so, first, by capitalizing on their indispensability for the performance of certain elite functions, notably, of course, those of economic development and administration; second, by constitutional revisions of the type which promote the values of conservatism rather than popular movements; third, by federation, which involves simultaneous limitation of local power and the transfer of control from popular leaders to a federal executive which substantially represents the interests of elite sections throughout the Caribbean; fourth, by prolonging their dependence on the metropolitan power for economic aid, and therewith the colonial status; or, fifth, by stressing the need for imperial or federal forces to guarantee the current social structure to encourage overseas investors; or finally, by the technique of buying out the popular leaders, which is not unknown in Jamaica. The point to notice in all this is that the introduction of liberal franchises and constitutions has been followed by an extension of political action to a federal field, and that these federal developments tend to restore control to those two social sections which formerly monopolized it. Thus the abrupt reversal of the political order of 1937 may yet prove to be pure illusion; and an effective restoration of this order may now be under way, with federation as its basis. In such a case, the federal association would simply replace the metropolitan link.

So far we have discussed only those social forms which provide the institutional core of the society, namely, the systems of kinship and marriage, religion, government, law and economy, education and occupational differentiation. There are also important differences between Jamaica's social sections in language, material culture, sport, associational patterns and value systems. In Jamaica a complete linguistic dichotomy does not obtain; but it has been found that 'middle-' and 'upper-class' natives do not know the meaning of 30 per cent of the words current in the Anglicized folk dialect (Le Page, 1956). It would also be surprising if those Jamaicans who habitually speak this folk dialect should know more than 70 per cent of the words commonly used by those who do not. Bilingualism in such societies is a characteristic of cultural hybridism, and such hybrid cultural adjustment is most typical of the intermediate section. Thus, while the small top section speaks and understands English, but not dialect, and while the large bottom section only speaks and understands dialect fully, the intermediate section tends to employ either linguistic form according to the occasion.

Recreational patterns also distinguish the three social sections. To begin with, recreation is typically an intrasectional activity, and has different organizational and activity forms in each section, cricket being the outstanding exception to this rule. Clubs taking part in a variety of sport competitions, and organized therefor, are typical of the intermediate section and rare among the lowest, whose usual sport association is the single-purpose cricket club organized on a community basis in rural areas among populations that are not institutionally differentiated. Competition between clubs of the upper section is not usual, and those which provide sport facilities normally hold open-entry individual tournaments in games such as golf or tennis, occasionally inviting foreign professionals to participate. Proprietary clubs organized for gambling, dancing and drinking are typical of the lowest section, while members' clubs are the typical forms of the upper two sections. Exclusive top-section clubs also offer facilities for the accommodation of members and guests, sometimes on a reciprocal exchange basis with certain of the London clubs. Club life among the top two sections is heterosexual and may include family units, but in the lowest section only men are members.

In their recreational activities the three sections differ even more strikingly than in their organization. Golf, polo, water-skiing, and certain other aquatic sports such as yachting are clearly limited to members of the top section, who do not take as active a part in track sports, football, or cricket as do the other two, especially the intermediate group. Tennis is commonly played among the upper and middle sections, together with billiards, bridge and certain other indoor games which do not, however, include dominoes or those gambling games typical of the lower section. Boxing, cricket, track, bicycling and to a lesser extent football, are the main outdoor games of the lower section. Such heterosexual activities as dancing and swimming are common to all groups, though the sex and age participation patterns, the forms of the activity, and the typical situations in which they occur also vary. It is almost a rule that intersectional participation in such activities as dancing, swimming, and the like should not take place. This restrictive sectional barrier has a considerable effect on the membership patterns of clubs in all sections.

Informal associations vary similarly among these social sections. Economic and political associations have already been mentioned. Excluding these, the clique is the typical form of association among the intermediate group, and is multifunctional in relation to occupation, mating, kinship, business, and recreation. Among the small dominant group, relations are both more specific and more widely distributed, the cocktail party attended by near-strangers and acquaintances being the stock alternative to the intimate dinner party. Among the lower section, cliques and parties are far less significant than are neighborhood, kinship, age-peer and workmate relationships.

To an outsider, the most striking differences between these sections are seen in their material culture. The material culture of the lowest section is symbolized by a chattel-house, few but gaudy clothes, and the cutlass for a tool. That of the intermediate section may be symbolized by the concrete bungalow, gadgets such as washing-machines and refrigerators, and the motor car or the typewriter for a tool. The upper section is characterized by 'the Great House', of which modern versions are still being built (though in different style), the team of servants, and the checkbook or telephone for a tool. Although the intermediate and higher sections have many elements of material culture in common, they also differ significantly, and the differences between the material culture of these two sections and that of the third are even more striking. Technological aims and differences also correspond with these differences of material culture.

The study of value-systems presupposes an adequate semantic analysis and an adequate body of data. Neither of these exists for Jamaica; but values, beliefs, ideals, goals, and norms are of such fundamental moment in social and cultural organization that even in the absence of these investigations, one may tentatively indicate the principal value-foci which differentiate the several sections of Jamaican society. It has already been shown that these sections differ in the modes of action, explanation, and proof which they employ. It can also be said that materialism provides the formative principle or reference point in the value-system of the upper section, whereas social status dominates the value-system of the intermediate section, and values of immediate physical gratification are central among the third section, spiritual as well as secular values reflecting these principles. This tentative differentiation of the sectional value-systems by their foci has two important implications. First, the moral axioms of one section are not the axioms of another, so that the same events or patterns are generally interpreted and evaluated differently by each of the three Jamaican social sections. Thus, the values and implications of color are peculiar to the intermediate section in the same way that the notions and values of spirit possession and manipulation are peculiar to the lowest section. Second, the coexistence of these divergent value-systems within a single society involves continuous ideological conflict. The need to express these differences of value and morality governs and reflects intersectional relations, and this insistence on the incompatibility of the sectional moralities is incessantly activated by the differing sectional reactions to common events, especially of course those which involve intersectional relations.

It is not merely that the same event has different meanings or value for the different sections; these differing interpretations compete continuously, and their competition is inherent in their coexistence, and in the corresponding cultural and social plurality which they express and represent. It follows that interpretations of events by reference to one or another of these competing moral systems is the principal mode of thought that characterizes Jamaican society, and also that such sectional moralizations normally seek to define a negative, extrasectional and disvalued pole in contrast to a positive, intrasectional and esteemed one. Thus Jamaicans moralize incessantly about one another's actions in order to assert their cultural and social identity by expressing the appropriate sectional morality. For such self-identification, negation is far more essential and effective than is its opposite; hence the characteristic appeal of negativism within this society, and its prevalence.

This summary describes a society divided into three sections, each of which practices a different system of institutions. The integration of these three sections within the larger society has never been very high; and for cohesion Jamaica has depended mainly on those forms of social control implicit in the economic system and explicit in government. Even so, patterns of interpersonal relations do not always correspond with these cultural divisions; and in every cultural section there are some persons who habitually associate with others who carry a different cultural tradition more regularly than with those of their own cultural community. The fewness of these marginal individuals is no adequate guide to their importance.

It may be argued that this account only delineates two institutionally differentiated sections, and that the white and brown strata described above are really two social classes which form a common section because they have a number of institutions in common. Clearly, the greatest cultural gulf within this society lies between the two upper sections and the large lower one; but although these two upper sections do share certain institutions, each also practices a number of institutions which is quite specific to itself, and since these sectional systems of institutions each tend to be integrated separately, I have regarded them as quite distinct.

References

BASCOM, W. R. (1952), 'The *esusu*: A credit institution of the Yoruba', *J. Roy. Anthropol. Inst.*, vol. 8, part 1, pp. 63–9.

CARMICHAEL, Mrs. (1833), *Domestic Manners and Social Customs of the White, Coloured and Negro Populations of the West Indies*, John Murray, 2 vols.

CLARKE, E. (1953), 'Land tenure and the family in four communities of Jamaica', *Social and Economic Studies*, vol. 1, no. 4, pp. 85–119.

CLARKE, E. (1957), *My Mother Who Fathered Me*, Allen & Unwin.

CURTIN, P. (1955), *Two Jamaicas: The Role of Ideas in a Tropical Colony; 1830–1865*, Harvard University Press.

EVANS, P. (1956), 'Legal aid to the poor', *The Daily Gleaner* (Kingston, Jamaica), November 30.

HENRIQUES, F. (1953), *Family and Colour in Jamaica*, Eyre & Spottiswoode.

KERR, M. (1952), *Personality and Conflict in Jamaica*, Liverpool University Press.

LE PAGE, R. B. (1956), Personal communication.

MINTZ, S. W. (1955), 'The Jamaican internal marketing pattern', *Social and Economic Studies*, vol. 4, no. 1, pp. 95–103.

MOSER, C. A. (1957), *A Study of Levels of Living, with Special Reference to Jamaica,* H M S O.

ROTTENBERG, S. (n.d.), 'Entrepreneurship and economic progress in Jamaica', *J. Inter-American Affairs*, vol. 7, no. 2.

SIMPSON, G. E. (1955), 'Political cultism in West Kingston', *Social and Economic Studies*, vol. 4, no. 2, pp. 133–49.

SIMPSON, G. E., (1956), 'Jamaican revivalist cults', *Social and Economic Studies*, vol. 5, no. 4.

SMITH, M. G. (1954), 'Slavery and emancipation in two societies', *Social and Economic Studies*, vol. 3, nos. 3 and 4.

SMITH, M. G., (1955), 'A framework for Caribbean studies', *Caribbean Affairs*, Extra-Mural Department, U C W I, Jamaica.

SMITH, M. G. (1956), *Labour Supply in Rural Jamaica*, Government Printer, Jamaica.

Part Eight
Race in Africa

Relations between black and white in Africa range from
poised hatred in South Africa, where both are native and
engaged in unequal competition, to unselfconscious
intermingling in Ghana where the Whites are expatriate
employees. Gluckman argues that even in the extreme case of
South Africa there were social and economic bonds within
the colour bar which linked members of the opposed segments
and hence provided a measure of social cohesion. Mitchell
examines two of a set of racial beliefs about White cultural
superiority held by White Rhodesians. He argues that their
ideas, though demonstrably false, are not amenable to rational
discussion because they form part of a body of myth which
explains the superior position in the social structure occupied
by Whites.

Burnham describes the part played by physical visibility
and racial myths in a region of the Cameroons in which a
number of culturally distinct populations reside, and then
examines the accord between a racialist ideology and aspects of
social organization in this complex pluralistic setting. *Les races*
in the colonial city described by Pons are ethnic rather than
racial groupings. Pons argues that an understanding of the
differentially successful accommodations to urban life made
by the different 'races' requires an examination of their work,
residential and educational situations.

22 Max Gluckman

The Bonds in the Colour Bar: South Africa

Reprinted from Max Gluckman, *Custom and Conflict*, Blackwell, 1955, pp. 137–65.

[. . .] Here we have a nation-state which is full of quarrels firmly set in custom and belief – quarrels between Whites and Blacks and Indians and Coloured, between Afrikaners and English, as well as between economic interest groups, and so forth. Does the general thesis that conflicts in men's allegiances in one set of relationships lead to cohesion over a wider range of relations, or through a longer period of time, apply to this sort of society? Clearly in South Africa the system is constantly changing, and with these changes the conflicts it contains are altering. But are the conflicts of allegiances themselves part of such social order as there is? I think they are.

This doesn't mean that I approve of these conflicts. Indeed, I don't. I am one of those South Africans who have reacted strongly against the racial discrimination of our country. I claim no prophetic vision in seeing disaster ahead of it. But I can try to examine objectively the sort of society which South Africa has created with the bonds of the colour-bar, Furthermore, I am trying to understand how this society keeps working. The divisions, the conflicts, the hatreds, between people and groups in South Africa are obvious enough. But how does the society keep going: wherein resides its cohesion? The striking problem here, as it was in feuding societies, is to show the order, not the quarrels, to see how quarrels are contained, not how they arise. And I find the same rule applies which applied to feuds – divisions in the ranks of any group, which link its members with its enemies in other relationships, exert pressure to prevent open fighting. But the whole system is so ill-balanced that each settlement leads to a change in the system, and to the breeding of new and more violent quarrels. Though until recently there were at least some cross-linkages between the colour-groups, later governments have been hard at work eliminating them.

I must say again that when I find cross-linkages between the colour-groups and suggest that these produce some stability in the larger system, I am not approving or disapproving. I am only describing and analysing and seeking to explain the difficult problem: why does not South Africa explode? I have always felt that research into the causes of peace would be more profitable than research into the causes of war.

Ultimately, of course, South Africa keeps going because the Whites wield superior force. They conquered the country by force of arms, or the threat of arms, and by patently superior technology. It is true that some African tribes sought protection; but this was often against other Whites, and these tribes saw they had no choice. To some extent, this same argument applies when they sought for protection against other tribes; it was superior arms, despite the smaller numbers of the colonists, which counted. Force established the authority of the Whites, and force keeps it going – not only actual arms, but better organization, central control, greater overall unity, telephones, and so forth. I am not going to keep mentioning this point, which Hilaire Belloc summed up: 'Whatever happens we have got the Maxim gun; and they have not!' I am sure that if the Whites did not have this police and military control of organization and firepower, they would not last very long. The Africans learnt how strong are this firepower and organization, with overseas reserves, in the course of early wars and a few revolts and riots: but it is not only the fear of this firepower which keeps them working in a whole series of relationships with other colour-groups. I say, keeps them working – may I say, *kept* them working – because I am going to talk about conditions in the mid-thirties, when I was doing social anthropological research in one part of South Africa. I then came to the conclusion that it was money, as well as guns, which keeps South Africa going. Money does so by giving Whites and Blacks reciprocal, if also competing, interests in the whole economic system; and money introduces divisions in the ranks of each colour group. Money is the prime factor, but there are, of course, also others which are important – education, religion, political alliances, even friendship.

I feel it is more profitable to examine this problem in a small area of South Africa. I choose Zululand, in Northern Natal, primarily because I studied it, and because I do not know of another analysis which has looked at the cohesive effect of conflict in a modern African situation. I have, of course, also used other studies in making my interpretation. I have been working with the general idea that wherever men act in relation to one another, it is possible by observation to find regularities in their actions. In short, the behaviour of men in society forms a system, which has a structure. This system, as Herbert Spencer pointed out long ago, is akin to an organic, rather than to a mechanical, system. We study in society both an anatomy and a physiology. And the idea of conflicts which are resolved within the overall system of the society, and which contribute to the continued operation of that system as a whole, has physiological parallels. The whole process of eating, digestion and excretion, exhibits the same kind of situation. But social systems, unlike organic systems, are fluid: they can change much more rapidly, and they can interbreed. Zululand is an area where different kinds of social systems have been interbreeding, and changing after interbreeding.

Social systems can interbreed with astonishing rapidity. But they also show a great capacity for absorbing intrusions without change. Both these processes can be seen in Zululand's history. When European mariners began to pass the region on their way to India from the sixteenth century onwards, some of them were shipwrecked among the Zulu peoples. Many were killed: the system eliminated them forthwith. Shaka, the man who created the Zulu kingdom early in the nineteenth century, told British traders that his ancestors had been afraid of the Whites, whom they regarded as a particular kind of sea-monster, and killed. If his statement was true, it means that before these shipwrecked Whites were eliminated, they were first absorbed into the Zulu beliefs as monsters. But there are records of other shipwrecked sailors among some tribes who were accepted into the society as if they were tribesmen. [...]

In 1818 Shaka, the head of the small Zulu tribe, conquered most of the region of Natal and established himself as king over a powerful nation of warriors. Six years later British traders settled at Port Natal, the present Durban, and began to trade with the king. They became habitués at Shaka's court, and were a source of great gratification to him. He established them as his chiefs at Port Natal: they were constitutionally absorbed into his political system. He began to use them in his dealings with his enemies, for he called on them to bring their muskets to assist his armies in fighting a tribe which was opposing his imperium. He also tried to send an embassy through them to negotiate an alliance with the British king. Here we see that the new body of British, few in numbers but powerful with firearms, and with their links to the Cape, were accepted into the system as strengthening the king in his foreign relations – they were accepted in terms of existing conflicts. Later, Shaka's brother and successor, Dingane, used the Boer trekkers who sought land from him to recover cattle which he alleged had been stolen from him by another chief. And another brother, Mpande, got the Boers to help him oust Dingane; forty-seven years later Mpande's grandson also called on the Boers for assistance in a civil war. I am citing these instances because they clearly exhibit that when the members of two societies come into relationship with one another, they quickly establish regularized relations, and the form of these relations may be shaped by internal conflicts in either society. British traders and Boer trekkers were hostile to one another; but when the Boer trekkers were massacred by the Zulu, the British turned against their patron, the Zulu king, and supported their fellow-Whites.

But once the British were established they did not continue as chiefs in the system equivalent to the king's other subordinate chiefs – though he called them 'my chiefs' at Port Natal. They began to gather about them tribesmen who had fled from the Zulu armies when these were conquering the region; and refugees from the harsh Zulu king fled to them for sanctuary. No ordinary chiefs could have granted such sanctuary. Relations between the king and his White chiefs became strained over this matter and a missionary, Captain Alan Gardiner, RN, had to negotiate a treaty under which the Whites agreed to accept no more refugees. In addition, these White chiefs and the Boers were the outliers of large White groups with a range of technology, goods and weapons, quite superior to those of the Zulu. Their settlement completely upset the balance of power in the region. Soon there were states of a different kind established in the Zululand region, ne Black and the other White.

These states were separated by a border, but many interrelationships existed across the border. The Natal Government intervened at the request of the Swazi to stop Zulu attacks on the Swazi. Traders and missionaries and hunters went from Natal, by the Zulu king's permission, into Zululand. Their own descriptions show that they were familiar figures among the Zulu, and that standardized modes of behaviour between Whites and Zulu had evolved. These manners generally emphasized the separateness of the two colour-groups, but there were also many customs for intercommunication. I am going to skip over this period, which I've used chiefly to show how easily social systems absorb new elements into their pattern of conflict and cohesion, and how easily distinct social systems interbreed. The process of social interbreeding merges more clearly after the final conquest of Zululand by Britain in 1887. The Zulu state was broken, and the Zulu king became one of many chiefs ruling small separate tribes in Zululand. Native Commissioners were established with troops to support their authority.[. . .]

The British finally decided to assume full control. Crops had not been planted, villages had been burned, life was insecure. The *Pax Britannica* seemed a blessing to many Zulu. Yet still the new Native Commissioners had to use force to get some of their orders accepted, even among the tribes which had been their allies. Force was the final factor in establishing British rule, but while that rule put an end to certain things which the Zulu valued, it satisfied other Zulu interests, both general and particular. As the desire to get the support of British or Boer weapons in their struggles had previously divided Black opposition to the coming of the Whites, so this new division of interests introduced conflicts into Zulu allegiances and thus facilitated the wider establishment of British rule. This led to the development of an intricate social system involving many relationships between Whites and Blacks.

Reports of the British Native Commissioners of this period show four main trends. First, the royalist section, which had fought to the end and had seen the king exiled, was described in

1891 as 'maintaining a kind of passive resistance to my authority'. But a month later the Commissioner joyfully reported:

I have had to adjudicate in two matters between prominent members of the [royalist] party. These are about the first cases of the kind that have been brought to me; and the fact may be of some importance as indicating a tendency on the part of these people towards acknowledging and accepting the authority of the magistrate.

With their leader in exile, possibly there was no Zulu superior to these men to settle their dispute, for at a meeting three years later the royalist leaders still showed open hostility to the Government. But the effect was as stated by the magistrate. Where litigants refused to obey Zulu judges, only Government could enforce its decisions, and thus settle cases among a people used to regular judicial procedures. Government was being accepted to settle internal disputes. Also, while at first royalists chiefs and leaders refused stipends offered them and compensation for crops lost in the settlement of tribal boundaries, after a few years they accepted the money. The payment of stipends to chiefs made it in their interest to be loyal to Government.

The second trend is that from the beginning certain chiefs were anxious to demonstrate their loyalty to Government, and deferred to the Native Commissioners. They helped to recover stolen cattle, to punish faction fighters in their tribes, to collect tax, and so forth. In 1888, just over a year after the first establishment of the magistracy, a chief who had been Prime Minister to the rebellious King, sent messengers to the Commissioner to say a murdered body had been found. They reported his words:

When I heard of the murder I summoned the people of that neighbourhood and acted according to my old habit in Zululand in order to fathom the matter. I did not mean any disrespect to Government by investigating the matter myself. Now I have sent for you to examine the following people . . .

This is typical of many acts by chiefs and commoners. In 1891 the Commissioner wrote to his superior that there had been reported to him many deaths from fever. He went on: 'The Natives are gradually becoming more accustomed to report their troubles to me ...' For the Zulu were ready enough to take advantage of Government's presence and what they could derive from it.

The third trend in these records is that the Commissioners tried constantly to make use of the chiefs in their administration. In 1889 the Commissioner asked that a chief be appointed over the royalist faction as it was 'exceedingly difficult' to administer them without a chief. Ruling through the chiefs was most economical, and money for staff was scarce. This method of rule was also quite satisfactory for Government purposes, even though the chiefs were not wholehearted servants of Government. So that, again, when in settling the boundaries of tribes Government found difficulty in making a definite allocation, it constituted a new tribe there and appointed a chief over the new tribe. A meeting of Zulu was informed: 'The present aide of the magistrate's court ... is to be appointed. As soon as he takes over the duty his connection with the magistrate's court will cease'. It is significant for later developments, that his connection with the magistrate's court has so effectively ceased that his heir is now absorbed into the Zulu nation's resurgent opposition to the Whites. [...]

The fourth and most important trend was the development of the Commissioner's work independently of the chief. He was the focus in his district of the whole Government machinery. Only he could act in matters across district boundaries, and in matters involving Whites. Especially as Zulu began to go out to mines and industries to earn money, only the Commissioner could handle many of the business and personal matters which arose for them and their kin. In tax-collecting, control of hunting, pass-laws, and like matters, a steadily increasing minimum of allegiance to the Commissioner was enforced. In 1891 chiefs lost their power to try criminal offences, and the Zulu had to rely on the Commissioner for protection against wrongdoers. But above all, the Commissioner, more than anyone else, represented White culture with its technical superiority and desirable advantages. As early as 1888 a chief asked the Commissioner to send a doctor to treat him, and in the next few years the Commissioner assisted the Zulu in several epidemics. Cattle diseases made him undertake veterinary work. He organized famine relief, built roads, shot troublesome game, handled missionaries, traders, and labour-recruiters. He began to employ Zulu in greater and greater numbers; as the chief had lost his right to collect tribute and to call up labour, he could not support his court and employed fewer and fewer men. An index of the increasing importance of the Commissioner, as contrasted with the chiefs, is that no new chieftainships have been created in Northern Zululand, while the original magisterial district has been divided into three – though obviously it was initially far bigger than any chieftainship. The Commissioner's subordinate White and Zulu staff has grown. Government brought with it a vast cultural apparatus, and it used some, though not all, European technical achievements in its administration. The first Commissioners carried out many works, and these in time came to be handled by separate technical departments – veterinary, agriculture, health, education, public works. Technical officers are supposed to consult with administrators, and do in general. But there are many conflicts between these different officers; and I wish I had time to tell the fascinating story of how Zulu try to exploit these conflicts for their own ends.

This growth in the local organization of Government went with many cumulative changes in the life of the Zulu. Peace was established. Zulu wanted money to pay taxes and buy the coveted goods of the Whites: most of them had to go out to work. They began to adopt White tools. Schools were opened and missionaries began to win converts to Christianity, as they had not been able to do under the Zulu kings. An Anglican missionary of the earlier period is reputed to have said: 'The only way to get Zulu Christians is to buy 'em and breed 'em'. The dependence of Zulu on an economic and political system established by the Whites increased steadily. Thus there emerged in Zululand a social system containing Blacks and Whites which had a cohesion of its own, arising from the common participation of Zulu and Whites in economic and other activities in which they became more and more dependent on one another. Force established White rule and the threat of force maintained it. But the Zulu want of money, and their desires for White goods and education, created a system of social relationships in which Whites and Zulu cooperated to earn their separate livings. Even White force was used to protect individual Zulu against breaches of law by other

Zulu, and by Whites. The system contained many sources of dispute and friction, but these arose largely out of new forms of cooperation between the colour groups.

It was the drive of the expanding White group which established this joint system of relationships, and which determined its form. Under it, the Zulu became largely peasants and wage-labourers, periodically entering distant industry to earn money and leaving the tribal areas where their families worked the land. But Zulu traditional territorial groups were absorbed into the system as administrative units, and chiefs as subordinate officials. Blacks and Whites, despite their cooperation, were sharply separated by custom and language, standards of living, types of work, marriage barriers, and social exclusiveness. But they were held together largely in the cohesion of a common social system – by money and cultural ties, as much as by the Maxim gun.

For my main argument, I want to emphasize that the system worked because from the beginning divisions of interest in the Zulu group led certain of its sections and individuals to seek alliances with certain White groups of individuals. Zulu kings sought the aid of White muskets against their Black enemies. Later, desires for peace, for White technical assistance, and for White money and goods, introduced conflicts in Zulu allegiances, and thus led some Zulu – eventually almost all Zulu – into cooperation with Whites. The whole process of establishing cross-linkages across the main Black–White division was quickly at work. Rarely did Zulu and Whites face each other only as solid, united groups in hostile relations – not even during the Zulu war when two sections went over to the British. The individual Zulu who sought cooperation with Whites did so partly out of conflicts in the Zulu group: they were chiefs who were hostile to the king; subjects who resented the rule of chiefs; younger sons who were not going to inherit the family herd; women who fought against patriarchal control of their marriages; ambitious commoners who saw more scope in service for the Commissioner than for the chief, and in education rather than in peasant cultivation. Similar divisions in the White group were operating. Missionaries who wanted to evangelize, educate, and improve Zulu approached them with interests very different from Boer farmers: churches of Zulu and Whites worshipping together arose. Traders and recruiters had other interests. Through these years the bonds of cooperation crossing the colour-bar were bonds between different sections in each group, for each group's members were divided by conflicting interests and values. And these conflicts existed in individuals who pursued various, and often conflicting, ends, in the new social system. These conflicts within each group and each individual led to cohesion in the emerging larger system.

This is an outline of the historical developments which produced the Zululand I studied in the middle thirties. [. . .]

But while individual Zulu, and groups of Zulu, acknowledged and used the Commissioner, their attitude to Government was mainly suspicious and hostile. They blamed it for the new conflicts which had emerged in their own community. They pointed to restrictive laws. They regarded even measures which Government appeared to intend in their interests as being designed to take from them their land and their cattle; and they cited in argument the encroaching of Whites on Zululand in the past, and what they regarded as a series of broken promises about their land. They did not trust any proposal emanating from Government – or any White man. My Zulu servant said to me: 'White men treat Blacks as they treat fish. The first day they throw meat into the water, and the fish eat it: it is good. The next day there is a hook in it'. And I have seen an old Zulu, after some of them had been discussing the very effective cattle-sales introduced by the then Commissioner, hold his hands apart – 'a White project is like this, and then' (reversing his hands around) 'we learn what is behind it. We Zulu will sell all our cattle, and then we shall cease to be a people'. A Zulu agricultural demonstrator complained to me that life was unpleasant for him as the people treated him as a spy (*ifokisi* – a fox). I heard a chief upbraid this demonstrator for coming to ruin his district, but the same chief pointed out to me how much better the maize in the demonstrator's garden grew than the maize in his own garden. He explained to me: 'I am not such a fool that I cannot see his methods are better than mine; but if we followed his methods the Whites would see that our land is good and take it away from us, as they have done before. We must not let them see how good our land is'. For this reason or rationalization, chiefs opposed the damming of a valley which would have brought prosperity to a dry region.

Thus the initial reaction of the Zulu in any situation in which Government officials proposed beneficial schemes, was to reject them. The result was that their chiefs, whom they expected to lead their opposition to Government but who were required by Government to assist it, were caught in insoluble conflicts. This position was clearly exhibited in 1938 when a chief who opposed the building of cattle-paddocks with rotational grazing was praised by his people, but condemned by Government officials. On the other hand, a chief who asked for cattle-paddocks was praised by officials, but condemned by his people. For the people look to their native leaders to examine Government proposals and 'stand up for the people' against them.

The Zulu are ready enough to express these feelings of opposition. They have a legend (I could not discover whether it is based on fact) – that when General Hertzog succeeded Smuts as Prime Minister and Minister of Native Affairs he came to Zululand to address a meeting. When he had finished speaking, no Zulu rose to reply. Finally, on the invitation of the local Commissioner, their own Prime Minister spoke. He is reported to have said:

This chief has spoken pretty words. We have listened, but we do not know what they have to do with us. We do not know this White man. Who is he? We were defeated by the English and became subjects of Queen Victoria. The English handed us over to the Boers, without consulting us. We are not children to be handed about thus, and do not recognize the change.

Again, in 1938, the Paramount Chief, then recognized by Government as social head of the Zulu nation, called a great meeting of Zulu to hear the report of their elected members of the newly formed Native Representative Council. He began by telling the crowd, which included many Whites, that he was a nominee of the Government on this Council: therefore they had not come to listen to him, for he was a 'a spy of Government' (an *ifokisi*). A great shout of laughter relieved the Zulu's apprehension that he was in fact a Government man.

Thus I found that Commissioner and chief had opposed

positions in the modern political structure of Zululand. The chief's powers had been radically curtailed; he had lost his relatively enormous wealth; he was surpassed in the new knowledge and skills by many of his people; the men had less time to devote to his interests; he could no longer levy tribute or labour. He could enforce only that allegiance which Government, in its desire to rule through chiefs, would make his people render. True, his disapproval was a serious sanction; but it could be faced. If he tried to oppress or exploit a man, this man could turn to the Commissioner for protection. But the chief had found a new basis for his power: to lead his people in their resistance to Government and to the Whites. If he too readily accepted Government proposals which he might well believe to be in his people's interests, they would turn against him.

But the chief not only led his subjects' opposition to Government. He also joined with them in a way no White official could do. The Commissioner could not cross the barrier between Black and White. He could talk with Zulu and discuss their troubles, but his social life was with the other Europeans in his district. And, of course, he had no kinship or marriage ties with Zulu. On the other hand, the chief's social life was with his people. He was related to many of his subjects by kinship ties and any of them might become so related by marriage. Though the chief was their superior, he was equal with them as against the Whites and (in their own words) 'felt together with them'. They told me: 'The chief has the same skin as we have. When our hearts feel pain, his heart feels pain. What we find good, he finds good.' No White man could do this, could represent them. For chiefs appreciated with other Zulu the value of many customs which were decried by Whites. [. . .]

My first conclusion was that opposition and hostility were absolute. But as I sat in chief's courts or at tribal meetings, and at the Commissioner's headquarters, I also became increasingly aware of the large amount of cooperation and cohesion. Chief and Commissioner were opposed, but in routine administration they worked together fairly well. Chiefs and their subordinate officers actively assisted the Commissioner in the administration of law and the carrying out of certain executive duties. The Commissioners were keen on their work and anxious to see their districts progress; indeed, some of them came into opposition against other Whites, and even against the Government that they represented, as they pressed measures in the interests of Zulu. And as individuals some of them won the trust of their people. But it was never complete, and the attitude of suspicion to Government as a whole and to Commissioners as authorities remained unchanged.

This attitude rarely came into the open, and then only over major issues. In day-to-day life the system worked. When major issues arose the superior power of Government could force a measure through unless it depended on the willing cooperation of chiefs and people. The Zulu, then, had little hope of resisting Government rule and passively accepted decisions, even if they avoided implementing them. At meetings of tribal councils they expressed their hostility. The proud, unquenched resentment of the Zulu under their subjugation has been magnificently embodied in Roy Campbell's poem, *The Zulu Girl*, where he speaks of

The curbed ferocity of beaten tribes,
The sullen dignity of their defeat.

I became aware thus of the routine functioning of the system. In time I observed something beyond this. The opposed balance between the authorities of Commissioner and chief shifted from situation to situation in Zulu life. A certain minimum of allegiance to both Commissioner and chief was enforced by Government; the influence of each might vary above that minimum with their characters and relations to each other. A sympathetic Commissioner who understood the Zulu would draw them to him, especially from an unsatisfactory chief; a harsh Commissioner kept the people away from him, and they went more to their chiefs. Even more I observed that the balance shifted for different individuals in the same situation, or for the same individual in different situations. A man who considered the chief biased against him, favoured Commissioners as impartial; but for him the chief was the source of justice when the Commissioner enforced an unwelcome law. The people rallied to the chiefs to oppose measures such as cattle-paddocking. If the chief tried to impress their labour, they compared him unfavourably with the Commissioner who paid for the labour he employed. They would say, however, at other times, that the Commissioner gaoled people for slight offences to get free convict labour and that was the purpose of prisons – then later they would praise imprisonment as the most sensible way of handling wrongdoers. The Zulu were constantly comparing Black and White political officers and switching their allegiance according to what was to their own advantage, or by what values they were being guided on different occasions. This switching of allegiance was not a matter of attitude only, but of action: I've largely deduced the attitudes from the actions.

Thus I found in the political system of Blacks and Whites some of the same processes that existed within the Zulu group. For the equivocal position of the Zulu chief in the relations between Government and people was an extreme form of the equivocality that attends every position of authority in an administrative system of this type. The officer represents the superior power to those below him: he represents those below him to the superior power. The situation was sharpened for the modern Zulu chief (or Baganda king) because there were such great differences in the values and interests of White and Black groups. The chief stood in this system in the same position as the village headman within a Zulu tribe: as the man at the bottom of the Government's hierarchy, moving among those ruled, he took the brunt of the conflict between authority and subjects. But the chief was drawn by his own skills and traditions for maintaining order and giving justice into cooperation with the Commissioner. He had special interests, in his stipend for example, in giving this cooperation. And he was pushed by the interests of some of his people in the new system into giving that cooperation, even though in other situations they expected him to oppose cooperation. A series of many conflicts developed the shape of modern Zululand polity, so that that polity worked – it had cohesion arising out of the conflicts.

In their actions towards these political leaders the Zulu did not form an undifferentiated group. The greatest division was into pagans and Christians. Christians, or schooled people, were in general readier to accept White innovations than pagans were; thus the Zulu group was divided into two groups, which were sometimes hostile to one another, though in most situations the individuals concerned cooperated as kinsmen and neighbours. Indeed, pagans often accepted innovations from a Christian relative which they resisted from Whites themselves. Missionaries entered into this situation as friendly though suspect characters: they remained on the other side of the colour-line. The majority of Christians had the same attitudes and acted as the pagans, operating similarly according to the situation. But their complaints against Whites and Government were often different from those of pagans. They tended to object, not to innovations, but to the slow pace of innovation. Some of the best educated among them, having come most strongly against the colour-bar, reacted away from White culture and reverted to their old culture, which they attempted to revive. There were also other sub-groupings, such as magistracy clerks, Zulu police, and Zulu technical assistants, who had special ties with Government. And overall there was the interest of all Zulu, as individuals and as breadwinners for their families, in earning some money for food, clothes, and the other means of subsistence, which led them to work for Whites. Thus they came into dependence on Whites. In this process Zulu met Whites in factories, churches, and White houses – for colour-groups did not meet as whole opposed blocks, but in smaller groupings and relationships within which their interests divided their allegiances from the standard loyalty of Zulu as against Whites. Conflicts of allegiance in the Zulu group were operating to produce cohesion in the larger system. Similar divisions and conflicts of allegiance were operating in the White group. The Commissioner was prepared to face Parliamentary hostility in Cape Town in order to do his job well in Zululand.

The central cleavage into colour-groups influenced almost every relationship. Missionaries evangelized Zulu who entered into churches with them: in response there developed separatist Zulu Christian sects reacting against White control. Simple paganism was not enough to oppose the churches, though some separatist churches embody pagan beliefs in their doctrines. Political associations split similarly. New conflicts in the Zulu group drove some people to accept White innovations, and involved some development of Zulu beliefs. The cult of the ancestors became obsolescent as family-heads tried to keep their Christian as well as their pagan kin. Beliefs in witchcraft and magic, which, unlike the ancestral cult, were not tied to relationship between kin, were applied in the many new relationships with strangers. At all points conflicts were influencing the large-scale, fragmented, but working, social system which was emerging. In the towns and the rural areas, groups embracing tribes to whom the Zulu were traditionally hostile emerged, and the Zulu chiefs had to establish linkages with trade union leaders, national congress leaders, and so forth. But all these groups were divided both by old loyalties and by new divisions of interest, leading to constant cooperation with Whites, so that continual open quarrelling was prevented.

I have been describing how conflicts within the Zulu and White groups broke into the solid loyalty of each group, by linking together sections and individuals. These conflicts divided the Zulu in their opposition to Whites, and introduced infirmity of purpose in each individual Zulu. But the conflicts were not by any means well balanced; and when a particular difference with a White had led to a change of action on the part of the Zulu he did not find that he had solved his immediate problem. He was faced with the same problem still or with a new problem. There was neither an accepted social system in which Zulu and Whites could come to satisfactory terms nor a moral order they would both accept. The colour-bar still divided them.

Therefore the ability of the Zulu to play off Commissioner against chief in different situations did not enable the Zulu to solve the problems of poverty, deteriorating land, inadequate wages, cultural strain, restrictive controls, and so forth, which they considered oppressed them. Ultimately neither set of authorities could meet their needs. Changes of the incumbents of offices, alterations of jobs, movements to new areas – no shifting of allegiances – could redress the fundamental cleavage of the colour-bar. Each new situation led not to the re-establishment of the old system, but to a changed system. The deep conflict which split the black-white society of Zululand within the Union of South Africa has continued to develop with aggravated severity. [...]

What I have tried to show is that the old Roman maxim,

'divide and rule', is not necessarily the Machiavellian trickery of self-seeking conquerors or rulers. Sociologically, the principle might be stated as, 'divide and cohere'. Hence I've called this analysis 'the bonds in the colour-bar' not because the Africans and Indians of South Africa are chained by discriminatory custom; but because discriminatory custom against the Africans and other coloured groups chains the dominant White group. This dominant group is separated so sharply from the other colour-groups that it loses its ability to manoeuvre and to establish links of friendship with Africans who, in other situations, may well be opponents. In the past, segregation policies were not applied consistently, and in social life consistence of logic counters systematic cohesion. I myself saw – and enjoyed – many friendly relationships between Whites and Blacks during the first years of my life, and while I was doing research in the field. But as the policy of *apartheid* is applied more and more consistently, any sort of amicable or loyal relations between Whites and Blacks become impossible. Those sections within the White group which were linked in some friendly relationship with sections of the Black group, are being attacked. This is symbolic of deepening, irresoluble, unbalanced conflict. If these sorts of links are eliminated, Black will deal with White only as authoritarian ruler and employer, always as an enemy, and never as an ally.

23 J. Clyde Mitchell

Myth and Society in Southern Rhodesia

Reprinted from J. Clyde Mitchell, 'Myth and society in Southern
Rhodesia', *The Listener*, vol. 75, no. 1936, 5 May, 1966, pp. 635–7.

I have just come from Rhodesia, having spent twenty years in
central Africa as a sociologist; the last ten years of these were in
the university in Southern Rhodesia. Most of my time was given
to the study of the social structure, both rural and urban, of the
African peoples in central Africa. Increasingly in latter years,
however, I came to appreciate that in some respects – especially
for the understanding of recent political events – a study of the
white population might have been more rewarding.

I did not conduct systematic inquiries among the Europeans
in Rhodesia but you can hardly live in a society and not have
certain aspects of thought and belief impressed upon you, in
much the same way that an anthropological fieldworker who
lives among some exotic people soon becomes aware of certain
themes which crop up regularly in daily life and which appear to
be highly significant to the people concerned. These are the folk
beliefs of the people. Malinowski, the anthropologist, pointed
out that privileged groups frequently hold sets of beliefs which
justify their position in the social structure. These beliefs are
often incorporated in myths and the myths are more than simple
rationalizations; they are made up of ideas which are impervious
to logical criticism and will survive in the face of strong factual
evidence to the contrary.

The salient feature of the social structure in Rhodesia is racial
distinction: skin colour is the most important single indicator of
social position. Although the Rhodesians of European descent
represent only one-twentieth of the total population, they occupy
the most important posts in business, in government and in the
professions. Their occupational status puts them in command
over capital and technical resources. They have better educational

opportunities open to them than the other peoples of Rhodesia, and have had, on the average, three or four times as much schooling. They earn on an average one-and-a-half times as much as the Asians, twice as much as the Eurafricans, and eight times as much as the Africans. They live in better housing at a much higher level of living than the other peoples. They are given preference, or assume it, in public places so that they are likely to be served before Africans in the shops; they have public facilities such as lavatories, swimming pools, hotels and restaurants reserved for their exclusive use. The voters who elect the majority of the members to the Legislative Assembly are almost entirely white and, not surprisingly, there is an overwhelming majority of whites in Parliament.

The white Rhodesians justify their dominance by their being the original bearers of western civilization and Christianity to Rhodesia. As such they feel that they are its present-day custodians. They contrast their cultural heritage unfavourably with the way of life of the indigenous African peoples, which they see at best as quaint or archiac, or more usually as savage and crude. This way of life they see as a characteristic of Africans, which goes with their skin colour and other physical features. Some believe firmly that Africans are genetically incapable of appreciating the finer points of western culture. Others, less extreme in their outlook, take an evolutionary point of view, strangely Victorian and out-of-date, that it will take Africans as long to be civilized as it did the Europeans – a period which is often fixed rather inexplicably at 2000 years. Western civilization, therefore, at present and for some time to come, is the peculiar perquisite of a racial category – the Europeans. They feel that they have a solemn duty to the whole of humanity to see that civilization is maintained in Rhodesia, and only they can do it.

Who built Zimbabwe?

The division of Rhodesian society into racial strata in which the numerically inferior are economically, politically, and socially superior, therefore rests on a set of beliefs about race – a set of beliefs that we can look upon as bearing the same relationship to the social structure in Rhodesia as the myths of simple peoples do in their social structure. Obviously there is an elaborate structure and development of these ideas but the way in which they operate might be illustrated by two rather different examples: 'Who were the builders of Zimbabwe?' and 'Are the chiefs the true representatives of their people?'

Zimbabwe is the most well-known of a number of ruins of spectacular stone buildings in Southern Rhodesia. These buildings are so unlike the meagre pole-and-daub dwellings of contemporary Africans that speculation about who their builders were has been rife ever since the ruins became known to Europeans in the latter half of the nineteenth century. The buildings of Zimbabwe are on an extensive scale and cover several square miles. The buildings at Dhlo-dhlo, Nalitale, Khami and elsewhere, though perhaps not quite so extensive, nevertheless provide evidence of building and architectural skills of some distinction. It is obviously difficult to reconcile the sophistication of this architecture with the crudity of modern pole and daub or the complexity of social organization which the ruins imply with the simplicity of present-day tribal life. Understandably, therefore, a surprising variety of theories have been advanced to account for the buildings. Among these have been the Phoenicians, the Persians, the Chinese, the Indians, the Arabs, and the Queen of Sheba. More recently I heard of one which held that they were built by a Roman legion which had apparently been dispatched to Britain under the command of an officer who was a bit of an oaf at map-reading. This motley collection of hypotheses shares one characteristic: they all exclude the possibility that the local Africans might have been the architects of the building.

Archaeological findings and a challenge

Trained archaeologists, however, starting with Caton-Thompson at the beginning of the century and continuing down to recent times, have put in many hundreds of manhours digging both at Zimbabwe and at the other ruins. They have all concluded, with due scientific reservation, that the buildings were erected – and re-erected on several occasions – by the forerunners of the present-day Shona-speaking peoples of Rhodesia who are known to have been in these parts at least since before AD 1500. To admit that the servant who digs the garden or serves the office tea or the peasant who scratches a miserable living from the soil in the Tribal Trust land had forebears capable of this degree of civilization challenges the justifying myth of the white Rhodesians. The opinion of any person, particularly if he has some academic pretensions, regardless of how relevant, or how sound they are, who supports a theory crediting the buildings to some non-African group immediately receives a sympathetic hearing.

Archaeological findings have not been entirely without effect on the myth. An interesting elaboration of it concedes that the African may in fact have built Zimbabwe – but only as unskilled workers under the supervision of some superior race, small in numbers, who provided the organization and design. This explains why the material culture which has been discovered by the archaeologists has mainly been Bantu in type. Some who have been convinced by the scientific evidence of the archaeologists have incorporated this evidence to support the myth in a way which is familiar to anthropologists who are used to studying witchcraft beliefs. Some accept the African origin of the buildings but emphasize their primitive architecture and the crudity of the building techniques employed. Others again accept that the buildings probably were of African origin but look upon them as a sort of 'freak of nature'. Whichever point of view is held the effect is the same: the African people of today are incapable of civilized arts of this order and by implication, therefore, are justifiably accorded an inferior position in the social structure of a modern civilized society.

When we turn to my second illustration, the beliefs about the position of the chief in modern Rhodesia, we find the same basic ideology operating, but in a rather different context. The method of ascertaining the views of African peoples on independence for Rhodesia has proved to be a stumbling block in the negotiation between the British Government and Mr Smith. Those who support the Rhodesian Front maintain, almost as an article of faith and in spite of a considerable body of evidence to the contrary, that the tribal chiefs can be the only true representatives of the African people.

Variable position of chiefs

History shows that the position of the chiefs over the last seventy-five years has been variable. Until 1910 they were virtually ignored by the Administration, which by-passed them and dealt directly with the people. But in that year they were accorded a place in the administrative system and given statutory rights and duties. The administration continued to work through the chiefs, trying to effect through them various reforms in land holding, agriculture, animal husbandry, and health practices. At this stage the native commissioners in their annual reports were describing the chiefs as backward and reactionary – a drag on the more progressive elements in African society.

But in the middle 1950s, largely as a result of the establishment of the Federation of the Rhodesias and Nyasaland without adequate consultation with the African peoples, organizations started to appear which began to express their opposition to the social order. These organizations were of the 'African Nationalist' type and sought support for their campaigns in the framework of a modern commercial and industrial order. From this point of view they were the adversaries of the chiefs. It is no accident that as African nationalism continued to increase in popularity, successive Rhodesian governments have sought to strengthen the position of the chiefs as functionaries in the administrative structure. A council of chiefs was formed and the Government has sought its advice on the independence issue as well as on other issues, their emoluments have been increased and they have been able to draw increasingly upon the power of the Administration to fortify themselves against their rivals and enemies – especially the nationalists in the tribal areas.

Nowadays approximately two-thirds of the men of working age are absent from the tribal areas earning wages. The increased pressure of population on land coupled with the declining crop yields have intensified the poverty of those left in the Tribal Trust land. This has made Africans from many different chiefdoms share a common envy of the large tracts of apparently unworked land owned by European farmers. Younger people who have been educated are aware of opportunities and are familiar with economic and political developments elsewhere. They are therefore conscious of the opportunities which are denied to them in Rhodesia. Africans in both town and tribal areas have a common cause on a national scale which the chiefs, because of their position in the administrative structure and their essentially parochial interests, appear to be unable to further. Nationalism is a common threat to both white Rhodesians and tribal chiefs. The myth is that the chiefs, by virtue of their being traditional leaders, are deemed to be representative of all Africans regardless of the degree of economic, social and political differentiation among them. Tribal institutions are peculiar to Africans, and therefore appropriate to them in all circumstances, in the same way that Christian western civilization is peculiar to Europeans and appropriate to them.

For the white Rhodesians to concede that the chiefs are not the representatives of the African people would be to raise the whole question of democratic representation and the inevitable confrontation with the opposition of the mass of the African people. When the chiefs *were* the representatives of the people these oppositions did not exist. By implication a return to those halcyon days can only be assured if the chiefs – and not the Nationalists – are seen to be the real leaders of the people. Hence in spite of a considerable amount of evidence which has been brought to show how unrepresentative the chiefs are in many important respects, the dictum that the chiefs are the true representatives of the people remains a firmly held element of white Rhodesian belief. It is part of the myth which justifies their political position.

When the sacrosanct character of the justifying myth is appreciated, it is easier to understand some particular features of Rhodesian beliefs and behaviour – the unenviable position of the scholar, for example. His scepticism towards all myths leads him to expose the shaky foundations of the social order and so he becomes inevitably a dangerous radical. Hence the white Rhodesian's constant mistrust of the University College and the activities of its staff and students. Hence also – and this is more sinister – the removal of certain Unesco literature concerning race relations from the reading lists of the Bulawayo teacher training college. It is clearly dangerous to have sceptics in a society based on this sort of myth.

It is clear that the white Rhodesians are not likely to give up beliefs that constitute the elements in the myth easily. They are likely to reject any argument and evidence which contradicts the myth. They are more likely to seek supporting evidence. As a result, in the last year or two a fair volume of literature from the southern States of America which supports segregation has appeared in Rhodesia. This literature significantly purports to provide scholarly justification for the racial myth.

I argue, then, that the sort of beliefs and attitudes of the white Rhodesians I have been describing stem from their position in the whole social structure, and that these beliefs justify the stand taken by the Rhodesians. It is unlikely that the Rhodesians will be persuaded to alter their attitudes or beliefs and so leave the way clear for a change in the social structure. This seems to me to be putting effect for cause. The change must be more fundamental – in the social structure itself – however that may be brought about.

24 Philip Burnham

Racial Classification and Ideology in the
Meiganga Region: North Cameroon

An original paper published here for the first time.

Although racial traits have no necessary or universal social
significance, they frequently form the basis for cultural classifications and evaluations that are of fundamental importance in
guiding social interaction. In this paper, I examine the past and
present significance of racial categories in the ethnically and
racially plural society of Meiganga *sous-préfecture*, one of the
administrative districts of the Adamawa region in the northern
part of the Federal Republic of Cameroon.[1]

In large-scale societies that are culturally and socially complex,
individuals continually face the need to interact with other
members of the society whom they have never met. A man walks
down a road and encounters a stranger approaching from the
other direction. How should he act toward this man? Should he
ignore him, greet him in a conventionalized manner, or avoid
stepping in his shadow? The behaviour chosen clearly depends
on an ability to determine, at the outset of the interaction, the
status of the stranger and then to act in a way that one's culture
defines as proper *vis-à-vis* such a status.

The more complex and pluralistic the society, the more numerous the relevant categories to which a person may be assigned.

1. My wife and I collected the data presented in this article during twenty-
one months of fieldwork in Cameroon from June 1968 to February 1970. I
would like to acknowledge the financial support of the University of
California at Los Angeles and the Wenner-Gren Foundation for Anthropological Research. Permission to quote from Derrick Stenning's *Savannah
Nomads* has kindly been granted by the International African Institute.
Thanks are also due to Professor M. G. Smith for his helpful criticism,
although responsibility for faults in the final product must remain with the
author.

To move effectively in such a setting, an actor needs to develop the ability to recognise all of the many socially significant categories of persons with whom he may interact. Generally, certain easily noticed traits including race, language, dress, bodily markings, occupation and gesture are available for use as labels for social groupings. Such traits can be symbolic of an individual's social personality, communicating information to the informed observer about the status of the person under observation.

The approach outlined thus far to the analysis of interaction between strangers in complex social settings conforms in most particulars to that embodied in Banton's discussion (1967, p. 57) of the concept of 'role sign'. I tend, however, to give more emphasis than does Banton to the fact that such signs refer to cultural conceptualizations of *groupings* of individuals within a society and that although interaction can be thought of as occurring between two isolated individuals (roles), the social significance of such interaction for the study of race relations is that these individuals are representing their respective social categories. Such categories can be thought of analytically (and not infrequently are viewed in a like manner by the actors as well) as possessing the characteristics of unique identity, standardized modes of recruitment, determinate membership, and presumed perpetuity and thus constitute relatively fixed points of reference for the structuring of a society (Smith, 1969, p. 31).

In societies where racial differentiae correlate highly with ethnic differences or patterns of social stratification, racial traits may seem the most trustworthy signs for actors to employ in categorizing strangers. Being genetically determined, racial traits are immutable during an individual's lifetime.

The desire and tendency of individuals to categorize people whom they meet on the basis of easily observable traits underlies the phenomenon of stereotyping, a common practice in multiracial settings. To be a completely effective predictor of the various components of a person's social status, however, a stereotype must be composed of traits which are in perfect association, such that the presence of one in an individual inevitably implies the presence of all the others. Such perfect correlation almost never occurs in real life. There are always the exceptions to the rule, the poor whites and the rich blacks in the Caribbean for example, that confound notions of how society is structured. In everyday interaction, the misplaced exactitude of stereotyping leads to incorrect assignment of persons to categories, manipulation of status by 'passing' from one category to another, and, perhaps, when stereotypes begin to consistently mispredict social status, the modification of the stereotype or the cognitions on which it is based.

Finally, the recognition of real or imagined associations of racial and cultural traits as expressed in commonly held stereotypes is often carried one step further, so that these interlinkages are popularly seen as having causal significance. The faulty logic that if an individual is of a certain race, then he must exhibit certain cultural traits as well, appeals to many peoples who have never benefitted from such scientific revelations as Boas' well known demonstration (Boas, 1940) of the independence of racial and cultural variables. Given such misguided causal theories, race can become reified as a cultural category in such a way that it does, in fact, take on a certain causal significance for behaviour *vis-à-vis* persons identified in terms of race.[2] Since certain racial characters are seen as necessarily linked to specified cultural and social traits, they may come to form the basis of legal codes or other prescribed behaviour patterns which are designed to ensure that race and culture do, in actuality, remain linked in morally defined ways.

Race and ethnicity in Meiganga today

As indicated above, race as a genetic phenomenon is not in itself sociologically significant but gains its importance in this regard from the social factors that are associated with it and the cultural beliefs that are based on it. For this reason, a discussion of race in Meiganga is best presented against a background of the ethnic groups resident in the area. The ethnic groups in the Meiganga region are, to a large degree, institutionally disparate and, to the extent that racial differences conform to ethnic boundaries, race derives its sociological attributes from its association with these discrete sets of institutions.

The majority ethnic group in the Meiganga area is the Gbaya

2. This is essentially the point made by Rex (1970, pp. 7 and 8).

numbering 33,850, a population of cultivators of negroid stock.[3] Next in numerical importance are the Mbororo, or pastoral Fulani, who total 19,218. Most Mbororo are tall, lithe, coppery-skinned people, and they are additionally distinguished by their economy which is based on transhumant cattle herding. Another Fulani group, the sedentary Fulani or Fulbe, also inhabit the Meiganga region in significant numbers (6617), practising a mixed economy of herding, trading, craft production and some agriculture. The Fulbe are a racially mixed population that arose through extensive interbreeding between sedentarized Fulani herders and the negroid populations which they dominated militarily, enslaved, and culturally assimilated.

The terminology to be applied to Fulani peoples in this paper must be made explicit since without careful definition, it is easy to confuse labels referring to cultural characteristics with those referring to genetically determined features. The potential for confusion arises from the commonly stated interpretation of Fulani culture history, based on oral traditions of the Fulani themselves, which suggests that the Fulani migrated into their present homeland as a culturally and racially uniform population of pastoralists. Since that time, different components of the Fulani population have adopted varying lifeways, which have resulted in highly variable patterns of intermarriage with surrounding negroid groups. Even if the notion of Fulani 'racial purity' was a genetically meaningful concept and could be objectively measured, it is almost certain that no such group could be located today.

Nonetheless, many members of Fulani groups exhibit a clearly defined physical type which differs markedly from the racial characteristics of the negroid groups near which they live. The most easily noticeable characteristics of such a Fulani is his lithe build, light coppery skin, aquiline nose and fine lips.[4] In this paper, when referring to such a complex of racial traits, I use the term 'Fulani'. I also employ the term 'Fulani' to refer to the common core of culture history which these peoples still

3. Census figures used are those of the 1966 Meiganga administrative census.
4. See Stenning (1959 p. 2), for added comments and bibliography on Fulani racial traits.

feel to be a socially binding force. I avoid confusion of the racial and cultural referents of 'Fulani' by carefully specifying my choice of meaning in the context in which I use the term. The terms 'Mbororo' and 'Fulbe' are used to denote the two main variants of the present-day culture of Fulani peoples, that of the pastoral Fulani as distinct from that of the sedentary Fulani.

The rest of the 64,022 population of the Meiganga region is distributed among ten census categories,[5] most of which refer to various negroid ethnic groups that have been fairly recent migrants to the region. There is considerable racial variability among these different negroid groups, particularly between the smaller forest peoples and the taller and more burly savanna-dwelling groups, yet these physical differences do not form the basis for social differentiation and thus need not be dealt with here.

The primary racial dichotomy[6] of significance to the peoples of the Meiganga region thus conforms to a certain degree to ethnic grouping; the majority population, the Gbaya, plus many of the smaller minorities resident in the area, are racially negroid while the second largest ethnic group, the Mbororo, is basically of Fulani racial type. Traditionally, Fulani peoples place a high value on their distinctive racial features and advance a racialist theory to account for what they perceive as a necessary interrelation between Fulani race and Fulani culture. In the Meiganga area, it is the Mbororo, the population that most closely accords with the Fulani racial ideal, who most ardently subscribe to this racially deterministic ideology. Because they are the most clearly enunciated and internally consistent system of belief, these

5. The ten 'ethnicities' listed in the 1966 Meiganga administrative census, in addition to the Gbaya, Mbororo, and Fulbe, were: Mbum, Bamileke, Hausa, Ewondo, Lakka, Bornuan, 'Congo' (immigrants from the neighbouring Central African Republic), 'Arabs' (North Africans and members of sub-Saharan ethnic groups speaking Arabic dialects), 'functionaries', and 'Europeans' (French and American missionaries plus a few merchants).

6. It could be argued that the white–black dichotomy in the former colonial African states remains the dominant racial ideology to the present day. This is probably true of the Meiganga region as well, although at present it is more latent than manifest due to the small number of whites (51) resident in the region. This article will therefore be focused only on what might be termed 'traditional' African ideologies of race.

Mbororo racialist theories usually serve as a reference point for discussion of the significance of race among Meiganga peoples. It seems appropriate, therefore, to describe the relations between race and culture in the Mbororo system prior to considering this topic for other ethnic groups.

The structural basis of Mbororo racial attitudes

The Mbororo share a number of cultural traits with their sedentary relatives, the Fulbe, including the use of *fulfulDe*[7] as a first language, the practice of Islam, a tradition of common origin, and a great interest in cattle. They are distinguishable from the Fulbe by their mobility as transhumant pastoralists, by the mode of exploitation of their cattle resources which emphasises the herd as a milk-producing unit rather than a beef herd, by their high rate of endogamy within the Mbororo group in general and their own patrilineal clans in particular, as well as by certain structural features in the political and kinship realms.

The traditional economy of the Mbororo is based entirely on the resources of their cattle herds although, as with many pastoral peoples, agricultural products contribute the majority of the calorie intake. These vegetal foods are normally secured through trade of milk and butter to neighbouring Gbaya cultivators. Increasingly, however, cash for food and clothes derives from sales of cattle to butchers and cattle traders. These occasional sales are normally more than balanced by the reproductive increase of the herd. The traditional Mbororo ethic strongly opposes such sales since they endanger the herding capital, and their regular occurrence indicates the increasing influence of the market economy over Mbororo values.

Older Mbororo informants believe that their distinctive way of life is endangered by the encroaching influences of surrounding sedentary societies. Cattle are the cornerstone of Mbororo life. Any sales or other tampering with the herds threatens more than a herder's standard of living; it imperils the very core of Mbororo

7. The spelling of *fulfulDe* words employed in this paper is basically that of Taylor, (1932). However, capital letters are employed to differentiate implosive 'B' and 'D' from the corresponding explosive consonants. Also, double vowels are substituted for Taylor's long vowels.

culture, for without sufficient cattle, an Mbororo is not free to practise his highly mobile lifeways. He is forced to settle down, to cultivate or to trade for a living, in short, to become a Fulbe.

Contact with the town also exposes an Mbororo to the risk of marrying a non-Mbororo, an act that automatically condemns him to a sedentary existence, since only Mbororo girls are trained or willing to support the difficult nomadic life. The Mbororo view this problem of intermarriage as a problem of dilution of racial purity, since possession of Fulani racial traits is thought to entail commitment to *pulaaku*, the traditional system of Fulani culture and values that is well suited to the herding life. This belief in the dangers of outbreeding finds structural expression in the Mbororo practice of *kooggal*, or preferential cousin marriage, which has been extensively documented by Stenning (1959).

The custom of preferential cousin marriage effectively links racial traits to success in cattle herding since, particularly in the patrilateral parallel cousin (father's brother's daughter) marriages that are most preferred by the Mbororo, endogamy ensures that the cattle owned by clan members are inherited within the clan. Specifically, herds that were split up due to the custom of partitive inheritance among male siblings are reconstituted when the children of these men intermarry in the next generation. Such patterns of endogamous marriage, of course, also preserve the genetic isolation of the clan so that inbreeding and succesful herd management are interconnected, if not in a causal manner. It is not surprising, in view of this clearly apparent, if non-causal, correlation between marriage patterns and control of cattle, that Mbororo ideology postulates a contingent relation between race and culture. As Stenning explains:

Kooggal marriage maintains and fortifies moral virtues, but also, though in a somewhat negative sense, conserves the physical type of the clan. The desirable physical qualities of a Fulani are a light colour, slight bone-structure, straight hair, thin lips, and, above all, a long narrow nose. Members of some WoDaaBe (an Mbororo sub-group) groups in which there has been a high degree of endogamy take pride in what is often their distinctive facial likeness, and in commenting upon it say: 'We are all of one stock' (*Min iriiri go'o*). But, in general Fulani can no longer correlate these desirable physical traits with lines of descent. Then the association becomes curiously reversed so that a man or woman possessing these features is regarded as being more likely to possess the moral virtues of a Fulani. A WoDaaBe proverb runs: *Raara kine nana gikku* – ('See the nose, understand the character'). By definition, Haabe, or non-Fulani, cannot possess these qualities, for they do not follow the Fulani way (1959, pp. 56–7).

In spite of the normative emphasis on the maintenance of Mbororo ethnic and racial boundaries via endogamy and assiduous management of cattle resources, there is a continual, if small, flow of population in and out of Mbororo society. This results both from the pressures to sell off the herd alluded to above and from the ecological fact that success in herd management is inevitably variable. Those who either fail to maintain a herd of viable size or those who are so successful as to develop particularly large herds tend to sedentarize, at least temporarily. Settlements exist in the Meiganga region of Mbororo whose members have been forced to undertake cultivation to secure an adequate subsistence, but these people are usually actively working to build up a herd again so that they may resume a transhumant life. Very successful Mbororo succumb to the ease of sedentary life – managing their numerous herds from a fixed location in or near a town. These individuals, particularly if elderly, tend to remain sedentary for the rest of their lives, and it is to their children that the choice is presented of permanently rejecting the old mobile ways in favour of a life modelled on that of the sedentary Fulbe town-dwellers. In the case of such sedentarized Mbororo, interbreeding with co-resident negroid populations inevitably occurs despite the value commitment against it. However, the offspring of these unions, contracted on the margins of Mbororo society, usually grow up as Fulbe rather than Mbororo. Children of miscegenous unions seldom return to the nomadic life and are thus only occasionally incorporated into the Mbororo category.

This phenomenon of loss of Mbororo population to the Fulbe category once again calls attention to this complex intermediate grouping, where certain traditional Fulani customs are practised by a population which, in the majority, is racially non-Fulani. Given traditional Fulani beliefs in racial and cultural interlinkages, the Fulbe category exhibits many contradictions between fact and ideology. Such contradictions are quite significant in that they allow considerable status mobility within the Fulbe social system. But, before considering the effects of these contradictions, it is necessary to explain briefly the historical development of Fulbe society so that we can see the sources of this racial heterogeneity.

The historical basis of Fulbe racial heterogeneity

The Fulbe presence in the Meiganga area dates at least to the early 19th century, when the Adamawa region of Nigeria and Cameroon was conquered in a Moslem holy war (*jihad*) by Fulbe clans owing allegiance to the emir of Yola. The town of Ngaoundere to the north of the Meiganga region, which had been founded by a section of the Mbum tribe, was conquered by one of the Fulbe groups and became the capital of a Fulbe principality which exercised nominal control over the Gbaya of Meiganga. The Fulbe were primarily interested in the Meiganga area and its environs as a source of slaves, which were captured in annual military expeditions during the dry season months. Initially, many Gbaya were taken in these raids, but soon important Gbaya clans entered into tribute-paying relations with the Fulbe of Ngaoundere and undertook to raid slaves from neighbouring tribes to pay this tribute. The Lakka tribe of southern Tchad took the brunt of these raids which continued well into the colonial period, the last recorded large-scale raid being held just prior to World War I.

The Fulbe who conquered the Adamawa region including Ngaoundere had migrated from Nigeria where they had been influenced by the Hausa and Kanuri patterns of political administration and slavery. (cf. Smith, 1954, pp. 239–91; 1959, pp. 239–52). Slaves (*machuBe*), when first captured in raids, were taken back to Ngaoundere where some were sent on to the emir of Yola as a part of the tribute due to him. The remaining slaves were distributed among the titled Fulbe nobles and the *laamiiDo*, the ruler of Ngaoundere. Most newly captured slaves were settled in slave villages (*duumDe*, singular – *ruumDe*), each of which owed an annual tribute in grain to its overlord. Such slave villages were the productive cores of Fulbe states and also supplied many of the foot soldiers in military operations. A noble's wealth and political following could be measured by the number of slave villages under his control. Some of these stemmed from his own slave raiding activities and others formed part of a corporate estate he controlled by virtue of being awarded a titled office by the ruler.

Other slaves became a part of the household of the ruler where they acted as a staff of servants and caretakers that was permanently attached to that office. Many of the female slaves were incorporated into the harems of the ruler and his nobles.

Second generation slaves (*riimaiBe*, singular – *diimaajo*, from the verb *rima* – 'to bear seed or produce young', (see Taylor, 1932, p. 158), who were raised as Moslems from birth, enjoyed certain advantages under Islamic law over first generation slaves. Such second generation slaves could not be sold, and their status became that of clients permanently attached to their master's household. Slave concubines who bore children by their masters were manumitted at his death. The offspring of these unions enjoyed equal jural status with children of the master's marriages to free women (*reedu rimDini mo* – the womb freed him) (cf. Taylor, 1932, p. 158; Stenning, 1959, p. 66). Slaves could also be freed (*rimDina* – to set free; *rimDinaaBe*, singular – *dimDinaa Do* – freed men) by their masters, and it was not uncommon that upon the death of the master, his testament would provide for the freeing of trusted slaves.

Certain slaves, particularly those in the service of the ruler, wielded great power even though they were not legally free. Frequently, the ruler relied more heavily on the trust of those slaves who served in key administrative positions than he did on that of his titled relatives who might enter into plots to wrest power from him.

If slave status was not a good guide to an individual's political power, membership in the Fulani racial section of Fulbe society was not a good criterion for judging political or economic status either. As indicated above, children of racially mixed unions between concubines and masters gained their status from their fathers and could inherit great wealth and power. On the other hand, competition between different branches of high-ranking Fulbe clans was intense and often resulted in the virtual destitution, both political and economic, of formerly high-ranking individuals despite their physical conformation to Fulani racial ideals. They became poor commoners (*talaka'en*, singular – *talakaajo*) but remained free men (*rimBe*, singular – *dimo*) with no directly traceable blot of slavery on their ancestry.

Thus, although the levels of social stratification in the Fulbe system based on wealth and power were not racially definable, race remained culturally significant because of its connection with the institution of slavery. The *fulfulDe* vocabulary relating to slave status contained implicit racial referents as shown in the following chart.

Table 1 Vocabulary relating to slave status

Term	Implicit racial referent
machuDo slave	non-Fulani
diimaajo second generation slave	non-Fulani (but Islamicized)
dimDinaaDo freed man	no more than one Fulani parent
dimo free man	at least one generation removed from slave (negroid) parentage

Race and social mobility in post-colonial Fulbe society

Slavery was abolished at the beginning of the colonial era and with its disappearance, one more institutional support to racial differentiation was removed. Opportunity for social mobility also expanded as economic development touched northern Cameroon and as the traditional Fulbe states surrendered much of their power to the national government. Cattle husbandry and trade presented particularly good chances for individual economic gain no matter what one's initial social status or racial affinities. The *gaynaako* (paid herdsman) system, which continues to be popular today, offered the chance for a man to constitute his own herd, since herdsmen were paid in calves. Although such work is arduous, a man can start with nothing and, with luck and diligence, eventually become independently wealthy in cattle.

In post-independence Cameroon, such economic possibilities are combined with the fact that the Cameroon national government and single political party is Fulbe-dominated and, at least in the regional government of north Cameroon, Fulbe have favoured access to political advantages and office. As a result of these and other economic and political facts it is currently highly advantageous to be identified with the Fulbe category, and many members of non-Fulani ethnic groups are becoming 'Fulbe-ized'. That such 'passing' from one ethnic group to another is possible is due, for the most part, to the highly heterogeneous racial composition of Fulbe society, which means that members of negroid ethnic groups wishing to join the Fulbe category cannot be identified as non-Fulbe purely on the basis of race. The Gbaya of Meiganga, the major negroid ethnic group which I studied, are involved in this phenomenon of 'passing' to a certain extent, although both my casual observation and reading on other negroid ethnic groups of northern Cameroon would suggest that they are perhaps not the best example of this phenomenon.

Gaining admission to Fulbe society is relatively simple, and an individual need qualify on only three counts – language, religion and overt consensus to Fulbe ideals of ethnic and racial superiority. Most inhabitants of northern Cameroon, regardless of their ethnic status, at least speak 'market' *fulfulDe* as a vehicular language. This 'pidgin' *fulfulDe* is a far cry from 'pure' *fulfulDe*, being most notably simplified through suppression of phonetic chiasmus and reduction in the number of verb tenses. However, there being no minimal accepted standard of accomplishment in *fulfulDe*, many 'Fulbe' speak miserable *fulfulDe*, having shifted ethnic allegiance and language during their lifetimes. Thus, language does not pose an effective barrier to admission to Fulbe life, although accomplishment in the language has sociolinguistic significance as an internal ranking mechanism.

The practice of Islam is likewise a *pro forma* prerequisite for entrance into Fulbe society. To demonstrate one's allegiance to the faith, it is only necessary to perform the five daily prayers and, since these may be said inaudibly, there is no means for others to check an individual's mastery of the Koranic verses. Like language, however, relative devotion to Islam allows great scope for internal Fulbe social ranking, with many institutions such as Koranic schools, religious orders, and the pilgrimage, and numerous symbols including writing tablets, charms, rosary beads, and various items of clothing forming the basis for differentiation of status of individuals in the religious sphere.

Consensus to Fulbe ideals of ethnic and racial superiority is also a simple step, formally speaking, although one might guess that it is the most difficult one from a physchological point of view. Fulbe are extremely disdainful of other peoples, openly using the insulting terms 'haaBe' (subject pagans), 'machuBe' (slaves), and 'baleejo' (black man) to refer to members of non-Fulani groups. To be a member of Fulbe society, one must be willing to join in such in-group talk, even when the insults are directed at one's previous ethnic group. This change in values appears to be most easily accomplished when an individual is living apart from members of his former ethnic group who might otherwise continue to interact with him in terms of his old culture.

This tendency for Gbaya to opt for Fulbe ethnic status when living outside their home region, in a Fulbe-dominated area is demonstrated by the fact that many Gbaya now living at the city of Ngaoundere have became acculturated to Fulbe custom, particularly to those traits which are highly visible in face-to-face interaction. For example, most Gbaya at Ngaoundere practice Islam (compared to only 44 per cent in Meiganga) (Callies, 1968, p.50)[8] and make overt displays of their daily prayers. Both men and women employ fulfulDe extensively, even in the home, so much so that when they return to their natal villages in Meiganga to visit, they have difficulty speaking Gbaya without a great admixture of fulfulDe vocabulary. Gbaya acculturation at Ngaoundere is also immediately noticeable in the style of dress and ornamentation of both men and women. Men prefer flowing robes to western-style dress. The women follow Fulbe styles including the wearing of a nose ring in the side of one of the nostrils, the use of a long piece of material as a head scarf so that it drapes down the back, and the application of cosmetics such as henna and antimony. In practising such behavioural traits,

8. Some authors see 'Islamicization' as the key to the process of acculturation operative in Northern Cameroon although I would argue that religious change is only one of many cultural adjustments experienced by individuals attempting to ally themselves with the dominant Fulbe presence.

Gbaya become indistinguishable, in casual interactions with strangers, from the rest of the Fulbe population. Their racial type is no clue to their ethnicity. Race is a particularly bad predictor of ethnic status at Ngaoundere, since there has been a very high rate of interbreeding between Fulani conquerors and Mbum (negroid) subjects for about one hundred and fifty years.

Back in Meiganga, Gbaya do not 'pass' to Fulbe ethnic status nearly as frequently. This is partly due to the fact, as suggested earlier, that manipulation of ethnic status is not as easy or useful when an individual is living among fellow Gbaya who have known him from birth. It is also due to the fact that an effective alternative model for social mobility through 'westernization' exists in the Meiganga region, which is in relatively close contact with the Christian and western influences of the educated black Africans of southern Cameroon. Since consideration of the competing influences of southern and northern Cameroon on the Gbaya of the Meiganga region is beyond the scope of this paper, I can only assert my view that the existence of an alternative model probably reduces the rate of 'Fulbeization' of the Gbaya.

Why do Fulbe racialist attitudes persist?

The main thrust of my discussion of race and social mobility in Fulbe society has been that, given certain legal, marital, economic, and political conditions, membership in the Fulani racial category is not a prerequisite for mobility in the economic or political hierarchies of Fulbe society. Analysing this situation from the deterministic point of view that racial classifications can only continue to function when they are symbolic of structurally generated patterns of stratification or ethnic grouping, one would be led to foresee the inevitable disappearance of Fulbe racialist attitudes. Such a causal sequence may operate in some cases, but the Fulbe example does not seem to support such a view. It has been over one hundred and fifty years since the Fulbe states in Adamawa were first established and over fifty years since slavery was effectively abolished – ample time, it would seem, for racial ideologies to come into line with a structural situation which offers virtually no concrete advantages to individuals of Fulani phenotypes. Why, then, has race remained significant in the Fulbe culture of Meiganga?

The answer to this problem relates to the phenomenon of reification of cultural categories discussed at the beginning of this paper and can be approached via consideration of Fulbe marital preferences and patterns and their genetic correlates. Throughout Fulbe society, there is a clearly expressed interest in marrying women who conform to the Fulani racial ideal. When I was in Cameroon, the vogue was to marry 'one of those light-skinned Garoua women', and rich men were prepared to pay bride prices in the neighbourhood of 100,000 CFA (about £150) for such wives. As several Fulbe informants expressed it to me, the rationale for marrying women of Fulani racial type, in addition to that of their superior beauty, was that they would produce light-skinned children who would be more intelligent because of their conformation to the Fulani racial ideal. When I remarked that Fulani women were notoriously less fertile than women of non-Fulbe groups, one informant responded that a few bright children were preferable to a host of dark-skinned dullards.

Of course, as explained above, rich men are not necessarily of Fulani racial type, and I noted a considerable number of marriages between light-skinned Fulbe women and very dark-skinned Fulbe (or Hausa or Choa Arab) merchants. On the other hand, given the Fulbe racialist ideology, it is to be anticipated that the parents of Fulani girls would prefer husbands for their daughters who were of similar racial type, if such a man was available who could afford the high bride price. Although Fulbe practise preferential cousin marriage to a much smaller extent than Mbororo the custom may contribute somewhat to positive assortative mating (i.e. like marrying like).

Despite these racially specific marital preferences, it seems hardly likely that there is sufficient positive assortative mating between members of Fulbe society of Fulani racial type to maintain anything like a 'pure stock'. In fact, as indicated at the outset of this paper, the assumption of the existence of such a 'pure Fulani stock' would be extremely tenuous even if such a concept made sense in terms of human population genetics. It seems virtually certain, given:

1. The differential reproductive success of the Fulbe versus surrounding negroid ethnic groups.[9]

2. The simple numerical preponderance of the total negroid population to the total Fulbe population in northern Cameroon, approximately 879,000 to 278,000 in 1961. (Callies, 1968, pp. 8, 9).

3. The continued 'passing' of non-Fulani into the Fulbe social category, that the modal racial characteristics of the Fulbe are progressively shifting toward the negroid end of the spectrum.

But, it is important to realise that in considering Fulani racial ideals, we are not dealing with absolutes. No member of Fulbe society today has seen what the Fulani of one hundred years ago looked like. The Fulani racial ideal is simply a relative concept; relative lightness of skin, relative narrowness of nose, relative wideness of lips, etc., are significant; not some objectively measured ideal racial characteristic. What is more, since skin colour and most bodily features are polygenetic traits, i.e. they are determined by genes at more than one chromosomal locus, it follows that there will normally be wide ranges of phenotypic variation in each of these characteristics in a heterogeneous population like that of the Fulbe, no matter whether mating is random or somewhat positively assorting (Stern, 1960, pp. 351–9). In practice, given Fulbe racial ideals, some positive assortative mating will certainly occur, which should make for even greater representation at the extremes of the distributions of racial traits. In short, there will inevitably be members of Fulbe society who look more 'Fulani' than the rest, and this variation will probably be sufficient to allow continued recognition of a 'Fulani ideal type'.

At this point, the economic and marital argument reinjects itself. Fulbe men continue to be willing to pay more for wives of Fulani racial type. Such girls would seem to have little in the way of utilitarian qualities to recommend them as wives: they cost more, they add nothing extra to the family income, they are not necessarily profitable as political alliances, and they are probably less fertile than non-Fulani women. If the only reason for their preference is that they will produce light-skinned child-

9. The average number of live births for a woman of north Cameroon was calculated at 4·8. The average for the Fulbe of the Adamawa region was 3·78. For the Gbaya, it was 5·22 (Callies, 1968, p. 62).

ren who are allegedly more intelligent, this is simply an indirect way of saying that cultural categorizations, not structural principles, are determining marital behaviour. The same is obviously true of marital preferences based on beauty or prestige. It seems clear that cultural categorizations, which historically developed out of differential incorporation of racially distinctive ethnic groups, have taken on causal significance of their own with respect to racially specific marital frequencies and brideprice rates in the Fulbe society of Meiganga today.

Conclusion

Although the analysis just presented concerning the importance of racial ideology versus social structure in Fulbe marriage choice has appeal, there are some indeterminate aspects of the argument that must be considered. To begin with, to say that present-day behaviour is being influenced by cultural values rooted in the past is to accept the primacy of historical explanations over those of sociology. Admittedly, Fulbe racialist ideologies may have been generated by structural conditions of fifty to one hundred years ago, yet we are then faced with a time lag of at least fifty years during which ideology would seem not to have adjusted to the abolition of slavery and other colonial and post-colonial structural changes.

Alternatively, it might be claimed that the racial ideology which plays such an important role in the marriage sphere is, in fact, generated by structural conditions operative at a more inclusive level. Thus, for example, de facto patterns of Fulbe political and economic favouritism may, in some parts of Cameroon, include racialist practices that are not particularly evident in the Meiganga region, which is somewhat removed from the centres of traditional Fulbe power further north and east. This de facto behaviour may, in turn, be the source of the racially-specific ideologies that continue to affect marital behaviour in Meiganga.

A comparable hypothesis might envision that Mbororo racialist ideologies, which are clearly structurally generated in their society, also affect Fulbe society and support positive assortative mating there as well. In Meiganga, Fulbe are in frequent contact with Mbororo and, in view of the historical connections between the two peoples, it is possible that Fulbe attempt to emulate their Mbororo cousins, who are representatives of a more 'pure' Fulani race and culture.

Both of these alternative hypotheses, however, raise theroetical problems which are beyond the scope of this paper and the pursuit of which would require more extensive field investigations. Traditional anthropology has been built on a concept of discrete societies ('tribes'), each with its own internally consistent set of beliefs and values. In complex and pluralistic social settings, anthropologists are somewhat at a loss to determine what beliefs relate to what social units, and the problem of boundaries looms correspondingly large in the analysis. There is also the problem that complex societies often are characterized by internally contradictory sets of beliefs, differing fundamentally, at least in theory, from the classic social anthropological model of the 'tribal' society where culture is usually considered to be a functional support to social structure. The Meiganga case illustrates many of these problems and provides the interesting contrast between Mbororo society with its consistent set of racial beliefs and Fulbe society with its structural and cultural conradictions.

References

BANTON, M. (1967), *Race Relations*, Tavistock.

BOAS, F. (1940), *Race, Language and Culture*, Macmillan.

CALLIES, J. M. (1968), *Enquête Démographique au Cameroun: Résultats definitifs pour la Région Nord, 1962–4*, Service de la Statistique, République du Cameroun.

REX, J. (1970), *Race Relations in Sociological Theory*, Weidenfeld & Nicolson.

SMITH, M. G. (1954), 'Slavery and emancipation in two societies', *J. Soc. and Econ. Stud.*, vol. 3.

SMITH, M. G. (1959), 'The Hausa system of social status', *Africa*, vol. 29, pp. 239–52.

SMITH, M. G. (1969), 'Institutional and political conditions of pluralism', in L. Kuper and M. G. Smith, (eds.) *Pluralism in Africa*, University of California Press.

STENNING, D. (1959), *Savannah Nomads*, International African Institute.

STERN, K. (1960), *Principles of Human Genetics*, W. H. Freeman.

TAYLOR, F. W. (1932), *A Fulani-English Dictionary*, Oxford University Press.

25 Valdo Pons

'Les Races de Kisangani':
Tribal Colonies in an African Town

Adapted by Valdo Pons from his *Stanleyville: An African Urban Community under Belgian Administration*, Oxford University Press for the International African Institute, 1969, pp. 62–100 and p. 145.

This reading presents an analysis of variations in the social configurations of tribal colonies in the Congolese town of Kisangani (formerly Stanleyville) as it was in the early 1950s. As in many African towns, the population was drawn from a variety of tribes and the consequent social and cultural heterogeneity had far-reaching significance in day to day life. The inhabitants commonly perceived and classified each other as persons with differing allegiances and loyalties, with differing modes and norms of behaviour, and with differing customs and traditions. Cultural diversity was a commonplace feature of the local scene, and its deep significance was strikingly underlined by the frequent use when speaking in French of the term *race* rather than *tribu* to refer to tribes. Thus, quite typically, on making enquiries about a new arrival or a new acquaintance, a man might well ask of another: '*Qui est-il? Quelle est sa race?*' Once a man's *race* had been established, certain predictions and assumptions could possibly be made about his social connections or about certain aspects of his behaviour.

Establishing an individual's tribal identity was, however, not always done through direct questioning. It could equally be a process conducted through observation over time. To appreciate this we have to consider the nature and variety of the ways in which members of different tribes could be identified. Some tribes or groups of tribes could be distinguished with varying degrees of precision on the basis of facial marks or other physical peculiarities (e.g. the elongated skulls of the Mangbetu and related tribes whose custom it was to strap heads in babyhood). Often, too, ethnic identification could be established with a relatively high degree of accuracy on the basis of certain features of dress and ornamentation, or on the possession of distinctive articles of native manufacture such as stools, kitchen utensils, and musical instruments, which commonly varied in type and style from one tribe to another or, perhaps, from one region or culture cluster of the hinterland to another. Again, identification was usually possible for persons with the requisite knowledge on the basis of speech which might be in a vernacular tongue or which, even if in Swahili or Lingala (the two *linguae francae* of the town), was liable to include a phrase in a vernacular tongue or particular expressions which betrayed one or other ethnic background. The very fact of whether a person tended to speak more spontaneously in Swahili or Lingala was an indicator of some reliability as to whether he or she came from the east or the west, and so on. Yet again, there were some gross behavioural indicators, such as style of native dancing, and there were more subtle ones in certain minor mannerisms. There were equally broad indirect indicators related to urban occupations and practices. Thus, for example, anyone who had lived in the town for some time would know that a white-collar worker was more likely, other things being equal, to be a Lokele than, say, a Topoke, though on the basis of a number of other possible criteria the cultural affinity between these two tribes might well have led to a man from the north or the east to fail to distinguish between them. Similarly, an experienced Kisangani dweller would always, other things being equal be more likely to assume that a fashionable *femme libre* was a Mubua, and that a woman trading on the market was a Lokele, rather than the other way round.

Various characteristics were frequently attributed to members of one or other tribe or *race*. Some of these were clearly associated with traditional customs and cultures though others stemmed from differences in the social configurations of the urban colonies of the various tribes. Differing histories and patterns of urban incorporation and settlement, and differing modes of urban economic involvement, had combined with both cultural and demographic differences to produce a wide variety of colonies. The purpose of the analysis which follows is to illustrate the extent of variation in their patterns of urban accommodation.

Tribal composition of the population and patterns of residence

At the time of this study the African population of Kisangani numbered about 41,000. With 6400 members the Lokele constituted 15·4 per cent of the total and were the largest single colony in the town. Next came the *Arabisés* who, though not a tribal group, constituted an equally distinctive ethnic element; with about 4,900 members they made up 11·8 per cent of the total. Following the Lokele and the *Arabisés* were seven tribes – the Babua, Bakumu, Topoke, Bambole, Babali, Balengola, and Bamanga with about 1000 to 4000 members each. The nine principal colonies together accounted for about two-thirds of the total population, the remaining third consisting of members of numerous, smaller colonies.

Some measure of residential concentration in Kisangani was a notable feature of most colonies, but there was considerable variation in its nature and extent. Some colonies were largely concentrated in only one of the three main townships of Kisangani with no appreciable concentration elsewhere. For example 89·4 per cent of the Bamanga lived in one township, and 74·6 per cent of the Bambole were in another. Other colonies were settled mainly in one township but also had a second smaller, though still substantial, concentration in another. The Babali, for example had 59 per cent of their members in one township, and 34·1 per cent in the second, but were scarcely represented in the third. Yet again, there were colonies, like the Topoke, with substantial proportions in each of the three townships.

The tendency towards residential concentration was in part a function of the geographical position of the townships in relation to routes of access from tribal areas in the hinterland. In most cases the main concentration of a tribe was found in the township closest to the roads, or in the case of the Lokele, to the river, of access to the towns from the countryside.

Although the degrees of dispersion and concentration varied considerably from one colony to another, the general pattern of settlement was one of significant concentrations in small neighbourhoods within the townships. In some areas there were marked tribal clusters in one or two avenues, and sometimes even in one section of a single avenue.

Three case histories

The cases of three particular tribes – the Lokele, the Babua, and the Topoke – may be used to illustrate the kind of relation encountered between differing modes of urban incorporation and differing social configurations in town.

The Lokele are a river people, whose tribal homes are situated in a narrow stretch of exceptionally fertile and densely populated land along the banks of the Congo River, starting a few miles downstream from Kisangani. They had the reputation in the town of being the most skilled fishermen and canoe navigators on the river. They first came to Kisangani when it was no more than a small commercial centre and administrative outpost. They settled on the left bank of the river where they were for years the only significant colony of immigrants, and where they continued to lead a domestic and neighbourhood life in many ways akin to that in their tribal areas. They were advantageously placed to engage in fishing and in the growing urban trade in articles of native manufacture and in agricultural produce. Their early establishment as an urban colony thus took place without creating any sharp discontinuity between town and village.

With easy access to their home areas and with cheap canoe transport on the river, Lokele women found themselves in a very favourable position to compete against women of other tribes for the control of the Kisangani markets in fish, vegetables and fruits. Over the years they came to be the dominant and most successful group of women traders in the town. Lokele men expected their womenfolk to trade regularly whereas the trading activities of most non-Lokele women were usually casual and intermittent. A Lokele woman brought to her marriage a dowry which she was expected to invest in trade, and there were some cases of Lokele women who made trading profits equal to or higher than the wages earned by their husbands.

The commercial success of Lokele women was a basic factor in the integration of Lokele urban society. It brought to the Lokele a measure of wealth which set them off from other tribes economically and contributed to the maintainance of their ethnic identity. The comparative wealth of Lokele families enabled boys of the tribe to compete with considerable success for education and for white-collar jobs. Nearly 20 per cent of Lokele men were white-collar workers, a figure significantly higher than for any other tribe; and, conversely, the proportion who were ordinary labourers was considerably lower than average. A small but important minority of Lokele men also entered retail trade in non-native goods such as bottled beer, tinned foods and cigarettes.

The Lokele's achievements in all these respects brought them the reputation of being 'clever' and 'superior' to most other tribes. In casual conversation people frequently named them as the tribe with an ability to get on, and they were sometimes held to rank with well-known African tribes of whom the local inhabitants either had no direct experience or whom they only knew through a few inhabitants in the town (e.g. the Baganda, the Hausa, the 'Senegalais', the 'Coastmen', and the Bakongo). At other times they were compared with the *Arabisés* who 'were the rulers here before the Europeans', or with the Azande who were sometimes singled out on account of their legendary military and technological prowess ('they knew how to make guns').

The comparative wealth of the Lokele combined with the success and industriousness of their women had contributed to the stabilization of their bridewealth payments at a very much higher-than-average level for the town. Few men who were not themselves Lokele could hope to marry a Lokele woman. Nor, under the normal circumstances, could a Lokele man meet obligations to his wife's family without considerable assistance from his own kinsmen. The woman of the tribe had the reputation of being particularly virtuous and the surveillance of Lokele parents over their daughters was claimed by some to be as strict in town as in their tribal villages. This was in turn related to the fact that the Lokele continued in their changing urban situation to attach exceptionally high value to the continuity of family life. It was rather exceptional for a Lokele woman to be unmarried. At the same time, there was, in sharp contrast to many other tribes, notably the Babua referred to below, a strong emphasis on the preservation of traditional values relating to a man's role as husband, father, and kinsman.

The Lokele remained residentially concentrated on the left bank of the river in an area of one township, where there were few non-Lokele. It was largely to this area that new Lokele immigrants turned to find accommodation and other assistance from kinsmen and friends on their first arrival in town. There was thus a whole complex of relations in which rural and urban life were intimately interwoven, while marriage, the rearing of children, and other aspects of domestic and neighbourhood life, continued in town, as in the country, to be largely enacted within a distinctively Lokele setting.

In sharp contrast to the Lokele, the Babua were said to have a weak sense of tribal solidarity associated with a relative indifference about the continuity of family life. They came from an area some 300 kilometres to the north of Kisangani and, on leaving their villages, they normally migrated to the small town of Buta in the first instance. In the early days of European colonization, they had acquired the reputation of making good soldiers. Substantial numbers had been drafted into the *Force Publique*, and the first settlement of Babua in the early days of Kisangani's growth was made up of discharged soldiers. In more recent years, they had acquired a similar reputation as good lorry drivers, a skill which they tended to pass on to new arrivals in the town. The survey sample of Babua wage-earners in fact contained 16 per cent of lorry drivers (as against 6 per cent in the population as a whole), and they also had appreciably higher-than-average proportions of mechanics and masons. Among European employers, the Babua had the general reputation of being good and efficient workers, and their services were much in demand.

As members of one of the oldest tribal colonies in the town, they enjoyed substantial advantages over more recent immigrants. We shall see that a high proportion of Babua household heads were title-holders of compounds, and that they frequently took in rent-paying tenants. We shall also see that only a small minority of Babua men had married in their tribal areas. Both at home and in Kisangani the tribe had a rate of fertility so low that it seems certain that as a population they were declining in numbers. The women of the tribe showed a strong spirit of independence from their men folk, a fact which commonly drew comments of disapprobation from members of tribes like the Lokele who placed great store on large families and on virtuous women. Moreover, Babua men and women commonly married members of other tribes. Over a third of all Babua men in the sample were married to non-Babua women and, for marriages taking place in Kisangani itself, the proportion was even higher. Nearly a half of all Babua men and women in the town were not married. In striking contrast to Lokele women it was not uncommon for Babua women to live singly or with partners to whom they were not married.

Both the Lokele and the Babua were among the tribes most involved in the life of the town, though in very different ways. The contrast between them makes the point that in studying different colonies we may be studying differing processes of urban incorporation. The Lokele were, in their family, domestic, and neighbourhood relations, a relatively 'closed' group, maintaining and developing a distinctively Lokele urban way of life, and their urban situation calls for analysis in the context of a social and cultural system embracing both town and village. In contrast, the Babua colony was made up of individuals many of whom were not in touch with their villages, and such relations as there were between town and tribal area were much less relevant to an analysis of their life in town than in the case of the Lokele. Moreover, the Babua's way of life in town had relatively little distinctive cultural content; there is a sense in which their way of urban life was 'the Kisangani way of life', developed by persons with little continuing participation in rural-tribal life.

Our third case, the Topoke, had a social configuration markedly different to that of either Babua or Lokele. Though coming from a tribal area adjacent to that of the Lokele and, in some parts, no further than 100 kilometres from Kisangani, the Topoke were in the early years of colonization little affected by the development of the wage-earning economy or by missionaries; it was not till the 1930s that they entered wage-earning employment to any appreciable extent, and the growth of their colony in Kisangani dates mainly from World War Two and the immediate post-war period. By 1952 they had about 3000 members settled in town and their rate of immigration far exceeded the rate for most of the principal ethnic colonies. Though many Topoke men had been to mission schools in their tribal area for a few years, they came to town principally as ordinary labourers. As compared to the Babua and Lokele, who had nuclei of well-established fellow-tribesmen in the town, the Topoke had less possibility of being accommodated by kinsmen on first arrival or of getting assistance in finding job openings or of acquiring a modicum of occupational skills from established specialized manual workers. Only a third of all Topoke households had their own dwelling compounds as against two thirds of the Lokele and three quarters of the Babua. And such dwelling compounds as were held by Topoke title-holders were usually crowded with subsidiary households of kinsmen and fellow villagers. Moreover, the colony had an excessively disproportionate ratio of men to women, many of the young men being unmarried or having left their wives at home. Such Topoke as could not find accommodation with kinsmen were commonly encountered as rent-paying tenants, sharing rooms in twos and threes on the compounds of members of other tribes.

The women were, with very few exceptions, married. Few Topoke families had been in town long enough to have adult urban-bred daughters, and the few women who found themselves widowed or divorced in the town seldom qualified – according to the administrative regulations in force under Belgian rule – to stay there as residents in their own right. Like the Lokele, the Topoke had a high birth rate and large families. Except for youths, a high proportion of the men were married, and the younger men who had come to town unmarried usually recruited brides from their home villages in preference to Kisangani women.

Being predominantly recent unskilled immigrants, few Topoke men had diverse sets of social relations such as those which typically linked the Babua, and even to some extent the Lokele, to other members of the urban population. They were known in the town as an 'uncivilized' and 'backward' tribe. Their wide dispersal through all three of the townships in Kisangani was a direct consequence of their late arrival on the urban scene and of their high rate of influx at the time of the present study. As new immigrants in a generally disadvantageous position to compete with other tribes in town, the Topoke attached exceptional importance to their home villages as sources of security and as places to which to return in the event of unexpected difficulties in town. At the same time the pressure of an increasing population in their tribal area was an important factor keeping them in town.

The Lokele, Babua and Topoke were all somewhat exceptional colonies. The Lokele were unique in being the only colony to enjoy the advantages of the particular combinations of cheap and easy access to the town, and an agricultural surplus in their home areas, and of a growing population and a well-established position in the town's markets, offices and workshops. The Babua and Topoke were not unique, but they were both exceptional in that each exhibited in high degree various characteristics which were common to many tribes but which were seldom found in such striking combinations. The Bamanga, for example, had a reputation similar to that of the Topoke for being 'backward' and 'uncivilized', but their position in town was less difficult owing to a longer history of wage-earning, to a lower current rate of immigration, and to having a somewhat larger nucleus of well-established urban dwellers. Or, to take another example, the Babali had many of the features of the Babua, but had been rather less successful in the field of employment.

Variation in social and demographic composition

The presence in one community of tribal colonies differing as markedly as did the Lokele, Babua, and Topoke, holds important implications for the study of urban social relations. Some of these implications emerge more clearly as we examine a series of data on the social and demographic composition of the nine largest tribal colonies in the town. On the basis of the demographic data we are able to detect three main 'types' of age and sex structures, and it will be seen that the Lokele, Babua and Topoke, are good examples of each of these three 'types'.

Figs 1 to 9 depict the population pyramids of the nine principal ethnic colonies. Inspection of the pyramids suggests that seven of the nine colonies fall into three 'types' and that the two remaining tribes can be seen as intermediate cases. Type A is represented by the Lokele (Figure 1): it has a broad base tending to become steadily narrower with increasing age. Type B is best represented by the Topoke (Figure 3): it has a broad base like the pyramid for Type A, but is pinched at the 'waist' (between the ages of five and fifteen years) and then broadens between the ages of fifteen and thirty-five years before again narrowing very rapidly above the age of thirty-five years. Type C, which is best represented by the Babali (Figure 9) is more in the shape of an onion than a pyramid: the base of children is narrow, the figure bulges in the middle, and the decline in the older age groups is more gradual than in Type B, leaving a proportion of adults over forty-five years approximately equal to the proportion of children below sixteen years of age. Of the remaining principal tribes, the Babua (Figure 8) and the *Arabisés* (Figure 7) fit Type C. fairly well, the Bambole (Figure 2) and Balengola (Figure 4) tend to fit Type B, while the Bamanga (Figure 5) and Bakumu (Figure 6) are the two intermediate cases which can be viewed as approximating to either Type B or Type C.

A partial explanation of these different 'types' of population emerges as we analyse further aspects of the nine populations and relate these to the three case studies of the Lokele, Babua, and Topoke. For this purpose some basic data are given in Table 1. The nine colonies showed a wide range of fertility ratios (number of live children aged five years or less as a ratio of women aged sixteen to forty-five years). For the entire population of Kisangani, the ratio was 489 (i.e. 489 children under five years of age for every 1000 women aged between sixteen to forty-five years) and for the nine principal colonies taken together it was 465. But between the nine tribes, the ratio ran from the high levels of 983 for the Lokele and 863 for the Bambole, to the extremely low levels of 181 for the Babua and 159 for the Babali.

Demographers have for long recognized that the ratio of children to women in any population is an exceedingly complex phenomenon. Firstly, this particular ratio is one which measures the effects not only of recent fertility but also of infant mortality. Secondly, reproduction is, we know, influenced by both biological and social factors. In examining any aspect of the problem we therefore need to distinguish between fecundity (the physical capacity for childbearing) and fertility (the reproduction actually achieved). Bearing this in mind it is evident that the systematic study of the factors underlying the differential tribal rates goes well beyond the scope of the present study. Yet it is of central importance for the analysis of different types of urban colony to note that differences in the fertility ratios of the nine tribes

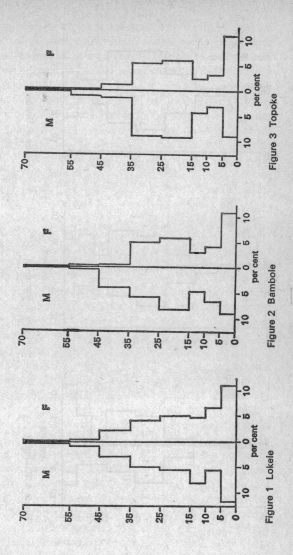

Figure 1 Lokele

Figure 2 Bambole

Figure 3 Topoke

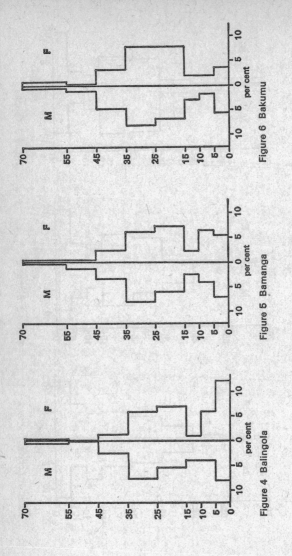

Figure 4 Balingola

Figure 5 Bamanga

Figure 6 Bakumu

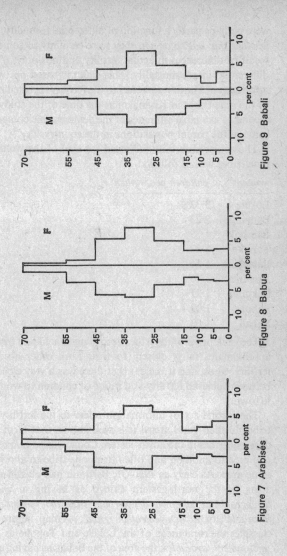

Figure 7 Arabisés

Figure 8 Babua

Figure 9 Babali

were perhaps partly a function of differential fecundity, and that, *whether this was so or not*, they were certainly to some extent a result of differences in actual fertility and not only, *if at all*, of differential infant mortality. This claim is based on two sets of information. The first set refers to the fertility reported by women of the nine tribes in Kisangani at the time of the study, and the second to available estimates of the demographic composition of some of the parent populations in the countryside.

The achieved fertility (adjusted for age) of the women of the nine tribes was as follows:

women	children per woman
Lokele	3·32
Bamanga	2·23
Bambole	1·89
Topoke	1·87
Balengola	1·56
Arabisés	1·46
Bakumu	1·27
Babua	1·09
Babali	1·03

The rank order of the tribes according to achieved fertility thus approximates fairly closely to their rank order according to fertility ratios, and it is clear that there was a very close relation between achieved fertility and ratios of children to women living in town.

The second set of information refers to the fertility of these tribes in their rural areas. It is well known that birth rates for different tribes in the north-eastern Congo varied markedly from one area to another, and often from one tribe to another in the same area. As early as 1930–31, Bertrand had classified various areas of the north-eastern Congo as having a '*mouvement démographique nettement défavorable*' or a '*mouvement nettement favorable*', or a '*mouvement incertain*'. A map he drew clearly classifies the rural areas of the Lokele and Topoke as having a '*mouvement favorable*', the area of the Babua as having a '*mouvement défavorable*' and the areas of the remaining principal tribes in Kisangani of 1952–53 as having a '*mouvement incertain*' (Bertrand 1931, p. 248). Since the time of Bertrand much evidence has accumulated to confirm his observation of marked differentials. For example, an investigation conducted in 1950 into the demographic composition of what were described by the author as 'specimen populations' from a number of rural areas in the Eastern Province yielded the following results for seven of the nine tribes with which we are here concerned: persons classified as 'children' constituted 21·0 per cent of the Babali, 22·7 per cent of the Babua, 27·8 per cent of the Balengola, 30·0 per cent of the Bakumu, 31·6 per cent of the Bambole, 39·7 per cent of the Bamanga, and 42·7 per cent of the Topoke (*Démographie Congolaise 1950*). Unfortunately, evidence of this kind is patently imprecise. But the frequency of similar reports by different observers at different times can reasonably be allowed to carry a good deal of weight.

Taking all such evidence into account and relating it to the data gathered in Kisangani, it appears that differences in fertility in the rural areas persisted in town and that the urban fertility ratios may be regarded as demographic features carried over into the town from parent populations in the countryside. As such, these differences have to be taken as given; they are differences which certainly affected social relations in the town, but which do not necessarily call for explanation in terms of these relations, nor in terms of the process of urbanization.

The age composition of adult men in the nine colonies taken together did not differ much from that of the total male population, but there were important variations between the nine tribes. Thus 45·6 per cent of Bambole men were between 16 and 25 years, whereas, at the other extreme, only 16·1 per cent of the Babua men fell into that age category.

The adult sex ratio of the nine colonies taken together did differ appreciably from that of the total population. As in other respects, however, there were marked differences between the nine colonies, ranging from ratios of 164·3 for the Topoke, and 140 for the Bambole, to 100 for the Bamanga and to only 70·1 for the *Arabisés*.

Turning to the information on lengths of residence in town, we find that the nine tribes taken together did not differ appreciably from the population of the town as a whole but there were again marked inter-tribal differences. Only 15·2 per cent of the Babali and 16·0 per cent of the *Arabisés* men had been in town for three years or less, but close on 40 per cent of the Topoke and Bambole were relative newcomers. Conversely, the proportions of men who had been in the town for more than ten years ran from 5·9 per cent for the Topoke to over 40 per cent for the *Arabisés* and Babali.

Taking such data into account we can begin to see the features of the three 'types' of population as aspects of three markedly different 'types' of tribal colony. The Lokele (Type A) had a high fertility ratio, a high proportion of young adults, and a high proportion of recent immigrants. In these associated respects they had a similar configuration to the colonies of Type B and especially to the Topoke and Bambole. But in some other respects Types A and B differed appreciably. Thus the Lokele had a significantly lower sex ratio than the colonies of Type B, as well as a significantly higher proportion of well-established urban residents. These observations suggest that the essential differences between the colonies of Types A and B were related to their differing histories of migration and urban incorporation and to associated differences in their patterns of rural-urban relations current at the time of the study. Both 'types' of colonies were drawn from tribes with high fertilities and increasing populations. Moreover, as it happens, they were tribes from contiguous areas of the town's hinterland and they had some cultural affinities which, for all we know, may well have been related to their high rates of fertility. But, as we have seen, the Lokele and the Topoke had significantly different histories of urban incorporation. And the same was to a large extent true of the Lokele as compared to the Bambole and Balengola, both of which tribes were, like the Topoke, relatively recent arrivals on the Kisangani scene, whose members were on the whole poorly established immigrants.

When we come to compare the configurations of Types B and C we find a wider range of differences deriving partly from differing histories of migration and urban incorporation and partly from differential fertility. The colonies of Type C had very low fertility ratios and appreciably lower-than-average proportions of recent immigrants from the countryside. Associated with these features, they had sex ratios ranging from very low in the case of the *Arabisés* to approximately average for the Babali, and they had low proportions of young adults and high proportions of longer-term residents. We have previously noted that in the case of the Babua some of these features were a function of their early settlement in the town, and the same was true of the *Arabisés* and Babali. All three were well-established tribes. This is reflected in Table 2, which shows that each had a high proportion of title-holders of dwelling compounds and thus also of home-owners. In sharp contrast to the Lokele who also had a large nucleus of well-established members, however, each of the three tribes of Type C had low rates of reproduction and of immigration. Like the Babua, the *Arabisés* had fared well in town in achieving a disproportionate number of better-paid jobs, but the Babali, though relatively well established as title-holders of compounds, had failed to distinguish themselves occupationally.

In general, then, the main differences between Types A and B were functions of differing histories of urban incorporation, whereas the differences between Types B and C were associated with differential fertility as well as with differing histories of urban incorporation. And differing histories of urban incorporation were in turn related to differing current patterns of rural-urban relations. The large volume of current immigration in colonies of Type B was associated with a lower level of involvement in town and, conversely, with a greater dependence for some measure of security on a continuing rural involvement.

Another pointer to varying degrees of rural and urban involvement is found in the proportions of men who had married their wives in Kisangani itself, in another centre of employment, and in tribal villages. This information is given in Table 3, from which it can be seen that whether we consider the positive indication of a high proportion of Kisangani marriages or the negative indication of a low proportion of marriages in tribal villages, the populations of Type C again emerge as substantially different to those of Type B. On this index, however, the Lokele (Type A) lie between Types B and C, which is what we would expect if we recall that their population contained appreciably large proportions of new immigrants as well as of longer-term residents.

Table 1 Summary of some salient demographic features of the nine principal tribal colonies.

Colony	'Type' of age and sex structure	Fertility ratio	Adult sex ratio	Per cent of adult men resident in the town 3 years or less	Per cent of adult men resident in the town 11 years or more	Per cent of adult men aged 16–25 years
Lokele	Type A	983*	114·6†	30·6*	35·1*	40·8*
Topoke	Type B	823*	164·3*	37·8*	5·9‡	42·8*
Bambole	Type B	863*	140·0*	39·3*	19·0†	45·5*
Balengola	Type B	691*	125·0*	33·8*	15·6‡	30·0†
Bamanga	Intermediate	392‡	100·0‡	23·4†	26·6‡	28·3†
Bakumu	Intermediate	242‡	104·4‡	24·5†	31·8†	29·4†
Babua	Type C	181‡	105·8‡	23·9†	32·4‡	16·1‡
Arabises	Type C	197‡	70·1‡	16·0‡	46·8*	19·8‡
Babali	Type C	159‡	116·9†	15·2‡	43·5‡	24·7‡
Nine principal colonies	—	465	105·9	26·5	30·5	30·1
All tribes in Kisangani	—	489	117·5	25·6	32·5	28·2

* Above average for the town
† Approximately average
‡ Below average

Table 2 Percentages for the nine principal colonies of household heads who were title-holders of dwelling compounds

Colony	'Type' of age and sex structure	Effective sample of household heads	No. of dwelling compound title-holders	Percentage of household heads who were title-holders of compounds
Arabisés	Type C	77	64	83·1
Babua	Type C	125	94	75·2
Babali	Type C	68	50	73·5
Bakumu	Intermediate	85	59	69·4
Lokele	Type A	145	95	65·5
Bambole	Type B	57	35	61·4
Balengola	Type B	43	22	51·2
Bamanga	Intermediate	42	15	35·7
Topoke	Type B	88	29	33·0
Nine principal colonies	—	730	463	63·4

'Closed' and 'open' colonies

I have previously implied that some tribal colonies in the town were relatively 'closed' (in the sense that members tended to restrict their personal relations to fellow members) as compared to others which were relatively 'open'. And I have pointed to the Lokele and Topoke as examples of relatively 'closed' colonies and to the Babua as an example of a more 'open' colony. We may now usefully examine the index of 'mixed' or non-tribal marriages in the nine largest colonies. The information is given in Table 4, from which it can be seen that 17·5 per cent of all the extant marriages of men in the nine colonies were non-tribal, but that this proportion fell to 6·4 per cent for marriages contracted in native villages, and rose to 21·1 per cent for marriages contracted in Kisangani and to the even higher proportion of 27·0 per cent for marriages contracted in labour centres other than Kisangani. The proportion of non-tribal marriages for the various colonies ranged from 2·9 per cent for the Bamanga to

36·0 per cent for the Babali and the Babua, and we may note that the table tends to corroborate our view of the Topoke and Lokele as relatively 'closed' colonies and of the Babua as more 'open'. But there are several difficulties of interpretation that have to be considered.

Firstly, when the marriages for each tribe are classified according to the places where they were contracted the numbers in some cells are too small for us to attach much significance to them. Secondly, and more fundamentally, the figures in the table could be used only as precise indices of the extent to which colonies were 'open' or 'closed' if we were in a position to compare the actual proportions of tribal and non-tribal marriages with the proportions expected under the assumption that marriage partners were selected at random. Unfortunately, this is not possible because

Table 3 Extant marriages of men in the nine principal colonies classified according to the place of the marriages

Colony	'Type' of age and sex structure	Married in Kisangani		Married in an employment centre other than Kisangani		Married in a native village		Total	
		no.	%	no.	%	no.	%	no.	%
Arabisés	Type C	99	75·0	16	12·1	17	12·9	132	100
Bakumu	Intermediate	46	53·5	9	10·5	31	36·0	86	100
Babali	Type C	26	52·0	11	22·0	13	26·0	50	100
Babua	Type C	43	50·0	36	41·9	7	8·1	86	100
Lokele	Type A	64	43·0	23	15·4	62	41·6	149	100
Bamanga	Intermediate	14	41·2	8	23·5	12	35·3	34	100
Bambole	Type B	15	30·0	8	16·0	27	54·0	50	100
Balengola	Type B	14	26·4	17	32·1	22	41·5	53	100
Topoke	Type B	15	19·0	20	25·3	44	55·7	79	100
Total		336	46·7	148	20·6	235	32·7	719	100

we have no means of establishing the tribal composition of the different universes of women to which men of the various tribes were exposed. Quite apart from variations in the age and sex composition of various tribes in town, there were large differences between the nine tribes in the proportions of men who had married in Kisangani, in native villages, and elsewhere. In principle we would therefore need to restrict our computations to marriages started in town. But we also know that many men in town commonly recruited brides from the countryside either out of preference or, in some cases, simply because of the scarcity of marriageable urban women. Thus, *even if we were to consider only marriages started in town*, it would be extremely difficult to establish the size and composition of the relevant universe from which brides were chosen. Finally, there is a third factor which has important methodological implications. We know that the various colonies were unevenly distributed in different parts of the town, and that social life tended to be strongly localized not only in the separate townships but also in smaller neighbourhoods within the townships. Thus the effective universes of potential marriage partners to which the inhabitants of various neighbourhoods were exposed were liable to vary markedly in tribal composition. In principle tribal *preferences* in regard to marriage partners could therefore be assessed only by relating the varying incidences of tribal or non-tribal marriages in the several tribes to a series of universes which took account of the layout of the town and of the neighbourhood composition of the townships. This is impossible on the basis of the data we have.

In view of the above considerations we cannot take the figures given in Table 4, as *necessarily* reflecting higher or lower preferences for marriage within the various colonies. Yet the figures are valuable in contributing to a general definition of the social environments within which people of various tribes interacted in town. For example, it is clearly important for us to know that only one Lokele man in ten was married to a non-Lokele woman whereas nearly four out of ten Babua men were married to non-Babua women. Or, to take an example of wider relevance, it is very important to note that there was a high degree of correlation between colonies ranked according to the incidence of non-tribal marriage and according to residential dispersion and concentration. Members of a tribe who tended to live close to each other were also more likely to be married to each other. This has importance irrespective of whether we are in a position to state that it

Table 4 Extant tribal and non-tribal marriages of men in the nine principal colonies classified according to the place of the marriages

1. Total number of marriages in sample.
2. Total number of non-tribal marriages.
3. Percentage of non-tribal marriages.
4. Number of marriages entered upon in Kisangani.
5. Number of non-tribal marriages in Kisangani.
6. Percentage of non-tribal marriages in Kisangani.
7. Number of marriages entered upon in other centres.
8. Number of non-tribal marriages in other centres.
9. Percentage of non-tribal marriages in other centres.
10. Number of marriages entered upon in native villages.
11. Number of non-tribal marriages in native villages.
12. Percentage of non-tribal marriages in native villages.

Tribe	1	2	3	4	5	6	7	8	9	10	11	12
Bamanga	34	1	2.9	14	1	7.1	8	0	0.0	12	0	0.0
Arabisés†	132	9	6.8	99	6	6.1	16	1	6.3	17	2	11.8
Topoke	79	8	10.1	15	3	20.0	20	4	20.0	44	1	2.3
Lokele	49	16	10.7	64	7	10.9	23	5	21.7	62	4	6.5
Bakumu	86	17	19.8	46	13	28.3	9	2	22.2	31	2	6.5
Balengola	53	12	22.6	14	4	28.6	17	8	47.1	22	0	0.0
Bambole	50	14	28.0	15	6	40.0	8	5	62.5	27	3	11.1
Babua	86	31	36.0	43	19	44.2	36	11	30.1	7	1	14.3
Babali	50	18	36.0	26	12	46.2	11	4	36.4	13	2	15.4
Total	719	126	17.5	336	71	21.1	148	40	27.0	235	15	6.4

† The Arabisés figures in this table are of limited significance for wives from other tribes *usually* became Islamized on marriage. A substantial proportion of Arabisés wives were in fact women drawn from a number of different tribes.

reflects differential preferences; the observation contributes to our assessment of the situations under which people interacted in the town.

Apart from the Lokele, Topoke, and Babua, there were other tribes which were generally regarded as either distinctly more 'closed' or distinctly more 'open' than the average; the Bakumu and the Bamanga were certainly viewed as relatively 'closed', while the Babali were regarded as more 'open' and more willing to mix with members of other tribes. These impressions are clearly in keeping with the data on non-tribal marriages in Table 4.

I have drawn attention to the fact of 'closed' and 'open' colonies as a general contribution to the description of the population. The notions of 'closed' and 'open' are, however, too crude to be of much value in the analysis of 'tribalism'. The factors making for 'open' or 'closed' colonies were various and variable. Thus, for example, the 'closed' colonies of the Lokele and Topoke exhibited both important similarities and marked differences. There was some cultural affinity between the two tribes and they were from adjacent areas of the hinterland where they were traditionally well known to each other. As we have seen, however, their histories of urban incorporation and participation were very different. The Lokele had a highly successful record in town, and were regarded as 'clever', 'independent', and 'exclusive'; they made up a 'closed' group tending to reject association with other tribes partly on account of their success. In contrast, the Topoke were a colony of recent immigrants, clinging to the social security of their village homes, and regarded as 'backward' and 'uncivilized' by other tribes; they were a relatively 'closed' group partly because most other tribes tended to reject them, and partly because of their own tendency to resist branching out and becoming more involved in urban life.

As a whole, the evidence shows, firstly, that different tribes had established markedly different forms of urban accommodation and, secondly, that these forms of accommodation were partly a function of the rural-urban relation. I contend that the set of urban-residential relations of colonies like the Babua, Babali and Arabisés could be fairly adequately studied without a parallel rural study, but that in the case of colonies like the Lokele and the Topoke, any adequate analysis would require urban-residential relations to be assessed within the framework of a wider rural-urban study. In either case, however, the evidence clearly is that the 'tribal' characteristics of different colonies in town were very far indeed from being solely, or even primarily, features of their respective traditional cultures. The study of inter-tribal or of 'racial' relations in Kisangani would thus require us to pay just as much or more attention to differences between the real situations of the colonies in town as to any cultural differences between them.

References

BERTRAND, M. le Colonel (1931), *Le problème de la Main-d'Oeuvre au Congo Belge*, Bruxelles.
CONGO BELGE (1950), *Démographie Congolaise*.

Part Nine
American Approaches

In America, the classic approach to race relations gave
primacy to social attitudes. The study of race relations became
the study of prejudice and scholars proposed that if attitudes
were changed, then the position of the Negro would be mitigated.
The fragment excised from Myrdal's monumental study of the
American Dilemma encapsulates this view. In it Myrdal pro-
pounds his major thesis, describing the dynamic of 'cumulative
causation' which determines the intensity of race prejudice.
Cayton and Drake follow a similar approach in their
discussion of the changing position of Negro hog butchers in
Chicago. An improvement in the black butchers' status is treated
as a small step toward the resolution of the American Dilemma.
Another element in the classic work on American race relations
is the use of the concept of caste to characterize the social
conditions of segregation. Warner explains this usage of caste
in a short and succinct essay. Now, with increasing black militancy
and with desegregation, the race relations scene has been transformed. A new sociology has developed to comprehend new
trends. Hannerz is our chosen representative.

26 Gunnar Myrdal

The American Dilemma

Excerpt from Gunnar Myrdal, *An American Dilemma*, McGraw Hill, 1944. First paperback edition 1964, pp. 75–80.

We hear it said nowadays that there is no 'race problem', but only a 'class problem'. The Negro sharecropper is alleged to be destitute not because of his color but because of his class position – and it is pointed out that there are white people who are equally poor. From a practical angle there is a point in this reasoning. But from a theoretical angle it contains escapism in new form. It also draws too heavily on the idealistic Marxian doctrine of the 'class struggle'. And it tends to conceal the whole system of special deprivations visited upon the Negro only because he is not white. We find also that as soon as the Negro scholar, ideologist or reformer leaves these general ideas about how the Negro should think, he finds himself discussing nothing but Negro rights, the Negro's share, injustices against Negroes, discrimination against Negroes, Negro interests – nothing, indeed, but the old familiar Negro problem, though in some new political relations. He is back again in the 'race issue'. And there is substantial reason for it.

The reason, of course, is that there is really a common tie and, therefore, a unity in all the special angles of the Negro problem. All these specific problems are only outcroppings of one fundamental complex of human valuations – that of American caste. This fundamental complex derives its emotional charge from the equally common race prejudice, from its manifestations in a general tendency toward discrimination, and from its political potentialities through its very inconsistency with the American Creed.

The theory of the vicious circle

A deeper reason for the unity of the Negro problem will be apparent when we now try to formulate our hypothesis concerning its dynamic causation. The mechanism that operates here is the 'principle of cumulation', also commonly called the 'vicious circle'.[1] This principle has a much wider application in social relations. It is, or should be developed into, a main theoretical tool in studying social change.

Throughout this inquiry, we shall assume a general interdependence between all the factors in the Negro problem. White prejudice and discrimination keep the Negro low in standards of living, health, education, manners and morals. This, in its turn, gives support to white prejudice. White prejudice and Negro standards thus mutually 'cause' each other. If things remain about as they are and have been, this means that the two forces happen to balance each other. Such a static 'accommodation' is, however, entirely accidental. If either of the factors changes, this will cause a change in the other factor, too, and start a process of interaction where the change in one factor will continuously be supported by the reaction of the other factor. The whole system will be moving in the direction of the primary change, but much further. This is what we mean by cumulative causation.

If, for example, we assume that for some reason white prejudice could be decreased and discrimination mitigated, this is likely to cause a rise in Negro standards, which may decrease white prejudice still a little more, which would again allow Negro standards to rise, and so on through mutual interaction. If, instead, discrimination should become intensified, we should see the vicious circle spiraling downward. The original change can as easily be a change of *Negro standards* upward or downward. The effects would, in a similar manner, run back and forth in the interlocking system of interdependent causation. In any case, the initial change would be supported by consecutive waves of back-effects from the reactions of the other factor.

The same principle holds true if we split one of our two variables into component factors. A rise in Negro employment, for

1. We call the principle the 'principle of cumulation' rather than 'vicious circle' because it can work in an 'upward' desirable direction as well as in a 'downward' undesirable direction.

instance, will raise family incomes, standards of nutrition, housing and health, the possibilities of giving the Negro youth more education, and so forth, and all these effects of the initial change, will, in their turn, improve the Negroes' possibilities of getting employment and earning a living. The original push could have been some other factor than employment, say, for example, an improvement of health or education facilities for Negroes. Through action and interaction the whole system of the Negro's 'status' would have been set in motion in the direction indicated by the first push. Much the same thing holds true of the development of white prejudice. Even assuming no changes in Negro standards, white prejudice can change, for example, as a result of an increased general knowledge about biology, eradicating some of the false beliefs among whites concerning Negro racial inferiority. If this is accomplished, it will in some degree censor the hostile and derogatory valuations which fortify the false beliefs, and education will then be able to fight racial beliefs with more success.

By this we have only wanted to give a hint of an explanatory scheme of dynamic causation which we are going to utilize throughout this inquiry. The interrelations are in reality much more complicated than in our abstract illustrations, and there are all sorts of irregularities in the reaction of various factors. But the complications should not force us to give up our main hypothesis that a cumulative principle is working in social change. It is actually this hypothesis which gives a theoretical meaning to the Negro problem as a special phase of all other social problems in America. Behind the barrier of common discrimination, there is unity and close interrelation between the Negro's political power; his civil rights; his employment opportunities; his standards of housing, nutrition and clothing; his health, manners and law observance; his ideals and ideologies. The unity is largely the result of cumulative causation binding them all together in a system and tying them to white discrimination. It is useful, therefore, to interpret all the separate factors from a central vantage point – the point of view of the Negro problem.

Another corollary from our hypothesis is practical. In the field of Negro politics any push upward directed on any one of those factors – if our main hypothesis is correct – moves all other factors in the same direction and has, through them, a cumulative effect upon general Negro status. An upward trend of Negro status in general can be effected by any number of measures, rather independent of where the initial push is localized. By the process of cumulation it will be transferred through the whole system.

But, as in the field of economic anti-depression policy, it matters a lot how the measures are proportioned and applied. The directing and proportioning of the measures is the task of social engineering. This engineering should be based on a knowledge of how all the factors are actually interrelated: what effect a primary change upon each factor will have on all other factors. It can be generally stated, however, that it is likely that *a rational policy will never work by changing only one factor*, least of all if attempted suddenly and with great force. In most cases that would either throw the system entirely out of gear or else prove to be a wasteful expenditure of effort which could reach much further by being spread strategically over various factors in the system and over a period of time.

This – and the impracticability of getting political support for a great and sudden change of just one factor – is the rational refutation of so-called panaceas. Panaceas are now generally repudiated in the literature on the Negro problem, though usually without much rational motivation. There still exists, however, another theoretical idea which is similar to the idea of panacea: the idea that there is *one* predominant factor, a 'basic factor'. Usually the so-called 'economic factor' is assumed to be this basic factor. A vague conception of economic determinism has, in fact, come to color most of the modern writings on the Negro problem far outside the Marxist school. Such a view has unwarrantedly acquired the prestige of being a particularly 'hard-boiled' scientific approach.

As we look upon the problem of dynamic social causation, this approach is unrealistic and narrow. We do not, of course, deny that the conditions under which Negroes are allowed to earn a living are tremendously important for their welfare. But these conditions are closely interrelated to all other conditions of Negro life. When studying the variegated causes of discrimination in the labor market, it is, indeed, difficult to perceive what precisely is meant by 'the economic factor'. The Negro's legal and political status and all the causes behind this, considerations by whites of social prestige and everything else in the Negro problem belong to the causation of discrimination in the labor market, in exactly the same way as the Negro's low economic status is influential in keeping down his health, his educational level, his political power, and his status in other respects. Neither from a theoretical point of view – in seeking to explain the Negro's caste status in American society—nor from a practical point of view—in attempting to assign the strategic points which can most effectively be attacked in order to raise his status – is there any reason, or, indeed, any possibility of singling out 'the economic factor' as basic. In an interdependent system of dynamic causation there is no 'primary cause' but everything is cause *to* everything else.

If this theoretical approach is bound to do away in the practical sphere with all panaceas, it is, on the other hand, equally bound to encourage the reformer. The principle of cumulation – in so far as it holds true – promises final effects of greater magnitude than the efforts and costs of the reforms themselves. The low status of the Negro is tremendously wasteful all around – the low educational standard causes low earnings and health deficiencies, for example. The cumulatively magnified effect of a push upward on any one of the relevant factors, is in one sense, a demonstration and a measure of the earlier existing waste. In the end, the cost of raising the status of the Negro may not involve any 'real costs' at all for society, but instead may result in great 'social gains' and actual savings for society. A movement downward will, for the same reason, increase 'social waste' out of proportion to the original saving involved in the push downward of one factor or another.

These dynamic concepts of 'social waste', 'social gain', and 'real costs' are mental tools originated in the practical man's workshop. To give them a clearer meaning – which implies expressing also the underlying social value premises – and to measure them in quantitative terms represents from a practical viewpoint a main task of social science. Fulfilling that task in a truly comprehensive way is a stage of dynamic social theory still to be reached but definitely within vision.

A theory of democracy

The factors working on the white side in our system of dynamic causation were brought together under the heading 'race prejudice'. For our present purpose, it is defined as discrimination by whites against Negroes. One viewpoint on race prejudice needs to be presented at this point, chiefly because of its close relation to our hypothesis of cumulative causation.

The chemists talk about 'irreversible processes', meaning a trait of a chemical process to go in one direction with ease but, for all practical purposes, to be unchangeable back to its original state (as when a house burns down). When we observe race prejudice as it appears in American daily life, it is difficult to avoid the reflection that it seems so much easier to increase than to decrease race prejudice. One is reminded of the old saying that nineteen fresh apples do not make a single rotten apple fresh, but that one rotten apple rapidly turns the fresh ones rotten. When we come to consider the various causative factors underlying race prejudice – economic competition; urges and fears for social status; sexual drives, fears, jealousies and inhibitions – this view will come to be understandable. It is a common observation that the white Northerner who settles in the South will rapidly take on the stronger race prejudice of the new surroundings; while the Southerner going North is likely to keep his race prejudice rather unchanged and perhaps even to communicate it to those he meets. The Northerner in the South will find the whole community intent upon his conforming to local patterns. The Southerner in the North will not meet such concerted action, but will feel, rather, that others are adjusting towards him wherever he goes. If the local hotel in a New England town has accommodated a few Negro guests without much worry one way or the other, the appearance one evening of a single white guest who makes an angry protest against it might permanently change the policy of the hotel.

If we assume that a decrease in race prejudice is desirable – on grounds of the value premise of the American Creed and of the mechanism of cumulative wastage just discussed – such a general tendency, inherent in the psychology of race prejudice, would be likely to force us to a pessimistic outlook. One would expect a constant tendency towards increased race prejudice, and the interlocking causation with the several factors on the Negro side would be expected to reinforce the movement. Aside from all valuations, the question must be raised: Why is race prejudice, in spite of this tendency to continued intensification which we have observed, nevertheless, on the whole not increasing but decreasing?

This question is, in fact, only a special variant of the enigma of philosophers for several thousands of years: the problem of Good and Evil in the world. One is remainded of that cynical but wise old man, Thomas Hobbes, who proved rather conclusively that, while any person's actual possibilities to improve the lot of his fellow creatures amounted to almost nothing, everyone's opportunity to do damage was always immense. The wisest and most virtuous man will hardly leave a print in the sand behind him, meant Hobbes, but an imbecile crank can set fire to a whole town. Why is the world, then, not steadily and rapidly deteriorating, but rather, at least over long periods, progressing? Hobbes raised this question. His answer was, as we know: the State, *Leviathan.* Our own tentative answer to the more specific but still overwhelmingly general question we have raised above will have something in common with that of the post-Elizabethan materialist and hedonist, but it will have its stress placed differently, as we shall subsequently see.

Two principal points will be made by way of a preliminary and hypothetical answer, as they influence greatly our general approach to the Negro problem. The first point is the American Creed, the relation of which to the Negro problem will become apparent as our inquiry proceeds. The Creed of progress, liberty, equality and humanitarianism is not so uninfluential on everday life as might sometimes appear.

The second point is the existence in society of huge institutional structures like the church, the school, the university, the foundation, the trade union, the association generally, and, of course, the state. It is true, as we shall find, that these institutional structures in their operation show an accommodation to local and temporary interests and prejudices – they could not be expected to do otherwise as they are made up of individuals with all their local and temporary characteristics. As institutions they are, however, devoted to certain broad ideals. It is in these institutions that the American Creed has its instruments: it plays upon them as on mighty organs. In adhering to these ideals, the institutions show a pertinacity, matched only by their great flexibility in local and temporary accommodation.

The school, in every community, is likely to be a degree more broadminded than local opinion. So is the sermon in church. The national labor assembly is prone to decide slightly above the prejudice of the median member. Legislation will, on the whole, be more equitable than the legislators are themselves as private individuals. When the man in the street acts through his orderly collective bodies, he acts more as an American, as a Christian, and as a humanitarian than if he were acting independently. He thus shapes social controls which are going to condition even himself.

Through these huge institutional structures, a constant pressure is brought to bear on race prejudice, counteracting the natural tendency for it to spread and become more intense. The same people are acting in the institutions as when manifesting personal prejudice. But they obey different moral valuations on different planes of life. In their institutions they have invested more than their everyday ideas which parallel their actual behavior. They have placed in them their ideals of how the world rightly ought to be. The ideals thereby gain fortifications of power and influence in society. This is a theory of social self-healing that applies to the type of society we call democracy.

The ideological compromise

After the War and Emancipation, the race dogma was retained in the South as necessary to justify the caste system which succeeded slavery as the social organization of Negro-white relations. In fact, it is probable that racial prejudice increased in the South at least up to the end of Reconstruction and probably until the beginning of the twentieth century. (Johnson, 1940).[2]

The North never had cleansed its own record in its dealing with

2. G. G. Johnson, 'History of racial ideologies', unpublished manuscript written for this study (1940). vol. 1, p. 149, *passim*; vol. 2, p. 331, *passim*.

the Negro even if it freed him and gave him permanent civil rights and the vote. In the North, however, race prejudice was never so deep and so widespread as in the South. During and after the Civil War it is probable that the North relaxed its prejudices even further. But Reconstruction was followed by the national compromise of the 1870s when the North allowed the South to have its own way with the Negroes in obvious contradiction to what a decade earlier had been declared to be the ideals of the victorious North and the policy of the nation. The North now also needed the race dogma to justify its course. As the North itself did not retreat from most of the Reconstruction legislation, and as the whole matter did not concern the average Northerner so much, the pressure on him was not hard, and the belief in racial inequality never became intense. But this period was, in this field, one of reaction in the North, too.

The fact that the same rationalizations are used to defend slavery and caste is one of the connecting links between the two social institutions. In the South the connection is psychologically direct. Even today the average white Southerner really uses the race dogma to defend not only the present caste situation but also *ante-bellum* slavery and, consequently, the righteousness of the Southern cause in the Civil War. This psychological unity of defense is one strong reason, among others, why the generally advanced assertion is correct that the slavery tradition is a tremendous impediment in the way of improvement of the Negro's lot. The caste system has inherited the defense ideology of slavery.

The partial exclusion of the Negro from American democracy, however, has in no way dethroned the American Creed. This faith actually became strengthened by the victorious War which saved the Union and stopped the Southerners from publicly denouncing the cherished national principles that all men are born equal and have inalienable civil rights. The question can be asked: What do the millions of white people in the South and in the North actually think when, year after year, on the national holidays dedicated to the service of the democratic ideals, they read, recite, and listen to the Declaration of Independence and the Constitution? Do they or do they not include Negroes among 'all men'? The same question is raised when we observe how, in newspaper editorials and public speeches, unqualified general statements are made asserting the principles and the fact of American democracy. Our tentative answer is this: In solemn moments, Americans try to forget about the Negroes as about other worries. If this is not possible they think in vague and irrational terms; in these terms the idea of the Negroes' biological inferiority is a nearly necessary rationalization.

The dogma of racial inequality may, in a sense, be regarded as a strange fruit of the Enlightenment. The fateful word *race* itself is actually not yet two hundred years old. The biological ideology had to be utilized as an intellectual explanation of, and a moral apology for, slavery in a society which went out emphatically to invoke as its highest principles the ideals of the inalienable rights of all men to freedom and equality of opportunity. It was born out of the conflict between an old harshly nonequalitarian institution – which was not, or perhaps in a short time could not be, erased – and the new shining faith in human liberty and democracy. Another accomplishment of early rationalistic Enlightenment had laid the theoretical basis for the racial defense of slavery; the recognition of *Homo sapiens* as only a species of the animal world and the emerging study of the human body and mind as biological phenomena. Until this philosophical basis was laid, racialism was not an intellectual possibility.

The influences from the American Creed thus had, and still have, a double-direction. On the one hand, the equalitarian Creed operates directly to suppress the dogma of the Negro's racial inferiority and to make people's thoughts more and more 'independent of race, creed or color', as the American slogan runs. On the other hand, it indirectly calls forth the same dogma to justify a blatant exception to the Creed. The race dogma is nearly the only way out for a people so moralistically equalitarian, if it is not prepared to live up to its faith. A nation less fervently committed to democracy could, probably, live happily in a caste system with a somewhat less intensive belief in the biological inferiority of the subordinate group. *The need for race prejudice is, from this point of view, a need for defense on the part of the Americans against their own national Creed, against their own most cherished ideals*. And race prejudice is, in this sense, a function of equalitarianism. The former is a perversion of the latter.[3]

3. The same principle operates also outside the Negro problem. The American Creed, in its demand for equality, has strong support from the very composition of the new nation. As immigrants, or the descendants of immigrants with diverse national origins, Americans have an interest – outside of the Negro problem – in emphasizing the importance of environment and in discounting inheritance. In order to give a human and not only political meaning to the legend *e pluribus unum*, they feel the need to believe in the possibility of shaping a new homogeneous nation out of the disparate elements thrown into the melting pot. This interest plays on a high level of valuations where the individual identifies himself with the destiny of the nation. In daily life, however, the actual and obvious heterogeneity in origin, appearance, and culture of the American people acts as a constant stimulus toward prejudiced racial beliefs.

27 Horace R. Cayton and St Clair Drake

Negroes as Hog Butchers for the World

Excerpt from Horace R. Cayton and St Clair Drake, *Black Metropolis*,
Cape, 1946, pp. 302–9.

The story of the integration of Negroes into Chicago's slaughtering and meat-packing industry provides a dramatic illustration
of the interplay between the forces of democratic idealism and
economic and political forces . . .

According to local tradition, the first Negroes to work in the
packing industry in Chicago were a beef-boner and a butcher,
who secured jobs in 1881. Although Negroes and whites are
today organized together in a union affiliated with the CIO,
where Negroes share positions of leadership with white workers,
the slaughtering and packing industry was once a racial battleground.

Between 1881 and 1894, a few Negroes filtered into the stockyards and packing plants without any apparent opposition from
the foreign born white workers who predominated in the industry.
During the Pullman Strike of 1894, when the stockyard workers
walked out in sympathy with the American Railway Union, a
large group of Poles were employed as strike-breakers. A few
days later, Negroes came into the yards in a similar capacity,
and union resentment was focused on them to such a degree that
a Negro was burned in effigy. After the strike a few Negroes
retained their positions, and although they were numerically
unimportant, their presence in the yards was interpreted as a
threat to the labor unions. In employing Negroes, management
had tapped an almost inexhaustible supply of cheap labor from
the South and simultaneously secured a labor force that seemed
very resistant to union organization.

The next large influx of Negroes into the yards occurred during
the strike of 1904. When the strike began, Negroes constituted
about five per cent of the labor force. Their numbers were

immediately increased, and hundreds of Negroes were smuggled into the plants on the same day that the white workers downed their tools. So large a number were employed that for a time it was thought that Negroes would predominate in the packing industry. The more extravagant estimates placed the number employed as high as ten thousand.

In this dispute, the role of the Negro worker differed from his role as strike-breaker in the 1894 strike. In the earlier dispute, Poles had been numerically more important, and, in spite of the publicity which attended their activities, Negroes played only an incidental part. But in 1904 their importance as strike-breakers was immediately recognized and an even more intense resentment by union men resulted.[1] After the strike had been settled, a small number of colored men retained their positions. The rest were discharged or displaced by returning union men. The packers were no longer in need of Negro workers, so they were loaded into special trains and sent back to the South.

Four years later, there were about 500 Negroes in the industry, and a small but steady stream of black workers continued to flow into the yards. Then, in 1917, because of the war labor shortage, the packers again tapped the southern labor pool, sending their agents into the Deep South to recruit Negro workers by the hundreds and even thousands. By 1920, one packing plant employed over 5000 Negroes, more than a quarter of its total labor force. The peak of Negro employment was reached in 1923, when 34 out of every 100 workers in the two largest packing establishments were colored. From 1922 until the Depression, the proportion of Negroes among all packing-house workers remained about 30 per cent.

Negroes and the old unions

After the strike of 1904, the packinghouse union was so weakened that its membership dropped from 34,400 in 1904 to 6200 in 1910. With the sudden increase in the number and proportion of Negroes in the industry, the Amalgamated Meat Cutters and

1. 'To the striking union men no scabs were as loathsome as the Negroes who took their jobs. Easily distinguishable, they were conspicuous among the strike-breakers and suffered the animus which is vented upon all scabs. Among the first of the strike-breakers to be hired, they were among the first to be asked to leave at the conclusion of hostilities.' (Herbst, 1932, p. 28.)

Butcher Workmen (AFL) began an organizational drive in 1916–17. The packers granted an increase of twenty cents an hour to unskilled workers, but the union continued to grow, and in 1917 the Stock Yards Labor Council was formed by the united action of all the craft unions with jurisdiction in the stockyards.

The problem of establishing a policy with respect to Negroes in the union organizations soon became pressing. Twenty of the various craft unions in the council drew the color-line sharply. The union officials appreciated the importance of organizing Negroes, and realized that a union organization could not succeed without them. Nevertheless, unanimity of opinion regarding a solution of the racial problem could not be achieved. Some union leaders urged that colored men be admitted to all the unions, but in some cases this was prohibited by constitutional provisions; in others, the racial prejudice of union officials had the same effect. A typical AFL solution was suggested – the organization of Negroes into separate locals. The Amalgamated Meat Cutters and Butcher Workmen, one of the craft unions involved, followed its traditional policy and admitted Negroes, but complications over racial matters soon developed.

Many Negroes joined unions, but on the whole the organizers were disappointed in the response of the colored workers. It was estimated that among northern-born Negroes 90 per cent became union members. Few southern-born Negroes joined, however, and at the height of the drive only about a third of the Negroes employed in the yards became affiliated with any union organization.[2]

At the beginning of the 1917 campaign, approximately 12,000 Negroes worked in the stockyards in Chicago. The number increased in direct ratio to the success of the unions in organizing the white laborers. Not only were the colored workmen regarded by management as almost immune to organization, and unreliable union members when they did join, but also the unions had no consistent policy toward Negroes.

2. Perhaps it should be pointed out explicitly that no one union existed in the yards at this time. There were as many different AFL craft unions represented as there were crafts in the packing industry. The largest union was the Amalgamated Meat Cutters and Butcher Workmen.

The packers, realizing that their hope of defeating unionism depended upon holding the allegiance of colored workmen, inaugurated a policy of increasing the number of Negroes in their plants, at the same time influencing them against unionism. In this connection, packing-house management made use of a colorful Negro promotor, Richard Parker, who was hired to organize a Negro union. A most enterprising person, Mr Parker started his activities by distributing about 20,000 handbills warning Negroes not to join the 'white man's union' but, instead, to affiliate themselves with his organization, the American Unity Labor Union. The argument was twofold: Negroes should not join white unions because the unions would not admit them on a basis of equality, and, secondly, white employers preferred non-union help. The following is a typical advertisement appearing in the Negro press at the time:

GET A SQUARE DEAL WITH YOUR OWN RACE

Time has come for Negroes to do now or never. Get together and stick together is the call of the Negro. Like all other races, make your own way; other races have made their unions for themselves. They are not going to give it to you just because you join his union. Make a union of your own race; union is strength. Join the American Unity Packers Union of the Stock Yards, this will give you a card to work at any trade or a common laborer, as a steamfitter, electrician, fireman, merchants, engineers, carpenters, butchers, helpers, and chauffeurs to drive trucks down town, delivering meat as white chauffeurs do for Armour's and Swift's or other Packers. A card from this Union will let you work in Kansas City, Omaha and St. Louis, or any other city where the five Packers have packing houses.

This union does not *believe in strikes*. We believe all differences between laborers and capitalists can be arbitrated. Strike is our last motive if any at all.

Get in line for a good job. *You are next . . .*

It was this Negro leader's proud boast that he had brought more Negroes to the city from the South than had any other man in Chicago. Parker's organization introduced considerable confusion into the union situation in the stockyards, and thus further weakened the AFL unions.

When a strike seemed imminent in 1917, a Federal arbitrator was appointed. The Stock Yard Council enjoyed some temporary success in recruiting Negro workers by telling them that the government would see that they got a raise if they joined the union. The Council planned a special drive to attract Negroes:

To this end a 'giant stockyards union celebration' was planned for 6 July. A workers' parade which was to include both races was scheduled . . . On the morning of the event, the packers asked the police to revoke the parade permit lest a race riot be precipitated. As the workers were not permitted to march together, two parades formed, a white and a colored, and marched to the Beutner playgrounds, where a Negro and white audience was assembled. The marchers were greeted by cheers from the colored workers who lined the streets. . . . One of the placards which dotted the procession read:

'The bosses think that because we are of different color and different nationalities we should fight each other. We're going to fool them and fight for a common cause – a square deal for all.'

In addressing the meeting, the secretary of the Stock Yards Labor Council [who some years later became the state chairman of the Communist Party] said:

'It does me good to see such a checkerboard crowd – by that I mean all of the workers here are not standing apart in groups, one race huddled in one bunch, one nationality in another. You are all standing shoulder to shoulder as men, regardless of whether your face is white or black.'

But this attempt to develop solidarity among the packing-house workers was abortive, partly because of the outbreak of the Chicago Race Riot in 1919. Probably one of the underlying causes of the Riot was the conflict between union members and packing-house employers for the allegiance of Negro workers.

Each group laid the responsibility for the riot upon the other. The riot resulted in a barrier to further union organization among Negroes and brought to an abrupt end the drive to enlist Negro packing-house workers.

On the Sunday afternoon when the Race Riot started, and throughout the week, there were sporadic clashes between whites and Negroes in the packing-house area. On Monday, union members were notified by management that arrangements had been made for the militia to protect the workers in the yards. A militant colored unionist proposed that rather than send for troops, the employers should recognize the closed-shop plan, and that the union would then assume responsibility for the conduct of all workers in the yards. Needless to say, the proposal was turned down by the employers. The employees refused to work under the guns of the soldiers, and thousands of them struck. After a few days the troops were withdrawn, and the workers were notified to return to the yards. Approximately 600 laborers, both white and colored, delayed a day and were dismissed.

The union organizations connected with the stockyards labored incessantly to maintain order during the two weeks of the riot. Editorials in union papers expressed not only sympathy for Negroes, but also a concern for the future existence of the union. One editorial observed:

Right now it is going to be decided whether the coloured workers are to continue to come into the labor movement or whether they are to feel that they have been abandoned by it and lose confidence in it.

The friendly attitude of union officials apparently brought some of the colored workers closer to the union. It was reported that 'the white and colored union men sustained each other in the main and ministered to the stricken. The financial aid and moral support which the union colored men received during the riot and immediately following it served to bring them to the headquarters of their organizations and to keep them "out of the packers" bread line'. It is to be remarked that both the packers and the union tried to aid the Negro workers – by feeding them and in other ways.

Under the circumstances, however, it was extremely difficult for Negroes to remain loyal to the union. The employers had replaced many staunch Negro union men with non-union Negroes, first when they refused to work without protection during the riot, and later when they refused to work under the guns of the militia. Negroes returning to work in the yards after the riot were glad to obtain employment under any terms and rapidly abandoned the union organizations.

Two years after the riot, another strike was called and lost in the yards, and the Amalgamated Meat Cutters and Butcher Workmen became a completely feeble organization. While the

1921 strike was brewing, Negro leaders expressed fear that the unorganized Negroes in the yards might become the target of another race riot. Thus the Chicago *Defender* wrote:

There is a phase to the situation which cannot be overlooked, and that is the possibility of recurring race troubles. Many of our people are employed at the yards. They are not members of the union and will not be inclined to leave their employment. The fear of being supplanted by white workers will hold them at work. Naturally, they will become the targets of pickets and strike sympathizers while going to and from their employment. Clashes under such circumstances are inevitable.

Negroes and the new union

Between 1921 and the Depression, the so-called company unions were dominant in the stockyards and packing plants. With the advent of the Depression, the AFL unions were revived, and a new union, the Packing-house Workers Industrial Union, also appeared on the scene. The latter union called several strikes in 1933 and 1934, but none of them were successful. Before the NRA, there had been fewer than 200 Negro members in the entire international organization of the AFL packing unions; but in the campaign that followed the passage of the blanket code, Negroes came into the union with the rest of the packing-house workers in large numbers. By January of 1935, there were more than 5000 Negroes enrolled in Chicago locals alone.

Most of the Negro members, however, were highly suspicious both of the wisdom of defying the packers' will and of the white workers' good intentions. When the union showed the first sign of weakness, many colored workers dropped out. Because of the half-hearted way in which the Amalgamated dealt with the problems arising out of Negro participation in the union's social, political and economic affairs, Negro workers became increasingly suspicious of this AFL union, but the Packing-house Industrial Workers Union, which was Communist-affiliated, never succeeded in making significant inroads among the workers, either colored or white.

When the CIO was formed in 1935, it immediately set itself the task of organizing the packing industry and breaking the hold of the company unions. Negroes responded enthusiastically to its appeal. Plant after plant was organized, until contracts had been negotiated with all of the major packers. Negroes and whites were organized together in the locals, and many Negroes were elected as officers. White workers under CIO leadership gave a convincing demonstration of solidarity with their colored fellow-workers, and Negroes responded by giving the union their confidence and loyalty.

A prominent Negro labor leader in 1937 described the relations of Negroes to the new union as follows:

In the yards, the dominant group is the Poles. They constitute 40 per cent of the workers. Negroes are 38 per cent. The rest are Lithuanians, Germans, Italians, and Croatians. The Negro is best informed on union procedure and is most articulate. The foreign groups understand, but aren't articulate because of language difficulties. We have our union literature printed in several languages so they will understand even though they can't speak English.

The best proof that the Negro is the best union member is that we have more Negro stewards and officers in our locals than any other group. And these were elected in mixed locals. In one local we have a Negro president. Local #6 is completely organised and a Negro is president of that local, too. The other officers are almost evenly distributed between Negroes and whites. The president of the local is white. The secretary is a Negro.

Negroes and whites in the same departments get practically the same pay. Of course, cleaner jobs go to white workers. There are more Negroes in the wool, glue, and sausage departments because this is dirtier work. Negro women are in the dirtier departments, too. These things will have to be ironed out after the union has agreements in all packing houses.

Testimony to the effectiveness of the union in improving Negro-white relations in the industry was offered by a rank-and-file Negro member, a stockyards laborer, who said to an interviewer in 1938: 'Now the union come and we has a friendlier feeling 'mongst us – we feels all together, 'stead of working 'gainst each other. That's a long ways from the time we was all fighting each other back in 1919 during the race riots. Then we was afraid to go to work for fear we would be kilt.'

Reference

HERBST, A. (1932), *The Negro in the Slaughtering and Meat Packing Industry in Chicago*, Houghton Mifflin.

28 W. Lloyd Warner

American Class and Caste

Reprinted from W. Lloyd Warner, 'American Class and Caste', *American Journal of Sociology*, vol. 42, 1936, pp. 234–7.

The social organization of the Deep South consists of two different kinds of social stratification. There is not only a caste system, but there is also a class structure. Ordinarily the social scientist thinks of these two different kinds of vertical structure as antithetical to each other. It is rare that the comparative sociologist finds a class structure being maintained together with a caste structure.

Caste as used here describes a theoretical arrangement of the people of the given group in an order in which the privileges, duties, obligations, opportunities, etc., are unequally distributed between the groups which are considered to be higher and lower. There are social sanctions which tend to maintain this unequal distribution. Such a definition also describes class. A caste organization, however, can be further defined as one where marriage between two or more groups is not sanctioned and where there is no opportunity for members of the lower groups to rise into the upper groups or of the members of the upper to fall into the lower ones. In class, on the other hand, there is a certain proportion of interclass marriage between lower and higher groups, and there are, in the very nature of the class organization, mechanisms established by which people move up and down the vertical extensions of the society. Obviously, two such structures are antithetical to each other, the one inflexibly prohibiting movement between the two groups and intergroup marriage, and the other sanctioning intergroup movement and at least certain kinds of marriage between higher and lower classes. Nevertheless, they have accommodated themselves to each other in the southern community we examined (Davis, Gardner and Gardner, 1941).

Perhaps the best way to present the configurations of the two kinds of vertical structure is by means of Figure 1. The diagonal lines separate the lower Negro caste (*N*) from the upper white caste (*W*), and the two broken lines in each segment separate the three general classes (upper, middle, and lower) in each caste from each other. The two double-headed vertical arrows indicate that movement up and down the class ladders in each caste can and does take place and is socially sanctioned, but that there is no movement or marriage between the two segments. The diagonal arrangement of the parallel lines which separate the two castes expresses the essential skewness created by the conflict of caste and class in the South. The gradual elaboration of the economic, educational, and general social activities of the Negro caste since slavery (and to some extent even before) has created new groups which have been vertically arranged by the society until certain fairly well-marked class groups have developed within the Negro caste. As the vertical distance of the Negro group has been extended during the years, the top Negro layer has been

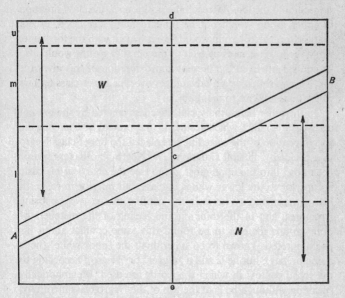

Figure 1

pushed higher and higher. This has swung the caste line on its axis (*c*), so that the top Negro group is higher in class than the lower white groups and is so recognized. (This recognition is expressed in circumlocutions and by unconscious actions, but is at times also consciously and openly stated by the members of both the white and the Negro groups.) If this process continues as it seems to be doing at the present time, it is possible, and indeed probable, that the lines *AB* might move on the axis *c* until they approximate the hypothetical line *de*. (Theoretically, of course, this process could go farther, but it seems unlikely). This tendency to bring the two groups out of vertical opposition and organization into a horizontal arrangement is being reflected at the present time in such movements as 'parallelism', as expounded by Dr DuBois. Such terms as 'parallelism' are kinds of collective representations which have come into existence and approximately express the social facts of the changing social structure; at the same time, of course, allowing the sentiments of some of the people who live in the structure also to find expression. Should the line *AB* reach the position *ed*, the class situation in either group would not be fundamentally disturbed, except that the top Negro group would be equivalent with the top white, while the lower classes in each of the parallel groups would also be equivalent. Even the present approximation of this gives the top Negro group certain advantages over his lower-class fellows which he is anxious to maintain.

On the other hand, the social skewness created by the present class-caste conflict which results in the process of changing the social location of the caste line has placed the upper-class Negro in a decidedly difficult situation. The Negro who has moved or been born into the uppermost group (see the chart) of his caste is superior to the lower whites in class, but inferior in caste. In his own personality he feels the conflict of the two opposing structures, and in the thinking and feeling of the members of both groups there is to be found this same conflict about his position. He is known to be superior to the 'poor white' (he is a doctor, say), but he is still a 'nigger' or 'Negro,' according to the social context in which the words are used. Metaphorically speaking, although he is at the top of the Negro class hierarchy, he is constantly butting his head against the caste line. He knows himself to be superior to the poor white, yet to the poor white the upper-class Negro is still a 'nigger', which is a way of saying the Negro is in a lower caste than himself. Furthermore, if it ever came to an issue, the supraordinate white class would maintain the solidarity of the white group by repudiating any claims by any Negro of superiority to the lower-class whites. This would be true even through the admission might be made privately that the Negro was superior to certain of the lower-class whites.

The present and past political behavior of the South has to be understood, it seems to me, in terms of the maintenance of the caste lines, and as an effort to prevent the continued elaboration and segmentation of the class groups within the lower caste. The unequal distribution of school funds and privileges are an excellent example of how the system tends to maintain itself through the changing generations.[1] The operation of the courts and the activities of the police also reflect the same concious or unconscious maintenance of control by the supraordinate white caste. For that matter, all social institutions in the South, including the family, school, association, clique, and church, are formed to fit the dominant caste social situation of the dominant social caste.

An interesting hypothesis may be built out of the skewed social position of the upper-class Negro. It seems possible that the instability of many of the individuals in this group (as compared, let us say, with the Negroes of the lower positions) may be due to the instability and skewness of the social situation in which they live. They are always 'off balance' and are constantly attempting to achieve an equilibrium which their society, except under extraordinary circumstances, does not provide for them.

1. The concepts of class and caste used here are briefly described in relation to the school system in Warner (1936).

References

DAVIS, A., GARDNER, B. B., and GARDNER, M. R. (1941), *Deep South: A Social and Anthropological Study of Caste and Class*, University of Chicago Press.
WARNER, W. L. (1936), *J. Educ. Sociology*, May.

29 Ulf Hannerz

Waiting for the Burning to Begin

Excerpt from Ulf Hannerz, 'Waiting for the Burning to Begin', *Soulside*, Columbia University Press, 1969, pp. 159–76.

Harlem 1964, Watts 1965, Chicago and Cleveland 1966 . . . The list of black ghetto risings in Northern cities was growing as the study of the Winston Street neighborhood began. The events of Harlem and Watts had already been incorporated into the history of black America, the newspaper headlines about Cleveland and Chicago were only a few weeks old. More was to follow, including Newark and Detroit 1967 and – toward the end of the study – Washington, D C, itself, in the days following the assassination of Martin Luther King in April, 1968. But by then an eruption of this kind could hardly come as a surprise. The circumstances understood to be at the basis of earlier risings had clearly been at work in Washington as well; besides, as the nation's attention moved from one violent ghetto crisis to another, people like those in the Winston Street neighborhood had also become concerned with the prospect of turmoil in their own community, its causes and its possible consequences. Although not an every-day subject of conversation for most ghetto dwellers, it seemed continuously present as a background understanding; when a verbal exchange concerning it occurred, practically everybody seemed to have pertinent experiences and opinions. There were also a number of incidents which pointed forward to more tumultuous times. The climate of large-scale trouble thus existed long before the outbreak became a fact. Here we will attempt to throw some light at grassroots conditions and events along the road to a ghetto rebellion, with an emphasis on the ghetto dwellers' own perspective toward it.

The sharing of discontent

Ghetto dwellers have much to resent about the way the outside world treats them: poor jobs, unemployment, unfair practices on the part of many employers, high rents for unsatisfactory housing, inadequate schools and health and welfare services, arbitrary, inefficient, and sometimes brutal police work, the poor performance and sharp practices of many businesses aiming at ghetto customers, as well as a host of major and minor expressions of prejudice and discrimination which may confront a member of the black minority as he goes about his everyday social traffic in American society.[1] Although such circumstances do not hit every member of the community with equal force, they provide each ghetto dweller with some basis for discontent, and probably they all play some role in the accumulation of grievances which may finally result in a rising. However, they do not seem to be equally prominent in the collective articulation of resentment which occurs spontaneously in the ghetto, and some of them are obviously of greater significance than others for the understanding of the form of ghetto rebellion. Some of the grievances are discontinuous and more private in their character, and one may perhaps only diffusely conceive of who is responsible for them. Thus complaints may be aired now and then about the insufficiency of garbage collection, about hours spent in waiting rooms, about a job a no better qualified white person got, or about a landlord who refuses to make repairs. But there are fewer of these, and they tend to be assimilated to the general body of knowledge about the hostile, distant white world. In the Winston Street neighborhood, at least, many more conversations about grievances dwell on white-owned businesses and the police; probably this is so because these are continuously present, represented by 'real people', on ghetto territory. This may make it easier for ghetto dwellers to share experiences directly and to see the relevance of one's own experience to that of others. Since merchants and policemen are also those outsiders who become most directly involved in the insurrection itself, we will pay

1. The Report of the National Advisory Commission on Civil Disorders (1968) may be consulted for a more general survey of ghetto dwellers' grievances. Mainstream institutional contacts with the ghetto are discussed by Jacobs (1966).

particular attention to how ghetto dwellers define their discontent with respect to these. This obviously does not mean that they are the only objects of 'real' grievances; rather, they seem to become the fact of concern toward which discontent is channeled also from other sources.[2] Thus they are particularly important in interpreting the insurrectionary mood of the ghetto in terms of social processes within the community.

As we have noted before, a great many of the business establishments in the ghetto are white-owned. Although some of these are quite modest enterprises – streetcorner groceries, carry-outs, variety stores and the like – most of the larger establishments are also among them, such as liquor stores, record stores, clothing stores, dry-cleaning operations, appliance and furniture stores, and auto dealers. Furthermore, there are the ghetto links of large supermarket and drugstore chains. The ghetto dwellers' attitude toward this white dominance behind the store fronts in their community is often one of bitterness. First of all this is based simply on the categorical relationship between blacks and whites. The people of the ghetto see that the meager resources allotted to them flow straight back to white people. It is very obvious to them that businessmen who are dependent on them for a living are doing much better than they. 'See, there goes our bread, but he'll be back for more tomorrow,' a streetcorner man says to his friends as they watch the owner of the liquor store across the street lock up his store and drive off in his car toward the suburb. But there is more to the resentment than this.

There is the question of prices, important all the way down the line from cars and TV sets to groceries. Since the ghetto dwellers are largely a low-income population, their desire for expensive goods – supported by TV and radio commercials, but also by the general affluence of the society surrounding them[3] –

2. Goldberg (1968, p.125) notes that only certain kinds of grievances seem to call forth risings directly. While this may be true and the police would then certainly have to be seen as an object of discontent particularly often involved – it seems questionable, as Rainwater (1967, p. 31) points out, if unrest would be prevented by dealing with factors which may be of a largely symptomatic nature. See also the comments at the end of this chapter.

3. In fact, some articles which could easily be seen as luxuries become necessities in a society where they are assumed to be everybody's property.

creates a demand for credit, and the businesses catering specially to a ghetto public thus specialize in instalment-plan sales. These often make items more expensive than they would ordinarily be.[4] Quite often high-pressure sales tactics are used, and advertising and information about sales conditions – on black radio stations and elsewhere – are frequently incomplete and misleading, so that the customers in due time find out that they will have to pay much more than they originally thought. Of course, few ghetto dwellers are so aware of the technicalities of instalment buying that they can protect themselves fully against unpleasant surprises. Thus they have personal or vicarious experiences of how they or friends or neighbors have been pursued by creditors or their agents, claiming debts which the ghetto dwellers feel are morally nonexistent. And such questionable debts are incurred not only by those in the community who are least well off but also by mainstreamers with steady and reasonably satisfactory incomes whose wishes for a comfortable and respectable life may lead them, for example, to acquire expensive furniture from one of the stores advertising their credit plans on ghetto radio.

Whether he knew what he was doing or not when he entered into debt, there are times when the ghetto dweller simply cannot make the payment which is due. The creditor may then have the debt attached through a routine court action to the debtor's salary, so that the latter's income is channeled straight to the creditor. This, of course, can cause great hardship on a poverty-stricken ghetto dweller, and it can also poison his relationship to his employer. When this method of claiming debts cannot be

---

The car is the best example. William Jackson, a teenager, was sitting in his mother's old station wagon, smoking cigarettes with a friend, when somehow the car caught fire. The two boys tried to extinguish the fire but failed: by the time the firemen arrived the car was destroyed, and Mrs Jackson had to stop working. She was a domestic in a distant Maryland suburb, and the taxi fare would be too expensive, while there was no reasonably convenient public transportation.

4. According to the Report of the National Advisory Commission on Civil Disorders, retail outlets specializing in instalment sales to ghetto dwellers in Washington charge an average 52 per cent more for furniture and appliances than other stores in the area (National Advisory Commission on Civil Disorders, 1968, p. 276).

used or for some other reason is not used, the merchandise in question may be reclaimed – and whether or not this is done in a justifiable manner, it is not likely to enhance the ghetto dweller's love for the merchants in his community. Freddy, living with his girl friend in a basement apartment, only had occasional income of his own but wanted the signs of success in street life. He made the down payment on an old Ford Thunderbird, and he and a friend of his spent days going over its engine, painting over its scratches, and cleaning it thoroughly – all a labor of love. At this time he was doing a little business in bootlegging, and as the time approached for the next instalment on the car, his apartment was raided by detectives. He was fined heavily, could not pay the car dealer, and lost the Thunderbird which was his pride. Rather understandably, he turned a little bitter. A girl swinger had a coat laid away for her in a store and had made a sizeable part of the payment as she lost her job and could not pay any more. She did not get the coat, nor was she given her money back, and she was not allowed to take something else and cheaper for what she had already paid. While she was sure the store had maltreated her, she felt she could no nothing about it.

The feeling that unfair business practices are involved is also directed toward the supermarkets and streetcorner stores catering to the ghetto dwellers' daily shopping needs. The opinion is widespread that chain stores charge more for an item in a ghetto branch than they do in more affluent areas, and that the food stuffs on sale in the ghetto are often of inferior quality. When it was reported that at least one supermarket chain hiked its prices on those days when welfare payments were made, this seemed rather generally accepted as the truth by people in the Winston Street neighborhood, although business officials denied it. One community organization posted pickets outside the stores involved, but business continued much as usual. One man had this to say:

Sure I can stop buying my groceries in those stores. But you know, then I have to buy everything from the old man up here at the corner, and he'll charge me even more. So I'll just have to go to the one who cheats me less.

It is undoubtedly true that it is generally more expensive to shop at the streetcorner groceries. It is not very difficult to give a couple of acceptable partial reasons why this is so: the small shopkeepers must make up for their limited turnover, and the small scale of their businesses also makes it difficult for them to stock up in an economical way. Yet it is not difficult for a ghetto dweller to believe that the streetcorner grocer is simply charging as much as he can possibly get away with.

The quality of the interaction between businessmen and ghetto dwellers is also often tense in a more personal way. Probably this is partially due to simple racial prejudice on the part of the white merchants; at least many ghetto dwellers complain about unjustified rudeness on the part of store owners. However, when shopkeepers appear to behave unnecessarily brusquely they may also be influenced by their fear of pilfering and even robbery which they understand to be common problems of ghetto business.[5] This is certainly particularly likely to hit those customers whose outward appearance is not altogether 'respectable': children, teenagers, or streetcorner men. But even if there is some basis for this fear it will anger a great many innocent people who find yet another reason to dislike white businessmen. This is evident as streetcorner men try to convince each other to make the visit to the liquor store with their collected funds; several of them hesitate to go because they 'don't like the man in there'. And when they send a child on an errand to the grocery store although they are idle themselves, one may also suspect that they want to avoid a confrontation with a disliked shopkeeper.

With the businessmen, the police are the representatives of the wider society who are most strongly in evidence on ghetto streets. According to the President's Commission on Crime in the District of Columbia (1966, p. 165), Washington's police force is about four-fifths white, despite the large black majority in the city. Thus most of the policemen patrolling the ghetto are also white. The relationship of the people of the ghetto to these policemen is markedly ambivalent and often tinged with more hostility than respect. True, as ghetto dwellers sometimes point out, 'You got to say this about them, they got a job to do.'. As we have noted before, the people of the ghetto feel that theirs is a dangerous environment; they are almost constantly conscious

5. Such problems for the shopkeepers may also contribute to higher prices.

of the potential of trouble. For this reason they are highly aware of the need for law enforcement, and they have nobody but the police to turn to. If there is a violent fight in the house next door some ghetto dwellers will indeed call the police, and occasionally a streetcorner man may report an enemy just to settle a score. Thus there is no consistent policy of non-cooperation. But one of the complaints ghetto dwellers have against the police is that a great extent it fails to protect them against the violence of the urban jungle. This laxity, they feel, is itself evidence of racial discrimination:

The police say, 'Let the niggers cut each other up.' They don't care as long as it is not in a white neighborhood. They're just watching out for the stores.

However, the kinds of actions the police do take is probably more important in causing ghetto resentment than what they do not do. Teenagers and streetcorner men feel they are being harassed quite unnecessarily in their everyday lives at the hangouts. As we have seen, for instance, public drinking and drunkenness are among the offences for which most arrests are made. The men who are drinking at the corner or in the back alley are constantly on guard against policemen and patrol cars; since they consider their drinking quite harmless to everybody else, they do not consider it any business of the police. It may indeed be impossible for them to find more privacy for their sociability than they do at their hangouts in public places; wives, mothers, sisters, or landladies may object to their getting together at home, and it is too expensive to drink at bars all the time. In fact, some policemen look the other way most of the time to avoid unnecessary arrests in such cases, but others seem to want to enforce the law to the letter, and the outcome is a feeling that the policemen act quite arbitrarily.

There are certainly a great many ghetto dwellers who take a much dimmer view of public drinking and drunkenness than these men do, and who would not mind if the police could actually enforce the law even more firmly in this field. Even so, they may concur in seeing the police as a source of trouble in their lives. A great many men can recall being arrested some time in their lives – if not recently, then quite often when they were young. In many of these cases they still consider the arrest to have been unjustified, and whether they do or not, they may reminisce about harsh treatment. One middle-aged man recounted a recent experience of his as follows:

I just got out of bed and had breakfast, and then I stood here on the stairs and thought about what I should do next, you know, and I had just decided to go over across the street and see some buddies when this police car came up, and the policemen called me. 'Hey boy', he said. So I said 'Yeah', And then he said, 'Get into the car.' 'What for?' I said. 'Just get into the car.' And then when we got down to the precinct I was booked as a drunk. So I said, 'Shi-it, I'm no more drunk than you are.' So they had to let me go, and I said I'd bring charges against them. Yeah, I really think I should, you know, but I won't, 'cause, see, if I do that he'll be bugging me every time he sees me, and charging me with one thing or another, and I don't want none of that. Would have been another thing if I had lived in another precinct.

Another man, complaining about his lack of exercise, said that he really should take to running around a few blocks each morning.

But I can't, 'cause if I do that I'll probably get busted. The police won't believe that you're up to any good if they see you running, see.

Only slightly later, it did indeed happen that a man was arrested while running toward the hospital where his mother lay dying.

Some such actions on the part of the police may well be simple harassment. The use of disliked epithets – 'boy', 'nigger', and so forth – shows that many policemen do not bother to hide their prejudice, and some excessive use of force cannot be understood as anything but police brutality. However, it seems that the police may also behave in ways unacceptable to the ghetto dwellers – or any public – because of the understandings they have of what the ghetto situation calls for from them as professionals.[6] To the police the ghetto is a high-crime district where the dangers of police work are great and where the public is generally suspect. Any strange behavior – and what is 'strange' to an outsider like a policeman need not at all be so to someone with a greater knowledge of the community – should

6. For a discussion of the professional ideology of ghetto policemen and other matters relating to their performance and standing in the ghetto community see Fogelson (1968).

be investigated, and if an infraction against the law has occurred, anybody who happens to be seen close to the scene of the crime soon afterwards is liable to be treated as a suspect, especially if he is young or if he does not look quite 'respectable'. Since a person who gets arrested in a high-crime community is thought to be potentially dangerous – he may resist arrest or even carry a weapon – the policeman may anxiously show a little extra strength just in case it should be necessary. With such rather primitive and categorical notions of how to treat ghetto dwellers, the policemen are apt to make arrests which should never have been made and to leave themselves yet more open to allegations of racism and police brutality. And since their actions may hit any member of the ghetto community, even its most law-abiding people may come to resent the police, not only for what they fail to do but also for what they do. One is not always ready to give the police the benefit of a doubt; the following notes from a street incident in the Winston Street neighborhood show how quickly the tensions between police and ghetto dwellers may escalate.

It was a rather cold Friday night in November, about 8 p.m. I was talking with Carl, George, Sonny, and Lee, one of the mainstreamer men in the neighborhood, outside Rubin's grocery. Outside the carry-out across the intersection a group of teenagers were talking and laughing loudly, with a couple of them engaging in a boxing bout. Two policemen walked up to the police telephone at the corner with a young man under arrest – apparently for drunkenness, as he had some difficulty walking. Another policeman came just after them. They called the precinct station for a car, then started searching the arrestee. To the bystanders they seemed to shake him with more force than necessary; he reacted with a jerk and shouted, 'Leave me alone, mother-fucker'. They found no weapon on him and continued to hold him in a firm grip. More people were coming by, and many of them stopped to watch. Before the police car arrived, there were people watching from each corner of the intersection. The teenagers outside the carryout were shouting insults at the police; a number of friends of the arrestee arrived in cars, and some got out. 'We'll make sure they don't do nothing to you', one of them said. The people in my group began speculating whether this was the start of a major clash. They felt the policemen would not dare beat the man while everybody was watching but that he would probably be brutalized in the car on the way to the precinct station, then sentenced for 'resisting arrest' which would serve to explain any marks on him. A couple of teenagers were threatening the policemen as daringly as was possible without yet coming to blows. Lee went over to them and said that policemen are dangerous and do not know what they are doing, so they had better not provoke them. Finally, after one of the policemen had made a new hurried call to the station, a patrol car came to take two of them and the arrestee to the station. Immediately afterwards, three police buses rushed in with lights flashing, coming to a halt at the intersection where each parked at a different corner. A number of policemen jumped out and shouted to people to leave, so as not to 'hinder traffic on the sidewalks'. Faced with this massive show of concern with the problems of pedestrians, everyone left.

This was obviously a routine arrest. It just so happened, however, that there were unusually many people outside for a late fall evening, and the policemen and the arrestee were highly visible to them for a rather long time. Both the policemen and the spectators seemed to overreact to each other. The ghetto people were quickly ready to interpret what they saw in terms of police brutality; the policemen feared a riot and bought in a force which may have stopped any further escalation but which to the ghetto dwellers constituted strong evidence that the police saw them all as an enemy. Thus a minor event became a basis for symmetrically schismogenetic interaction between the police and the ghetto as they progressively strengthened their showing and understanding of animosity.[7] As the spectators walked off from the scene they were talking about what might be happening at the precinct station; it was generally held that the police have turned to beating prisoners over their heads through telephone books. It is said to hurt just as badly but to leave no marks.

As the ghetto dwellers experience the behavior of white businessmen and policemen and work out interpretations of it together, they arrive at a collective definition of their grievances. They chuckle as they see a good friend and neighbor leave by the back door as the bill collector enters through the front door. They find themselves under constant surveillance from slow-moving patrol cars and feel they know what the policemen inside are thinking about them. They note that the 'fresh greens'

7. Bateson (1935) defines symmetrical schismogenesis as the process whereby two parties progressively react to each other by strengthening those similar responses which indicate the conflict between them.

at the grocery look like they have been around for some time, and that the children they send to the store on an errand often seem to get too little change in return. And they know of instances when policemen 'accidentally' shot those suspected of only minor offenses – something they can only see as gross disregard for black lives. Of course, a great deal of the interaction between the ghetto dwellers and these white outsiders in their territory flows quite smoothly. Quite possibly, too, the outsiders may be able to explain satisfactorily some of that behavior of theirs which from the ghetto dwellers' point of view is only evil. But what matters is that the people of the ghetto do in fact accumulate and share among themselves so much evidence of injuries to their interests and honor, and that they find little or no reason not to see the merchants as exploiters and the police as oppressors. Thus there is a withdrawal of legitimacy from these as community institutions; for they seem to be working against the community rather than for it. With the ghetto dwellers continuously strengthening this interpretation with new data, the foundations for rebellion against these outside powers exist long before the eruption comes.

The tradition of being oppressed

One should not, however, understand the ghetto view of the police and the ghetto merchants only in terms of their own ability to cause resentment. They have the additional burden of being the most accessible representatives of the white world as a whole, a world by which black people have a tradition of being exploited and oppressed. It is indeed a tradition; to many ghetto dwellers the relationship to whites does not seem to have changed much in recent times, and the white problem is still defined in terms reminiscent of the racist politics of the Deep South. The typical black-and-white joke at the Howard Theatre is still about the Ku Klux Klan. Whether or not the understanding of white people's racial attitudes which this reflects remains correct today, the institutionalized segregation of ghetto dwellers prevents many of them from finding out much about the current state of white opinion at first hand. Just as black people are taught about the meaning of blackness by other blacks, they learn about white people and race relations within the ghetto community rather than in face-to-face contacts with whites. White people are being typed by black people, as 'crackers', 'grays', 'Whitey', 'Mr Charlie', 'ofays', 'PWT' (poor white trash), 'honkies', or 'blue-eyed blond devils' (a Muslim term), just as white people among themselves are typing black people. In both cases the vocabulary becomes a cultural storehouse for hostility, a part of the community's own information about its external affairs which is seldom contradicted by other sources. Perhaps the white suburbs do not all share the views of the Klan, but the unemployed streetcorner man who hardly knows any white people personally does not necessarily know. As far as he is concerned, the machinery of the society may still seem like a Klan device to keep him down, and it is not impossible to fit ghetto merchants, the police, and many fleeting contacts with other whites into such an interpretation. In his state of isolation from mainstream society, a ghetto dweller may well view institutionalized segregation as a direct expression of average white personal prejudice. Whether he is correct in this or not, the impact of this is such that he will take any not obviously prejudiced white person with whom he comes in contact to be an exception to the rule. There are shopkeepers in the ghetto who can hardly be said to be 'liberals on the race question' but are yet hailed by neighborhood people as 'good white people', and the moderator of one TV talk show whom a fair number of white people would certainly consider strongly conservative was believed by many Winston Street people to be a 'typical white liberal'.

The ghetto community can thus keep alive its traditional representation of the relationship between white and black America without being confronted with much contrary evidence. To the notion of racism as a dominant force in the wider society is added that of racketeering – this understanding is probably a Northern ghetto innovation. Many ghetto men hint in conversations to 'the Syndicate' as one of the great powers in society, if not even the greatest. Some of the facts of ghetto life which cannot be easily explained in terms of racism may be blamed on large-scale white racketeering, with influences extending into government – 'the Syndicate' is said to have its own congressmen. One former alcoholic threw light on his conception of the power of racketeers in this statement.:

I'd rather smoke pot than be a juicehead, you know, you can stay cool, you don't piss in your clothes, you don't get into fights with your friends, and you can have some whenever you want it and you can afford it. Look, it's these ordinary cigarettes that give you cancer and you get addicted to, and they're legal, but pot which only makes you feel good is outlawed. You know why? Because if pot was legal, all those racketeers couldn't make so much money – that's why they keep pot illegal.

Most of the talk about these racketeers is independent of most ghetto dwellers' personal experiences, and their ideas about big crime are very hazy. If the imagery about 'the Syndicate' is not entirely without foundation, it certainly seems rather exaggerated. Even so, it must be taken into account as a part of many ghetto dwellers' model of black - white relations. The power imputed to racketeers constitutes a further reason for the ghetto dwellers to deny the morality of white dominance in their community.

The young and the old

If there is continuity in the tradition of oppression, its impact on the oppressed may yet be changing. There is a growing feeling that white dominance need not be accepted. A strong generational cleavage is noticeable at this point, for the younger people are clearly much more militant than the older. In the Winston Street neighborhood this shows up in how people regard the idea of black power. Hardly anyone feels that more power for black people to manage their own affairs would be a bad thing, but particularly the middle-aged and the elderly are worried that any kind of action against white dominance would hurt nobody more than it would hurt the ghetto dwellers themselves. They feel that 'black power' may be taken as a licence for unruly teenagers to go around knocking down people, black and white, thus starting a white avalanche which would come to destroy ghetto lives and homes. That is, the older people still believe much more in white power than in black, and they feel that the less noise they make about the latter, the less risk is there that the former will engage in retaliation. When a well-known spokesman of a black power organization paid a visit to the neighborhood some of these older people were afraid that he would start trouble there. Afterwards they expressed their support of a bootlegger's wife who went out into the street to tell him in no uncertain terms that although she surely had no more love for white people than he did, she wanted him out of there. It may be, of course, that her action was partially motivated by her particular concern for the family business which could be harmed if police attention were drawn to the neighborhood; this was the view of some of her more cynical young neighbors.

Among the younger people, on the other hand, many more are willing to listen to the black power message and acknowledge that 'it makes a lot of sense'. Many of them know little or nothing about the older civil rights organizations; they are familiar with the Nation of Islam (the 'Black Muslims') with which some of the streetcorner men in the neighborhood sympathize, but they are rather skeptical of it. The Muslim ideology seems notoriously unhip with its bans on pork, liquor, tobacco, dancing, flirtation, and so forth, and there is a feeling that the Muslims who were once in the front line of militant protest are accommodating themselves to co-existence with white power, despite their continuing rhetoric.[8] Besides, Elijah Muhammed gets his share of the suspicion that religious leaders are con-men. Thus for the younger generation at least, black power seems more in line with their own thinking. Although they usually continue to stay away from organized political participation, they can accept it as a rallying concept; this does not necessarily mean that they are aware of all its implications. But the black power movement gives some coherence to their own notions of what is wrong with the ghetto condition, and particularly to the discontent with white power. In so doing, it serves as a catalyst for ghetto change.

While the older people are concerned with the rebelliousness of the younger men and women, the latter feel that the preceding generations have too often been 'conned by the white man' into a complacency which has taken them nowhere. The middle-aged and the elderly have been 'Uncle Toms', 'handkerchief heads'. If there is some truth to this, there may be a good reason for it in that the generations have to a great extent lived their lives under

8. The routinization of the Nation of Islam is discussed by Parenti (1964); Essien-Udom (1962) gives a general account of the movement.

different circumstances. More of the o'der people are still to a great extent black Southerners. They have had their own experiences of being under constant white scrutiny in a much more personal way than is possible in the large Northern ghetto. What this meant not too long ago was made clear by John Dollard in *Caste and Class in a Southern Town* (1937); for instance, it was possible to punish by whipping those black persons who had been found to subscribe to Northern Negro newspapers. Perhaps the older ghetto generation of migrants are still more prone to 'watch their step' as they begin new lives in the North. One of the streetcorner men at Winston Street clearly had this opinion about his neighbors:

Those people around here ain't gonna do nothing they'd think a cracker wouldn't like. They're all from the Carolinas, you know – North Carolina and South Carolina. They just say 'Yes, sir', 'no sir'. They gonna shuffle forever.

The younger people 'ain't gonna shuffle no more'. In fact, it is questionable whether they, as born ghetto dwellers, ever had reason to shuffle very much. Harsh as the circumstances of life may be in the ghetto, black-white relationships in the North are seldom so close that the white party needs constantly to reassert its dominance, and the anonymity of the large ghetto also provides greater personal freedom for black people. It is, at least, a freedom to be relatively more militant in one's views and to be more daring in one's behavior.

The lack of politics

As we have noted, grievances were strongly felt and openly articulated in the Washington ghetto before the April rising. Yet most ghetto dwellers took no part in those organized political expressions which occurred. Civil rights groups and others carried on their work but seemed to draw little interest from most people in the community who agreed with what the groups did but paid little or no attention to them. The black power groups were to some extent an exception, both because they made some attempts to take their message to the streets and because mass media took a noticeable interest in them. Generally, however, there was no concerted political activity. Many people, of course, still felt it could be dangerous. They continued to look to the South for examples and had no trouble finding them. The weekend before Martin Luther King was killed a few men at a Winston Street corner were talking about the Poor People's March he was planning for Washington, DC; King had just participated in a march in Memphis in connection with the sanitation workers' strike, and the march had broken up in disorder. Reinhardt Ross, one of the men, was skeptical of marching:

They don't get me to walk in one of those marches and get my head busted. So where was King when all those people were beaten up by the police? On his way to the airport! You see? On his way to the airport! That's what happens every time with those protests, the leaders run off and the people who have been dumb enough to follow them get busted. No, he ain't gonna have no march here, King ain't gonna have no march here.

More often, however, the organized political activities were simply not of a kind which most ghetto dwellers would regard as any of their business, such as public meetings. When asked if they planned to go to some meeting coming up, most people in the Winston Street neighborhood were obviously surprised at the idea, and in this they seemed to represent well the ghetto as a whole. Attendance at public meetings tended to confirm the ghetto dwellers' lack of concern with this kind of organized activity. In the fall of 1966, when the black power concept was fairly new and widely debated, in the ghetto as well as outside, the local branch of the NAACP held a public meeting to discuss it. The meeting was held at the YMCA in the middle of the ghetto and included the local SNCC representative as a main speaker, but although the meeting was well advertised, few other than the predominantly middle-class, outer-city NAACP supporters showed up. More people came to a meeting on police brutality, called by all the better-known militant black groups and personalities, centrally located in a black church and again widely publicized. The ghetto population was also clearly better represented; plainclothes policemen in the audience were pointed out and asked to leave. Yet considering the size of the Washington ghetto, attendance was still small. At neither of these two meetings was anybody from the Winston Street neighborhood present. A third meeting was held by a civic group in order to discuss urban renewal plans for a large area including Winston Street. It was advertised through leaflets distributed to all households in the area, but only one resident of the Winston Street neighborhood attended, a preacher from a storefront church who took a greater than ordinary interest in community affairs.

Another test case for ghetto activism was a plan for a May Day boycott of public schools, to protest against conditions in ghetto schools and against the reappointment of an unpopular school superintendent. This boycott was largely a failure. Few children, on Winston Street or elsewhere in the community, stayed home. In this case, however, black groups were not united behind the boycott.

Although school conditions were not talked about a great deal in everyday ghetto conversations, at least in the Winston Street neighborhood, black power and police injustice certainly were recurrent topics, and neighborhood renewal was certainly a matter of concern. The very limited number of people who went to meetings such as these seems to show, then, that organized political activity did not reach the majority of ghetto dwellers. Although groups and meetings were involved in articulating ghetto grievances, their work had very little noticeable impact on the everyday lives of the majority of ghetto dwellers. Successes which could dramatize their activity were largely lacking. Meanwhile, other ghettos showed a radical way out of muteness.

The state of readiness

It did not escape the ghetto dwellers of Washington that the characteristics of other Northern ghettos were similar to those of their own community, and as Watts, Detroit and others burned, this was easily seen as a forecast for Washington. The mass media certainly strengthened this view as they detailed the conditions likely to lead to an eruption and spoke grimly of long hot summers to come. Over the afternoon paper Bee Jay could comment that if there were a rising in Washington it would be really bad; he thought there were firearms in practically every house. (This was probably greatly exaggerated.) But he would go along with it, for he would always be with his people. His friend disagreed. They could not win, and there was too much to lose 'If anything happens here I'll go and hide in the basement till it's over,' he said. But although opinions were divided about what to do in case of an eruption, few doubted that there might be one coming. Now and then as someone felt poorly treated by a ghetto business, he could mutter that 'a place like that ought to be burned to the ground'. Mass media showed quite clearly what goes on in a rising, and further information was supplied by friends who came to visit from cities where risings had already occurred – or who were visited there by Washingtonians. While some of this evidence was clearly unfavorable, there were visitors who evinced enthusiasm about their own rebellions. Sonny ran into an old musician acquaintance who had just returned to Washington from Detroit and who told him the ghettos of the two cities were a lot alike; 'you ought to do it here, too'. And at the meeting against police brutality mentioned above, a young man stood up to say that he had recently arrived from Watts – 'the brothers back there wonder what's going on in Washington, if you're all a bunch of Toms or something.' Obviously visitors such as these gave risings a political interpretation. These were rebellions, acts of black self-assertion – not just riots, outbreaks of selfish plundering, lawlessness, and irrational violence. Although the terminology varied, the general idea was clear. It was obviously one which many ghetto dwellers could develop on their own; but if they were so inclined, ideological support from experienced outsiders would do nothing to diminish their readiness for rebellion.

The Washington ghetto dwellers did not only take note of turmoil at a distance. There were also a number of incidents involving their own community. During the 1966 Easter holidays there was a disturbance caused by black teenagers in an amusement park outside the city; reportedly those in the Winston Street neighborhood knew of it in advance. In late summer that year there was a considerable rise of tension and some violence between the police and the inhabitants of a distant ghetto area in Southeast Washington. For some time afterwards Washington newspapers focused their attention on the 'breakdown of law and order' in this area, particularly on the problems of shopkeepers. Ghetto dwellers in other areas also acknowledged that there was 'a lot of trouble' going on there. The next major period of crisis came the following summer. As the risings of

Newark and Detroit had followed closely on each other many asked the question whether Washington was next in line. Some younger men in the Winston Street neighborhood alleged that there were newcomers to the city who were propagating the opinion that a rising would be a good thing; with the high death figures in Detroit and Newark in mind, they were themselves among those who were worried by the prospect of a repetition in their city. Therefore they very consistently argued strongly against a rising when conversations turned to this topic. During this period a number of rumors about agitators and incidents were flying and given varying credence. One very real incident occurred in the Northwestern corner of the ghetto where a young man left in charge of a delicatessen shot two youths who were allegedly trying to rob the store. Other young men in the area reputedly felt that there was something odd about the circumstances of the shooting. For some time people in this neighborhood were brooding over what had occurred, and at one point an angry crowd assembled close to the store. Apparently it was dissolved by a leader of a local civil rights group who dissuaded the people present from taking violent action. The situation was generally understood as one which could have been the starting point of general turmoil.

There came an outburst of looting and burning a rainy summer night, largely concentrated to the lower ghetto end of Seventh Street in the Northwest section of the city where there were a number of used furniture stores. Comparatively few stores were damaged, however, and there were not many arrests. Compared to what people expected could have happened, this was only a minor outbreak involving mainly a rather small number of teenage boys – it was generally believed that the rain had contributed strongly in keeping people off the streets. Those in the Winston Street neighborhood who had feared a large-scale rebellion with police and military reprisals on the model of Newark and Detroit seemed almost relieved. Many saw only a temporary respite, however; this was certainly not the expression of pent-up feelings which they thought would be as natural in Washington as it had been elsewhere. One swinger with a far-ranging network who usually appeared to have a good idea of what was going on in the community had this to say:

I think maybe that's it for this summer, but a lot of people I know would be in that kind of thing didn't even hear about this one till it was over. The rain did a lot, you know. And then a lot of people are a little scared right now, with all those people who got killed in Newark and Detroit, and they might be ready again when they've forgot about that. Next year they could start all over again.

In late October there was a tumultuous ending to a rock-and-roll show at the Washington Coliseum which was crowded to more than capacity with an audience of 6000 to 8000 people, most of them young; there was a noticeable amount of gatecrashing. It was an attractive bill including the popular duo Peaches and Herb and the comedian Clay Tyson as emcee; the stars of the show and thus last to appear were the Temptations, one of the leading Motown groups. Since there had been few major musical events in the community this fall even the Coliseum which usually has many empty setas was not large enough. People were standing in the aisles, and anybody who left his seat during the show – and there are always people moving around – could not be sure to get it back. Thus there was considerable commotion throughout the show. Finally, soon after the Temptations came on stage, a crowd surged forward toward it, dancing, walking, and pushing. This is not unusual at such shows, although it is discouraged by the management. In this case, however, the people who were moving ahead pushed one of the special policemen guarding the stage area to the ground. He apparently panicked as he felt he might get trampled to death; thus he reached for his gun and fired in the air. With the kind of expectation of violence prevalent among ghetto dwellers, this started a panic. People in the hall cried in alarm, one young woman could be heard shouting, 'They're shooting! No, No!', and while many fled, others joined those pushing toward the stage which was quickly vacated by the Temptations. Several people were hurt in the throng. Rufus 'Catfish' Mayfield, the well-known leader of a recently formed ghetto work corps, went on stage to ask people to return to order but was greeted with hostility or indifference. Chairs and others objects were flying as it was announced that the show would not be resumed. In the next hours there was rock throwing, window breaking, and looting in the area around the Coliseum; a few policemen were injured but not many arrests were made.

The years and months preceding the insurrection of April were thus far from uneventful to the ghetto dwellers. Again and again they were reminded of the possibility of violent conflict. Apart from the incidents which became more generally known there were such neighborhood happenings as the Friday night streetcorner arrest described earlier in this chapter. If the quick response of part fear, part violence by the Coliseum audience at the Temptations show gave a glimpse of how ready many ghetto dwellers were to see danger and violence in a situation, such an incident as this fall evening arrest showed the ghetto dwellers that the police were thinking in similar terms. As the next spring approached, it was a very obvious question whether there was another long, hot, violent ghetto summer beyond it.

The insurrection[9]

Like most people those in the Winston Street neighborhood were used to thinking of ghetto risings as phenomena of the summer; the street scene is more lively then, so escalation comes quicker, and the summer unemployment of high school students may add to the unrest. Among young people with a higher degree of political awareness it was pointed out now and then that turmoil could very well occur any time of the year, but as April came there was no widespread expectation that anything would happen very soon. One of the first evenings of the month there was an incident at a drug store at the always restless corner of Fourteenth and U Street, but it was reportedly calmed through the intervention of black power militants. Only two days later Martin Luther King was assassinated in Memphis, and the same street corner was soon again in the midst of the action.

As the news of the Memphis shooting – and somewhat later, of King's death – came over radio and television, neighbors on Winston Street quickly told each other about it, and many of those who had telephones called friends and relatives to see if they had heard about it. They speculated about what might happen. As the black radio stations turned to religious music the

9. The brief account of the April rising which follows was compiled from personal observations, conversations with ghetto dwellers (most of them from Winston Street) and the reports of the *Washington Post* and the *Evening Star*.

disc jockeys counseled their listeners to be calm. On WOL Nighthawk asked everybody to stay off the streets; King would not have wanted anybody to take to arms. But it could hardly be avoided that crowds formed to vent their united anger. Apparently there were more of them at the corner of Fourteenth and U Streets than anywhere else. As Stokely Carmichael appeared from the SNCC office on Fourteenth Street just north of the corner, a crowd gathered around him. He went around to those businesses which were still open, asking them to close in honor of Dr King, and they did so. In a couple of instances he advised those around him against violence, pointing to the overwhelming power of the adversary. Yet he could not contain the anger of the people on the streets whose numbers grew as the news of the assassination spread. Store windows started breaking and looting followed. After a while Carmichael gave up his attempt to keep the protest orderly and left the area. While he may have influenced the ghetto's contemporary ideology of discontent, he had little power over its ultimate expression. One young man who had been out on the streets this night commented a few days later:

You know, this thing had been building up for a long time, and so when something like this happens you can't just say, 'Hey, cool it, it's dangerous.' People felt they just got to do something, you know, and I guess most people don't believe too much in marching and that kind of stuff any more.

There were few policeman in the area as looting began, and the looters apparently did not feel very constrained by their presence. (According to one report, the police were told when crowds started to assemble that a conspicuous presence on their part could only exacerbate feelings.) Soon there were also attacks on stores on other main business streets in the ghetto. According to eye witnesses euphoria was added to anger as people felt they were finally striking back. When more police arrived on the scene bottles, bricks, and other objects were thrown at them; they were still too few to confront the larger groups involved in ransacking the stores, but a heavy rain began to fall during which the number of people on the streets decreased. However, looting did not stop. One young man on upper Fourteenth Street apparently shouted a few words out of a popular James Brown hit: 'We all get together, in any kind of weather ...' Fires began to burn along the street, but with fewer people around the police were slowly regaining control, partly with the use of tear-gas. Toward the early morning hours the community seemed largely quiet again.

This was Thursday night. On Friday morning people on Winston Street were debating what would happen that evening; ghetto streets are always lively on weekend nights, with more people than usual moving about, and people were still angry. 'This ain't over yet', one of the mainstreamer men said. 'It could go on a couple of more days.'

He was quite right; already that morning people were throwing bricks at cars passing through the ghetto, and looting and burning began again. Some groups went downtown but looting there was rather limited – as we have noted once before, it was particularly men's fashion stores that were hit – and there was hardly any burning outside the ghetto, where most of it continued to be concentrated on the main shopping streets. Some groups seemed to concentrate on going around 'opening up' stores which had closed early – that is, they broke doors and windows to leave the way in open to looters. This made it possible for a great many to join in who had qualms about taking the first step themselves. One young mother said afterwards:

Well, you could see all the stuff lying there and all those people going in and out, and somebody was gonna take it, so I thought I could as well get some for myself.

Of course, a great many ghetto dwellers took no part in the looting. There were those who felt it safest to stay home, perhaps following what was happening on radio and television. One young man on Winston Street accounted for his weekend this way:

I got myself a bottle of gin on Friday morning when the stores were still open, and then when I came home from work and saw all those people running around I just sat down and switched on the television. And that's what I did all the time, drinking and watching those crazy people taking care of business.

Some older people disapproved more directly of what was going on, seeing it not as a rising but as theft and destruction. This was the view of a middle-aged woman expressed a few days later:

I was really sorry to see it. Some of the people I saw should have a lot better sense. They was just stealing, that's what I think. Some of the people in them stores hadn't done nothing wrong.

As far as most of the people on the streets were concerned however, they did not appear to think that they were doing anything immoral; rather they were affirming an emergent community morality. It was as if goods hoarded by somebody who had no right to it were suddenly released for general consumption. Although profits were derived from looting, it could be easily understood as a political act against white oppression and exploitation. At the very least there was little question of 'theft' on the part of any individual participant, as previous ownership became simply irrelevant when the stores came temporarily under generous community control. Furthermore, the burning which often followed on looting was obviously to be seen within the framework of black – white conflict nobody could profit directly from throwing Molotov cocktails. Even more important, the participants abided quite strictly by their definition of the ghetto moral community and generally did not harm businesses with 'soul brother' or 'soul sister' signs. (There were at least one 'sole brother' and one 'sold brother' sign; ghetto-specific culture is largely non-literate.) Any harm to ghetto dwellers' lives and properties was thus unintentional yet it was rather extensive, as fires spread to black-owned businesses as well as to the apartments where ghetto dwellers lived above white business establishments. To the residents on the large business streets, then, the firebombing was a great danger. Fats, who had recently moved from Winston Street to a building just off Fourteenth Street, where the fires were heaviest, said afterwards that if he had seen anybody trying to set fire to his building he would have shot him.

During much of the Friday the police were alone in trying to halt the rising. However, they were much too few to do so successfully. Their presence in small numbers had little effect as their authority was not recognized. There were acts of hostility against them as well as against firemen: however, they were under orders to use their weapons only with the greatest restraint, so direct violence between ghetto dwellers and police was limited. Very few sniping incidents were reported; afterwards there were many comments to the effect that ghetto dwellers could well have responded in kind had the police started shooting. As it was, the police often seemed simply irrelevant as the looting and burning continued.

Those who went on radio and television to ask people to leave the streets did not seem to have a great influence either. On Saturday, as the rising was drawing toward an end, they were joined by 'soul brother number one', James Brown; this must have been one of the few times when many young ghetto dwellers reacted to him only with derision. Otherwise the black radio stations had a very restrained coverage of what was going on in the city, as it had been claimed that the news media had helped intensify earlier risings through their reporting. One station returned repeatedly to a gospel hit by the Violinaires, 'I don't know what this world is coming to', with this bewildered beginning:

Demonstration and protest
putting brother 'gainst brother
juvenile delinquency
putting child against mother

While this responded to the sentiments of some ghetto dwellers, others found it simply ridiculous.

In the Winston Street neighborhood, a few blocks away from ghetto business centers, there was no burning, but some of the businesses at neighborhood street corners were raided. Liquor stores were particularly heavily hurt as people swarmed in and around them on Friday afternoon. However, those neighborhood people who took part in the looting did so mainly on the principal shopping streets. Most of them were swingers and teenagers, but there were also streetcorner men and younger children.

After the turmoil

On Friday evening the National Guard and federal troops were called into action in Washington, and through their massive presence, rather than through much use of force, they put an end to the rising. During Saturday looting and burning gradually ceased. Soldiers were standing guard outside the stores that were left, but along long stretches of the main business streets only ruins remained. While white radio stations reported that the soldier's guns were unloaded, black radio stations said nothing about this. In the Winston Street neighborhood small boys who had been to see the military encampment at a nearby school were practicing marching, while adults stood in small groups gossiping and joking about the last few day's events. On Sunday things were returning to normal. People hurried to do their shopping at those chain stores which were still in existence and which opened for a little while to meet the needs of those customers who had not been able to do any shopping in the past days. Some neighborhood people went over to the large shopping streets to see what they looked like; there they could mix with sightseeing white suburbanites whose movie cameras, steadily aimed at the ruins, were spinning out of the windows of slow-moving cars.

First people wondered what would happen on Tuesday when Martin Luther King was buried in Atlanta; then the question arose if something might not happen again the following weekend which was Easter holiday. Fires were set to several ghetto business establishments in the days which followed, and acute tenseness remained for some time as many were not yet convinced that the turmoil was over. There was a good laugh as somebody appeared in a new outfit he had not had before the rising, and one could hear of exchanges as well as goods for sale – some had gotten the wrong size, and there were obviously those who had taken booty not only for their own consumption. In the Winston Street neighborhood there appeared to be rather few who strongly resented the rising.[10] Nobody there had been greatly harmed by it, while those ghetto dwellers who had lost homes, belongings, and jobs may well have had another opinion. Fats, coming back to see his friends from his new home, complained that there was nowhere to go shopping in the area of upper Fourteenth Street, but even so he was only rather slightly inconvenienced. Even those, particularly among the mainstreamers, who did not approve of what had happened were usually ready to explain it in terms of ghetto grievances, although some of them then continued to propose rather superficial remedies,

10. Obviously there were tendencies toward the growth of what Tomlinson (1968) has called a 'riot ideology', supporting or at least showing sympathetic understanding toward risings.

such as more youth workers on the recreation department pay-roll. (However, they thought of this as a black power program.) Others looked at the rising from a more humorous angle – looting was made to resemble trickster behavior, a familiar ghetto theme. The illegality of taking from the oppressor could be recognized, but it was a wickedness it was easy to empathize with. Younger people, in particular, looked at the rising in the most strictly political terms, expressing the hope that 'they gotta do something now'. Thus for some, participation in the rising, if only a matter of momentary anger at first, or fun and conveni-ence later, may have become an act of political commitment – at least public meetings held in the months after the rising seemed to draw larger audiences than most earlier meetings.[11]

However, what would actually happen continued to be un-certain. It would probally take long before ghetto business streets were rebuilt, and it was very likely that many of the white merchants would not come back even then. A considerable number probably did not want to, and with insurance rates in black ghettos soaring, even more of them could not afford to. Perhaps this could leave niches open for black enterprises, since only their 'soul brother' signs seemed to be as valuable as a lot of insurance.

As far as the police force is concerned, the other focus of discontent which we discussed above, its relationship to the community continued to deteriorate in the months following the April rising. A number of incidents were quite widely talked about, and black power groups emphasised the demand for some kind of community control of the police. Undoubtedly it would help to have more black policemen, recruited from the ghetto. After all, a policeman's role is to a great extent that of an officer of the peace; if the goal of keeping the peace is best pursued by his staying off the streets, as it seems to have been in many recent critical ghetto situations, he is obviously a failure.[12] Black officers might be better able to calm feelings in the community by virtue of their skill in the interaction idiom of the ghetto

11. Black militant groups seems also to have become stronger after the risings in Watts, Newark, and Detroit.

12. For a discussion of the policeman as a peace officer see Banton (1964, particularly pp. 166–76).

dwellers, even if it is true that they are no less harsh than others if violence does erupt. It is also likely that their common-sense knowledge of ghetto life would make them more sure of themselves and thus much less vulnerable to accusations of arbitrariness and brutality. But in the current situation of conflict between the police and the community, it may not be easy to recruit ghetto dwellers to the force, as they could well come to be seen as renegades. Even if it were possible, there could come a reaction on the part of ghetto militants against attempts to manipulate the community by putting a black man on the beat. So perhaps there is no other way of restoring confidence in the police than granting some form of community control.

But after all, if demands for greater black participation in ghetto business and law enforcement were met, the problems of the relationship between the ghetto and mainstream society would still have been dealt with only in a marginal way. The questions of income and employment, for instance, would probably not be greatly influenced.[13] Because they are based within ghetto territory, shopkeepers and policemen are particularly easily touched by ghetto protest, but they are only the most accessible symbols of the whole body of ghetto grievances against the wider society. And, we must conclude, for the wider society to try to deal only with the symbols may be an unrealistic solution, since symbols could possibly be exchanged.

13. Unless, of course, black enterprises in the ghetto expanded so as to take on a great part of the ghetto labor force.

References

BANTON, M. (1964), *The Policeman in the Community*, Tavistock.
BATESON, G. (1935), 'Culture Contact and Schismogenisis', *Man*, vol. 35, pp. 178–83.
DOLLARD, J. (1937), *Caste and Class in a Southern Town*, Harper & Row.
ESSIEN-UDOM, E. U. (1962), *Black Nationalism*, University of Chicago Press.
FOGELSON, R. M. (1968), 'From resentment to confrontation: the police, the Negroes, and the outbreak of the 1960s riots', *Political Science*, vol. 83, pp. 217–47.
GOLDBERG, L. C. (1968), 'Ghetto riots and others: the faces of civil disorder in 1967', *J. of Peace Research*, vol. 5, pp. 116–31.
JACOBS, P. (1966), *Prelude to Riot*, Random House.

NATIONAL ADVISORY COMMISSION ON CIVIL DISORDERS (1968), *Report of the National Advisory Council on Civil Disorders*, Bantam Books.

PARENTI, M. (1964), 'The Black Muslims: from revolution to institution', *Social Research*, vol. 31, pp. 175–94.

PRESIDENT'S COMMISSION ON CRIME IN THE DISTRICT OF COLUMBIA (1966), *Report on the President's Commission on Crime in the District of Columbia*, US Government Printing Office, Washington, DC.

RAINWATER, L. (1967), 'Open letter on white justice and the riots', *Trans-action*, vol. 4, no. 9, pp. 22–3.

TOMLINSON, T. M. (1968), 'The development of a riot ideology among urban Negroes', *American Behavioral Scientist*, vol. 11, no. 4, pp. 27–31.

Part Ten
New Zealand

Though they are still a relatively deprived minority,
the Maori have emerged, after a bloody colonial bashing and
a period of rural isolation, as comparatively well adapted
city dwellers who intermarry relatively extensively with the
dominant white majority. Walker describes Maori adaptation
with particular reference to settlement in a suburb.

30 R. J. Walker

Urbanism and the Cultural Continuity
of an Ethnic Minority: The Maori Case

An original paper published here for the first time.

The Maori People

When New Zealand was colonized in the early nineteenth
century the Maori population was estimated as approaching
200,000 (Census Report, 1926). By 1900, as a result of colonization and wars over land (during which some Europeans advocated
extermination; Miller, 1966, pp. 35, 105), the Maori population
had fallen to 40,000. The members of the two races had drawn
apart and were watching one another with angry eyes across
the frontier that few men wished to cross (Miller, 1966, p. *xi*),
and European humanitarianism was directed at 'smoothing the
pillow of the dying race' (Ramsden, 1948, p. 36). But an indi-
genously led regeneration combined with improved housing,
better education and medicine enabled a rapid population
increase, so that by 1966 there were 201,159 Maoris in an overall
population of 2,676,919.

A new Maori migration

Following their defeat in the Land Wars of the 1860s, the
Maori withdrew to the remnants of their tribal lands, and until
as late as 1926, 91 per cent lived in isolated rural communities
(Hunn, 1960, p. 19). This was the time when New Zealand's
image of itself as a racially harmonious society came into being.
By 1936 rapidly growing numbers (Metge, 1964, p. 14) and
pressure on land resources (Hohepa, 1964, p. 41), spurred urban
migration (Metge, 1964, p. 128). The rate increased during and
after World War Two, with some encouragement and assistance
from the Government (Rose, 1967, p. 38), so that by 1966 50
per cent of the Maori lived in towns. Metge has called this shift

of population 'A new Maori migration', emphasising thereby that it was a conscious and deliberate process.

The problem of urban adjustment

I studied Otara, a satellite town of metropolitan Auckland, which had been built in the 1960s. Maori made up more than 6000 of a total population of 20,000 – sufficient therefore to enable me to examine how far Maori sub-culture and forms of social organization had survived transplantation to an urban environment.

Auckland has a population of over a half a million and a complex of industrial, commercial and professional enterprises, and it is obvious that the Maori must 'accept the city as something given, as a datum with which he must come to terms' (Epstein, 1968, p. 47). The problems of adjustment are two-fold. First, a Maori has to learn the ways of the city. Second, he has to give consideration to the maintenance of his cultural identity. Living alongside the dominant Europeans forces the Maori to face, perhaps for the first time, the possibility of being assimilated.

Ethnic identity and minority group status

The majority of first-generation migrants bring with them their physical and ethnic identity as Maoris. This identity is an objective category perceived by both Maori and European and sets up mutual expectations in their social relations.

The Maori perceives the European as a racial category in terms of the visible characteristics of white skin, light hair and eye colouring and sharp facial features. For this racial category the Maori uses the word 'Pakeha', meaning 'strange' to distinguish him from the Maori meaning 'normal'. The Maori is perceived as a distinctive racial group from the Pakeha by both Maori and Pakeha in terms of the same physical characteristics of brown skin, dark eyes, dark hair and more rounded facial features.

The ideology of racial equality was signalled as long ago as 1840 by Captain William Hobson's remark at the signing of the Treaty of Waitangi, 'We are now one people' (Buick, 1914, p. 131), but the Maori is still a long way from being the social equal of the European. His ethnic identity clearly marks him as a member of an underprivileged minority group.

There is a wide gap in educational achievement between Maori and European; many thirteen year old Maori children 'may be retarded up to 3 or 4 years in reading ... have no occupational goals ... developed a hostility to school, and ... see little relevance in school learning' (MEF, 1966, p. 8). The Maori pass rate in the School Certificate examination fluctuates between 19 per cent and 23 per cent compared with the national average of 50 per cent (MEF, 1966, p. 7). In 1965, 85·5 per cent of pupils left school without any recognized educational qualifications (MEF, 1966, p. 6), while Maori representation at universities is only 1 : 1541 compared to 1 : 185 for the Europeans (Hunn, 1960, p. 25).

The Maori farm migrant, because of his poor education, 'finds it easier to obtain employment of a relatively unskilled type and typically he finds employment as a labourer or as a factory worker'. (Rose, 1967, p. 42). In Wellington and Auckland, 39 per cent of the Maori work force is in manufacturing industries compared with 29·5 per cent (Rose, 1967, p. 43) of the European. In 1966 the median income for Maori males was $1871 per annum compared with $2191 for non-Maori.

Maori educational, economic and social disadvantages are reflected in their relatively high conviction rate. 'Maoris offend against the person at a much greater rate than does the European population ... The rate of sexual offences involving Maoris was about four times and of assaults over six times the statistical expectancy' (Department of Justice, 1968, pp. 208–9); while in the Auckland Police area, the charge rate for Maoris is more than four and a half times that for Europeans (Duncan, 1970, p. 120). The conviction rates for crimes against the person and property are also correspondingly high; the annual average convictions per 100 of the male population for the period from 1954 to 1968 was 8·71 for the Maori and 1·88 for the European (Duncan, 1970, p. 45). Thus, it is clear that the Maori form both an ethnic minority group and constitute a substantial sector of the socio-economically depressed class.

The cultural background

The traditional sub-culture of the Maori underpins Maori identity; a fact which clearly differentiates the minority position of the Maori from that of the American Negro, and provides him with an alternative value system to that derived from Euro-American culture. In many respects, this makes up for the disadvantages he experiences in that other culture.

The majority of Maoris living in urban centres have been socialized in predominantly Maori rural communities, in which an individual distinguishes himself as a person of the land (*tangata whenua*) as against strangers (*tangata huere mai*) (Metge, 1964, p. 27). A person of the land has certain rights and obligations, such as ownership of land and the right to speak on the village courtyard (*marae*).[1] Kinsmen express their kinship by giving help to each other during periods of social crisis such as funerals (*tangi*), the unveiling of headstones, and at weddings and twenty-first birthday celebrations (Metge, 1964, p. 48). The sense of communal life between both kin and non-kin was also expressed in the reciprocal sharing of meat and the exchange of machinery and labour during the harvest. Leadership was diffused and informal. Although the elders were highly respected and regarded as the 'proper' leaders (Metge, 1964, p. 84), leadership was, in fact, spread across kin groups and through different voluntary associations, such as the tribal committee, Maori committee and Maori Women's Welfare League.

Metge reports that informal social controls such as ostracism, gossip and withdrawal of support were only weakly developed (Metge, 1964, p. 90), but Hohepa has shown how the collective moral force of the community was mobilised against individuals who offended against the social code as, for example, by indulging in pre-marital sexual relations (Hohepa, 1964, pp. 82–3).

A description of the rural sub-culture is outside the scope of this paper, but the features mentioned above and listed in the following paradigm are sufficient to establish that membership of it clearly distinguishes the Maori from the European:

1. Early socialization in a predominantly Maori rural community.

1. The *marae* refers to the open space of ground in front of the ancestral meeting house.

2. Identification and affiliation with one or more *marae* in a tribal territory.

3. Early life characterized by:
   (a) Economic depression, poor housing, cash cropping, small land holdings and seasonal labouring,
   (b) Labouring for parents for food and keep,
   (c) Care and responsibility for younger siblings,
   (d) Introduction to Maori food preferences.

4. Recognition that life in the community is kin-based in the tribe and sub-tribe, marked by support in times of crisis, and the sharing of food and property.

5. Early acquaintance with death and with Maori mortuary customs.

6. Attendance at Maori meetings and observation of village courtyard etiquette such as oratory, order of precedence and hospitality.

7. A deep and abiding respect for elders.

8. Belief in *tapu* associated with death and cemeteries; this is symbolized by the simple purificatory rite of washing hands.

9. Belief in ghosts (*keehua*), second sight (*matakite*), monsters (*taniwha*), premonitions, guardian spirits, faith-healing and superstitions about the taking of shellfish from the sea.

10. A commitment to religion in its widest sense, 'as a belief in a will controlling natural law' (Schwimmer, 1966, p. 149).

Maoris are conscious of themselves as forming an entity (30,261) in Auckland, and of being an ethnic minority in an alien and threatening environment. Maoris, at work or in the shared neighbourhood of a suburb or a housing estate, associate with each other more readily than they do with their European workmates and neighbours. Through being concentrated in employment such as driving, labouring in freezing works and on wharves, production process work and as craftsmen (51·24 per cent in 1956 of the male population; Hunn, 1960, p. 29), Maoris in the city build up a network of social relations which complements their kinship links. Strangers first relate to each other by establishing the town or village from which they originate and then search for mutual kin or acquaintances and, once such a connection has been established, a bond is formed.

Shared group status, economic depression, experiences on a housing estate and cultural values have fostered the emergence of a pan-Maori identity which runs across former tribal divisions. Although kinship and tribal associations do flourish in the city, wider and more embracing Maori associations have developed, which are symbolized by the adoption of names such as 'Wellington tribe' (*Ngaati Poneke*) and 'Otara tribe' (*Ngaati Otara*) for the new quasi-tribes of the city.

The problems of family life

The Department of Maori Affairs has aimed to provide new houses for immigrant Maoris. It was assumed that such provision, combined with a policy of 'pepper-potting' Maori houses among those of Europeans, would ensure the easy integration of the Maori into the social mainstream of New Zealand life. But the transition was fraught with more difficulties than the Department had foreseen. Maoris, because of their poor education and limited social experience, were not fully equipped to be self-reliant in a metropolis. Urban life represented escape from parental authority and the close scrutiny of the small community into independence, individuality and anonymity. Above all, better paid employment and assistance from the State Advances Corporation gave Maori the chance to attain the New Zealand ideal of individual home ownership.

Few Maoris had ever owned new homes and fewer still had been inside European homes. Their only model was the glamourized picture presented by advertisers. Thus, many assumed that all Europeans began home life with completely furnished homes. Therefore in order to take his place with self-respect alongside his European neighbour, a Maori felt obliged to buy the best by contracting long-term hire-purchase commitments. People who had never owned a washing machine or refrigerator considered them necessary adjuncts to urban living. Of the hundred households surveyed in Otara, 95 had TV, 89 a refrigerator and 83 a washing machine. Recurring accounts for rates, water, electricity, gas and rent or mortgage repayments had often been forgotten when the hire-purchase agreements were signed. A consequence, exacerbated by a minor economic recession in 1967, was that many ended up in arrears with their rates, rent or electricity bills as they tried to stave off repossession of their home appliances. In some extreme cases water, electricity, gas and telephones were disconnected. In some cases all that kin could provide was temporary refuge in their own homes until the services were restored. City people harassed by creditors cannot rely on kinsmen to help them out. Firstly, because kin have been left behind in the country or are scattered across the suburbs of the metropolis. Secondly, the very facts of urban living itself have compelled each household to become an independent autonomous unit. Ninety of the hundred households surveyed were based on the nuclear family; thirty-eight included one or two close kin of the householder or his spouse. Such arrangements, however, were considered to be temporary accommodations for visiting relatives or recently arrived job-seekers.

The adaptive role of voluntary associations

The key to successful adjustment to urban life and the establishment of the minor system of Maori social organization within the major system of the European metropolis is voluntary association.

Banton (1957, p. 168), and Little (1955, p. 222) when discussing the 'Ambas Gedda' and the 'Dancing Compins' respectively in African towns, have emphasised the integrative functions of voluntary associations in multi-tribal situations. Epstein (1968, p. 47) has also indicated that voluntary associations concerned with welfare appeared as an early feature of urban African society. To a certain extent Maori experience in Auckland parallels that of African migrants. In the city, Maori people come together in voluntary association to meet their needs for fellowship, mutual aid, the assertion of group norms, the expression of Maori values and the enjoyment of dancing, singing and oratory.

Family clubs and bereavement societies can ease the financial insecurity of the urban family. Families with sufficient kin in the city come together and, by the adoption of a constitution and formal offices, formalize their kinship links and create a family club or bereavement society. Some of these eventually founder through non-payment of dues or withdrawal of contributions. But, when membership of family clubs is restricted to close kin and leadership is invested in an elder, such clubs have proved effective in meeting funeral costs or helping the bereaved family to take their dead back for burial in ancestral ground, and tiding members through short periods of illness, unemployment or loss of time at work.

Where Maoris are employed in large numbers in one enterprise, they form their own clubs to run 'socials'[2] and organize basketball and football fixtures with other works teams. The games are usually played on Sunday afternoons and followed by beer and food cooked in an earth oven. Most European organized games are competitive, played on Saturdays and training is a serious business, whereas Maori teams play for fun. No one trains or plays very hard and even the overweight and unathletic can participate. Competition only enters when an occasional field day is organized in order to raise funds for a home village courtyard. Occasionally a 'Pakeha' (European) mate is included in such a team.

Maori culture clubs are also an important feature of urban life. Recruitment is variable. Sometimes a group of families in an urban neighbourhood meet in each others' homes to practise their war dances and action songs. Sometimes inmates of hostels or students form clubs to meet both their needs for fellowship and their desire to give expression to their culture and to ensure its transmission. The most stable and enduring culture clubs are those run by different church denominations or those in suburbs where there are strong Maori communities. A marked feature of urban culture clubs is the inclusion of Europeans. Although many Europeans are given inclusion simply because they wish to share in Maori culture, the high rate of Maori-European intermarriage, almost 50 per cent in Auckland (Harré, 1966, p. 143), ensures the inclusion of some Europeans in most Maori social and cultural activities.

Maori welfare committees in particular provide some measure of continuity for the social organization of the Maori, and pro-

2. A social is an evening function where music is provided for dancing and alcohol is served. In order not to contravene the liquor laws, tickets are pre-sold to members and their friends and no money is taken at the door.

vide an acceptable and recognizable link with the tribal committees which were established under the Maori Social and Economic Advancement Act, 1945. (The later Maori Welfare Act of 1962 gave recognition to the urban shift of the Maori people by redesignating 'tribal committees' as 'Maori committees'. The granting of statutory authority to voluntary associations is peculiar to New Zealand). Maori committees are elected to office for a triennial period and are charged under the Act with the following functions:

1. To promote the social and economic advancement of the Maori people.

2. To promote harmonious relations between Maoris and other members of the community.

3. To assist Maoris in their physical, economic, educational, social, moral and spiritual wellbeing.

4. To help Maoris enjoy the full rights, privileges and responsibilities of New Zealand citizenship.

Maori committees are expected to cooperate with schools, departments of state and other voluntary associations. The statutory authority vested in them provides an immediate outlet for legitimate leadership in the urban, multi-tribal situation, where the traditional criteria of leadership, such as age, descent and skill in oratory, although desirable, are not primary requirements. There is a trend towards a more democratic type of leadership which takes into account education, administrative skill and the ability to negotiate with Europeans, though an aspirant leader still has to make astute use of his kinship and personal networks to build up his position. In a committee that I studied between 1967 and 1969, the leader bound his followers to himself by budgeting eighty clients and shielding them from the threats of creditors, repossessors and bailiffs while promoting other followers to office as committee members, wardens and honorary welfare officers. The statement by Wolf (1966, p. 16–17) fits exactly:

The offerings by the patron are more immediately tangible. He provides economic aid and protection against both the legal and illegal exactions of authority. The client in turn pays back in more intangible assets.

There are first demonstrations of esteem. . . . A second contribution by the client to the patron is offered in the form of information on the machinations of others. A third form of offering consists in the promise of political support. Here the element of power emerges which is otherwise marked by reciprocities.

The Maori court

Maori wardens and honorary welfare officers, nominated by Maori committees and appointed by the Minister of Maori Affairs, act as the 'eyes and ears' of a committee; they locate problems of social maladjustment and try to deal with them. Difficult cases are taken before a committee which, under the Act, can assume the functions of a court and has power to impose a penalty of up to $20 or to impose a prohibition order on individuals who neglect their family responsibilities.

Four committees sometimes invoke their judicial powers, but generally committees aim to deal with minor offences before they get to the Magistrate's Court, thereby shielding Maori from the full weight of the impersonal European Court of Law. The effectiveness of the courts which I observed lay in the expression of the collective moral force which they mobilized against an offender. This is evident in admonitions such as:

'When you are called a dirty Maori it reflects
on us your Maori people.'

'When you fall, we fall, when you succeed, we succeed.'

'When you die, who will mourn you? We your Maori people will.'

When an offence has been committed, the Maori community closes its ranks, reaffirms its solidarity, and reintegrates the offender into itself. He is reminded that the anonymity of urban life does not absolve him of his minority group status and that his every action, for good or ill, impinges on 'his' Maori people.

The urban marae

The most urgent need of the urban Maori is for urban *marae* as a focal point for community sentiment, as the most appropriate place to hold a funeral (*tangi*), and as a platform where they can give voice to their needs and grievances in the face of the dominant European majority. A Maori thinks of the *marae* as an institution where he is king, where he is exalted to the front rank and his minority group status is not apparent.

In 1950 the only *marae* in Auckland was demolished by the municipal authorities as a blot on the landscape (Kawharu, 1968, p. 176). A substitute *marae* at the community centre catered for the needs of the first wave of migrants into the inner city, but in later years, as the people dispersed to the outer suburbs, the desire arose to build *marae* there. At present seven *marae* are being planned or have been started in Auckland to supplement the two which have been built during the last five years. The sponsors of urban *marae* have to find answers to ideological and practical questions such as: should projects be called *marae* or community centres; should they be exclusively Maori or multiracial? At the practical level, the problems of unifying Maoris owing allegiance to different kin groups and voluntary associations have to be solved; different committees, kin groups and church groups tend to favour projects of their own.

Of the two existing *marae* one is recruited on the traditional principle of kinship and the other is recruited by religious affiliation.

Conclusion

The urban migration of the last twenty or so years has brought about a new confrontation, but despite European dominance, the Maori has adjusted to the practical demands of city life and succeeded in establishing his culture there, which provides social and cultural satisfactions which cannot be found in the major European system. With the establishment of urban *marae*, its transmission into the foreseeable future is also assured.

References

BANTON, K. (1957), *West African City*, Oxford University Press.
BUICK, T. L. (1914), *The Treaty of Waitangi*, S. & W. Mackey, Wellington.
DUNCAN, L. S. W. (1970), *Crime by Polynesians in Auckland*, unpublished M.A. thesis, University of Auckland.
DEPARTMENT OF JUSTICE, (1968), *Crime in New Zealand*, R. E. Owen, Government Printer.
EPSTEIN, A. L. (1968), *Politics in an Urban African Community*, Manchester University Press.

HARRÉ, J. (1966), *Maori and Pakeha*, A. H. & A. W. Reed,
  Wellington.
HOHEPA, P. W. (1964), *A Maori Community in Northland*, University of
  Auckland.
HUNN, J. K. (1960), *Report on the Department of Maori Affairs*,
  Government Printer, Wellington.
KAWHARU, I. H. (1968), *Urban Immigrants and Tangata Whenua*,
  The Maori People in the Nineteen-Sixties, edited by E. Schwimmer,
  Blackwood and Janet Paul, Auckland.
LITTLE, K. (1955), 'Structural change in the Sierra Leone Protectorate',
  Africa, vol. 25.
M.E.F. (1966), Maori Education Foundation, *Annual Report*.
METGE, J. (1964), *A New Maori Migration*, The Athlone Press.
MILLER, H. (1966), *Race Conflict in New Zealand*, Blackwood and Janet
  Paul, Auckland.
RAMSDEN, E. (1948), *Sir Apirana Ngata and Maori Culture*,
  A. H. & A. W. Reed, Wellington.
ROSE, W. D. (1967), *The Maori and the New Zealand Economy*,
  Department of Industries and Commerce, Wellington.
SCHWIMMER, E. (1966), *The World of the Maori*, A. H. & A. W. Reed,
  Wellington.
WALKER, R. J. (1970), *Maoris in a Metropolis*, unpublished Ph.D.
  thesis, University of Auckland.
WOLF, E. R. (1966), 'Kinship, friendship, patron-client relations, in
  complex societies', in M. Banton (ed.), *The Social Anthropology of
  Complex Societies*, A.S.A. Monograph, no. 4, Tavistock.

Part Eleven
Situations and Encounters

The writings in this section treat race as an element
in social situations and encounters. Regularity in social life
is seen to derive from the replication of encounters of
particular types within situations which can themselves be
typified. The analyses proceed from the experience of social
interaction rather than from societal institutions and structures.
Where race is concerned, this kind of analysis is particularly
useful as it captures something of the poignancy inherent in
reactions to race.

31 Charles Rogler

Some Situational Aspects of Race Relations in Puerto Rico

Reprinted from C. Rogler, 'Some situational aspects of race relations in Puerto Rico', *Social Forces*, vol. 27, 1949, pp. 72–7.

The popular conception of race distance, or the degree of social isolation between races, is derived mainly from cursory observations of race relations in a particular situation; or, at the most, in a very limited number of situations. From these limited and cursory observations, the observer will more than likely derive his overall conception of the racial situation.

His common sense will often lead him into one or the other of these extreme views: He will conclude that racial intimacy is the general rule if the particular situation he observes so indicates; or, he will conclude that racial discrimination is the general rule, if, by chance, he is an observer of a situation in which racial discrimination is practiced.

But more or less active participation in many Puerto Rican situations, and the observations of the behavior of persons participating therein, yielded the fact that in some situations the Negro, and persons who were conspicuously negroid in appearance, could participate fully alongside whites; while in other situations, Negroes, and mixed types with marked negroid characteristics, were discriminated against.

With this initial fact of situational difference in the degree of 'race distance' established beyond question, the next logical step is to raise and attempt to give a sociological answer to the question: Why is there little or no social distance between races in one situation while in other situations race distance is a conspicuous fact?

From the point of view of race relations, the problem so stated immediately suggests a workable way of classifying situations for analysis, namely on the basis of the varying degree of moral value that whites place on the anatomic facts of race or color in different situations.

Two representative types of situations will be presented for analysis: first, the bi-racial situation in which race has little or no moral value; and second, situations which are either implicitly or explicitly indicative of discriminative practice against the Negro, or mixed persons who are socially defined as Negroes.

From the situational point of view, the differences in degree of race distance and the explanation as to how they came about may be conceptualized by the expression, *definition of the situation*. This concept subsumes the following situational phenomena: (a) the typical behavioral patterns of the participants in the situation; (b) the expected and actual roles and statuses of the participants; (c) and whether the level of social interaction in the situation is predominantly critical and ideational, or whether predominantly emotional or traditionally sentimental.

The two situations selected as indicative of little or no race distance, or wherein race has little or no moral value, will be descriptively and functionally different; yet both will be similar in the sense that the participants are indifferent to race. This approach will be duplicated for the two situations which exemplify racial discrimination.

Finally, an attempt will be made to formulate the evidence presented in each case into some sociological principle, or principles, that will serve as deductive tools for the analysis of similar situations elsewhere.

Situation 1: a political situation

The discussants in this situation are two prominent leaders of a Puerto Rican political party. Mr A is an upper-class white man; Mr B is a Negro, or at least a person with conspicuously negroid traits, whose social position, owing to his political accomplishments, is locally defined as 'on the borderline' of the upper class.

Their meeting was arranged, and the purposes of it are mutually understood. The immediate purpose is to achieve, through the give and take of discussion, a plan of action which it is hoped will further the chances of winning the election. The discussion proceeds on an impersonal level. Ideas, not race, are the objects for attention and of interest. Plans and counter-plans are offered and weighed, and a compromise plan of action is sooner or later achieved. Personal references and informalities may be injected from time to time into the discussion, but these digressions are 'tension releasers', or incidental convivial digressions from the definitive nature of the meeting.

If the two discussants are equally astute and articulate, leadership will shift from one to the other. But in this case Mr B, the Negro, was more astute and dominated the discussion; and, for this reason, he was the primary leader for the duration of the situation.

Both men owe their leadership to the same political process. Both have come to their positions the hard way, which is up from the ranks. There is, therefore, comparatively little in their political background that would socially differentiate them into diverse personality types. Deferential, condescending, or patronizing attitudes are ruled out in the face of the mutual desire to win the election. The interaction is defined in terms of this desire. Both persons are controlled in their behavior by rules of political expediency. Because of this, Mr A does not evince racial sentiment. It is inexpedient for him to permit extraneous racial factors to prejudice his suggestibility to the ideas of Mr B.

Political process in Puerto Rico is so characteristically unbalanced by rapid shifts from schismatic movement to compromise and coalition that there is little to encourage either the development or maintenance of strong party sentiment. And, for the same reason, it is unlikely that the political process would tend to create and stabilize attitudes and values on a racial basis.

If political behavior is defined in terms of expediency, if the social definition of the political situation is so characteristically one of dynamic redefinition, it may be safely said that any individual effort to give race a moral context would, of itself, tend to be an immoral act.

Situation 2: an informal lower-class dance

The participants are whites, a few Negroes and several mulattoes. The time and place of the dance are arranged. Anyone in the neighborhood who is interested may attend. The younger set is numerically dominant. To the outsider, the typical picture would probably be one of unbearable congestion. But to them it means that they are having a good time. The definition of a good dancer is indicative of this cramped condition: 'He is one who knows how to dance on a board.'

The rule for the host is graciousness, hospitality, and solicitude for the pleasurable well-being of his guests; it is the maximum of personal pleasure achieved through uninhibited action. Drinking of alcoholic beverages, which is socially approved, tends to lessen social distance, but the general rules of propriety are not abandoned. This is a culturally produced leisure-time situation, not a revelous, nor an orgiastic one. It is important to keep these moral norms in mind because, thereby, the leisure-time pattern for the situation becomes a pertinent index of the definitive nature of lower-class situations in general, whether they be of a work-a-day or play-a-day type.

Personal rivalry, insofar as it exists, or any other force that has a status-giving significance, is not defined along racial lines. In fact, the general attitude towards status and the values that produce it tends strongly to be one of indifference.

If and when race distance is indicated in some subtle form, it tends to be directed along sex lines, the women being somewhat more race and status conscious than the man. This slight difference sometimes appears in the choice of a dancing partner.

It is sometimes assumed that race distance varies inversely with the degree of familiarity that is definitive of the situation. A lower-class dance is a very familiar situation, measured by any criterion. Likewise, it is apparent that any white person at the dance can see who is a Negro and who is not a Negro. Why, then, does the white man not assume a racial attitude towards the Negro? The proximate answer, as already given, is owing to comparative indifference to status and status-producing values. This indifference is the consequence of socio-economic forces that minimize competition and struggle in this class.

Questions of status are of slight importance to a class of people whose economic condition has for generations remained on a subsistence level, and whose folkways, attitudes, moral and religious values are so closely woven into this subsistence economy as to produce a comparatively well organized person. This condition tends to produce a class whose wishes lie close to social reality. Forces which produce competition, social differentiation, conflict, and struggle for status are constrained by this traditional social inertia.

In the lower class, where the only 'stable' factor is economic insecurity, where slight advantages in economic status continuously shift from person to person, and where mutual aid is a survival expedient, there is neither need of nor any process to produce any socially differentiated set of traditional status-producing values. Dominance and subordination on any basis are out of character within a comparatively isolated class whose activities are organized around the elemental process of satisfying basic human needs.

Such conditions do not nurture fears that Negroes will displace whites. Fear that the Negro will achieve equal or higher status is of little consequence when status and the values that promote it are incidental and transitory. As in the previous situation, race relations at the lower-class dance must be understood in the light of the definition for the situation and against the situational patterns of this class, which in turn must be set in a cultural area where sharp racial practice is not the rule.

What common social forces operate to minimize race distance in these two situations whose definite patterns and functions are fundamentally different? In both situations there is an absense of those types of processes that tend to create race distance, hence any attempt to postulate the maintenance of a racially differentiated pattern along traditionally sentimental lines is meaningless. In the last analysis, this means that the race relations in a lower-class convivial, emotional dance situation are determined by the same basic social forces that operate to define race relations in the secular political situation participated in by two influencial political leaders.

The next two situations will exemplify discrimination against persons who are socially defined as Negroes. The salient fact in these two situations is denial to the Negro of the privilege of enjoying situational prerogatives that are commensurate with his accomplishments.

Situation 3: a casino dance

The casino is an esoteric, upper-class men's leisure-time club. General rules for admission are laid down in the casino's constitution and bylaws. As far as known, there is no provision specifically excluding the admission of Negroes. Owing to the absence of Negro members and the absense of rules forbidding their admission it may be assumed that exclusion is sanctioned by custom and sentiment on the part of the members who, themselves, rated admission because of a reputable family name, personal prestige, or the solicitation of influential friends.

Before proceeding to the analysis of this situation, this question needs to be asked and answered: How does the casino exemplify discrimination to the point of exclusion of the Negro when it is known that all lower-class white persons are excluded, too? Where vertical mobility is quantitatively negligible, where socio-economic conditions are such as to favor a closed class system, the odds against achieved upper-class status by any lower-class person are fractional.

But if the local casino excludes Negroes in a community inhabited by a more or less numerous Negro population there is *prima facie* evidence that he has been discriminated against. If this circumstantial evidence is buttressed by further evidence showing that lower-class white persons do occasionally, although very rarely, become eligible for admission because of their outstanding accomplishments, while at the same time Negroes with equal or even greater accomplishment are not eligible for admission, the proof that the Negro has been discriminated against is quite conclusive. These latter facts are known to exist.

The casino has high institutional prestige. It is old and deeply rooted, both in Spanish and Spanish-American culture. By definition and function it epitomizes the 'best', the acme of social position. It engrosses in a traditionally sentimental form all of the behavioral manifestations of upper-class prestige in general, and the upper-class family in particular.

Although the casino is by constitutional definition an upper-class male recreational club, its convivial life is frequently highlighted by dances. This activity automatically introduces into the casino situation a definition based on sex values. All of the artifices and formalities that advertise high social position are operative. Ostentation in dress, conspicuous formality, and symbolisms indicative of high status are the behavioral characteristics of the women. Gallant, solicituous, differential and preferential treatment of women is the expected male role.

The sentiment that the 'best' in life is the traditional prerogative of this in-group correspondingly implies a prejudice against persons who do not belong. The 'we' response of the casino group towards the Negro is the traditional feeling that he is inferior, which may be rationalized more or less as follows: The Negro was a slave. Therefore, he is inferior in spite of his intrinsic abilities. This out-group racial attitude prevails as a social force in the casino situation in the comparative absence, past or present, of racial competition, rivalry or conflict in the larger culture.

From the point of view of race relations, the central and crucial factor in the casino situation is the upper-class family. In spite of the fact that functions of the casino are more narrowly defined, it is essentially an institution that advertises the family's prestige. It shares with the family the in-group sentiments and prerogatives of the 'best'. It would seem that casino life is one of the most effective ways of publishing to the world the importance of the status and roles of the family groups that are represented therein. The casino group's conception of its status and its conception of the role it plays in the maintenance of upper-class family values automatically creates a discriminatory attitude towards any outsider who may damage these conceptions. The Negro is an out-group, hence he is excluded.

Case 4: a legislative caucus

From the point of view of race relations, the problems involved in this case grew out of a series of political maneuverings and compromises that deprived an outstanding Negro politician of a leadership position in the legislative body which position he would have had, had his abilities and the legislative traditions been the primary considerations.

Legislative procedure in Puerto Rico generally follows the practice of selecting as Speaker of the House or President of the Senate the outstanding party leader who is elected to each chamber. In this particular case a prominent Negro politician was deprived of this customary prerogative.

On the basis of the analysis presented in the political situation previously discussed, it would be easy to jump to the conclusion that the racial factor is not present in any political situation. But the facts presented in this situation will show the dangers of overgeneralizing even where, to all general appearances, the definitive characteristics of this situation are the same as those presented in the aforementioned political situation.

Vertical movement of leaders even in the secular area of political action entails identification with new values and new forces. The core set of secular political facts may continue to define social situations in this vertical process and, hence, tend to blind the observer to the existence of values, other than secular, that progressively become more restrictive as the Negro approaches the apex of the vertical movement.

The Negro political leader who is involved in this vertical movement will find that what was once secular – what was once governed by rules of political expediency – has come to be a blend of secular and traditionalized sentiment with the latter tending to be the controlling factor. This is a new situation. A new definition exists for it. It is not feasible to dichotomize the secular and the traditionally sentimental in this situation. They blend. If the white political leader is involved, the secular tends to dominate; if the Negro leader is involved, upper-class sentiments tend to dominate.

As a working basis for the analysis of the racial aspect of this situation the following ideal construct may be formulated. Race would have a neutral, non-moral significance if status and role were defined solely in terms of achievement, or if all values that define status and role were completely secularized, or if social processes were such as not to create social differentiation along racial lines.

This ideal is most nearly realized among the lower classes. Among the upper classes it is most nearly approached in those situations wherein the person of color has advanced his status in and through secular values, such as in the amassing of wealth or the gaining of professional prominence.

Those who resented the exclusion of this prominent Negro leader attributed it to American influence. They rationalized somewhat as follows: Legislative procedure brings Puerto Rican leaders into close contact with the Americans whom they know have strong prejudices against Negroes. Therefore, they compromise their own non-biased racial attitudes and assume an American racial bias as a means of catering to their American political overlords. This argument has frequently been heard in connection with similar discriminatory incidents, so it merits some analysis for the light it may throw on this case, as well as others of a similar nature that appear from time to time.

There is strong suspicion that the racial factor would be considered by local political leaders in connection with the selection of a candidate for Resident Commissioner in the Federal Congress. But this does not necessarily mean that controlling forces in these cases are placed correctly when they are attributed solely to American influence. The meaning of discriminatory racial practice is materially affected by whether the local sentiment is for or against it; or, more particularly, the sentiment of that group or class which has traditionally dominated political action. The claim that race discrimination is based on political expediency does not necessarily mean the absence of a ruling-class sentiment in favour of discrimination.

One possible way of understanding racial discrimination in the area of political activity would be to observe the status and role-playing prerogatives of outstanding Negores in those predominantly secular areas that are not subject to American influence. In no area of secular endeavor is it possible for the outstanding Puerto Rican Negro to enjoy the situational prerogatives that are consonant with his abilities. This situational constraint on his social movement is apparent not only in activities that are directly in line with professional accomplishment, but also in those ancillary situational areas where privileges are often enjoyed because of achievement. For example, a skillful Negro physician will have fewer white patients than his white colleague with equal or even less skill. Furthermore, the proportion of patients would be even less among upper-class whites. In addition, the Negro physician would enjoy fewer ancillary situational prerogatives than his white colleague.

So, it would appear that there are traditional sentimental forces operating in this situation that exclude the Negro. And, as in the previous case which was marked by an absence of secular values, the upper-class traditional sentiment of the 'best' tends to create an out-group attitude towards Negroes who have risen high in their respective fields of endeavor.

A personal factor also tends to operate: Personal rivalry and envy are accentuated as political leaders advance into the higher ranks where struggle for status is keener owing to the selective elimination of the less competent. Under such conditions it is comparatively easy to direct discriminative behavior towards rivals whose race marks them apart.

The following principles governing race relations are proposed for the situations that have been analyzed:

1. If the definition of the situation is secular and impersonal, the behavior in the situation evinces little or no race distance.

2. In lower-class, leisure-time situations where familiarity, informality, and conviviality are the definition of the behavioral patterns and where uninhibited personal satisfaction is the function, there is little or no race distance because the socio-economic forces are such as to neutralize status-producing values, and to bar social differentiation along racial lines.

3. In upper-class, leisure-time situations, as exemplified in casino life, the traditional in-group sentiment that the 'best' is their prerogative produces a prejudicial out-group attitude towards the Negro, and he is excluded.

4. In the top levels of secular achievement, the situational definition is a complex of secular and traditionally sentimental values. In situations so defined, such as the legislative one, the sentimental in-group feeling of the 'best' tends to prevail and deny to the Negro situational privileges consonant with his intrinsic abilities.

32 Harold Finestone

Cats, Kicks and Colour

Harold Finestone, 'Cats, Kicks and Colour', *Social Problems*, vol. 5,
July, 1957, pp. 3–13.

Growing recognition that the most recent manifestation of the
use of opiates in this country has been predominantly a young
peoples' problem has resulted in some speculation as to the
nature of this generation of drug users. Is it possible to form an
accurate conception as to what 'manner of man' is represented by
the current species of young drug addict? Intensive interviews
between 1951 and 1953 with over fifty male colored users of
heroin in their late teens and early twenties selected from several
of the areas of highest incidence of drug use in Chicago served
to elicit from them the expression of many common attitudes,
values, schemes of behavior, and general social orientation. Moreover, since there was every reason to believe that such similarities
had preceded their introduction to heroin, it appeared that it was
by virtue of such shared features that they had been unusually
receptive to the spread of opiate use. Methodologically, their
common patterns of behavior suggested the heuristic value of the
construction of a social type. The task of this paper is to depict
this social type, and to present a hypothetical formulation to
account for the form it has taken.

No special justification appears to be necessary for concentrat-
ing in this paper on the social type of the young colored drug
user. One of the distinctive properties of the distribution of drug
use as a social problem, at least in Chicago, is its high degree of
both spatial and racial concentration. In fact, it is a problem
which in this city can be pinpointed with great accuracy as having
its incidence preponderantly among the young male colored
persons in a comparatively few local community areas. The following delineation of the generic characteristics of young colored
drug users constitutes in many respects an ideal type. No single

drug addict exemplified all of the traits to be depicted but all of them revealed several of them to a marked degree.

The young drug user was a creature of contrasts. Playing the role of the fugitive and pariah as he was inevitably forced to do, he turned up for interviews in a uniformly ragged and dirty condition. And yet he talked with an air of superiority derived from his identification with an elite group, the society of 'cats'. He came in wearing a non-functional tie clip attached to his sport shirt and an expensive hat as the only indications that he was concerned with his appearance and yet displayed in his conversation a highly developed sense of taste in men's clothing and a high valuation upon dressing well. He came from what were externally the drabbest, most overcrowded, and physically deteriorated sections of the city and yet discussed his pattern of living as though it were a consciously cultivated work of art.

Despite the location of his social world in the 'asphalt jungle' of the 'Blackbelt' he strictly eschewed the use of force and violence as a technique for achieving his ends or for the settling of problematic situations. He achieved his goals by indirection, relying, rather on persuasion and on a repertoire of manipulative techniques. To deal with a variety of challenging situations, such as those arising out of his contacts with the police, with his past or potential victims, and with jilted 'chicks', etc. he used his wits and his conversational ability. To be able to confront such contingencies with adequacy and without resort to violence was to be 'cool'. His idea was to get what he wanted through persuasion and ingratiation; to use the other fellow by deliberately outwitting him. Indeed, he regarded himself as immeasurably superior to the 'gorilla', a person who resorted to force.

The image of himself as 'operator' was projected onto the whole world about him and led to a complete scepticism as to other persons' motives. He could relate to people by outsmarting them, or through openhanded and often ruinous generosity, but his world seemed to preclude any relationship which was not part of a 'scheme' or did not lend itself to an 'angle'. The most difficult puzzle for him to solve was the 'square,' the honest man. On the one hand the 'square' was the hard-working plodder who lived by routine and who took honesty and the other virtues at their face value. As such he constituted the prize victim for the cat. On the other hand the cat harbored the sneaking suspicion that some squares were smarter than he, because they could enjoy all the forbidden pleasures which were his stock in trade and maintain a reputation for respectability in the bargain.

The cat had a large, colorful, and discriminating vocabulary which dealt with all phases of his experience with drugs. In addition, he never seemed to content himself with the conventional word for even the most commonplace objects. Thus he used 'pad' for house, 'pecks' for food, 'flicks' for movies, 'stick hall' for pool hall, 'dig the scene' for observe, 'box' for record player, 'bread' for money, etc. In each instance the word he used was more concrete or earthier than the conventional word and such as to reveal an attitude of subtle ridicule towards the dignity and conventionality inherent in the common usage.

His soft convincing manner of speaking, the shocking earthiness and fancifulness of his vocabulary, together with the formidable gifts of charm and ingratiation which he deployed, all contributed to the dominant impression which the young drug user made as a person. Such traits would seem to have fitted naturally into a role which some cats had already played or aspired to play, that of the pimp. To be supported in idleness and luxury through the labors of one or more attractive 'chicks' who shoplifted or engaged in prostitution or both and dutifully handed over the proceeds was one of his favorite fantasies. In contrast with the milieu of the white underworld, the pimp was not an object of opprobrium but of prestige.

The theme of the exploitation of the woman goes close to the heart of the cat's orientation to life, that is, his attitude towards work. Part of the cat's sense of superiority stems from his aristocratic disdain for work and for the subordination of self to superiors and to the repetitive daily routine entailed by work, which he regards as intolerable. The 'square' is a person who toils for regular wages and who takes orders from his superiors without complaint.

In contrast with the 'square', the cat gets by without working. Instead he keeps himself in 'bread' by a set of ingenious variations on 'begging, borrowing, or stealing.' Each cat has his 'hustle' (Finestone, 1957, pp. 60 – 85), and a 'hustle' is any non-violent means of 'making some bread' which does not require work. One of the legendary heroes of the cat is the man who is such a skillful con-man that he can sell 'State Street' to his victim. Concretely, the cat is a petty thief, pickpocket, or pool shark, or is engaged in a variety of other illegal activities of the 'conning' variety. A very few cats are actually living off the proceeds of their women 'on the hustle'.

The main purpose of life for the cat is to experience the 'kick'. Just as every cat takes pride in his 'hustle', so every cat cultivates his 'kick'. A 'kick' is any act tabooed by 'squares' that heightens and intensifies the present moment of experience and differentiates it as much as possible from the humdrum routine of daily life. Sex in any of its conventional expressions is not a 'kick' since this would not serve to distinguish the cat from the 'square', but orgies of sex behavior and a dabbling in the various perversions and byways of sex pass muster as 'kicks'. Some 'cats' are on an alcohol 'kick', others on a marihuana 'kick', and others on a heroin 'kick'. There is some interchangeability among these various 'kicks' but the tendency is to select your 'kick' and stay with it. Many of these young drug users, however, had progressed from the alcohol to the marihuana to the heroin 'kick'. Each 'kick' has has its own lore of appreciation and connoisseurship into which only its devotees are initiated.

In addition to his 'kick' the cat sets great store on the enjoyment of music and on proper dress. To enjoy one's 'kick' without a background of popular music is inconceivable. The cat's world of music has a distinctive galaxy of stars, and the brightest luminaries in his firmament are performers such as 'Yardbird' (the late Charlie Parker) and disc jockeys such as Al Benson. Almost every cat is a frustrated musician who hopes some day to get his 'horn' out of pawn, take lessons, and earn fame and fortune in the field of 'progressive music'.

The cat places a great deal of emphasis upon clothing and exercises his sartorial talents upon a skeletal base of suit, sport shirt, and hat. The suit itself must be conservative in color. Gaiety is introduced through the selection of the sport shirt and the various accessories, all so chosen and harmonized as to reveal an exquisite sense of taste. When the cat was not talking about getting his clothes out of pawn, he talked about getting them out of the cleaners. With nonchalant pride one drug user insisted that the most expensive sport shirts and hats in the city of Chicago were sold in a certain haberdashery on the South Side. The ideal cat would always appear in public impeccably dressed and be able to sport a complete change of outfit several times a day.

The cat seeks through a harmonious combination of charm, ingratiating speech, dress, music, the proper dedication to his 'kick', and unrestrained generosity to make of his day to day life itself a gracious work of art. Everything is to be pleasant and everything he does and values is to contribute to a cultivated aesthetic approach to living. The 'cool cat' exemplifies all of these elements in proper balance. He demonstrates his ability to 'play it cool' in his unruffled manner of dealing with outsiders such as the police, and in the self-assurance with which he confronts emergencies in the society of 'cats'. Moreover, the 'cat' feels himself to be any man's equal. He is convinced that he can go anywhere and mingle easily with anyone. For example, he rejects the type of music designated 'the blues' because for him it symbolizes attitudes of submission and resignation which are repugnant and alien to his customary frame of mind.

It can be seen now why heroin use should make such a powerful appeal to the cat. It was the ultimate 'kick'. No substance was more profoundly tabooed by conventional middle-class society. Regular heroin use provides a sense of maximal social differentiation from the 'square'. The cat was at last engaged, he felt, in an activity completely beyond the comprehension of the 'square'. No other 'kick' offered such an instantaneous intensification of the immediate moment of experience and set it apart from everyday experience in such spectacular fashion. Any words used by the cat to apply to the 'kick', the experience of 'being high', he applied to heroin in the superlative. It was the 'greatest kick of them all'.

In the formulation now to be presented the cat as a social type is viewed as a manifestation of a process of social change in which a new type of self-conception has been emerging among the adolescents of the lower socio-economic levels of the colored population in large urban centers. It is a self-conception rooted in the types of accommodation to a subordinate status achieved historically by the colored race in this country, a self-conception which has become increasingly articulated as it responded to and selected various themes from the many available to it in the milieu of the modern metropolis. Blumer's classification (1939, pp. 255–78) of social movements into general, specific, or expressive, appears to provide a useful framework for the analysis of the social type of the cat.

In terms of these categories the cat as a social type is the personal counterpart of an expressive social movement. The context for such a movement must include the broader community, which, by its politics of social segregation and discrimination, has withheld from individuals of the colored population the opportunity to achieve or to identify with status positions in the larger society. The social type of the cat is an expression of one possible type of adaption to such blocking and frustration, in which a segment of the population turns in upon itself and attempts to develop within itself criteria for the achievement of social status and the rudiments of a satisfactory social life. Within his own isolated social world the cat attempts to give form and purpose to dispositions derived from but denied an outlet within the dominant social order.

What are these dispositions and in what sense may they be said to be derived from the dominant social order? Among the various interrelated facets of the life of the cat two themes are central, those of the 'hustle' and the 'kick'. It is to be noted that they are in direct antithesis to two of the central values of the dominant culture, the 'hustle' versus the paramount importance of the occupation for the male in our society, and the 'kick' versus the importance of regulating conduct in terms of its future consequences. Thus, there appears to be a relationship of conflict between the central themes of the social type of the cat and those of the dominant social order. As a form of expressive behavior, however, the social type of the cat represents an indirect rather than a direct attack against central conventional values.

It is interesting to speculate on the reasons why a type such as the cat should emerge rather than a social movement with the objective of changing the social order. The forces coercing the selective process among colored male adolescents in the direction of expressive social movements are probably to be traced to the long tradition of accommodation to a subordinate status on the part of the Negro as well as to the social climate since the Second World War, which does not seem to have been favourable to the formation of specific social movements.

The themes of the 'hustle' and 'kick' in the social orientation of the cat are facts which appear to be overdetermined. For example, to grasp the meaning of the 'hustle' to the cat one must understand it as a rejection of the obligation of the adult male to work. When asked for the reasons underlying his rejection of work the cat did not refer to the uncongenial and relatively unskilled and low paid jobs which, in large part, were the sole types of employment available to him. He emphasized rather that the routine of a job and the demand that he should apply himself continuously to his work task were the features that made work intolerable for him. The self-constraint required by work was construed as an unwarranted damper upon his love of spontaneity. The other undesirable element from his point of view was the authoritarian setting of most types of work with which he was familiar.

There are undoubtedly many reasons for the cat's rejection of work but the reasons he actually verbalized are particularly significant when interpreted as devices for sustaining his self-conception. The cat's feeling of superiority would be openly challenged were he to confront certain of the social realities of his situation, such as the discrimination exercised against colored persons looking for work and the fact that only the lowest status jobs are available to him. He avoided any mention of these factors which would have forced him to confront his true position in society and thus posed a threat to his carefully cherished sense of superiority.

In emphasizing as he does the importance of the 'kick' the cat is attacking the value our society places upon planning for the future and the responsibility of the individual for such planning. Planning always requires some subordination and disciplining of present behavior in the interest of future rewards. The individual plans to go to college, plans for his career, plans for his family and children, etc. Such an orientation on the part of the individual is merely the personal and subjective counterpart of a stable social order and of stable social institutions, which not only permit but sanction an orderly progression of expectations with reference to others and to one's self. Where such stable institutions are absent or in the inchoate stages of development, there is little social sanction for such planning in the experience of the individual. Whatever studies are available strongly suggest that such are the conditions which tend to prevail in the lower socioeconomic levels of the Negro urban community (Drake and Cayton, 1945, pp. 564–99). Stable family and community organization is lacking in those areas of the city where drug use is concentrated. A social milieu which does not encourage the subordination and disciplining of present conduct in the interests of future rewards tends by default to enhance the present. The 'kick' appears to be a logical culmination of this emphasis.

Accepting the emergence of the self-conception of the cat as evidence of a developing expressive social movement, we may phrase the central theoretical problem as follows: What are the distinctive and generic features of the cat's social orientation? Taking a cue from the work of Huizinga (1955) as developed in *Homo Ludens*, we propose that the generic characteristics of the social type of the cat are those of play. In what follows, Huizinga's conception of play as a distinctive type of human activity will be presented and then applied a tool of analysis for rendering intelligible the various facets of the social orientation of the cat. It is believed that the concept of play indicates accurately the type of expressive social movement which receives its embodiment in the cat.

According to Huizinga (1955) the concept of play is a primary element of human experience and as such is not susceptible to exact definition.

· 'The *fun* of playing resists all analysis, all logical interpretation ... Nevertheless it is precisely this fun element that characterizes the essence of play.' (p.3) The common image of the young colored drug addict pictures him as a pitiful figure, a trapped unfortunate. There is a certain amount of truth in this image but it does not correspond to the conception which the young colored addict has of himself or to the impression that he tries to communicate to others. If it were entirely true it would be difficult to square with the fact that substantial numbers of young colored persons continue to become drug users. The cat experiences and manifests a certain zest in his mode of life which is far from self-pity. This fun element seemed to come particularly to the fore as the cat recounted his search for 'kicks', the adventure of his life on the streets, and the intensity of his contest against the whole world to maintain his supply of drugs. Early in the cycle of heroin use itself there was invariably a 'honeymoon' stage when the cat abandoned himself most completely to the experience of the drug. For some cats this 'honeymoon' stage, in terms of their ecstatic preoccupation with the drug, was perpetual. For others it passed, but the exigencies of an insatiable habit never seemed to destroy completely the cat's sense of excitement in his way of life.

While Huizinga declines to define play, he does enumerate three characteristics which he considers to be proper to play. Each one of them when applied to the cat serves to indicate a generic feature of his social orientation.

1. 'First and foremost . . . all play is a voluntary activity.' (p.7) 'Here we have have the first main characteristic of play: that it is free, is in fact freedom.' (p.8).

The concept of an expressive social movement assumes a social situation where existing social arrangements are frustrating and are no longer accepted as legitimate and yet where collective activity directed towards the modification of these limitations is not possible. The cat is 'free' in the sense that he is a pre-eminent candidate for new forms of social organization and novel social practices. He is attempting to escape from certain features of the historical traditions of the Negro which he regards as humiliating. As an adolescent or young adult he is not fully assimilated into such social institutions as the family, school, church, or industry which may be available to him. Moreover, the social institutions which the Negroes brought with them when they migrated to the city have not as yet achieved stability or an adequate functioning relationship to the urban environment. As a Negro, and particularly as a Negro of low socio-economic status, he is excluded from many socializing experiences which adolescents in more advantaged sectors of the society take for granted. He lives in communities where the capacity of the population for effective collective action is extremely limited, and consequently there are few effective controls on his conduct besides that exercised by his peer group itself. He is fascinated by the varied 'scenes' which the big city spreads out before him. Granted this setting, the cat adopts an adventurous attitude to life and is free to give his allegiance to new forms of activity.

2. ... A second characteristic is closely connected with this (that is, the first characteristic of freedom), namely, that play is not 'ordinary' or 'real' life. It is rather a stepping out of 'real' life into a temporary sphere of activity with a disposition all of its own. Every child knows perfectly well that he is 'only pretending,' or that it was 'only for fun'. . . . This 'only pretending' quality of play betrays a consciousness of the inferiority of play compared with 'seriousness', a feeling that seems to be something as primary as play itself. Neverthelesss. . . the consciousness of play being 'only a pretend' does not by any means prevent it from proceeding with the utmost seriousness, with an absorption, a devotion that passess into rapture and, temporarily at least, completely abolishes that troublesome 'only' feeling.
(Huizinga, 1955, p.8)

It is implicit in the notion of an expressive social movement that, since direct collective action to modify the sources of dissatisfaction and restlessness is not possible, all such movements should appear under one guise, as forms of 'escape'. Persons viewing the problem of addiction from the perspective of the established social structure have been prone to make this interpretation. It is a gross oversimplification, however, as considered from the perspective of the young drug addict himself. The emergence of the self-conception of the cat is an attempt to deal with the problems of status and identity in a situation where participation in the life of the broader community is denied, but where the colored adolescent is becoming increasingly sensitive to the values, the goals, and the notions of success which obtain in the dominant social order.

The caste pressures thus make it exceedingly difficult for an American Negro to preserve a true perspective of himself and his own group in relation to the larger white society. The increasing abstract knowledge of the world outside – of its opportunities, its rewards, its different norms of competition and cooperation – which results from the proceeding acculturation at the same time as there is increasing group isolation, only increases the tensions.
(Mydral, 1944, p. 760).

Such conditions of group isolation would appear to be fairly uniform throughout the Negro group. Although this isolation may be experienced differently at different social levels of the Negro community, certain features of the adaptions arrived at in response to this problem will tend to reveal similarities. Since the struggle for status takes place on a stage where there is acute sensitivity to the values and status criteria of the dominant white group, but where access to the means through which such values may be achieved is prohibited, the status struggle turning in on itself will assume a variety of distorted forms. Exclusion from the 'serious' concerns of the broader community will result in such adaptions manifesting a strong element of 'play'.

Frazier in *Black Bourgeoisie* (1957) discusses the social adaption of the Negro middle class as 'The world of make-believe.'

The emphasis upon 'social' life or 'society' is one of the main props of the world of make-believe into which the black bourgeoisie has sought an escape from its inferiority and frustrations in American society. This world of make-believe, to be sure, is a reflection of the values of American society, but it lacks the economic basis that would give it roots in the world of reality. (p. 237).

In the Negro lower classes the effects of frustrations deriving from subordination to the whites may not be experienced as personally or as directly as it is by the Negro middle class, but the massive effects of residential segregation and the lack of stable social institutions and community organization are such as to reinforce strong feelings of group isolation even at the lowest levels of the society.

It is here suggested that the function performed by the emergence of the social type of the cat among Negro lower class adolescents is analogous to that performed by 'The World of Make-Believe' in the Negro middle class. The development of a social type such as that of the cat is only possible in a situation where there is isolation from the broader community but great sensitivity to its goals, where the peer group pressures are extremely powerful, where institutional structures are weak, where models of success in the illegitimate world have strong appeals, where specific social movements are not possible, and where novel forms of behavior have great prestige. To give significance to his experience, the young male addict has developed the conception of a heroic figure, the 'ideal cat,' a person who is completely adequate to all situations, who controls his 'kick' rather than letting it control him, who has a lucrative 'hustle', who has no illusions as to what makes the world 'tick', who is any man's equal, who basks in the admiration of his brother cats and associated 'chicks', who hob-nobs with 'celebs' of the musical world, and who in time himself may become a celebrity.

The cat throws himself into his way of life with a great deal of intensity but he cannot escape completely from the perspective, the judgments, and the sanctions of the dominant social order. He has to make place in his scheme of life for police, lockups, jails, and penitentaries, to say nothing of the agonies of withdrawal distress. He is forced eventually to confront the fact that his role as a cat with its associated attitudes is largely a pose, a form of fantasy with little basis in fact. With the realization that he is addicted he comes only too well to know that he is a 'junky', and he is fully aware of the conventional attitudes towards addicts as well as of the counter-rationalizations provided by his peer group. It is possible that the cat's vacillation with regard to seeking a cure for his addiction is due to a conflict of perspectives, whether to view his habit from the cat's or the dominant social order's point of view.

3. Play is distinct from 'ordinary' life both as to locality and duration. This is the third main characteristic of play: its secludedness, its limitedness. It is 'played out' within certain limits of time and place. It contains its own course and meaning.
(Huizinga, 1955, p. 9)

It is this limited, esoteric character of heroin use which give to the cat the feeling of belonging to an elite. It is the restricted extent of the distribution of drug use, the scheming and intrigue associated with underground 'connections' through which drugs are obtained, the secret lore of the appreciation of the drug's effects, which give the cat the exhilaration of participating in a conspiracy. Contrary to popular conception must drug users were not anxious to proselyte new users. Of course, spreading the habit would have the function of increasing the possible sources of supply. But an equally strong disposition was to keep the knowledge of drug use secret, to impress and dazzle the audience with one's knowledge of being 'in the know'. When proselyting did occur, as in jails or lockups, it was proselyting on the part of a devotee who condescended to share with the uninitiated a highly prized practice and set of attitudes.

As he elaborates his analysis of play, Huizinga brings to the fore additional aspects of the concept which also have their apt counterpart in the way of life of the cat. For instance, as was discussed earlier, the cat's appreciation of 'progressive music' is an essential part of his social orientation. About this topic Huizinga remarks, 'Music, as we have hinted before, is the highest and purest expression of the *facultas ludendi*.' (1955, p. 187). The cat's attitude toward music has a sacred, almost mystical quality. 'Progressive music' opens doors to a type of highly valued experience which for him can be had in no other way. It is more important to him than eating and is second only to the 'kick'. He may have to give up his hope of dressing according to his standards but he never gives up music.

Huizinga also observes, 'Many and close are the links that connect play with beauty' (1955, p.7). He refers to the 'profoundly aesthetic quality of play' (1955, p. 2). The aesthetic emphasis which seems so central to the style of living of the cat is a subtle elusive accent permeating his whole outlook but coming to clearest expression in a constellation of interests, the 'kick', clothing, and music. And it certainly reaches a level of awareness in their language. Language is utilized by the cat with a conscious relish, with many variations and individual turns of phrase indicating the value placed upon creative expression in this medium.

It is to be noted that much of the description of the cat's attributes did not deal exclusively with elements unique to him. Many of the features mentioned are prevelent among adolescents in all reaches of the status scale. Dress, music, language, and the search for pleasure are all familiar themes of the adolescent world. For instance, in his description of the adolescent 'youth culture' Talcott Parsons would appear to be presenting the generic traits of a 'play-form' with particular reference to its expression in the middle class.

It is at the point of emergence into adolescence that there first begins to develop a set of patterns and behavior phenomena which involve a highly complex combination of age grading and sex role elements. These may be referred to together as the phenomena of the 'youth culture'. . . .

Perhaps the best single point of reference for characterizing the youth culture lies in its contrast with the dominant pattern of the adult male role. By contrast with the emphasis on responsibility in this role, the orientation of the youth culture is more or less specifically irresponsible. One of its dominant roles is 'having a good time' . . . It is very definitely a rounded humanistic pattern rather than one of competence in the performance of specified functions.

(1949, pp. 220–21).

Such significant similarities between this description and the themes of the social type of the cat only tend to reinforce the notion that the recent spread of heroin use was a problem of adolescence. The cat is an adolescent sharing many of the interests of his age-mates everywhere but confronted by a special set of problems of color, tradition, and identity.

The social orientation of the cat, with its emphasis on non-violence, was quite in contrast to the orientation of the smaller group of young white drug users who were interviewed in the course of this study. The latter's type of adjustment placed a heavy stress upon violence. Their crimes tended to represent direct attacks against persons and property. The general disposition they manifested was one of 'nerve' and brashness rather than one of 'playing it cool'. They did not cultivate the amenities of language, music, or dress to nearly the same extent as the cat. Their social orientation was expressed as a direct rather than an indirect attack on the dominant values of our society. This indicates that the 'youth culture' despite its generic features may vary significantly in different social settings.

In his paper, 'Some Jewish types of personality', Louis Wirth made the following suggestive comments about the relationship between the social type and its setting.

A detailed analysis of the crucial personality types in any given area or cultural group shows that they depend upon a set of habits and attitudes in the group for their existence and are the direct expressions of the values of the group. As the life of the group changes there appears a host of new social types, mainly outgrowths and transformations of previous patterns which have become fixed through experience. (1926, p. 112).

What are some of the sources of the various elements going to make up the social type of the cat which may be sought in his traditions? The following suggestions are offered as little more than speculation at the present time. The emphasis upon non-violence on the part of the cat, upon manipulative techniques rather than overt attack, is a stress upon the indirect rather than the direct way towards one's goal. May not the cat in this emphasis be betraying his debt to the 'Uncle Tom' type of adjustment, despite his wish to dissociate himself from earlier patterns of accommodation to the dominant white society? May not the 'kick' itself be a cultural lineal descendant of the ecstatic moment of religious possession so dear to revivalist and store-front religion? Similarly, may not the emphasis upon the exploitation of the woman have its origin in the traditionally greater economic stability of the colored woman?

W. I. Thomas in one of his references to the problems raised by the city environment stated, 'Evidently the chief problem is the young American person' (1926, p.46). In discussing the type of inquiry that would be desirable in this area he states that it should

. . . lead to a more critical discrimination between that type of dis-organization in the youth which is a real but frustrated tendency to organize on a higher plane, or one more correspondent with the moving environment, and that type of disorganization which is simply the abandonment of standards. It is also along this line . . . that we shall gain light on the relation of fantastic phantasying to realistic phantasying. . . .
(1926, p.47).

Posed in this way the problem becomes one of evaluating the social type of the cat in relation to the processes of social change. This social type is difficult to judge according to the criterion suggested by Thomas. Since many of the cat's interests are merely an extreme form of the adolescent 'youth culture', in part the problem becomes one of determining how functional the period of adolescence is as preparation for subsequent adult status. However, the central phases of the social orientation of the cat, the 'hustle' and the 'kick', do represent a kind of disorganization which indicates the abandonment of conventional standards. The young addicted cat is 'going nowhere'. With advancing age he cannot shed his addiction the way he can many of the other trappings of adolescence. He faces only the bleak prospect, as time goes on, of increasing demoralization. Although the plight of the young colored addict is intimately tied to the conditions and fate of his racial group, his social orientation seems to represent a dead-end type of adjustment. Just as Handlin in *The Uprooted* suggests that the first generation of immigrant peoples to our society tends to be a sacrificed generation (1951, p. 243), it may be that the unique problems of Negro migrants to our metropolitan areas will lead to a few or several sacrificed generations in the course of the tortuous process of urbanization.

The discussion of the social type of the cat leads inevitably to the issue of social control. Any attempt to intervene or modify the social processes producing the 'cat' as a social type must have the objective of reducing his group isolation. For instance, because of such isolation and because of the cat's sensitivity to the gestures of his peers, the most significant role models of a given generation of cats tend to be the cats of the preceding age group. Where, in a period of rapid change, the schemes of be-behavior of the role models no longer correspond to the possibilities in the actual situation, it is possible for attitudes to be transmitted to a younger generation which evidence a kind of 'cultural lag'. Thus the condition of the labor market in Chicago is such as to suggest the existence of plentiful employment opportunities for the Negro in a variety of fields. But because such openings are not mediated to him through role models it is possible that the cat is unable to take advantage of these opportunities or of the facilities available for training for such positions.

The social type of the cat is a product of social change. The type of social orientation which it has elaborated indicates an all too acute awareness of the values of the broader social order. In an open class society where upward mobility is positively sanctioned, an awareness and sensitivity to the dominant values is the first stage in their eventual assimilation. Insofar as the social type of the cat represents a reaction to a feeling of exclusion from access to the means towards the goals of our society, all measures such as improved educational opportunities which put these means within his grasp will hasten the extinction of this social type. Just as the 'hoodlum' and 'gangster' types tend to disappear as the various more recently arrived white ethnic groups tend to move up in the status scale of the community (Bell, 1953, p. 131–54), so it can confidently be expected that the cat as a social type will tend to disappear as such opportunities become more prevalent among the colored population.

References

BELL, D. (1953), 'Crime as an American way of life', *Antioch Review*, vol. 13, pp. 131–54.

BLUMER, H. (1939), 'Social movements', in R. E. Park, (ed.), *An Outline of the Principles of Sociology*, Barnes & Noble.

DRAKE, St C., and CAYTON, H. R. (1945), 'Lower class: sex and family', *Black Metropolis*, Harcourt, Brace & Co.

FINESTONE, H. (1957), 'Narcotics and criminality', *Law and Contemporary Problems*, vol. 22, Winter, pp. 60–85.

FRAZIER, E. F. (1957), *Black Bourgeoisie*, Free Press.

HANDLIN, O. (1951), *The Uprooted*, Grosset and Dunlap.

HUIZINGA, J. (1955), *Homo Ludens, A Study of the Play Element in Culture*, Beacon Press.

MYRDAL, G. (1944), *An American Dilemma*, Harper & Row.

PARSONS, T. (1949), 'Age and sex in the social structure', *Essays in Sociological Theory Pure and Applied*, Free Press.

THOMAS, W. I. (1926), 'The problem of personality in the urban environment', in E. W. Burgess, (ed.), *The Urban Community*, University of Chicago Press.

WIRTH, L. (1926), 'Some Jewish types of personality', in E. W. Burgess, (ed.), *The Urban Community*, University of Chicago Press.

33 Durward Pruden

A Sociological Study of a Texas Lynching

D. Pruden, 'A sociological study of a Texas lynching', *Studies in Sociology*, vol. 1, no. 1, 1936, pp. 3–9.

Part 1: the story of the lynching

One Saturday morning in the spring of the early 1930s the Negro laborer on a White man's farm, near Leeville,[1] Texas, came to his employer's house to collect his wages. On being told by the farmer's wife that her husband had gone to town and had not left the wages, the Negro, disappointed, left the house, but returned shortly with a shotgun, forced the woman into her bedroom, and assaulted her several times. Fearing that the woman's five-year-old son in the back yard might give an alarm, the Negro went to look for him, but first tied his victim to the bed, telling her he would return soon. She broke loose and fled across a field to a neighbor's house where the sheriff was telephoned. Meanwhile, some men came walking along the road, and the Negro fled toward a creek bottom.

Although the above is the commonly accepted story of the crime, there are other versions, as is frequently the case in charges of this nature. Most of the Leeville Negroes and some Whites believe that no assault occurred. Medical records show that the illicit relationship did occur.

The arrest and beginnings of mob action

One deputy sheriff came to the scene and arrested the Negro, who, it is claimed, fired at him. The Negro confessed, agreed to plead guilty, waived all rights, and was secreted in a jail in a town some miles distant from Leeville. The next Monday night a small group of men and boys loitered near the Leeville jail.

1. Fictitious names are used throughout the article. The population of Leeville is 15,000.

By Tuesday many exaggerated versions of the details of the assault were being repeated on the street. Tuesday night a large group of boys and men appeared at the jail and demanded the Negro. They refused to leave until the sheriff allowed some of their leaders to go through the jail and see that the Negro was not there. There were no more attempts at mob action until the next Friday, the date set for the trial.

The attempt at trial

On the morning of the trial many people came to the Leeville business center, both local residents and others from farms and small communities of the adjacent trading area. The judge refused to change venue, but had four Texas Rangers present to guard the court. The Rangers took the Negro into the courthouse early in the morning before the crowd gathered. All morning, as the jury was being selected, the crowd around the courtyard and in the courthouse halls grew larger and more belligerent. Just as the situation was hanging in the balance between an orderly trial and a riot, a rumor was circulated that the governor of the state had telegraphed the Rangers not to shoot anyone in trying to protect the Negro. Although the rumor was untrue, yet it was accepted by the mob and so encouraged its members as to make the Rangers practically helpless without extensive bloodshed. The precipitating event which changed the huge, curious crowd into a vicious and active mob, was the bringing of the woman from the hospital to the courthouse in an ambulance, and carrying her on a stretcher through the crowd into the courtroom. This was about 1 o'clock. After that the mob went wild. It broke in the courtroom, and was repeatedly driven back by the Rangers, with drawn guns and tear gas. Several shots were fired. The judge at last decided to change venue, and the Negro was hurried into the second-floor, fireproof vault room of the district clerk's office.

Burning the courthouse

When the mob saw that the Rangers were determined to hold the courthouse, they determined to burn it. A group of teenage boys, led by an excited and vociferous woman dressed in red, broke out the courthouse windows with rocks, threw gasoline in, and fired the building about 2.30 in the afternoon. The fire department used its ladders to carry the people from the second floor courtroom. There was some objection to the rescuing of the judge, county attorney, sheriffs, and Rangers; but, finally, all were removed except the Negro in the district clerk's vault. As the firemen tried to fight the blaze during the afternoon, the mob cut the fire hose and sometimes attacked the firemen.

The battle with the soldiers

The Rangers, who had left the courthouse, telephoned the governor for assistance, and about 4 p.m. a small detachment of National Guards arrived from a neighboring town. They marched around the falling ruins of the courthouse, saw that they were too far outnumbered to restore order, and returned home. About 6 p.m. a larger unit of fifty-two soldiers from a large city to the south arrived. Leaving a detachment to garrison their headquarters at the county jail three blocks west of the courthouse, the remainder deployed around the smoldering courthouse ruins to push the crowd back from the hanging walls. As darkness fell, the spirit of the mob became uglier. They reasoned that if the governor would not let the Rangers shoot at them, he surely would not let soldiers shoot either. They began to abuse the soldiers, and soon a pitched battle ensued in which the troops were forced to retreat the three blocks back to the jail, followed by the angry mob throwing bricks, rocks, pieces of timber, chunks of concrete, broken bottles, sticks of dynamite, etc. Several soldiers were badly cut and beaten, others had their rifles taken from them, and some of the mobsters received minor bullet wounds. Reinforced by their comrades at the jail the troops made a determined stand there and started shooting into the air. The mob then withdrew and returned to the courthouse square to open the vault and get the Negro, about whose condition there was much speculation.

From around 8 p.m. to midnight various efforts were made to open the upper room of the great two story steel and cement vault. A gigantic crowd packed the entire square and side streets. Finally, the mob leaders confiscated an acetylene torch; and, working from the top of a ladder, were able to open a hole large enough to insert dynamite and blow out a hole which the mob leader entered and threw out the dead body of the Negro.

The corpse was dragged behind a Ford roadster containing two young men and two girls to the Negro business section, a distance of seven blocks. Thousands of people followed in a frenzied midnight parade, yelling, singing, tooting horns of automobiles. At an important corner in the Negro section the body was drawn up to the limb of a cottonwood tree in front of a Negro drug store. The store was forcibly entered and ransacked, the money and valuables pocketed, confections passed out to the crowd, and the furniture and furnishings piled under the Negro's body for fuel. Some versions have it that the leader unsexed the Negro in the presence of the crowd of men, women, and children before lighting the fire. The crowd gave a mighty cheer as flames enveloped the Negro's body. After the burning of the body some of the crowd – the onlookers – went home, but the more vicious elements continued ransacking and burning with gasoline the Negro business places including a hotel, drug store, two cafes, two barber shops, two dentists' offices, a doctor's office, two undertaking establishments, an Odd Fellows' Hall, a Knights of Pythias building, a theater, a lawyer's office, a life insurance office, a cleaning and pressing shop, and several residences. They swore that they would 'run all the damn niggers out of Leeville'. Many of the remaining mob were very drunk. The fire department was not permitted to put any water on the fires except on nearby property owned by Whites.

Exodus of the Negroes

Meanwhile all of Leeville's 2000 Negro inhabitants were under cover. Some were given refuge by White friends and employers in Leeville; the others, with their old people, their sick, their babies and children, hurried away in old automobiles, wagons, buggies, on mules, and by foot. Some reached Negro friends in adjacent cities; less fortunate individuals spent a harrowing night in ditches, ravines, clumps of bushes, under houses or bridges, etc.

Martial law

About 1 o'clock Saturday morning 150 more National Guards arrived with machine guns, rifles, side arms, and tear gas. They, together with the previously mentioned soldiers at the jail, were at last able to break the mob and disperse it. At 3 a.m. more troops arrived. At dawn the soldiers had the town under control with machine guns mounted at strategic points. Martial law was declared and arrests began. During the next few days there were continual rumors that the mob would reassemble on the outskirts of town at dark, make a new march against the soldiers, and complete their avowed job of burning all Negro dwellings and driving their occupants out of town permanently. The armed force was increased to 419 men and more arms were brought in, but nothing more of importance occurred. A notice was found tacked on a White employer's office door warning him to fire his Negro workers and engage Whites. Warnings to leave town were discovered on some Negro dwellings. A military court of investigation turned over twenty-nine persons and 600 typewritten pages of confidential evidence to the civil authorities, who indicted fourteen men and boys. They were removed to jail in the large metropolitan city to the south; a citizen's committee to maintain order was organized; and the troops left Leeville after being there nine days.

Legal dispositions

After many seemingly unnecessary delays on the part of the Leeville county attorney, the rioters were brought to trial in the aforementioned metropolitan city, where, to the surprise and chagrin of the judge, a jury of urban men could not be found who would agree to convict even if the defendants were proved guilty. On another change of venue to the state capital city, one young man was finally given a two-year term for arson. This was more than a year after the lynching. The defendant was already at odds with the law on other charges. Before ending his sentence he was released by the governor on petition of Leeville citizens on account of the illness of his mother. The other thirteen men were never tried.

Aftermath

Race relations in Leeville continued very strained for many months. The Negro citizens (most of whom returned) were abused and persecuted severely before the situation became normal again.

Part 2: conclusions and interpretations

Economic decadence and Negro competition

Government and financial statistics show that although Leeville had at the beginning of the century been a leading Texas city financially, industrially, and culturally, yet during the decade preceding this riot it definitely lost ground in population as well as in business, and at the time of the lynching was feeling the pinch of economic decadence severely.

Negroes are not allowed in many communities near Leeville, and in that city they are excluded from work at most industrial institutions, having to content themselves with what money sifts down from the wealthier Whites for such odd jobs as car washing, lawn mowing, shoe shining, and day labor on the farms. In spite of this situation the more ambitious Negroes had managed to accumulate some property, and several had become quite prosperous. Meanwhile due to the economic decadence, many of the poorer Whites were having financial difficulties. Proof of their resentment of the propertied Negroes is shown in the riot by the destruction of Negro property, the plans to burn all Negro homes, the mob slogan of 'run all the niggers out of Leeville', the posting of notices on the Negro shacks warning the occupants to leave, the notice on the establishment of a White employer warning him to discharge Negro help and employ Whites, and the period of persecution of the Negroes during the months immediately after the lynching. It seems safe to say that in Leeville the racial attitude of the wealthier Whites is still paternalistic, while the poor Whites hate the Negro as an economic competitor, whose color furnishes a good attacking point.

Attitudes relating to the lynching

Individuals: individual attitudes toward the lynching were of three rather distinct types based on the economic status of the individual:

1. On the whole, the wealthier people, who did not compete with the Negro but used him for odd jobs, disapproved heartily of the lynching, not for intellectual or humanitarian reasons, particularly, but because
(a) they emotionally preferred to have law and order, and

(b) they hated to see their town receive the consequent adverse publicity.

2. Generally speaking, the middle class economic group disapproved of the affair not because of the loss of life involved but because it distressed them to see property destroyed. Many of them were present at the lynching as 'observers', and a few became excited enough to lend moral support to the actual lynchers. Their usual comment was, 'I blame the judge. When he saw the terrible mob, he should have ordered the sheriff to start back to the jail with the Negro. Then the mob could have got him without burning the courthouse.'

3. The lowest economic group, who compete with the Negro, furnished the actual mob and will be discussed later in this article.

Churches: the attitude of the Leeville churches was colored by the economic factor. Pastors of the four largest churches, which are attended principally by the wealthier and the middle economic groups, condemned the lawlessness. Pastors of the outlying churches – in the poorer districts around the cotton mill, railroad shops, etc. – avoided discussion of the lynching because they knew that many of their members were in sympathy with it. One pastor on the east side of town, who was bold enough to censure the mob from his pulpit, was immediately waited upon by a committee of his members and advised to refrain from further mention of the subject if he expected to retain his position.

The Press: although the Leeville daily paper undoubtedly contributed to the rise of the mob by carrying detailed stories of the crime, and by publishing the rumor about the Rangers being ordered not to shoot, yet this effect seems to have been an inadvertent one arising from the usual newspaper practices. On the other hand, after the lynching occurred, the editor continually condemned the mob caustically, saying editorially the next day:

The mob is never right. It is always wrong, and unreasonable, and dangerous – Leeville's name has been dishonored by the people of her own county. It will take a generation to outlive the stain on her honor, if it ever can be done.

Small weeklies in the nearby villages confined themselves, for the most part, to reporting only the news items about the lynching.

Officials: the Rangers undoubtedly did their best to protect their prisoner against unusual handicaps. On the whole, the sheriff's force did its duty, especially up until the courthouse was fired. The young National Guardsmen showed unusual discipline in their fights with the crowd, and they and their officers did an excellent piece of work during the period of martial law in ferreting out the mobsmen and turning them over to the civil authorities.

It is highly probable that the judge refused to change venue in the first place because he little suspected that such an outrage could occur in Leeville. But some of his fellow citizens believe that he was interested in the political advantage of a notorious trial.

The county attorney was courageous in helping protect the Negro before the trial. But he seemed interested primarily in another death penalty for his record and in a widely publicized case in which he would be cast in a popular role. He obtained the help of a man who lived near the assaulted woman to point out veniremen from her community, enabling him to select a biased jury. Furthermore, it seems that it was not necessary for him to have the woman brought to court to get a conviction, because the death penalty was, in his words, 'a cinch'; and the trial, had it been completed, would have been another 'legal lynching'. He became heated in talking to the writer about the Negro and referred to him as a 'damn black son-of-a-b———'.

The city firemen at first made an effort to extinguish the courthouse fire, but, after the riot, failed almost unanimously to help identify mob members who cut their hose and attacked them.

The city police made practically no effort either during or after the lynching to help uphold law and order. During the lynching they confined most of their activity to directing traffic. It is, perhaps, significant to note that the assaulted woman was a relative of one of the most popular policemen.

Attitudes reflected by degree of cooperation with military investigation: during the next few days after the outbreak the military authorities conducted a thorough investigation court. All public spirited citizens were invited to give them information and were promised secrecy. Practically none of the real community leaders as pastors, teachers, attorneys, college alumni, bankers and big business men took advantage of this opportunity to help punish the mob members. The records of this court show that practically all of the sixty-four people not suspected of complicity who testified before the court were given specific individual orders to appear, and a few were brought in forcibly by the officers. Twenty-three were cooperative; the cooperation of ten others was doubtful; and thirty-one were plainly evasive, either because of sympathy for the mob, or fear of retribution from mob members. Witness after witness answered under oath that he had been in the crowd all day, that he had lived all his life in and around Leeville and thus knew most of its inhabitants, and yet he could not remember having recognized anyone among the thousands of people present during the day. Particularly was this the attitude of all but a few of the city firemen and policemen.

The mob personnel

Perhaps there should be some distinction made between the terms 'crowd' and 'mob'. In the great crowd of thousands of curious spectators there were three types:

1. Many fine citizens who opposed the lawlessness, but dared not do anything about it – mostly of the upper economic group.

2. Many more who did not participate, but were either indifferent or in favor of the lynching – mostly of the middle economic group.

3. The active mob – mostly of the lowest economic group who may be said, in general, to compete with the Negro.

The active mob

A compilation of data on the men and boys charged or suspected by the military authorities, and some others revealed by private investigation, gives a fairly accurate sample of the active mob. Table 1 classifies fifty-eight of these individuals by occupational status:

Table 1—Active mob members classified by occupational status

Do not work, or do odd jobs	8
Unemployed teenage boys	6
High-school boys	5
Total unemployed	19
Mill and factory workers	7
Road workers	4
Truck driver	1
Shrubbery worker at nursery	1
Total common laborers	13
Farmers and farm-hands	8
Total farmers	8
Mechanics	4
Welder-plumber	1
Cement worker	1
Bricklayer	1
Railroad switchman	1
Total skilled laborers	8
Grocery store operators	2
Filling station operator	1
Dry goods store operator	1
Total owners of small town businesses	4
Gin operator	1
Advertising manager of a department store	1
Bank clerk (a youth)	1
Total salaried people	3
Fruit peddler	1
Banjo player and singer	1
Insurance agent	1
Total miscellaneous	3

At least eleven of the active participants in the riot were known to have had previous police records. Nine had been in the hands of the law for stealing, fighting, or bootlegging (this was before repeal). Two were under suspended sentence for stealing; and one, a hobo, had spent twelve years as an inmate of an insane asylum.

Pertinent facts about the most active lynchers[2]

The acknowledged leader of the mob was a man, forty years old, who could neither read nor write, and had no particular profession, but occasionally did a little cattle trading and 'bronc bustin' in rodeos. He drank a great deal, and was described by officers as 'a rough and ready bully'. He had been before the courts several times as a bootlegger. With his wife and little daughter he lived in a shabby part of town near some Negro shanties. He owned no property, and belonged to no church. The wife provided most of the family's support by taking in washing. His attitude at the opening of the vault was described as that of a great benefactor – a protector of womanhood – doing his duty in a brave and dramatic manner. A few years after the lynching he was killed in a drunken brawl on a South Texas sheep ranch.

The boy who was given the two-year prison term was seventeen years old, his father was dead, and his mother was a low paid worker at a shirt factory. At an early age he began truanting from school, stealing chickens, coming into the hands of the police, and was eventually brought before the courts for cattle stealing. At this time he had returned from prison and had again been before the courts for stealing.

One of the men who helped open the vault later had trouble with a farmer because he raped the farmer's wife. Another commited suicide some years after the lynching, indicating emotional instability. Still another mob member was an inebriate; and the hobo member, at the time of the lynching, was sleeping in a city park and confessed that his breakfasts consisted of bread and milk stolen early in the morning from various grocery stores. He had often been picked up for vagrancy in other cities following his release from the insane asylum. An eighteen year old boy who fought the firemen was described by those who knew him as 'a sort of a half-wit'. Only one of the fourteen indicted owned a home.

2. For detailed case studies of mob members see complete thesis, Pruden (1935).

The five high-school participants are all described by school officials as problem boys, 'overgrown and hungry for notoriety'. The mother of one was a prostitute, and the father of one (a city fireman) committed suicide recently. Two boys from fairly well fixed homes were involved.

A summation of the evidence about the personnel of the mob indicates that the active leaders and participants – mostly from the lowest economic group – included:

1. Some vicious criminals.

2. Many teenage, excitable youths, impatient at restraints of the law.

3. Many propertyless, uneducated, unattached men of the domino-parlor clientele type.

A mixed-race sexual theory

The question has often been raised why white men and sometimes white women become so insanely infuriated at sex relations, either forced or voluntary, between Negro men and White women. There is usually no intense excitement when a white man rapes a white woman. Such a case recently occurred in the county where murder as well as rape was committed. Yet the white culprit received an orderly trial. When a Negro man assaults a Negro woman in Leeville, the customary penalty is a fine of $12.50. Furthermore, the investigation disclosed that some of the young white boys and older loafers of Leeville patronize Negro prostitutes, and some of the white farm laborers arrange illicit relations with rural Negro women.

In the light of these facts the following theory – not a proved conclusion – is suggested: it is a well known tenet of Freudian psychology that when a human mind contains some thought material which is repulsive to the morals of the group, such material is forcibly relegated to deep corners of the subconscious mind to make the consciousness more comfortable. Buried in the subconscious, these thoughts struggle for release and expression. Many times they evade the social censor of consciousness by finding expression in reversed forms or indirect activities. Could it be that these men of the lowest (and sometimes the highest) social strata become so infuriated at a Negro's rape of a white woman because of the guilty enjoyment they have received from socially disapproved sex play with Negro women? Or, again, do they have an almost subconscious curiosity as to whether or not their own white women folk would likewise enjoy mixed-race sex relations? Or yet again, perhaps they have had mental imageries and reveries of obtaining satisfying sex experiences by assault, near-assault, or seduction methods; and, therefore, have a subconscious resentment against the Negro's doing what they, themselves, dare not, or, perhaps, have not had the opportunity to do. Furthermore, could it be that these loud and boisterous women taking leading parts in lynchings of Negroes are giving indirect expression to subconscious reveries they themselves may have had of such mixed-sex relations?

Final general conclusion

The rape case was only an excuse for overt conflict that would eventually have come anyhow, because of the irritation of the poor whites at the increased prosperity of the business and professional Negroes. The lynching, however, was more than an economic struggle at the bottom. It was aided and abetted by the passive attitude, indifference, or open approval of the upper economic classes, and was therefore, a community phenomenon.

Sources

1. Hundreds of interviews with the people of Leeville and surrounding territory, National Guard Officers, sheriff's force, and other officials.

2. Two volumes of secret testimony taken by the Military Court of Investigation.

3. Files of newspapers of Leeville and the nearby city dailies, including some Negro papers.

4. Pamphlets, books, and other data published by the Commission on Interracial Cooperation.

5. For further sources and complete bibliography, see Pruden, (1935).

Reference

PRUDEN, D. (1935), *A Sociological Study of a Texas Lynching*, Southern Methodist University.

34 Robert E. Park

The Marginal Man

Excerpt from Robert E. Park, 'Introduction' to E. V. Stonequist,
The Marginal Man, Scribner, 1937, pp. xiii–xviii.

William Graham Sumner, in what is probably the most frequently quoted passage in the *Folkways*, tells us that we should conceive primitive society as a congeries of small ethnocentric groups scattered over a territory. In such a society each group thinks of itself in the first person and regards itself as 'the center of everything'. It is a 'we-group'. Others are outsiders. They are part of the landscape.

The size of such a group is determined 'by the conditions of the struggle for existence, and its internal organization corresponds to its size but is further conditioned by its relations with all the others. This is because order and discipline in each 'we-group' or 'in-group' depends upon the exigences of war and peace with the 'others-groups' or 'out-groups'. Thus society, primitive society at least, turns out to be 'a group of groups', in which the normal relation of each to every other is 'one of war and plunder, except so far as agreements have modified it'. Under these circumstances 'the relation of comradeship and peace in the we-group and that of hostility and war towards others-groups are correlative to each other'. The loyalties that bind together the members of the little world – the world of the family, the clan and the tribe – are in direct proportion to the intensity of the fears and hatreds with which they view their enemies and rivals in the larger intertribal and international world outside.

In the course of the long historical process from which the modern world has emerged this picture of primitive society has been progressively altered. Now that the aeroplane has wellnigh abolished the distances that once separated the nations and peoples and the radio has converted the world into one vast whispering gallery, the great world – intertribal, interracial, and international – the world of business and politics – has grown at the expense of the little world, the world of intimate, personal loyalties in which men were bound together by tradition, custom, and natural piety.

Nevertheless the general patterns of primitive society still persist and human nature is, on the whole, what it has been. It is still in the family and under the influence of the tribe, the sect or the local community, as Cooley insisted, that the individual acquires those habits, sentiments, attitudes and other personality traits that characterize him as human.

On the other hand, it was and is in the market place where men from distant places come together to chaffer and bargain, that men first learn the subtleties of commerce and exchange; the necessity for cool calculation, even in human affairs, and the freedom to act, as individuals, in accordance with interests rather than sentiments. It is with the expansion of the market, as a matter of fact, that intellectual life has prospered and local tribal cultures have been progressively integrated into that wider and more rational social order we call civilization.

Thus the vast expansion of Europe during the last four hundred years has brought about changes more devastating than in any earlier period in the world's history. Europeans have invaded every part of the world, and no part of the earth has escaped the disturbing, even if vivifying, contacts of European commerce and culture. The movements and migrations incident to this expansion have brought about everywhere an interpenetration of peoples and a fusion of cultures. Incidentally it has produced, at certain times and under certain conditions, a personality type, a type which if not wholly new is at any rate peculiarly characteristic of the modern world. It is a type to which some of us, including the author of this volume (Stonequist, 1937), have given the title 'The marginal man'.

The marginal man, as here conceived, is one whom fate has condemned to live in two societies and in two, not merely different but antagonistic, cultures. Thus, the individual whose mother is a Jew and whose father is a Gentile is fatally condemned to grow up under the influence of two traditions. In that case, his mind is the crucible in which two different and refractory cultures may be said to melt, and, either wholly or in part, fuse. One runs across individuals who are caught in this conflict of cultures in the most unlikely places.

Readers of George Santayana's *The Last Puritan* will hardly fail to discover – even if the subtitle, 'A memoir in the form of a novel', did not advertise the fact – that the story it tells, if not an autobiography, is nevertheless, in some subtle and symbolic way, autobiographical. Obviously the two leading characters, Oliver and Mario, are the symbols of the two cultures, which the author united in his own person, and the almost mystical friendship which, in spite of differences of temperament and tradition, unites them indicates how intimately the traditions they represent were related in the mind of the author.

In the epilogue the author refers to this novel as a 'fable,' and Mario, with whom he represents himself as discussing the import of the fable, adds, that 'perhaps there is a better philosophy in it than in your other books.'

Perhaps the best philosophy is one that achieves, as in the case of Plato, its fullest and happiest expression in fables. In any case a man's philosophy is always an aspect, if not an integral part, of his personality, and Santayana's philosophy reflects the effect, upon a mind conscious of a conflict in its natural loyalties, of an effort to achieve an inner harmony and consistency; such a harmony and consistency as is essential to that 'life of reason' which he has so persuasively set forth in the volumes he has written under that title.

Santayana was born in Spain of Spanish parents, but fate ordained that he should get his education and live most of his life in America and England. It is evident from his account of life in Boston, that he lived there with his mother, as he did in fact in Spain with his father, more or less as an alien, always conscious of a different tradition and of intimate and indissoluble connections with another and a different world. In fact his life in both Spain and America seems to have been that of the typical 'stranger', as described by Simmel in his *Sociology*; that is, one who lives in intimate association with the world about him but never so completely identified with it that he is unable to look at it with a certain critical detachment. In Santayana's case this detachment has become, as Edman expresses it, an intimate but 'compassionate understanding' of his world (See introduction Edman, 1935, p. *lvi*).

In an article, contributed to a symposium on the subject of contemporary American philosophy, Santayana (see Edman, 1935, pp. 1–20) has described 'the mixed associations' under which his 'opinions' came into existence, subjected as they were to the strain of his 'complex allegiances'. He says: 'My philosophy may be regarded as a synthesis of these various traditions, or an attempt to view them from a level from which their several deliverances may be justly understood'.

Of himself a little later, he adds:

I felt like a foreigner in Spain, more acutely so than in America, although for more trivial reasons. . . . English had become my only possible instrument, and I deliberately put away everything that might confuse me in that medium. English, and the whole Anglo-Saxon tradition in literature and philosophy, have always been a medium to me rather than a scholarship, and learning of any sort seemed to me a means, not an end. . . . Thus in renouncing everything else for the sake of English letters I might be said to have been guilty, quite unintentionally, of a little stratagem, as if I had set out to say plausibly in English as many un-English things as possible. (Santayana, pp. 4–5)

The Last Puritan, whether it be an 'indirect memoir' of the author, as Edman assumes, or a philosophy in the form of a fable, as Santayana himself suggests, is in any case for the students of human nature a human document in which the conflict and fusion of cultures, as it actually takes place under certain circumstances and in certain minds, is clearly reflected.

The fundamental notion upon which this present study of the so-called marginal man is based is, I should say, the conviction that the individual's personality, while based on instincts, temperament and the endocrine balance, achieves its final form under the influence of the individual's conception of himself. The conception which each individual inevitably forms of himself is determined by the role which fate assigns to him in some society, and upon the opinion and attitude which persons in that society form of him – depends, in short, upon his social status. The individual's conception of himself is, in this sense, not an individual but a social product.

The marginal man is a personality type that arises at a time and a place where, out of the conflict of races and cultures, new societies, new peoples and cultures are coming into existence. The fate which condemns him to live, at the same time, in two worlds is the same which compels him to assume, in relation to the worlds in which he lives, the role of a cosmopolitan and a stranger. Inevitably he becomes, relatively to his cultural milieu, the individual with the wider horizon, the keener intelligence, the more detached and rational viewpoint. The marginal man is always relatively the more civilized human being. He occupies the position which has been, historically, that of the Jew in the Diaspora. The Jew, particularly the Jew who has emerged from the provincialism of the ghetto, has everywhere and always been the most civilized of human creatures.

From what has been said one may infer that the marginal man is an incidental product of a process of acculturation, such as inevitably ensues when peoples of different cultures and different races come together to carry on a common life. He is, as I have suggested, an effect of imperialism, economic, political and cultural; an incident of the process by which civilization, as Spengler has said, grows up at the expense of earlier and simpler cultures (Spengler, 1926).

The Marginal Man is concerned finally and fundamentally less, as the title might suggest, with a personality type, than with a social process, the process of acculturation. The distinction is that, in the latter case, the author has chosen to investigate the process less from the point of view of the person than of the society of which he is a part; less from the point of view of custom and culture than from habit and personality.

References

EDMAN, I. (1935), *The Philosophy of Santayana: Selections from the Complete Works of George Santayana*, Constable.
SPENGLER, O. (1926), *The Decline of the West*, Knopf.
STONEQUIST, E. V. (1937), *The Marginal Man*, Scribner.

35 Graham Watson

Passing for White in South Africa

Excerpts from Graham Watson, *Passing for White: A Study of Racial Assimilation in a South African School*, Tavistock, 1970, pp. xiii–xiv, 18–26.

[...] Frequent allusions are made to Nature by propagandists of apartheid; but the division of mankind into races is an invention not of Nature but of Man. Races and the divisions which exist among them in South Africa reveal the hidden hand of nothing more elemental than the bureaucracy of Pretoria. If this is kept firmly in mind, there is no cause for bewilderment in the facts that brothers and sisters can belong to different *races*, that *White* adults can start life as *Coloured* children, that men can live as *Coloureds* but work as *Whites*. It happens quite often.

Those who at some stage of their lives have been Coloured – in South Africa the term denotes those of mixed White and non-White ancestry – but who, by subterfuge, have subsequently succeeded in being accepted as White are known as *pass-Whites*. Whites know little about them, and the secrecy which envelops the process of passing ensures that this will always be so. ....[1]

'We want no mixing of languages, no mixing of cultures, no mixing of religions, and no mixing of races' (van Rooy, quoted by Bunting, 1964, p. 194) is a statement which accurately reflects

1. For an introduction to the literature on South African race relations the reader can do no better than to consult van den Berghe (1965) and the select bibliography contained therein. Patterson (1953) is perhaps the best-known work on the coloured people. Dickie-Clark (1966), while more limited in scope, is unrivalled in the field. Cilliers (1963) is a useful compendium of information, based largely on the 1960 *Census Report*.
There is no lengthy treatment of passing for White in non-fictional volumes on South Africa, but the topic is dealt with cursorily by Dover (1937); *Report of the Commission of the Cape Coloured Population of the Union* (1937); Patterson (1953); Millin (1954); Stonequist (1961); Dickie-Clark (1966). Well-known fictional works dealing specifically with the topic include Millin (1924) and Fugard (1964).

the philosophy embodied in the plethora of legislation affecting schooling in South Africa. White children must, by law, attend schools reserved for Whites only and must secure instruction through the medium of the mother tongue, be it Afrikaans (the language of the Afrikaner White majority) or English, and Coloured children must attend Coloured schools. Yet, twenty years after the nakedly racist Nationalist Party came to power, there still exists in the land of apartheid a number of public schools reserved by law for Whites of English mother-tongue, which, contain a considerable proportion of swarthy pass-White pupils of Afrikaans extraction. Colander High School is by no means unique. ...

The process of passing for White is made feasible, in the first place, by the fact that the cultures of the White and Coloured peoples are very similar, though there are differences. Some of the differences, such as the Mohammedan religion of the minority, are obvious. Also obvious is the use of Afrikaans as a home language. The pass-White will often adopt English as his first language, but if he does not he will at least expunge from his vocabulary words and phrases which can be identified as belonging specifically to the Coloured argot. Equally obvious is the relative poverty of the Coloured people, and with it, the rumbustious way of life which seems to be associated with low-status groups the world over. This the aspirant must relinquish. There are also various other differences, such as loyalty to a coon troupe, or a taste for dagga, which must be concealed. The subtler differences, a desire for certain foods, perhaps, or a pronounced anti-Muslim prejudice, are not so readily recognized by White persons as primarily Coloured traits and, for this reason, aspirants are more careless about owning to them.

Passing for White is made feasible, in the second place, by the fact that there are infinite gradations between White and non-White skins and physiognomies, so that it is often not possible to tell from physical features alone to which race a particular person belongs. These infinite gradations owe their existence to the extensive miscegenation which began with the earliest Dutch settlement in South Africa and which has continued ever since (c.f. MacCrone, 1957, ch 3; Marais, 1957, ch.1; Anon, 1953). Jeffreys (1959) argues convincingly that since by the end of the

Graham Watson 459

seventeenth century there were fewer than four hundred White colonists at the Cape, and that 15–30 per cent of all marriages at the time were 'mixed', 'It is fairly safe to say that where any family has been in the country for more than two hundred years, the chance of having no infusion of colour is rather remote'. Van den Berghe (1965, p. 42) argues that 'One can safely estimate that anywhere from one-tenth to one-quarter of the persons classified as 'White' in the Cape Province are of mixed descent, and that every 'old family' from White Cape Society has genealogical connections with Coloured families.' Findlay (1936) estimated that at least 733,000 persons of 'mixed blood' were included in the 1·9 million persons then recorded as Whites in South Africa.

The difficulties experienced by those whose task it is to classify South Africans in terms of racial categories under the Population Registration Act No. 30 of 1950 (which provides for the issue of identity cards on which is recorded the race of the bearer) are as nothing compared to the embarrassment and tragedy which can be the lot of those classified. A Member of Parliament (Russel, 1963) cites the case of a married couple who had their race classification altered five times. They were declared Coloured in 1953; in 1955 they were accepted as White. In 1957 they were reclassified as Coloured; in 1958 as White; in 1959 as Coloured; subsequently as White. Horrell (1958) recounts many similar cases. The following case study, collected by the author in Colander and the only one of its kind ever published, exposes the arbitrary nature of racial classification by demonstrating how different members of the same family can be classified disparately for the purposes of legislation and how each member may act over time and in varying circumstances as a member of more than one race.[2]

Ego's paternal great-grandfather (1) (see Figure, 1, p. 461) was born in Scotland and emigrated to Stellenbosch, where he worked on the railways in an unknown capacity. He married a White woman, whom he later divorced. He then remarried, this time to a Coloured woman. They produced a son who remained in Stellenbosch as a produce farmer. He lived and worked as a White, and was married to a girl from St Helena, about whose parents nothing is known.

They had nine children, seven sons and two daughters. Two of their

2. Some details have been altered to preserve anonymity.

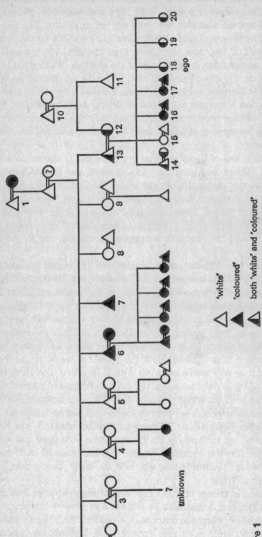

Figure 1

sons, (2) and (3), remained in Stellenbosch. One was a produce farmer and the other owned a store. Both lived and worked as Whites, and married women who also lived and worked as Whites. The two men died before the era of race classification. Their widows survive, but it is not known if and how they have been classified. One couple was barren, and nothing is known about the children of the other.

One son, (4) moved to Colander, where he worked as an engine driver. He lived and worked as a White, but died before being classified. He married a woman who lived as White; her classification is not known. Neither their son, a teacher, nor their daughter, a cutter in the clothing industry, is married. Both live, work, and are classified as Coloured.

Another son of Ego's paternal grandfather, (5) moved to a small farm at Phillipi, and from there to Crawford, and then to Sunnyside. This area was declared Coloured under the Group Areas Act, so he moved to Lansdowne, for both he and his wife lived, worked, and were classified as White. Their unmarried daughter lives, works, and is classified as White, and is a typist. Their married daughter, a shop assistant, and her husband, a tramway mechanic, are in the same position.

Another son of Ego's paternal grandfather, (6), moved to Lansdowne where he lived and worked as a Coloured teacher. He died before race classification. His wife lived as Coloured, but her classification is unknown. Their son became a carpenter, and their three daughters each married teachers. All these children and their spouses live, work, and are classified as Coloured. Yet another son of Ego's paternal grandfather, (7), lives with his brother in Vasco. He lives as a Coloured, but his classification is not known. He is the darkest of the family, and is not allowed to answer the door or to sit at the table when visitors are present.

One of Ego's paternal aunts, (8), lived as White and married a man who also lived as White and who had a private income. Both died before classification. They lived in Parow and had no children.

The other paternal aunt, (9), moved with her husband, who had an unspecified job in the navy, to Parow, where both lived and worked as White. She was classified White – but her husband died prior to classification. Their only son, who is in the army, lives, works, and is classified as White.

Nothing is known of Ego's maternal great-grandfather except that he was Dutch and that both he and his wife severed connection with Ego's mother when she married a Coloured man. Ego's maternal grandfather, (10), a tobacco farmer from Stellenbosch, married a woman who, like himself, lived and worked as White. Both died before classification.

They had two children. Nothing is known about the son, (11), except that he lives as White and that he severed connection with his sister, Ego's mother, (12), when she married a Coloured. She married the remaining son of Ego's paternal grandparents, (13), and moved from Stellenbosch to Maitland; thence to Tiger Valley and Crawford. Her husband was a carpenter. Both live and work as Coloured, yet both are classified as White; they find this amusing.

They had seven children, six daughters and a son. The son, (14), a clerk, lives as a Coloured, works as a White, and is not yet classified. His wife is in a similar predicament. One daughter, (15), married a shop manager. Both live and work and are classified as White. The two other married daughters, (16) and (17), one of whom is a clerk live, work, and are classified as Coloured, Their husbands – a clerk and a carpenter – are in the same position. Ego, (18), is unmarried and lives and works as White, but had delayed applying for her Population Registration Card for fear that she might be classified Coloured. She has once been dismissed employment because she refused to produce her unemployment registration card: she previously worked as Coloured and this is stated on the card. Her two unmarried sisters, (19) and (20), a shop assistant and a nurse, both live as Coloureds but work as White, and are classified as White.

Thus, of Ego and her siblings, two live, work, and are classified as Coloured; one lives as Coloured, works as White, but remains unclassified; two live as Coloured but work and are classified as White; one lives and works as White but is unclassified; and one lives and works and is classified as White: their parents live and work as Coloureds but are classified as White. Thus do the architects of apartheid separate the races.

Most of those who pass belong, claim informants, to the artisan and skilled worker group. It seems probable that those who rank above this group in the internal status hierarchy are tempted to remain within the Coloured camp, sometimes out of political loyalty to their compatriots, and sometimes perhaps for fear of increased economic competition within the White group. Those who rank below the artisan group seldom possess the characteristics necessary for successful passing. The most important of these characteristics is, of course, a fair skin, and this is found mainly among the élite and artisan group (cf. Cilliers, 1963; Patterson, 1953).[3]

3. It is surely misleading to describe South Africa as a caste or caste-like society. The term caste focuses our attention upon barriers to inter-group mobility and blinds us to the kind of miscibility described here.

But a fair skin is not the only qualification necessary for successful passing. Cultural criteria must also be taken into account. And here again it is the elite and artisan groups who possess the most qualifications for passing. It is they who are able to afford the education necessary to enter White occupations, the relatively high rent payable on properties bordering White homes, the standard of living and articles of dress which most Whites enjoy. It is they who most commonly speak English as their first language, or who have stayed at school long enough to acquire proficiency in it as a second language.

To facilitate the process of passing, Coloureds will, it is commonly said, often move from the town or province where they are known.[4] One hears of Coloureds who have moved from Johannesburg to Cape Town for this purpose, and of others who have moved from Cape Town to Johannesburg.[5] Dr Wollheim estimates that there are at least 25,000 pass-Whites in Johannesburg today (*Cape Times*, 5 July, 1961). Many others migrate to England, Canada, and elsewhere. But the strongest movement is probably from the districts of the South-Western Cape – the area which is bounded by Swellendam on the west and Uitenhage on the east, and which includes George, Knysna, Mossel Bay and Oudtshoorn – to Cape Town itself. The South-Western Cape was traditionally a farming area and the movement to town is in part a consequence of increasing mechanization on the farms. It is also an area of traditional intermarriage across the colour line. The Afrikaans names Van Rensburg, Groenewald, Jacobs, Marais, Oktober, Veldsman, Booysens, and others, occur frequently among Coloured families, many of whom claim blood relationship with their 'White cousins'. There was a secondary strain of English intermarriage, especially in the areas of George and Knysna, where the names MacKay, Martin, Dunn, Owen, Benn, and Bailey are not uncommon among Coloured families. The offspring of such intermarriages seldom find them-

4. Migrations were deliberately planned for this purpose, but it is probable that, more often than not, this was just one of those factors taken into consideration when planning a move.
5. In the *Cape Times* of 4 April 1963 a member of the School Board is reported as advising the father of a dark complexioned child to send his son to a school in the Transvaal where it is easier for such a child to enrol in a white school.

selves fully accepted by their White relatives, while they themselves feel superior to their Coloured relatives: they needs must move in order to establish themselves as White. Today 60 per cent of the Cape Coloureds live in towns and cities, 25 per cent in Greater Cape Town alone (Cilliers, 1963, pp. 16-17).[6]

Many live in the older, run-down parts of Cape Town, near the city centre, and along the railway line to the southern suburbs. Others live in recently established townships such as Athlone and Kensington, on the fringes of the city. According to the 1960 census report they slightly outnumber the Whites of Colander.

Such is the attraction of Colander to Coloured people that, while the numbers of White residents declined by about one-third between 1936 and 1960 (because, as one informant put it, 'The roof leaks, the Jew exploits, and I'm moving away from the skollies') the number of Coloureds increased in the same period by almost half. The proportion of Coloureds to the total population of Colander has risen steadily from approximately 30 per cent in 1936 to approximately 50 per cent in 1960.

Colander and its environs has for many years attracted 'better-class' Coloured residents. Its attraction for them is, in the first place, proximity to employment, for most Coloured housing estates, such as Bonteheuvel, are far from the factories of Colander which provide many Coloured persons with work. The income of most Coloureds is decidedly lower than that of most Whites, and the extra expense involved in travelling to work from these outlying areas is seen as a heavy burden. A second attraction of Colander is that rents, compared with other White areas, are low. But probably the greatest attraction of the district for Coloured persons, according to informants, is the fact that there White and Coloured housing intermingle. Whites and Coloureds live side by side as neighbours, though there is a tendency for the two groups to live on different sides of the same street, and a tendency for Coloureds to concentrate in densely populated pockets west of the main road. This intermingling provides an opportunity for relatively fair Coloured persons to acquire White status through residence in a nominally White area – one necessary condition of passing for White.

6. A map of the distribution of the coloured population in South Africa can be found in M. Cole (1961, p. 663).

The reaction of Coloured people to those of their number who pass varies from the sympathetic to the hostile. [...]

Those who pass during working hours but return to their families and friends at night, or at least at frequent intervals, appear to escape the full force of their relatives' enmity; indeed, they are likely to be given every assistance. This reaction might be interpreted as a reflection of that aspect of the White ethic which encourages the individual to exact maximum advantage within fair rules and to obtain the best employment he can. But those who cut themselves off completely from their relatives are likely to be regarded with varying degrees of hostility. Here is a case in point.

The brothers Jannie and Piet are both of relatively fair complexion and possess European physiognomies. Piet, who is the fairer of the two, decided to pass, while, after a few humiliating experiments, Jannie decided otherwise. Jannie married an obviously Coloured woman and brought her to live in the paternal home in lower Colander. Piet married a woman of fair complexion, and moved to a house east of the main road, where there were more Whites, and cut himself off completely from his brother and other relatives. About two years ago, unbeknown to Jannie, he moved to a White suburb far from Colander and his old acquaintances.

When the father died, Piet, the eldest, made arrangements for the funeral. Jannie offered to help, but his offer was brusquely refused. He was told to keep away from the ceremony, lest his brother be embarrassed. Nevertheless, he attended. Few were present, and, as it happened, there were not enough pall-bearers. Piet cast about himself in desperation but, though the need was pressing, deliberately overlooked his swarthy brother. After some hesitation Jannie wordlessly aligned himself with the other pall-bearers, and carried his father to his grave. While the grave was yet open his brother accosted him, deeply angered. 'I thought we understood each other . . .' he hissed. So Jannie lost his temper and threatened to knock Piet into the grave. They broke up amid bitter recriminations.

Jannie despises his brother for cutting himself off from his family of origin and for assuming a form of speech and mannerism which is, allegedly, superciliously White: 'I can't talk to him any more,' he complained. 'We grew up together; but now he is White and I am not.' On the other hand, he has no objection to passing in some circumstances. He himself attends White cinemas and public houses and offers to fight anyone who challenges him. He has enrolled his own son at a

White technical college. This son, after remaining at the college for only a few weeks, burst into the headmaster's office and exclaimed, in a highly emotional state, 'I don't fit in here. I am Coloured. I want to leave.' When Jannie heard this he gave his son a severe beating for jeopardizing his chances of apprenticeship to a White trade.

But whether or not Coloureds approve of or resent those who pass, they invariably see the process as involving tragedy: 'The dark children go to Coloured school and the fair ones to a European school, and then they come home and sit together around the table. How can that be right? It's breaking up families. How can that be right? Why do they have to make a law?

To sum up, . . . upward social mobility among Cape Coloureds can fruitfully be conceived as proceeding along a continuum at one end of which is the farm labourer and towards the other end of which occurs a bifurcation, one branch leading to élite status, the other to White status. Persons situated at the point of bifurcation may, if their complexion is sufficiently fair, choose to pass for White. The process of passing is facilitated by cultivating the ways of the White man, by leaving towns in which the passer's identity as a Coloured is known, and by moving to a district, such as Colander, where Whites and Coloureds intermingle. The act of passing evokes reactions among Coloured people varying from connivance to sharp antagonism.

References

ANON. (1953), 'The origin and incidence of miscegenation at the Cape during the Dutch East India Company's regime 1652–1795', in *Race Relations Journal*, vol. 20, no. 2.

BUNTING, B. (1964), *The Rise of the South African Reich*, Penguin.

CILLIERS, S. P. (1963), *The Coloured People of South Africa*, Banier, Cape Town.

COLE, M. (1961), *South Africa*, Dutton.

DICKIE-CLARK, H. F. (1966), *The Marginal Situation*, Routledge & Kegan Paul.

DOVER, C. (1937), *Half-Caste*, Secker & Warburg.

FINDLAY, G. (1936), *Miscegenation*, Pretoria News Publishers.

FUGARD, A. (1964), *The Blood Knot*, Simondium, Cape Town.

HORRELL, M. (1958), *Race Classification in South Africa – its Effects on Human Beings*, South African Institute of Race Relations.

JEFFRYES, M. D. W., (1959), 'Where do Coloureds come from?', *Drum*, nos. 102–6 and 108.

MacCrone, I. D. (1957), *Race Attitudes in South Africa*, Witwatersrand University Press.

Marais, J. S. (1957), *The Cape Coloured People*, Witwatersrand University Press.

Millin, S. G. (1924), *God's Stepchildren*, Constable.

Millin, S. G. (1954), *The People of South Africa*, Knopf.

Patterson, S. (1953), *Colour and Culture in South Africa*, Routledge & Kegan Paul.

Report of the Commission of the Cape Coloured Population of the Union (1937), U.G. 54.

Russel, H. (1963), *Cape Times*, 19 February.

Stonequist, E. V. (1961), *The Marginal Man*, Russell & Russell.

van den Berghe, P. (1965), *South Africa: A Study in Conflict*, Wesleyan University Press.

Further Reading

The following are good and readily available general studies of race relations:

M. Banton, *Race Relations*, Tavistock, 1967.

P. Mason, *Race Relations*, Oxford University Press, 1970.

J. Rex, *Race Relations in Sociological Theory*, Weidenfeld and Nicolson, 1970.

P. L. van den Berghe, *Race and Racism*, Wiley, 1967.

S. Zubaida (ed.), *Race and Racialism*, Tavistock, 1970.

Part One

A. Barnett, *The Human Species: A Biology of Man*, MacGibbon & Kee, 1950; Penguin, 1965.

C. D. Darlington, *Genetics and Man*, Penguin, 1966.

C. D. Darlington, *The Evolution of Man and Society*, Allen & Unwin, 1969.

T. Dobzhansky, 'The genetic nature of differences among men' in Stow Pearson (ed.) *Evolutionary Thought in America*, chapter three, Yale University Press, 1950.

S. M. Garn, *Readings on Race*, Charles C. Thomas, Springfield, 1960·

F. S. Hulse, 'Some factors influencing the relative proportions of human racial stocks'. In *Cold Spring Harbour Symposia on Quantitive Biology*, vol. twenty two, pp. 34–45, 1957.

A. R. Jensen, 'How much can we boost I Q and scholastic achievement?' *Harvard Educ. Review*, vol. 39, Winter, 1969.

O. Klineberg, *Race Differences*, Harper & Row, 1935.

F. B. Livingstone, 'Anthropological implications of sickle cell gene distribution in West Africa,' *American Anthropol.*, vol. 60, pp. 533–62, 1958.

F. B. Livingstone, 'Human Populations', in Sol Tax (ed.), *Horizons of Anthropology*, Aldine, 1964, Allen and Unwin, 1965.

F. B. Livingstone, and T. Dobzhansky, 'On the non-existence of human races', *Current Anthropology*, vol. 3, pp. 279–281. 1962.

R. R. Race and R. Sanger, *Blood Groups in Man*, Blackwell, (5th edn.), 1968.

J. C. Trevor, 'Race', in *Chambers Encyclopedia*, Pergamon Press, 1967.

P. E. Vernon, *Intelligence and Cultural Achievement*, Methuen, 1969.

Parts Two and Three

M. Banton (ed.), *Darwinism and the study of Society*, Tavistock, 1961.

M. Banton, 'Race as a social category', *Race*, vol. 8, no. 1, pp. 1–16. 1966

R. Benedict, *Race and Racism*, Routledge and Kegan Paul, 1942.

C. Bolt, *Victorian Attitudes to Race*, Routledge and Kegan Paul, 1971.

J. S. Hiller, Jr, 'The species problem: nineteenth century concepts of racial inferiority in the origin of man controversy', *American Anthropologist*, vol. 72, 1970, pp. 1319–29.

G. Jahoda, *White Man: a Study of the Attitudes of Africans to Europeans in Ghana before Independence*, Oxford University Press, 1961.

C. Lévi-Strauss, *Race and History*, The Race Question in Modern Science Series, UNESCO, Paris, 1952.

V. S. Naipaul, *The Middle Passage: The Caribbean Revisited*, Deutsch, 1962; Penguin, 1969.

Parts Four and Five

J. Baldwin, *The Fire Next Time*, Dial Press, 1963; Penguin 1964.

C. Brown, *Manchild in the Promised Land*, Macmillan & Co. 1965; Penguin 1969.

S. Carmichael and C. V. Hamilton, *Black Power: The Politics of Liberation in America*, Cape, 1968.

C. Himes, *Pinktoes*, Arthur Barker, 1961; Corgi, 1970.

J. W. Johnson, *The Book of Negro Poetry*, Harcourt Brace & World, 1922.

G. Moore and U. Beier (eds.), *Modern Poetry from Africa*, Penguin, 1963.

Présence Africaine, A Cultural Review of the Negro World, Published in both French and English editions by Présence Africaine, Paris, 1947. and continuing.

L. S. Senghor, *Selected Poems*, 1964, *Prose and Poetry*, 1965. Translated by John Reed and Clive Wake, Oxford University Press.

Richard Wright, *Black Boy*, World Books, 1950; see also his other novels and short stories.

Part Six

H. Codere, 'Power in Ruanda', *Anthropologica*, (n.s.), vol. no. 4, pp. 45–85, 1962.

E. F. Frazier, *Black Bourgeoisie*, Free Press, 1957.

L. Kuper, *An African Bourgeoisie: Race, Class, and Politics in South Africa*, Yale University Press, 1965.

R. Lemarchand, 'Power and stratification in Ruanda: a reconsideration', *Cahiers d'Etudes Africaines*, vol. six, no. 24, pp. 592–610, 1966.

R. Segal, *The Race War*, Cape, 1966; Penguin 1967.

K. M. Stampp, *The Peculiar Institution: Negro Slavery in the American South*, Knopf; Eyre and Spottiswood, 1956.

C. M. Turnbull, *The Forest People*, Chatto and Windus, 1961.

E. E. Williams, *Capitalism and Slavery*, University of North Carolina Press, 1944.

Parts Seven to Eleven

J. H. Boeke, *Economics and Economic Policies of Dual Societies: as Exemplified by Indonesia*, International Secretariat, Institute of Pacific Relations, Allen & Unwin, 1953.

C. R. Boxer, *Race Relations in the Portuguese Colonial Empire 1415–1825*, Clarendon Press, 1963.

Neils Winther Braroe, 'Reciprocal Exploitation in an Indian-White Community', *Southwestern J. of Anthropol.* vol. 21, pp. 166–178, 1965.

'Colour and race', A special issue of *Daedalus, Journal of the American Academy of Arts and Sciences*, vol. 96, no. 2, 1967.

A. Davis and J. Dollard, *Children of Bondage: the Personality development of Negro Youth in the Urban South*, American Council on Education, 1940.

A. Davis, B. B. Gardner, and M. Gardner, *Deep South: a Social Anthropological Study of Caste and Class*, University of Chicago Press, 1941.

J. P. Davis, 'The influence of race on social stratification: the Dominican republic', in *The American Negro Reference Book*, Prentice Hall, 1966.

J. Dollard, *Caste and Class in a Southern Town*, Harper & Row, 1937; third edn., Doubleday, 1957.

L. Dumont, 'Caste, racism and "stratification": reflections of a social anthropologist', *Contributions to Indian Sociology*, vol. 5, pp. 20–43, 1961. Also in French, *Cahiers Internationaux de Sociologie*, 29, pp. 91–112, 1960.

F. Fanon, *The Wretched of the Earth*, MacGibbon & Kee, 1965; Penguin, 1967.

P. Foot, *Immigration and Race in British Politics*, Penguin, 1965.

E. F. Frazier, *The Negro in the United States*, Macmillan & Co., 1949.

G. Freyre, *The Mansions and the Shanties: the Making of Modern Brazil*, Knopf, 1963.

R. Frucht (ed.), *Black Society in the New World*, Random House, 1970.

J. S. Furnivall, *Colonial Policy and Practice: a Comparative Study of Burma and Netherlands India*, Cambridge University Press, 1948.

M. Gluckman, *Analysis of a Social Situation in Modern Zululand*, Rhodes-Livingstone Papers no. 28, Manchester University Press, 1958. A reprint of an article in *Bantu Studies*, vol. 14, pp. 1–30, 147–74, 1940.

J. Harré, *Maori and Pakeha*: A. H. and A. W. Reed, Wellington, N.Z., 1966 and Pall Mall Press, for Institute of Race Relations, 1966.

C. S. Hill, *How Colour Prejudiced is Britain?*, Gollancz, 1965.

H. Hoetinck, *Two Variants in Caribbean Race Relations: a Contribution to the Sociology of Segmented Societies*, Oxford University Press for Institute of Race Relations, 1967.

R. Hooper (ed.), *Colour in Britain*, British Broadcasting Corporation, 1965.

H. Kuper, *The Uniform of Colour: a Study of White-Black Relationships in Swaziland*, Witwatersrand University Press, 1947.

L. Kuper and M. G. Smith (eds.), *Pluralism in Africa*, University of California Press, 1970.

J. D. Loman and Dietrich C. Reitzes, 'Notes on race relations in mass society', *Amer. J. of Sociol.* vol. 58. pp. 240–6, November, 1962.

S. Patterson, *Dark Strangers*, Tavistock London, 1963; Penguin 1965.

L. Rainwater, *Behind Ghetto Walls: Black Families in a Federal Slum*, Aldine, 1970 and Allen Lane, The Penguin Press, 1971.

J. Rex and R. Moore, *Race, Community and Conflict a Study of Sparkbrook*, Oxford University Press, 1967.

R. T. Smith, *The Negro Family in British Guiana: Family Structure and Social Status in the Villages*, Routledge, & Kegan Paul, 1956.

P. Worsley, *The Trumpet Shall Sound; a Study of 'Cargo' Cults in Melanesia*, MacGibbon & Kee, 1957.

Acknowledgements

Permission to reproduce the following Readings is acknowledged to the following sources:

1 South African Institute of Race Relations
2 *The American Journal of Physical Anthropology*
3 Arthur H. Stockwell Ltd
4 University of Washington Press
5 U N E S C O
6 International Institute of Differing Civilizations
7 University of Chicago Press and George Weidenfeld & Nicholson
8 Addison-Wesley Publishing Co. Inc.
9 University of Chicago Press
10 Studies in British History and Culture
11 University of Wisconsin Press
12 Professor H. R. Isaacs
13 Holt, Rinehart and Winston Inc.
14 Cambridge University Press
15 Mr Wole Soyinka
16 The Institute of Race Relations
17 The Clarendon Press
18 Mr Oliver Cromwell Cox
19 International African Institute
20 University of North Carolina Press
21 Routledge & Kegan Paul Ltd
22 Basil Blackwell Publisher
23 Professor J. Clyde Mitchell
24 Professor Philip Burnham
25 International African Institute
26 Harper & Row Inc.
27 Harcourt, Brace and Jovanovich Inc.
28 University of Chicago Press
29 Columbia University Press
30 Dr R. J. Walker
31 University of North Carolina Press
32 The Society for the Study of Social Problems
33 Dr Durward Pruden
34 Professor E. Stonequist
35 Tavistock Publications Ltd

Author Index

Subject Index

Abanyaruanda, Banyarwanda, 78, 83, 221
Adolescence, behaviour patterns of, 436
African 'character', European images of, 138–9
servants, 133
Africans' 'place in nature', 130
Age and attitudes, 380–82, 394
Alienation theme in *négritude*, 166–8
American 'creed', 243, 252–5, 351
Apartheid, 82, 293
Arabisés, 321–42
Assimilation, French policy of, 168
Associations
African-credit thrift, 264
Jamaican informal, 271
Maori voluntary, 405–8
Sports, 270–71
Australoid, 20–21, 40

Babali, 321
Babua, 321
Bahutu *see* Hutu
Bakumu, 321
Balengola, 321
Bamanga, 321
Bambole, 321
Banyarwanda *see* Abanyaruanda
Batutsi *see* Tutsi
Batwa *see* Twa
Black comedians, 163–4
Black
Muslims, 381
'Power', 381–4
Buhake system, 224
Bushmen, 21, 25

Cameroon (North), 301–18
Cape Coloured *see* Coloureds

Caribbean writers, 169–70, 178
Caste
and class in America 77, 247, 249, 251–4, 364–7
defined, 224
in India, 248
and Negroes, 249, 252–3, 432
and race in USA, 219–20
structure in Rwanda, 224–6
Caste-prejudice as aspect of culture prejudice, 215, 220
Castes, stereotype characteristics of social-racial, 221
'Cat'
extinction of type, 439
rejection of work by, 429
and social change, 437
social type defined, 423
Caucasoid, 20–22, 22, 23
Celt and Saxon dichotomy, 128
Celts, 124
Chicago
Negroes in meat-packing industry, 356
race and drug use in, 423–39
race riots in, 360
Chiefs
in South African administration, 283, 290, 292
in Rhodesian administration, 297–300
Christ-killer, 106
Class
and caste in America, 77, 247, 249, 251–4, 364–7
and racial structure, 94–6
and trade unions, 252
Clientage systems, 226
Colonial system, and racial ideology, 167
Colour
associations, reversal of, 174
implications of (Jamaica) 272–3